"When any person is known to be considering the new Religion, all his relations and acquaintances rise en masse; so that to get a new convert is like pulling out the eyetooth of a live tiger."

— Adoniram Judson

Pulling the Eye Tooth from a Live Tiger

A Memoir Of the Life and Labors of Adoniram Judson
Volume 1
by Francis Wayland

Audubon Press
& Christian Book Service

AUDUBON PRESS
2601 Audubon Drive / P.O. Box 8055
Laurel, MS 39441-8000   USA

Orders: 800-405-3788
Inquiries: 601-649-8572
Voice: 601-649-8570 / Fax: 601-649-8571
E-mail: buybooks@audubonpress.com
Web Page: www.audubonpress.com

© 2006 Audubon Press edition

All rights reserved.

Printed in the United States

Cover design by Crisp Graphics

ISBN # 0-9742365-7-8

Original Publication:

To preach the Gospel in regions beyond... – 2 Cor. 10:16

In Two Volumes

Volume 1

Boston: Phillips, Sampson, and Company
London: Nisbet and Company
1853

Stereotyped at the Boston Stereotype Foundary

All Scripture quotations are from the KJV

PREFACE.

WHEN, in compliance with the request of the Executive Committee of the American Baptist Missionary Union, and of the widow of the late Dr. Judson, I undertook to compile the following Memoir, I supposed that a large amount of his correspondence and other writings would be easily accessible. In this respect, however, I was entirely disappointed. From peculiar views of duty, Dr. Judson had caused to be destroyed all his early letters written to his family, together with all his papers of a personal character. Mrs. Ann H. Judson, from prudential reasons, during their captivity in Ava, destroyed all his letters in her possession. Manuscripts were also consumed by the burning of Mr. Stevens's house in Maulmain. Dr. Judson's correspondence with Dr. Staughton perished by the shipwreck of a vessel on the passage from Philadelphia to Washington. Last of all, his letters to his missionary brethren in Burmah were lost by the foundering of the ship which was conveying them to this country. My materials, therefore, consisted chiefly of his official correspondence, much of which had been published in missionary periodicals. To these I have been able to add such letters as had escaped destruction, together with very valuable reminiscences from the pen of Mrs. Judson. Enough, however, has been preserved to present his missionary character with remarkable distinctness. His opinions on many subjects can never be recovered, but the record of his deeds is beyond the reach of both fire and flood.

My grateful acknowledgments are due to the secretaries of the American Baptist Missionary Union, the Rev. Solomon Peck, D. D., and the Rev. Edward Bright, D. D., for the facilities which they have afforded in the prosecution of my labors. They have placed at my disposal every paper on their files which could add to the interest of the Memoir, and have rendered me efficient aid in every part of my undertaking. To Dr. Bright especially I am under great obligations for superintending the press, when, from circumstances beyond my control, I was unable to perform this labor myself.

To the Rev. Rufus Anderson, D. D., the senior secretary of the American Board of Commissioners for Foreign Missions, I am greatly indebted. Not only has he caused to be copied for my use every paper in his possession relating to the connection of Dr. Judson with that society, but he has at all times granted me the aid of his eminent abilities and profound acquaintance with every department of missionary service.

Whatever value this Memoir may possess must be ascribed, in no small degree, to the assistance which I have received from Mrs. Judson. She arranged for me all the letters and papers, furnished me with information which no other person could possess, and has communicated notes and reminiscences which will be found to be among the most interesting portions of the work.

I should do injustice to my own feelings were I to close this preface without recording my obligations to the publishers, Messrs. Phillips, Sampson, & Co. Their arrangements have been characterized by great liberality; their promptness and punctuality have left nothing to be desired; and the interest which they have taken in the publication can only be appreciated by those whose duty it is to labor in this sometimes harassing vocation. An acknowledgment of my obligations is also due to the gentlemen of the Boston Stereotype Foundry, for the fidelity and taste with which they have carried forward their part of the work.

In the humble hope that these volumes will throw some valuable light upon the subject of Christian missions, and thus serve the cause to which the life of Dr. Judson was devoted, they are submitted to the candid consideration of the Christian public.

BROWN UNIVERSITY, *August* 5 1853.

CONTENTS

OF THE FIRST VOLUME.

CHAPTER I.

PARENTAGE. — CHILDHOOD AND YOUTH. — LIFE IN COLLEGE. ENTERS THE THEOLOGICAL SEMINARY AT ANDOVER, . 11

CHAPTER II.

RESIDENCE AT ANDOVER. — CONVERSION. — FIRST IMPULSES TOWARDS MISSIONARY LABOR. — MISSIONARY ASSOCIATIONS. — ORIGIN OF THE AMERICAN BOARD OF COMMISSIONERS, ... 27

CHAPTER III.

MISSION TO ENGLAND. — CAPTURE, AND DETENTION IN FRANCE. — INTERVIEWS WITH THE DIRECTORS OF THE LONDON MISSIONARY SOCIETY. — RETURNS TO THE UNITED

STATES. — APPOINTED A MISSIONARY OF THE AMERICAN BOARD OF COMMISSIONERS FOR FOREIGN MISSIONS. — MARRIAGE AND ORDINATION. — RELATIONS WITH THE BOARD, ... 63

CHAPTER IV.

EMBARKATION. — ARRIVAL IN INDIA — CHANGE OF VIEWS ON BAPTISM. — COURSE OF THE EAST INDIA COMPANY. — ESCAPE TO THE ISLE OF FRANCE. — PASSAGES TO MADRAS AND RANGOON. — FORMATION OF THE BAPTIST GENERAL CONVENTION FOR FOREIGN MISSIONS, ... 93

CHAPTER V.

THE BURMAN EMPIRE. — EXTENT. — RIVERS. — POPULATION — RESOURCES. — GOVERNMENT. — RELIGION, ... 128

CHAPTER VI.

ENTRANCE UPON MISSIONARY WORK. — HIS VIEWS OF THAT WORK. — ACQUISITION OF THE LANGUAGE. — PROGRESS OF THE MISSION. — VOYAGE TO MADRAS, ... 154

CHAPTER VII.

CONFIDENCE IN GOD. — VIEWS OF THE IMPORTANCE OF PREACHING THE GOSPEL. — THAT WORK COMMENCED. — OPENING OF THE ZAYAT. — FIRST CONVERTS TO THE CHRISTIAN RELIGION. — PREPARATIONS FOR VISITING AVA, . 204

CONTENTS.

CHAPTER VIII.

FIRST VISIT TO AVA. — RETURN TO RANGOON. — PROGRESS OF THE GOSPEL. — NEW STATION AT CHITTAGONG. — FAILURE OF MRS. JUDSON'S HEALTH. — VOYAGE TO BENGAL, . 246

CHAPTER IX.

RETURN TO RANGOON. — GROWTH OF THE CHURCH. — INCREASED ILLNESS OF MRS. JUDSON. — SAILS FOR THE UNITED STATES. — THE MISSION RE-ENFORCED. — SECOND VISIT TO AVA. — TRANSLATION OF THE NEW TESTAMENT COMPLETED, ... 288

CHAPTER X.

HOPEFUL PROSPECTS OF THE MISSION — PASSAGE UP THE IRRAWADI. — WAR BETWEEN THE ENGLISH AND BURMANS. — IMPRISONMENT OF DR. JUDSON AT AVA AND OUNG-PEN-LA. — HIS RELEASE. — PERSONAL REMINISCENCES, . . . 326

CHAPTER XI.

MISSION TRANSFERRED TO THE TENASSERIM PROVINCES. — REMOVES TO AMHERST. — EMBASSY TO AVA. — SYSTEM OF MISSIONARY REGULATIONS. — DEATH OF MRS. JUDSON. — DEATH OF HIS ONLY CHILD. — REMOVES TO MAULMAIN. — DEATH OF HIS FATHER, ... 401

CHAPTER XII.

LABORS AT MAULMAIN. — ORDINATION OF BURMESE PASTORS. — MUNIFICENT GIFT. — LETTER TO SIR ARCHIBALD CAMPBELL. — VIEWS OF HIGHER ATTAINMENTS IN RELIGION. — PREPARATION OF WORKS FOR THE PRESS. — SECLUSION, ... 445

CHAPTER XIII.

REVISITS RANGOON. — PASSAGE TO PROME. — SOJOURN AT PROME. — RESIDENCE AT RANGOON. — PROGRESS IN TRANSLATING THE SCRIPTURES. — RETURN TO MAULMAIN. — REVIEW OF HIS AUSTERITIES. — THE KARENS. 485

MEMOIR OF DR. JUDSON

CHAPTER I.

PARENTAGE–CHILDHOOD AND YOUTH.—LIFE IN COLLEGE.—
ENTERS THE THEOLOGICAL SEMINARY AT ANDOVER.

1788–1808.

Adoniram Judson, the senior Baptist missionary to Burmah, was born in Malden, Massachusetts, on the 9th of August, 1788. He was the eldest son of Adoniram and Abigail Judson.

Rev. Adoniram Judson,* the father, was born in

---

* I am indebted to the Rev. S. Hopkins Emery, of Taunton, Massachusetts, for the following memoranda of the Judson family. In some cases both the names and dates differ from those which I have received from the family. I am unable to explain the discrepancy between the two accounts. "Adoniram Judson, father of the missionary to Burmah, was the son of Elnathan and Rebecca (not Mary) Judson."

Elnathan, the father of Adoniram senior, married Rebecca Minor, June 30, 1736. This Rebecca was the daughter of Ephraim and Rebecca Minor, and granddaughter of Captain John Minor, the first settler of Woodbury, and Indian interpreter. She was born January 30, 1712. Captain Elnathan Judson died December 14, 1796, aged eighty-four years.

They had children as follows:

1. Ephraim, (a clergyman, some time settled in Taunton, Massa-

(11)

Woodbury, Connecticut, in June, 1752, and was the youngest son of Elnathan and Mary Judson. He was married November 23, 1786, to Abigail Brown, a native of Tiverton, Rhode Island, born December 15, 1759, eldest daughter of Abraham and Abigail Brown.

The children of Adoniram and Abigail Judson were,

1. Adoniram, born in Malden, Massachusetts, August 9, 1788.

2. Abigail Brown Judson, born in Malden, Massachusetts, March 21, 1791, now residing in Plymouth.

chusetts, and afterwards in Sheffield, Connecticut,) born December 5, 1737, baptized December 11, 1737.

2. Thaddeus, baptized October 14, 1739.
3. Mary, baptized October 18, 1741.
   Married to Edward Pond, November 7, 1765.
4. Noah, baptized July 15, 1744.
5. Elisha, baptized July 20, 1746.
6. Elisha 2nd, baptized November 8, 1747.
7. Adoniram, baptized July 15, 1750.

Elnathan, the grandfather of the missionary, was born May 8, 1712. He had brothers, Elisha, who died young, Elisha 2nd, and Peter; also sisters Abigail, Martha, and Jerusha. They were the children of Jonathan Judson, who married Mary Mitchell, daughter of Deacon Matthew Mitchell, August 22, 1711.

Jonathan, the great-grandfather of the missionary, was born December, 1684. He was the son of John Judson, who married, 1673, Elizabeth Chapman, of Stamford; and was again married in 1699, to Mrs. Mary Orton, of Farmington. Jonathan had two brothers and two sisters.

Their father, John was the son of Joseph, who came to this country at the age of fifteen, lived first at Cocord, then at Stratford, and married Sarah Porter, of Windsor. Joseph had eleven children.

His father was named William, the progenitor of the Judsons in this country. He came from Yorkshire, England, in 1634m bringing three sons, Joseph, Jeremiah, and Joshua.

The above facts were collected from the Stratford and Woodbury records, by William Cothen, Esq., of Woodbury, Connecticut, who is making out a genealogical account of the family.

3. Elnathan Judson, born in Wenham, Massachusetts, May 28, 1794. He was a surgeon in U. S. N., and died in Washington, District of Columbia, 1829.

4. Mary Ellice Judson, born in Wenham, February 18, 1796, and died September 12 of the same year.

Rev. Adoniram Judson, the father, was first settled in the ministry, if I mistake not, at Malden, Massachusetts. This must have been prior to the year 1788. He was invited to become the pastor of the church in Wenham in November, 1792, and was installed there in the following December. He continued the pastor of this church until the close of the year 1799, when, at his own solicitation, he was dismissed. In 1802, he was installed as pastor of one of the churches in Plymouth. Here he remained about fifteen years. Having changed his sentiments on the subject of baptism, he was dismissed in 1817. He died at Scituate, Massachusetts, November 25, 1826, aged seventy-six.

Mr. Judson was a man of vigorous mind, resolute will, and strong common sense. His judgments were generally accurate, and his reliance upon them implicit. He was rather fitted to command than to obey, and his system of domestic government, probably, belonged more to the patriarchal than to the present dispensation. Though not, so far as I discover, ambitious of personal distinction, he appears to have coveted eminence for his children with more than a wise eagerness; and to have been in the habit of stimulating his son to exertion by the assurance that he would certainly become a great man. The propriety of creating these anticipations in the minds of the young is at best doubtful. Talent generally reveals itself, at a sufficiently early period, to the consciousness of its possessor. To have done a thing is the proper proof to a young man that he can do it. It is, besides, the only reliable evidence of his actual ability. To encourage extravagant anticipations of success in the mind of a child is commonly to sow the seeds of oddity and arrogance, and render ultimate failure almost inevitable.

I had once or twice the pleasure of spending a few hours with Mr. Judson, after he had passed the seventieth year of his age. His appearance has left a deep impression on my recollection, now that nearly thirty years have glided away. He was, as I remember him, a man of decidedly imposing appearance. His stature was rather above the average height. His white hair, erect position, grave utterance, and somewhat taciturn manner, together with the position which he naturally took in society, left you somewhat at a loss whether to class him with a patriarch of the Hebrews, or a censor of the Romans. He was, through life, esteemed a man of inflexible integrity, and uniform consistency of Christian character.

The son, at an early age, gave promise of unusual ability. His intellect was acute, his power of acquisition great, and his perseverance unflagging. To these elements of character he added a love of preëminence which seems to have been carried somewhat to excess. His temper was amiable; specially so in his own family. From early years he seems to have been remarked for uncommon self-reliance. Thus endowed, it may readily be believed that he was generally the acknowledged leader in the little circles to which he became attached.

Young Judson was taught to read by his mother, when only three years old. His father had gone from home on a short journey, and she, wishing to surprise her husband, took the opportunity to teach the child to read during his absence. He learned so rapidly that he was able to give his father a chapter of the Bible on his return. In speaking of this and other similar things, he said that he was not aware of being injured by the forcing system, but he should certainly not prescribe it for his children.

On the 17th of August, 1804, Mr. Judson entered Providence College, now Brown University, one year in advance. He was then in his sixteenth year. His contemporaries all unite in representing him to have been a young man of studious and secluded habits, attaining to perfection in every exercise, and scrupulously careful to devote every moment of his time to intellectual improvement. During a part of his collegiate course, he was engaged in the instruction of a school in Plymouth. At the close of his senior year, he received the highest appointment for commencement, an English oration, with the valedictory addresses.

This appointment was sufficient to prove that Mr. Judson was, in the opinion of his instructors, the first scholar in his class. But it is evident that, beyond this, they considered him a young man of rare attainments and extraordinary promise. The late Rev. Dr. Messer, then president of the university, a man chary of praise, and eminently cautious in his judgments, wrote the following letter to the father of the future missionary during the first year of his collegiate residence: —

BROWN UNIVERSITY, April 30, 1805.

REV. SIR: Notwithstanding the greatness of my present hurry, I must drop you a word respecting your son; and this,

I can assure you, is not by way of complaint. A uniform propriety of conduct, as well as an intense application to study, distinguishes his character. Your expectations of him, however sanguine, must certainly be gratified. I most heartily congratulate you, my dear sir, on that charming prospect which you have exhibited in this very amiable and promising son; and I most heartily pray that the Father of mercies may make him now, while a youth, a son in his spiritual family, and give him an earnest of the inheritance of the saints in light.

I am, very respectfully,
Your friend and servant,
ASA MESSER.

Shortly after leaving college, Mr. Judson published a work on English Grammar. A recommendation of the book by his former instructors, Rev. Drs. Messer and Park, holds the following language: —

PROVIDENCE, February 15, 1808.

SIR: In expressing our opinion of your "Elements of English Grammar," we ought, perhaps, to remind you, that that opinion may possibly be affected by a recollection of the very worthy and honorable manner in which you pursued the whole of your collegiate course, and in which, when less than twenty years old, you finished it at the last commencement. Be this as it may, you may be certain that the work has given us much gratification. It exhibits a fresh instance of the ingenious literary enterprise and perseverance of its author; and should you conclude to give it to the public, it will, we hope, meet, as it merits, a generous patronage.

We remain, with respect,
Your affectionate friends,
ASA MESSER.
CALVIN PARK.

The fo lowing reminiscences of young Judson extend from his early boyhood until a short time after his graduation. They contain all that can be elicited from the recollections of his surviving relatives respecting this period of his history.

Dr. Judson's sister remembers, with an interest which, no doubt, obtained a very important accession from the events of after life, that, at the age of four years, little Adoniram used to collect the children of the neighborhood about him, and mounting a chair, go through with the exercises of the pulpit with singular earnestness, and greatly to the admiration of his auditors. This was a favorite reminiscence of his parents; and they never forgot that the hymn usually put forth on these occasions was the one commencing, " Go preach my gospel, saith the Lord."

Adoniram was about seven years old, when, having been duly instructed that the earth is a spherical body, and that it revolves around the sun, it became a serious question, in his mind, whether or not the sun moved at all. He might have settled the point by asking his father or mother; but that would have spoiled all his pleasant speculations, and probably would have been the very last thing to occur to him. His little sister, whom alone he consulted, said the sun did move, for she could see it; but he had learned already, in this matter, to distrust the evidence of his senses, and he talked so wisely about positive proof, that she was astonished and silenced. Soon after this, he was one day missed about midday; and as he had not been seen for several hours, his father became uneasy, and went in search of him. He was found in a field, at some distance from the house, stretched on his back, his hat with a circular hole cut in the crown, laid over his face, and his swollen eyes almost blinded with the intense light and heat. He only told his father that he was looking at the sun; but he assured his sister that he had solved the problem with regard to the sun's moving, though she never could comprehend the process by which he arrived at the result.

He was noted among his companions for uncommon acuteness in the solution of charades and enigmas, and retained a great store of them in his memory, for the purpose of puzzling his schoolfellows. On one occasion, he found, in a newspaper, an enigma rather boastfully set forth, and accompanied by a challenge for a solution. He felt very sure that he had "guessed riddles as hard as that," and gave himself no rest until he had discovered a satisfactory answer. This he copied out in as fair a hand as possible, addressed it to the editor, and with no confidant but his sister, conveyed it to the post office. But the postmaster supposed it to be some mischievous prank of the minister's son, and he accordingly placed the letter in the hands of the father. The poor boy's surprise and discomfiture may be imagined, when he saw it paraded on the table after tea. "Is that yours, Adoniram?" "Yes, sir." "How came you to write it?" Silence. "What is it about?" Falteringly, "Please read it, father." "I do not read other people's letters. Break the seal, and read it yourself." Adoniram broke the seal, and mumbled over the contents, then placed the letter in his father's hands. He read it, called for the newspaper which had suggested it, and after reading and re-reading both, laid them on the table, crossed his hands on his knees, and looked intently into the fire. Meantime Adoniram stood silently watching his countenance, speculating on the chances of his being treated as a culprit, or praised for his acuteness. But the father woke from his revery, the subject of conversation was changed, and the letter never heard of afterwards. The next morning, Adoniram's father gravely informed him that he had purchased for his use a book of riddles, a very common one, but as soon as he had solved all that it contained, he should have more difficult books. "You are a very acute boy, Adoniram," he added, patting him on the head with unusual affection, "and I expect you to become a great man." Adoniram seized upon the book of riddles joyfully, and was a good deal surprised and disappointed to find it the veritable arithmetic which the larger boys in Master Dodge's school were studying. But then his father had praised him, and if there was any thing puzzling in the arithmetic, he was sure he should like it; and so he prepared to enter upon the study with alacrity.

Before reaching his tenth year, he had gained quite a reputation for good scholarship, especially in arithmetic. A gentleman residing in the neighboring town of Beverly sent him a problem, with the offer of a dollar for the solution. Adoniram immediately shut himself in his chamber. The reward was tempting; but, more important still, his reputation was at stake. On the morning of the second day, he was called from his seclusion to amuse his little brother, who was ill. He went reluctantly, but without murmuring, for the government of his parents was of a nature that no child would think of resisting. His task was to build a cob house. He laid an unusually strong foundation, with unaccountable slowness and hesitation, and was very deliberately proceeding with the superstructure, when suddenly he exclaimed, "That's it! I've got it!" and sending the materials for the half-built house rolling about the room, he hurried off to his chamber to record the result. The problem was solved, the dollar was won, and the boy's reputation established.

At the age of ten he was sent to one Captain Morton, of whom he took lessons in navigation, in which he is said to have made decided progress. In the grammar school he was noted for his proficiency in the Greek language. His schoolmates nicknamed him Virgil, or (in allusion to the peculiar style of the hat which he wore, as well as to his studious habits) "old Virgil dug up." As a boy, he was spirited, self-confident, and exceedingly enthusiastic, very active and energetic, but fonder of his books than of play. His sister has a vivid recollection of his affectionate tenderness towards her, and of his great kindness to inferior animals. He was very fond of desultory reading; and as there were no books for children at that period, he alternated between the books of theology, found in his father's library, and the novels of Richardson and Fielding, or the plays of Ben Jonson, which he was able to borrow in the neighborhood. It is not probable that his father encouraged this latter class of reading; but the habits of self-dependence which he had thought proper to cultivate in his son, left his hours of leisure mostly untrammelled; and seeing the greediness with which the boy occasionally devoured books of the gravest character, it very likely had not occurred to him that he could feel the least possible interest in any work of the imagination.

Before Adoniram was twelve years of age, he had heard visitors at his father's talk a great deal of a new exposition of the Apocalypse, which they pronounced a work of rare interest. Now, the Revelation was the book that, of all others in the Bible, he delighted most to read; and he had searched the few commentators his father possessed without getting much light upon its mysteries. The new exposition was owned by a very awe-inspiring gentleman in the neighborhood; but Adoniram felt that he *must* have it, and after combating a long time with his bashfulness, he at last determined on begging the loan of it. He presented himself in the great man's library, and was coldly and sternly refused. For once, his grief and mortification were so great that he could not conceal the affair from his father. He received more sympathy than he anticipated. "Not lend it to you!" said the good man, indignantly; "I wish *he* could understand it half as well. You shall have books, Adoniram, just as many as you can read, and I'll go to Boston myself for them." He performed his promise, but the desired work on the Apocalypse, perhaps for judicious reasons, was not obtained.

When about fourteen years of age, his studies were interrupted by a serious attack of illness, by which he was reduced to a state of extreme weakness, and for a long time his recovery was doubtful. It was more than a year before he was able to resume his customary occupations. Previous to this, he had been too actively engaged to devote much time to thought; but as soon as the violence of the disease subsided, he spent many long days and nights in reflecting on his future course. His plans were of the most extravagantly ambitious character. Now he was an orator, now a poet, now a statesman; but whatever his character or profession, he was sure in his castle building to attain to the highest eminence. After a time, one thought crept into his mind, and imbittered all his musings. Suppose he should attain to the very highest pinnacle of which human nature is capable; what then? Could he hold his honors forever? His favorites of other ages had long since been turned to dust, and what was it to them that the world still praised them? What would it be to him, when a hundred years had gone by, that America had never known his equal? He did not wonder that Alexander wept when at the summit of his ambition; he felt very sure that he should have wept too. Then he would become alarmed at the extent of his own wicked soarings, and try to comfort himself with the idea that it was all the result of the fever in his brain.

One day his mind reverted to religious pursuits. Yes, an eminent divine was very well, though he should of course prefer something more brilliant. Gradually, and without his being aware of his own train of thought, his mind instituted a comparison between the great worldly divine, toiling for the same perishable objects as his other favorites, and the humble minister of the gospel, laboring only to please God and benefit his fellow-men. There was (so he thought) a sort of sublimity about that, after all. Surely the world was all wrong, or such a self-abjuring man would be its hero. Ah, but the good man had a reputation more enduring. Yes, yes, his fame was sounded before him as he entered the other world; and that was the only fame worthy of the possession, because the only one that triumphed over the grave. Suddenly, in the midst of his self-gratulation, the words flashed across his mind, "Not unto us, not unto us, but to Thy name be the glory." He was confounded. Not that he had actually made himself the representative of this last kind of greatness; it was not sufficiently to his taste for that; but he had ventured on dangerous ground, and he was startled by a flood of feelings that had till now remained dormant. He had always said and thought, so far as he had thought any thing about it, that he wished to become ruly religious; but now religion seemed so entirely opposed to all his ambitious plans, that he was afraid to look into his heart, lest he should discover what he did not like to confess, even to himself—that he did not want to become a Christian. He was fully awake to the vanity of worldly pursuits, and was, on the whole, prepared to yield the palm of excellence to religious ones; but his father had often said he would one day be a great man, and a great man he had resolved to be.

He entered college at sixteen, a year in advance; and having lost his fifteenth year by illness, he was obliged to devote himself very closely to his studies, and seldom gave himself any respite, even during the vacations. He was ambitious to excel; and a classmate says of him, he has "no recollection of his ever failing, or even hesitating, in recitation." He had a powerful rival in his friend Bailey,* and this probably added zest to his ambition. When he received the highest appointment in the commencement exercises, his delight knew no bounds. He hurried to his room, and wrote, "Dear father, I have got it. Your affectionate son, A. J." He then took a circuitous route to the post office, that he might quiet the beatings of his heart, and appear with propriety before his classmates, and especially before his rival friend.

It was at this period that French infidelity was sweeping over the land like a flood; and free inquiry in matters of religion was supposed to constitute part of the education of every man of spirit. Young Judson did not escape the contamination. In the class above him was a young man by the name of E——, who was amiable, talented, witty, exceedingly agreeable in person and manners, but a confirmed Deist. A very strong friendship sprang up between the two young men, founded on similar tastes and sympathies; and Judson soon became, at least professedly, as great an unbeliever as his friend. The subject of a profession was often discussed

---

* The late Hon. John Bailey, member of Congress from Massachusetts.

between them. At one time, they proposed entering the law, because it afforded so wide a scope for political ambition; and at another, they discussed their own dramatic powers, with a view to writing plays.

Immediately on closing the school at Plymouth, Judson set out on a tour through the Northern States. After visiting some of the New England States, he left the horse with which his father had furnished him with an uncle in Sheffield, Massachusetts, and proceeded to Albany to see the wonder of the world, the newly-invented Robert Fulton steamer. She was about proceeding on her second trip to New York, and he gladly took passage in her. The magnificent scenery of the Hudson had then excited comparatively little attention, and its novelty and sublimity could not fail to make a deep and lasting impression on one of Judson's ardent and adventurous spirit. Indeed, during his last illness, he described it with all the enthusiasm that he might have done in his youth. His name was frequently mistaken for that of Johnson; and it occurred to him that, in the novel scenes before him, he might as well use this convenient disguise, in order to see as deeply into the world as possible. He therefore, without actually giving out the name with distinctness, or ever writing it down, became Mr. Johnson. He had not been long in New York before he contrived to attach himself to a theatrical company, not with the design of entering upon the stage, but partly for the purpose of familiarizing himself with its regulations, in case he should enter upon his literary projects, and partly from curiosity and love of adventure.

Before setting out upon his tour he had unfolded his infidel sentiments to his father, and had been treated with the severity natural to a masculine mind that has never doubted, and to a parent who, after having made innumerable sacrifices for the son of his pride and his love, sees him rush recklessly on his own destruction. His mother also, was no less distressed, and she wept, and prayed, and expostulated. He knew his superiority to his father in argument; but he had nothing to oppose to his mother's tears and warnings, and they followed him now wherever he went. He knew that he was on the verge of such a life as he despised. For the world he would not see a young brother in his perilous position; but "I," he thought, "am in no danger. I am only seeing the world — the dark side of it, as well as the bright; and I have too much self-respect to do any thing mean or vicious." After seeing what he wished of New York, he returned to Sheffield for his horse, intending to pursue his journey westward. His uncle, Rev. Ephraim Judson, was absent, and a very pious young man occupied his place. His conversation was characterized by a godly sincerity, a solemn but gentle earnestness, which addressed itself to the heart, and Judson went away deeply impressed.

The next night he stopped at a country inn. The landlord mentioned, as he lighted him to his room, that he had been obliged to place him next door to a young man who was exceedingly ill, probably in a dying state; but he hoped that it would occasion him no uneasiness. Judson assured him that, beyond pity for the poor sick man, he should have no feeling whatever, and that now, having heard of the circumstance, his pity would not of course be increased by the nearness of the object. But it was, nevertheless, a very restless night. Sounds came from the sick chamber — sometimes the movements of the watchers, sometimes the groans of the sufferer; but it was not these which disturbed him. He thought of what the landlord had said — the stranger was probably in a dying state; and was he prepared? Alone, and in the dead of night, he felt a blush of shame steal over him at the question, for it proved the shallowness of his philosophy. What would his late companions say to his weakness? The clear-minded, intellectual, witty E——, what would he say to such consummate boyishness? But still his thoughts *would* revert to the sick man. Was he a Christian, calm and strong in the hope of a glorious immortality? or was he shuddering upon the brink of a dark, unknown future? Perhaps he was a "freethinker," educated by Christian parents, and prayed over by a Christian mother. The landlord had described him as a *young* man; and in imagination he was forced to place himself upon the dying bed, though he strove with all his might against it. At last morning came, and the bright flood of light which it poured into his chamber dispelled all his "superstitious illusions." As soon as he had risen, he went in search of the landlord, and inquired for his fellow-lodger. "He is dead," was the reply. "Dead!" "Yes, he is gone, poor fellow! The doctor said he would probably not survive the night." "Do you know who he was?" "O, yes; it was a young man from Providence College — a very fine fellow; his name was E——." Judson was completely stunned. After hours had passed, he knew not how, he attempted to pursue his journey. But one single thought occupied his mind, and the words, Dead! lost! lost! were continually ringing in his ears. He knew the religion of the Bible to be true; he felt its truth; and he was in despair. In this state of mind he resolved to abandon his scheme of travelling, and at once turned his horse's head towards Plymouth.

Mr. Judson graduated Bachelor of Arts on September 2, 1807. On the 17th of the same month, he opened a private school in the town of Plymouth, where his parents then resided. February 25, 1808, he completed his "Elements of English Grammar." I have before me a copy of this work. It was published in Boston, by Cushing & Lincoln, and is, I presume, a good epitome of the forms and laws of the language. In July of the same year, he completed and published "The Young Lady's Arithmetic," which was, at the time, a valuable text book for schools. The preparation of two works of this kind, in addition to the labors of a school, indicates that, at this early period, he had inured himself to strenuous and enterprising labor.

August 9, 1808, he closed his school, and commenced the journey through the Northern States, of which mention is made in the preceding memoranda. He returned to Plymouth, September 22, with his mind deeply impressed with the necessity of personal religion. At this crisis, the Rev. Dr. Griffin and the Rev. Moses Stuart, both professors in the Theological Seminary at Andover, visited his father. They proposed that he should enter that seminary. He seems to have been for some time undecided, and a few days afterwards engaged himself as an assistant to a teacher in Boston. This situation, however, he soon relinquished, and proceeded to Andover to connect himself with the seminary. He entered the institution in October, not as a professor of religion and candidate for the ministry, but as a person deeply in earnest on the subject, and desirous of arriving at the truth.

CHAPTER II.

RESIDENCE AT ANDOVER. — CONVERSION. — FIRST IMPULSES TOWARDS MISSIONARY LABOR. — MISSIONARY ASSOCIATIONS — ORIGIN OF THE AMERICAN BOARD OF COMMISSIONERS.

1808-1810.

Mr. Judson removed to Andover October 12, 1808. He was at first admitted as a special student; that is, he was permitted to attend the various courses of instruction in the seminary; but, having made no profession of religion, he could not be received as a member in full standing. As he entered at once upon the studies of the second year, he must already have made considerable proficiency in the languages of the Old and New Testaments.

At this period, he had no hope of pardon through Christ. He had become thoroughly dissatisfied with the views of life which he had formerly cherished. Aware of his personal sinfulness, and conscious that he needed some great moral transformation, he yet doubted the authenticity of revealed religion, and clung to the deistical sentiments which he had lately imbibed. His mind did not readily yield to the force of evidence. This is by no means an uncommon case; nor is it at all difficult of explanation. A deeply-seated dislike to the humbling doctrines of the cross frequently assumes the form of inability to apply the common principles of evidence to the case of revealed religion. Men of unusual strength of will, and a somewhat too confident reliance on the decisions of their individual intellect, are peculiarly liable to fall into this error.

Mr. Judson's moral nature was, however, thoroughly aroused, and he was deeply in earnest on the subject of religion. The professors of the theological seminary encouraged his residence at the institution, wisely judging that so diligent an inquirer must soon arrive at the truth. The result justified their anticipations. In the calm retirement of Andover, guided in his studies by men the praise of whose learning and piety is in all the churches, with nothing to distract his attention from the great concerns of eternity, light gradually dawned upon his mind, and he was enabled to surrender his whole soul to Christ as his atoning Savior. This event occurred in November, about six weeks after his removal to Andover. On the 2d of December, 1808, as he has recorded, he made a solemn dedication of himself to God. On the 28th of May, 1809, he made a public profession of religion, and joined the Third Congregational Church in Plymouth, of which his father was then pastor.

The change in Mr. Judson's religious character was not attended by those external indications of moral excitement which are frequently observed. The reformation wrought in him was, however, deep and radical. With unusual simplicity of purpose, he yielded himself up once and forever to the will of God, and, without a shadow of misgiving, relied upon Christ as his all-sufficient Savior. From the moment of his conversion, he seems never, through life, to have been harassed by a doubt of his acceptance with God. The new creation was so manifest to his consciousness, that, in the most decided form, he had the witness in himself. His plans of life were, of course, entirely reversed. He banished forever those dreams of literary and political ambition in which he had formerly indulged, and simply asked himself, How shall I so order my future being as best to please God? The portions of his correspondence which belong to this period indicate an earnest striving after personal holiness, and an enthusiastic consecration of every endowment to the service of Christ.

In June, 1809, he received and declined the appointment to a tutorship in Brown University.

In September of the same year, he read, for the first time, Buchanan's " Star in the East." It was this that led him to reflect upon the personal duty of devoting his life to the cause of missions. The subject occupied his prayerful attention until February, 1810, when he finally resolved, in obedience to what he believed to be the command of God, to become a missionary to the heathen.

The following letters and reminiscences will, I think, enable us to form a tolerably definite conception of Mr. Judson's religious character during his preparation for the ministry, and of the impression which he made upon his instructors and friends: —

From the Rev. Gardner Spring, D. D., to Mrs. Emily C. Judson.

. . . Your departed husband and I were members of the same class; met daily for religious and scholastic purposes; and our intercourse was uniformly, and to the last, of the most pleasant kind. His youthful heart was glowing with zeal for the extension of the gospel to this lost world. He often conversed on the subject with me, and once desired me to ascertain the views of my deceased father* in regard to the practicability and wisdom of the enterprise which issued in his own personal devotement to the missionary cause. There were other young men in the seminary of like sympa-

---

* The late Rev. Dr. Spring, of Newburyport.

thies, whose names you know. They formed a lovely cluster of the fruits of the Spirit, whose fragrance has many a time diffused itself over my own barren heart, and is allied to some of the sweeter memories of my ministry.

From the Rev. Dr. Woods, of Andover, to Mrs. Emily C. Judson.

I wish I could do more in compliance with your request than I am able to do. I have had letters from Dr. Judson; but they were on business, and are not now easily found. My recollections of him are very distinct and very interesting. When he first came to Andover, he was, as he described himself in the church at Hamilton, destitute of the love of God, altogether in darkness and unbelief. But he was soon visited, I trust, with renewing grace, and, after some time, set his heart upon the salvation of the heathen. He was of an ardent temperament, and his ardor showed itself in every thing he undertook. His mind was very active, and he excelled in scholarship. When he visited this country, my intercourse with him at Andover and at Hamilton was very delightful. I thought he had made great advances in the divine life, and was adorned with the beauties of holiness. He now is regarded by the Christian world, and that very justly, as a distinguished missionary — eminent in labors, in sufferings, and in usefulness. His memory is blessed, and God has been glorified in him.

Miss Mary Hasseltine, the sister of Mrs. Ann H. Judson, has furnished me with the following reminiscences of this period: —

My recollections of his youthful efforts as a preacher are, that he was solemn, impassioned, logical, and highly scriptural, without much of the hortatory, with no far-fetched figure or studied ornament of phrase. I can see his erect, commanding figure in the sacred desk, his manly countenance glowing with celestial fire, laboring intensely to excite in his hearers an interest in those high and holy themes that so fill his own vision. Methinks I hear his strains of eloquence as he proceeds:

FIRST IMPULSES TOWARDS MISSIONARY LABOR. 31

"See you that Christless youth, a scorner of God and goodness? His steps take hold on death, his vicious career hastens him onward to the verge of time. At this dread moment, 'terrors take hold on him as waters, as a storm hurleth him out of his place.' He drops into those dark abodes, where hope never comes; his affrighted spirit shrieks out, How long am I to stay in this place of torment? From every part of those doleful shades is reverberated, Forever, forever, forever." His eloquence and oratory were a transcript of Dr. Griffin's.

His first introduction to our family was in the summer of 1810, at the general association of Massachusetts, which met at Bradford. But we had no acquaintance with him until the succeeding autumn. He was then in all the ardor of his first love. It may literally be said, that he was a man of one idea, and that was, love to Jesus, and a desire to manifest it in all its varied forms. Yet he was by nature ardent, impetuous, and ambitious, with the most unshaken confidence in his own judgment, irrespective of the advice of his seniors. Of these propensities he was fully conscious, and against them continually warred.

Mrs. Ann H. Judson gives the following testimony to his piety, in a letter to her sisters, after a residence with him of eleven years. She says, "I feel that there is not a better man on the globe than my husband; not one who labors more strenuously to overcome every unhallowed emotion of his spirit." She further adds, "I have known him to spend whole days in fasting and prayer, taking no nourishment but a little fruit in the morning, passing the day at the zayat, and returning in the evening languid and pale." While at Calcutta, the subject of a situation in the college at Fort William was mentioned to him. He remarked, "It would suit my ambitious feelings, but I would by no means indulge them." It was remarked by the excellent Dr. Spring,* that he was aware of young Judson's ambition; but when God should have disciplined him with trials, he will be admirably fitted for his great work. Should

---

* Of Newburyport.

he be located in a place where a translation of the Scriptures would be required, he was so fine a linguist that he would be the very man to prosecute the arduous task.

Some of the letters which follow were written at a later date than the period comprehended within the present chapter. They all, however, relate to the same subject, — the religious sentiments of Mr. Judson previous to the time of his embarkation for India, — and I have therefore grouped them together in this place.

Letters to Miss Ann Hasseltine.

ANDOVER, December 30, 1810. Sunday Eve.

I have been through the labors of another Sabbath. A preacher can say with Pope, "E'en Sunday shines no day of rest to me." Brother Nott preaches this evening; but, on account of a cold, I stay at home. I am persuaded that the chief reason why we do not enjoy religion is, that we do not try to enjoy it. We are not like a good man who resolved that he *would* grow in grace. We pervert the doctrine of our dependence to indulging indolence and sinful ease. I have enjoyed some religion to-day, and I think by means of resolving in the morning that I would avoid every thing displeasing to God. I have some hope that I shall be enabled to keep this in mind, in whatever I do — *Is it pleasing to God?* To assist my memory, I have used the expedient of inscribing it on several articles which frequently meet my sight. Is it not a good plan? But after all, it will be of no use, unless I resolve, in divine strength, instantly to obey the decision of conscience.

December 31. Monday Eve.

It is now half after nine, and I have been sitting fifteen minutes with my pen in hand, thinking how to begin. I have this day attained more than ever to what I suppose Christians mean by the enjoyment of God. I have had pleasant seasons at the throne of God. Those lines of Watts have been very sweet to me : —

> "Till thou hast brought me to my home,
> Where fears and doubts can never come,
> Thy countenance let me often see,
> And often thou shalt hear from me."
>
> 78th of 1st Book.

God is waiting to be gracious, and is willing to make us happy in religion, if we would not run away from him. We refuse to open the window shutters, and complain that it is dark. We grieve the Holy Spirit by little sins, and thus lose our only support. Perhaps the secret of living a holy life is to avoid every thing which will displease God and grieve the Spirit, and to be strictly attentive to the means of grace. God has promised that he will regard the man that is of a broken and contrite spirit, and trembleth at his word. He has promised that they that wait upon him shall renew their strength. The Almighty, the immutably faithful, has made this promise. He is not a man, that he should lie, and his arm is not of flesh. Wait, then, upon the Lord. Of how much real happiness we cheat our souls by preferring a trifle to God! We have a general intention of living religion; but we intend to begin to-morrow, or next year. The present moment we prefer giving to the world. "A little more sleep, a little more slumber." Well, a little more sleep, and we shall sleep in the grave. A few days, and our work will be done. And when it is once done, it is done to all eternity. A life once spent is irrevocable. It will remain to be contemplated through eternity. If it be marked with sins, the marks will be indelible. If it has been a useless life, it can never be improved. Such it will stand forever and ever. The same may be said of each day. When it is once past, it is gone forever. All the marks which we put upon it it will exhibit forever. It will never become less true that such a day was spent in such a manner. Each day will not only be a witness of our conduct, but will affect our everlasting destiny. No day will lose its share of influence in determining where shall be our seat in heaven. How shall we then wish to see each day marked with usefulness! It will then be too late to mend its appearance. It is too late to mend the days that are past. The future is in our power. Let us, then, each morning, resolve to send the day into eternity in such a garb as we shall wish it to wear forever. And at night let us reflect that one more day is irrevocably gone, indelibly marked. Good night.

January 1, 1811. Tuesday Morn.

It is with the utmost sincerity, and with my whole heart, that I wish you, my love, a happy new year. May it be a year in which your walk will be close with God; your frame calm and serene; and the road that leads you to the Lamb marked with purer light. May it be a year in which you will have more largely the spirit of Christ, be raised above sublunary things, and be willing to be disposed of in this world just as God shall please. As every moment of the year will bring you nearer the end of your pilgrimage, may it bring you nearer to God, and find you more prepared to hail the messenger of death as a deliverer and a friend. And now, since I have begun to wish, I will go on. May this be the year in which you will change your name; in which you will take a final leave of your relatives and native land; in which you will cross the wide ocean, and dwell on the other side of the world, among a heathen people. What a great change will this year probably effect in our lives! How very different will be our situation and employment! If our lives are preserved and our attempt prospered, we shall next new year's day be in India, and perhaps wish each other a happy new year in the uncouth dialect of Hindostan or Burmah. We shall no more see our kind friends around us, or enjoy the conveniences of civilized life, or go to the house of God with those that keep holy day; but swarthy countenances will every where meet our eye, the jargon of an unknown tongue will assail our ears, and we shall witness the assembling of the heathen to celebrate the worship of idol gods. We shall be weary of the world, and wish for wings like a dove, that we may fly away and be at rest. We shall probably experience seasons when we shall be "exceeding sorrowful, even unto death." We shall see many dreary, disconsolate hours, and feel a sinking of spirits, angu'sh of mind, of which now we can form little conception. O, we shall wish to lie down and die. And that time may soon come. One of us may be unable to sustain the heat of the climate and the change of habits; and the other may say, with literal truth, over the grave —

> "By foreign hands thy dying eyes were closed;
> By foreign hands thy decent limbs composed;
> By foreign hands thy humble grave adorned;"

but whether we shall be honored and mourned by strangers, God only knows. At least, either of us will be certain of *one* mourner. In view of such scenes shall we not pray with earnestness, "O for an overcoming faith," &c.?

JUDSON.

Letter to Miss Abigail Hasseltine.

DIVINITY COLLEGE, ANDOVER, October 25, 1810.

I am at a loss what appellation to use in addressing you; so believe I will use none.

Meeting to-day with one Mr. Osgood, from Pembroke, an odd fancy came into my head, that I would write to you; though I have never seen you, and know scarcely any thing of you, more than that you are Ann's sister, and, I hope, a lover of Jesus. The latter circumstance alone would not have afforded sufficient ground to write; so you must charge this letter to Ann's account.

In mentioning these two circumstances, however, I have mentioned a great deal. From the first I conclude certainly that you are a person by whom this letter will be honored by being received. From the other I am led infinitely higher, even to consider you (is it possible for sinners to attain it?) an heir of God, and joint heir with Christ to an inheritance, &c. How much is implied in that one phrase, lover of Jesus! It contains a claim to all the real blessings of this world, and to an eternity of blessings. Love to Jesus is a sure title to the greatest possible happiness; for Jesus is omnipotent, and has determined to make his friends happy, and surely will not forget a single one in whose heart is enkindled one spark of love. Nor does he intend a partial happiness for his friends. It will be as great as their capacity will admit. Nor does he intend a temporal happiness. It will never have an end. Nor does he intend a happiness eternally stationary. It will be eternally increasing. The happiness of his friends will not only be complete, so as to fill their capacity, but as their capacities will be eternally enlarging, the quantity of happiness they enjoy will be eternally increasing; and not merely eternally increasing in the same ratio, but eternally increasing in an eternally accelerated ratio. So that there will unquestionably arrive a moment in the ages of eternity when the additional happiness, that instant superadded to the happiness already enjoyed by each glorified spirit, will almost infinitely outweigh the whole sum of human happiness enjoyed in this world. To all this may he aspire who is a lover of Jesus. Blessed Jesus, thou art no "niggard provider." When thou givest, thou givest like a God.

How little do we, sinful, shortsighted worms of the dust, realize these things! If we did realize them, could we possibly be agitated by the trifles which daily occur? Would it be possible for Christians to be impatient under their light afflictions, which are but for a moment? Should we be unwilling to bear all the hardships and sufferings which Jesus lays upon us in this world, if we had a realizing conviction that the torment, superadded at some one instant in eternity to the torment already endured by each condemned soul, will almost infinitely outweigh all the pain ever suffered in this world?

Reminiscences of Conversations with Dr. Judson.

I have often heard Dr. Judson speak of his introduction to Andover, and of the state of utter darkness, and almost despair, in which he was at the time. I have also heard him tell of the gradual change which came over him; but there was nothing sufficiently striking in it to fasten on the memory.

There was none of his characteristic impetuosity exhibited

in his conversion; and he had none of those overpowering, Bunyan-like exercises, either before or after, that would be looked for in a person of his ardent temperament. He was prayerful, reflective, and studious of proofs; and gradually faith, trust in God, and finally a hope through the merits of Christ, took possession of his soul, he scarcely knew how; and from the moment that he fully believed, I think he never doubted. He said he felt as sure that he was an entirely new creature, actuated by new motives and governed by new principles, as he was sure of his own existence. His old habits of thought and feeling, to some extent, clung to him, but they were made subservient to higher purposes; and though he might still have his objects of ambition, they could never again be of the first moment. The change, though gradual, was too marked, too entire, to admit of a moment's doubt. He had no exercises on the subject of entering the ministry; it became a matter of course immediately on his indulging a hope.

Dr. Judson's letter to Dr. Chapin describes his first meeting with Buchanan's "Star in the East," and its effect upon him. He has often related the same circumstances to me, sometimes giving ludicrous descriptions of his own conduct, but usually ending by thanking God that he had been granted, in any way, such a vivid conception of his duty as to preclude all subsequent hesitancy or faltering. But however extravagant his conduct may have been, I doubt whether his feelings, even then, were stronger than they remained in after life. His missionary views were always of the most comprehensive and engrossing character; and his remarks in our monthly concerts, and more especially at the close of a day's work in private, were characterized by a high-wrought enthusiasm seldom found in persons of his maturity of years and judgment.

He devoured with great greediness every scrap of information concerning Eastern countries; and it was finally Colonel Symes's "Embassy to Ava" which first turned his thoughts to Burmah. These glowing and overwrought pictures were peculiarly congenial to his romantic spirit; but it is again remarkable that the interest thus excited was never lost; that, on the contrary, it grew deeper and stronger as the brilliant fancy colors faded. He did not think exclusively of Burmah however, though his predilections for that country were strong. His heart from the first was turned entirely to the East, and he was impatient of any thing short of a life devotement.

He spent the winter vacation, 1810, at Plymouth, and attended a meeting at Old Dedham, where there was a great revival. Up to this time his parents had not been made acquainted with his missionary views. He felt an exceedingly great reluctance to break the matter to his father, whose ambitious views with regard to him he very well knew, and who was not likely, he thought, to fall in with a plan of this sort. One evening his father threw out some hints of splendid prospects in the future, and his mother and sister showed by smiling innuendoes that they were in the secret. Adoniram became alarmed, and begged his father to explain himself, as their views with regard to the future might not coincide, and it was desirable to have an understanding on the subject. His father was very sure there would be no difference of opinion, and then proceeded to explain that the Rev. Dr. Griffin had proposed his son as his colleague in "the largest church in Boston." "And you will be so near home!" added his mother. His heart seemed bursting, and he could not answer either of them. But soon his sister joined in the conversation, and to her he replied, "No, sister; I shall never live in Boston. I have much farther than that to go." Steadily and calmly, but most fervidly, he proceeded to describe the course which he had marked out for himself; and though it occasioned his mother and sister very many tears, his father scarcely offered a word of opposition. He wisely acquiesced in what he probably saw was inevitable.

Dr. Griffin had conferred thus early with the elder Judson, with regard to his son, that he might prevent him from committing himself to any other plan.

While at Andover, Mr. Judson's attention was first called to the subject of health. He was thought to possess a certain delicacy of constitution, with a tendency to consumption. It occurred to him, that, if he became a missionary, it was important that he should study the best mode of promoting health and prolonging life, as on these his usefulness would in a great measure depend. He therefore entered into a careful study of physiology, and arrived at certain practical rules, which always afterwards governed him. Among these, the first was, frequently to inhale large quantities of air, so as to expand the lungs to the utmost; the second, daily to sponge the whole body in cold water; the third, and above all, to take systematic exercise in walking. All these he carried out to the end of his life, insisting that no exercise, such as gardening, riding, &c., could be substituted for walking; that is, could answer as a *full* substitute. How much the length of his life depended on this, it is impossible to say; but it is at least illustrative of his character. No man was ever more ready to expose himself to dangers and privations; but even when doing what would appear to worldly men the most reckless things, he studied every precaution, and provided himself with every comfort that the case would admit of, and always strove to impress on his missionary associates a similar daring with a similar thoughtfulness.

The preceding letters show that, from the time of his self-consecration to the missionary service, he became, in the highest sense, a man of one idea. He offered himself up a living sacrifice on the altar, and seemed to look forward with pleasure to suffering and affliction, if it were to be endured in the path of Christian duty.

It has been already mentioned, that in September, 1809, Mr. Judson first began to consider his personal duty in relation to missions. In February, 1810, he resolved to become a missionary to the heathen. In the interval between these two dates, several young men, whose names have now become familiar to us as household words, joined the seminary from Williams

College. Among them were Samuel J. Mills, Jr., James Richards, and Luther Rice. They had already formed a missionary society in college, the object of which was to train themselves for the work of missions to the heathen. The second article of their constitution was in the following words: "The object of this society shall be to effect, in the persons of its members, a mission or missions to the heathen." In the fifth article it is provided, that "no person shall be admitted who is under an obligation of any kind which shall be incompatible with going on a mission to the heathen." The sixth article is as follows: "Each member shall keep himself absolutely free from every engagement, which, after his prayerful attention, and after consultation with the brethren, shall be deemed incompatible with the object of this society, and shall hold himself in readiness to go on a mission when and where duty may call."

This constitution was signed September 7, 1808, about a month before Mr. Judson entered the seminary at Andover.

The most active promoter of this missionary association in Williams College, I think, without doubt, was Samuel J. Mills. He entered college in 1806, having, as it seems, relinquished secular pursuits, and entered upon a course of education, for the purpose of preparing himself for missionary labor. While in college he presented the subject to James Richards, Luther Rice, and Gordon Hall. With them he united in the formation of this same missionary fraternity, and his whole life, from that time forward, was exclusively devoted to the work of missions.

Several of the members of this society entered the Theological Seminary in 1809. They were here joined by Rev. Samuel Nott, Jr., who, a year before, while studying theology with his father, the Rev. Samuel Nott, D. D., of Franklin, Connecticut, had been deeply impressed with the conviction of his duty to carry the gospel to the heathen. Judson was already considering the subject, and in the following February came to a decision. We thus perceive that, in these several places, the Spirit of God was leading different individuals to dedicate themselves to the cause of the heathen. In 1809 and 1810 they were brought together at Andover, and becoming known to each other, were soon united in bonds of Christian affection. Henceforward their plans were formed in common. One leading impulse moved them all. They conversed together, they prayed together, and they labored together to kindle the missionary flame in Andover, in many of the colleges in our country, and among the churches wherever they were called to preach. In this manner they cultivated the spirit of self-devotion in their own hearts, and were anxiously looking for those indications of divine Providence which should point out the way in which their desires might be accomplished.

Mr. Judson's name was not affixed to the constitution of this missionary association until 1811. The reason of this apparent delay is, I presume, found in the fact that the society existed for several years, in Williams College, before it was removed to Andover; and he probably, in this formal manner, united with his brethren as soon as an opportunity was afforded.

It has been supposed that the young men at Williams College, and all their associates but Judson, had directed their attention exclusively to western missions, until they met him at Andover. This opinion is, I think, incorrect. Mr. Nott, in 1808, had thought *only* of eastern missions. The constitution of the society refers in general to *heathen*, without any indication of a preference for either the East or the West.

If missions to our own Indians were first thought of, I imagine that this idea was very soon merged in a more comprehensive one. Mills, during a visit to New Haven, became acquainted with Henry Obookiah, a native of the Sandwich Islands. He at once devised means for giving him a Christian education, that he might go back and evangelize his countrymen. In writing to Mr. Hall on this subject, under date of December 20, 1809, Mr. Mills says, " What does this mean, brother Hall? Do you understand it? Shall he be sent back unsupported to reclaim his countrymen? Shall not we consider these southern islands a proper place for the establishment of a mission? Not that I would give up the heathen tribes to the westward. I trust that we shall be able to establish more than one mission in a short time, at least in a few years. I mean that God will enable us to extend our views and labors farther than we have before contemplated. We ought not to look only to the heathen on our own continent. We ought to direct our attention to that place where we may, to human appearance, do the most good, and where the difficulties are the least. . . . The field is almost boundless; in every part of which there ought to be missionaries. In the language of an animated writer, ' O that we could enter at a thousand gates, that every limb were a tongue, and every tongue a trumpet, to spread the gospel sound! The man of Macedonia cries, Come over and help us. This voice is heard from the east and from the west, from the north and from the south.'" This was written by S. J. Mills before he had been at Andover, and about three weeks after Judson had first turned his thoughts especially to missions. In the same letter, however, the following remark is made about Judson, which shows that his views of missions were known to his brethren, and that he had turned his attention to the evangelization of the East: " With regard to Andover, two of the brethren are there; I think it likely I shall go there myself soon, or within four or five weeks. I heard previously of Mr. Judson. You say he thinks of offering himself as a missionary to the London Society, for the East Indies. What! is England to support her own missionaries and ours likewise? O, for shame! If he is prepared to go, I would fain press him forward with the arm of a Hercules, if I had the strength; but I do not like this dependence on another nation, especially when they have already done so much, and we nothing."

From all the facts within my knowledge, I think it probable that Messrs. Judson and Nott, who were specially intimate, had their minds, in the first instance, turned to the East, as a field of missions; and that Mr. Judson had specially fixed his eye on Burmah.

The brethren at Williams College, while devoting themselves to missions in general, had their attention at first directed to the aborigines on our own continent. Their views, however, immediately expanded as the field opened before them; and they looked at heathendom as their appropriate province, prepared to enter it at any point, wherever the providence of God should direct. It is possible that the brethren who went to Andover before Mills had not expanded their views as rapidly as he. When, however, they met together and compared their purposes, they were easily convinced that Asia, with its idolatrous myriads, was the most important field on earth for missionary effort. The attention of the whole company seems henceforth to have been turned almost exclusively to the East.

Another subject here presents itself, on which it is necessary to bestow a passing notice. It has been frequently said that the world is indebted to the young men at Andover for the formation of the American Board of Commissioners. That they were the *occasion* of the formation of the board, is, I think, true. It is also true that, but for them, the board would not have been formed at that particular time. But, if we would ascertain the whole truth, I think we must look also at that condition of the public mind which, at their first application for missionary service, shaped itself into so important an organization.

It is well known that as early as May 28, 1799, an association was formed in Boston under the name of the Massachusetts Missionary Society. The object of this society was, "to diffuse the knowledge of the gospel among the heathens, as well as other people in the remote parts of our country, where Christ is seldom or never preached." In 1804, the constitution of this society was so modified that the article defining its object was made to read as follows: "The object of this society is, to diffuse the gospel among the people of the newly-settled and remote parts of our country, among the Indians of the country, and through more distant regions of the earth, as circumstances shall invite, and the ability of the society shall admit." In 1803, this society commenced the publication of the Massachusetts Missionary Magazine, of which the object was, to circulate missionary intelligence, and awaken and diffuse a missionary spirit among the Congregational churches in New England. This periodical was continued until 1808, when it was merged in the Panoplist, which, in turn, gave way to the present Missionary Herald. The General Assembly's Missionary Magazine, or Religious Intelligencer, was commenced in January, 1805, and was conducted with singular ability. In 1806, the Rev. Dr. Griffin delivered the annual missionary sermon before the General Assembly in Philadelphia. In this discourse the claims of the heathen are urged with an eloquence which has seldom been surpassed. Mr. John Norris, a wealthy merchant of Salem, was deeply interested in the cause of the heathen, and made a large donation to the Andover Theological Seminary, because such an institution would aid in carrying forward his favorite object. Robert Rallston, Esq., of Philadelphia, at one time remitted to the Baptist mission at Serampore, for himself and others, three thousand three hundred and fifty-seven dollars and sixty-three cents. Dr. Carey acknowledged the receipt of six thousand dollars from American Christians during the years 1806 and 1807. The interest of our churches in missions to the East was also, from time to time, quickened by the arrival of missionaries from England, on their way to India, or on their return home, as, at that time, they could not obtain passage in any of the ships of the East India Company. I well remember, in my boyhood, the temporary residence of such missionaries in New York, and the deep interest which their presence occasioned in all the churches in that city. In 1809, the Rev.

Dr. Worcester delivered the annual sermon before the Massachusetts Missionary Society — a discourse which, for depth of earnestness and power of appeal, may be advantageously compared with the most eloquent missionary sermons that have yet appeared. Buchanan's " Star in the East," which was published in the course of the year 1808 or 1809, must have increased and disseminated much more widely the missionary spirit which was already awakened in the community.*

Such was the condition of the Congregational and Presbyterian denominations. The same spirit, to a considerable degree, animated the Baptist churches, though their number was small, and their means but feeble. The Baptist Missionary Society of Massachusetts was formed in 1802. In the next year, Dr. Baldwin, at the request of the society, commenced the publication of the Massachusetts Baptist Missionary Magazine. This periodical had an extensive circulation throughout the Northern States. It was principally occupied by the journals of missionaries in our frontier settlements, narratives of revivals in our churches, and missionary intelligence from abroad. Dr. Baldwin was a correspondent of Dr. Carey, of Fuller, and of Ryland; and, being imbued with their spirit, he delighted to coöperate with them in spreading before his brethren the accounts which they furnished of the triumphs of the cross.

In the year 1812, the Salem Bible Translation and Foreign Mission Society was formed, under the fos-

---

* For the above facts, and many others on this subject, I am indebted to the Rev. Dr. S. M. Worcester's deeply interesting life of his father, the Rev. Samuel Worcester, D. D., the distinguished secretary of the A. B. C. F. M.

tering care of the late Rev. Dr. Bolles. This society, until the establishment of the Baptist General Convention, contributed its collections in aid of the Baptist missions in the East Indies. Nor would it be just to omit, in this place, the name of the Rev William Staughton, D. D., pastor of the Sansom Street Church, Philadelphia, and afterwards secretary of the Baptist General Convention. He had been, when in England, the friend and associate of the most efficient friends of missions there. He was in frequent correspondence with all of them, and was, perhaps, the most direct channel by which their spirit was diffused among our churches. Distinguished for eloquence, varied accomplishments, and most animating views of the progress of the gospel, the triumph of the cross was always a favorite theme in his discourses. Many of our most successful ministers were his students in theology; and they imbibed in a happy degree his characteristic sentiments.

Of course, I do not assume that the missionary spirit was at this time universal. Far from it. It is by no means universal now. Men of enlarged views, steadfast faith, and ardent piety, in various denominations, had become, to a good degree, interested in the subject of missions, and their influence was diffusing itself among their less favored brethren. The beams of the sun had only fallen upon the tops of the mountains; they had not yet rested upon the hillsides; much less had they penetrated into the valleys. But the mountain tops testified that the sun had risen.

As yet, no general organization had been formed for carrying the gospel to the heathen. Nor is this to be wondered at. It was much less easy to form general organizations then than at present. That was not the age of steamboats, railroads, or telegraphs. Besides this, our national character has changed greatly in the course of forty or fifty years. We were then by no means conscious of our strength. There were then comparatively few things in which we had tried what we could do. This want of national confidence affected all our public decisions, and it, of course, had its effect on our views of what was practicable in the missionary enterprise.

In this state of public feeling, all that was wanted was the occurrence of some event which should impose upon the friends of missions the necessity for immediate action. Such an event was found in the application of the young men at Andover, to the General Association of Massachusetts, for an appointment as missionaries to the heathen.

The more important facts relating to this transaction are, I think, the following: The Andover brethren had made it a point to interest in their enterprise the most influential clergymen in that vicinity. Opportunity was afforded for this purpose in their various excursions for the supply of vacant pulpits in the surrounding towns. They had also frequently presented the subject to their instructors, the professors of the seminary. In consequence of these preliminary labors, "by a concerted arrangement, Drs. Spring and Worcester met the professors, with a few others, for consultation, at the house of Professor Stuart, at Andover, on Monday, June 25, 1810. It was a meeting never to be forgotten. Advice was given to Mills and his associates to submit their case to the General Association, which was to meet the next day at Bradford, and which Dr. Spring and Dr. Worcester were expecting to attend as delegates. When this advice was given, the idea of such a body of men as 'The American Board of Commissioners *for Foreign Missions*' had not been suggested."* Dr. Worcester, in a letter dated March 23, 1821, only three months before his lamented death, has given the following account of the first conception of the American Board : " The day of small things is in fresh remembrance. On the 25th of June, 1810, serious deliberation, attended with fervent prayer, was held at Andover, relative to the burning desire of three or four theological students there to be employed as missionaries to the heathen. The result was to refer the momentous question to the General Association of Massachusetts. The next day, Dr. Spring took a seat in my chaise, and rode with me to Bradford, where the General Association was to convene. In the conversation on the way, the *first idea*, I believe, of the American Board of Commissioners for Foreign Missions was suggested ; the form, the number of members, and name were proposed. On the 27th, the question came before the association, and the report of the committee, which was adopted by that body, was the substance of the result of the conversation in the chaise." †

The application was made to the General Association according to the suggestion here spoken of, on the 28th of June, 1810, and referred to a committee. On the following day, a report was presented and adopted, and the first board of commissioners elected. This seems to have been the manner in which it pleased God to unite the labors and counsels of the fathers, into whose breasts he had breathed the missionary spirit, with the self-denying zeal of their younger

* Life of Worcester, vol. ii. p. 99. † Ib. p. 106.

brethren, who had solemnly dedicated themselves to God, as the heralds of his gospel to the heathen.

I am aware that, to the young missionaries, the fathers, who became the pillars of the enterprise, appeared at first slow of heart to believe, and backward in committing themselves to this great undertaking. Though they always spoke in public in favor of missions, yet they seemed to them not fully prepared to carry their principles into practice. Nor is this to be wondered at. Between the adoption of a principle and the carrying it out into practice, under new and untried circumstances, there is an interval over which the wisely resolute are prone to step with caution. They instinctively watch for the leadings of divine Providence. They hesitate to pledge themselves before they are in possession of all the facts in the case, and until the time for action has arrived. They are also cautious in the selection of their associates, and are unwilling to become responsible for the actions of men whose character and principles they do not fully understand. To young men of ardent hope and burning enthusiasm, who, gazing intently on the object, are liable to overlook the means by which it is to be accomplished, such conduct seems frequently timid and unbelieving, if not over-cautious and half-hearted. All this, in the commencement of an important undertaking, is reasonably to be expected. A few years of experience enables both parties to look at the subject through the same medium. The old acquire confidence by putting forth their strength, and the young learn to respect caution by suffering the penalties of rashness. Divine wisdom thus makes use of the opposite impulses of good men to carry into effect its own merciful designs.

ACCOUNT OF EARLY MISSIONARY IMPRESSIONS. 51

It was while visiting Bradford, to attend the meeting of the General Association, that Mr. Judson first became acquainted with Ann Hasseltine, who afterwards became so well known to the Christian world as Mrs. Ann H. Judson.

On the 5th of September, 1810, Mr. Judson was admitted to the degree of Master of Arts in Brown University. On the 24th of the same month, he completed his course of education in the Theological Seminary at Andover. On the 17th of May preceding, when on a visit to Vermont with some of his brethren, he had been licensed to preach by the Orange Association of Congregationalist Ministers in that state.

The following letters will present, in detail, the facts which have been briefly alluded to in the foregoing pages: —

To the Rev. Dr. Chapin, President of Columbian College, Washington.

MAULMAIN, December 18, 1837.

VERY DEAR BROTHER: Yours of March 21st I have received with great pleasure, and shall be glad to answer your inquiries, and give you any information in my power.

I had addressed a letter to brother Rice, dated July 13, 1836, which could not, however, have reached him before his death. As that letter contains considerable information which has a bearing on the subject of your inquiries, I will first transcribe it, and then subjoin remarks on some other points. "My dear Brother Rice: You ask me to give you some account of my first missionary impressions, and those of my earliest associates. Mine were occasioned by reading Buchanan's 'Star in the East,' in the year 1809, at the Andover Theological Seminary. Though I do not now consider that sermon as peculiarly excellent, it produced a very powerful effect on my mind. For some days I was unable to attend to the studies of my class, and spent my time in wondering at my past stupidity, depicting the most romantic scenes in missionary life, and roving about the college rooms, declaiming on the subject of missions. My views were very incorrect, and my feelings extravagant; but yet I have always felt thankful to God for bringing me into that state of excitement, which was perhaps necessary, in the first instance, to enable me to break the strong attachment I felt to home and country, and to endure the thought of abandoning all my wonted pursuits and animating prospects. That excitement soon passed away; but it left a strong desire to prosecute my inquiries, and ascertain the path of duty. It was during a solitary walk in the woods behind the college, while meditating and praying on the subject, and feeling half inclined to give it up, that the command of Christ, 'Go into all the world, and preach the gospel to every creature,' was presented to my mind with such clearness and power, that I came to a full decision, and though great difficulties appeared in my way, resolved to obey the command at all events. But, at that period, no provision had been made in America for a foreign mission, and for several months, after reading Buchanan, I found none among the students who viewed the subject as I did, and no minister in the place or neighborhood who gave me any encouragement; and I thought that I should be under the necessity of going to England and placing myself under foreign patronage.

"My earliest missionary associate was Nott; who, though he had recently entered the seminary, (in the early part of 1810,) was a member of the same class with myself. He had considered the subject for several months, but had not fully made up his mind. About the same time, Mills, Richards, and others joined the seminary from Williams College, where they had, for some time, been in the habit of meeting for prayer and conversation on the subject of missions; but they entered the junior class, and had several years of theological study before them. You were of the same standing, but from some engagement, (a school, I believe,) did not arrive so soon, though you ultimately finished your course before the others, and joined the first party that embarked.

"Newell was the next accession from my own class. As to Hall, he was preaching at Woodbury, Connecticut. I heard that he once thought favorably of missions, and wrote him a short letter. He had just received a call to settle in that place, and was deliberating whether it was his duty to accept it or not, when the letter was put into his hand. He instantly came to a decision, and the next rising sun saw him on the way to Andover. I think that he arrived about the time of the meeting of the General Association of Ministers at Bradford, in the summer of 1810. I do not, however, recollect him present at that meeting, nor was his name attached to the paper which we presented to the association, and which was originally signed by Nott, Newell, Mills, Rice, Richards, and myself, though, at the suggestion of Dr. Spring, your name and Richards's, which happened to stand last, were struck off, for fear of alarming the association with too large a number.

"I have ever thought that the providence of God was conspicuously manifested in bringing us all together, from different and distant parts. Some of us had been considering the subject of missions for a long time, and some but recently. Some, and indeed the greater part, had thought chiefly of domestic missions, and efforts among the neighboring tribes of Indians, without contemplating abandonment of country, and devotement for life. The reading and reflection of others had led them in a different way; and when we all met at the same seminary, and came to a mutual understanding on the ground of *foreign* missions and *missions for life*, the subject assumed in our minds such an overwhelming importance and awful solemnity, as bound us to one another, and to our purpose, more firmly than ever. How evident it is that the Spirit of God had been operating in different places, and upon different individuals, preparing the way for those movements which have since pervaded the American churches, and will continue to increase until the kingdoms of this world become the kingdoms of our Lord and of his Anointed!

Letter to his Parents.

ANDOVER, June 29, 1810.

HON. PARENTS: The following is a copy of the letter which I directed to Dr. Bogue: —

DIVINITY COLLEGE, ANDOVER, MASS., April, 1810.

REV. SIR: I have considered the subject of missions nearly a year, and have found my mind gradually tending to a deep conviction that it is my duty personally to engage in this service. Several of my brethren of this college may finally unite with me in my present resolution. On their as well as my own behalf, I take the liberty of addressing you this letter. My object is to obtain information on certain points — whether there is at present such a call for missionaries in India, Tartary, or any part of the *eastern* continent, as will induce the directors of the London Missionary Society to engage new missionaries; whether two or three young, unmarried men, having received a liberal education, and resided two years in this Divinity School, wishing to serve their Saviour in a heathen land, and indeed susceptible of a *"passion for missions,"* — whether such young men, arriving in England next spring, with full recommendations from the first Christian characters in this country, may expect to be received *on probation* by the directors, and placed at the seminary in Gosport, *if that be judged expedient;* and whether, provided they give satisfaction as to their fitness to undertake the work, all their necessary expenses after arriving in England shall be defrayed from the funds of the society, which funds will, it is hoped, be ultimately reimbursed by supplies from the American churches.

We have consulted our professors on this subject, particularly Dr. Griffin, professor of oratory. He intends writing to several in England, and perhaps to Dr. Bogue. But his engagements being such as will prevent his writing at present, and wishing *myself* to receive a letter from you *immediately*, containing the desired information, I have written myself. I close with an earnest request that you will please to transmit me an answer as soon as possible, and a prayer that your answer may be favorable **to** my most ardent wishes.

(Signed,)   ADONIRAM JUDSON, JR.

Rev. Dr. Bogue, Gosport, England.

P. S. I shall deem it a favor if you do not confine your remarks to the points which I have proposed, but are pleased to give such general *information* and *advice* as you may think will be useful to me and my brethren.

The following is a copy of the petition laid before the General Association, this week convened in Bradford, composed of delegates from several associations in this state, and from the General Associations of New Hampshire and Connecticut.

The undersigned, members of the Divinity College, respectfully request the attention of their reverend fathers, convened in the General Association at Bradford, to the following statement and inquiries : —

They beg leave to state that their minds have been long impressed with the duty and importance of personally attempting a mission to the heathen; that the impressions on their minds have induced a serious, and, as they trust, a prayerful consideration of the subject in its various attitudes, particularly in relation to the probable success and the difficulties attending such an attempt; and that, after examining all the information which they can obtain, *they consider themselves as devoted to this work for life,* whenever God, in his providence, shall open the way.

They now offer the following inquiries, on which they solicit the opinion and advice of this association: Whether, with their present views and feelings, they ought to renounce the object of missions, as either visionary or impracticable; if not, whether they ought to direct their attention to the eastern or the western world; whether they may expect patronage and support from a missionary society in this country, or must commit themselves to the direction of a European society ; and what preparatory measures they ought to take, previous to actual engagement.

The undersigned, feeling their youth and inexperience, look up to their fathers in the church, and respectfully solicit their advice, direction, and prayers.

    Signed,   ADONIRAM JUDSON, JR.
              SAMUEL NOTT, JR.
              SAMUEL J. MILLS.
              SAMUEL NEWELL.

I wrote the above petition at the instance of Dr. Spring and Mr. Worcester, with whom I had previously conversed. Yesterday we went to Bradford, and met the association in the meeting house. After the paper was read, we presented ourselves, and severally made a statement of our motives and intentions. A committee of three was then appointed to consider and report on the subject. We were dismissed, and returned to Andover. I have not yet received the result of the association. If I receive it to-morrow, and it is not too long, I will insert it.

July 11. I have been waiting thus long for a copy of the result from Mr. Worcester, the scribe. I understand that the council entirely approved of our movements, and appointed a Board of Commissioners, to take some efficient measures. Some of these are President Dwight, Governor Treadwell, General Huntington, Dr. Lyman, Dr. Spring, Mr. Worcester, and Mr. William Bartlet. I have not heard the *precise* object of these commissioners, nor when they are to meet. But one general object is to concentrate the efforts of the several missionary societies to this point, or to form a new *foreign* society. Dr. Spring and Professor Stuart have engaged in the business "*pedibus et unguibus.*" Dr. G. has at length written to England. Mr. Gordon Hall, whom I have mentioned to you, has joined us. He had a call to settle in Woodbury, with a salary of six hundred dollars. He came here to inquire into the missionary business before he decided, and has now written back a negative answer. He is one of the first of young men, and promises fair to be one of the pillars of the mission. He is sensible, judicious, learned, pious; has been preaching nearly a year, and quite united the Woodbury people. There are now four of us who are ready to start, at three months' warning, for any part of the world — Hall, Newell, Nott, and myself. There are *at least* four others in the junior class who are ready to support the mission, wherever it shall be established. We are in a state of suspense as to any immediate measures; our eyes are directed to an arrival from England. Our chief object in laying the business before the association, was to excite a general attention to the subject in this country, hardly expecting that such measures will be seasonably taken as shall preclude our soliciting British aid.

My missionary essay appeared in the twelfth number of the last volume of the Panoplist. That magazine will be the chief vehicle of missionary intelligence in this country. The first number of the new volume came out last month. Mr. Evarts, of Connecticut, is the new editor — a young man of distinguished science, sound sentiment, and evangelical piety. He has lately gone to Charlestown, to take the sole charge of the publication. There ought to be two dozen of the Panoplist taken in Plymouth. The treasurer of the Cent Society ought to undertake the business. It would be doing a piece of general benevolence. Is no one willing to do this little for the diffusion of religious information?

I preach sometimes on the Sabbath in neighboring towns, commonly without notes. I hardly think that I shall write any more sermons. Why should I spend my time in attempting the correctnesses and elegances of English literature, who expect to spend my days in talking to savages in vulgar style? Why not cultivate extempore speaking altogether, when that will soon be my only mode of preaching for life? Spring * is warmly attached to the missionary project, and either in Boston or New York will, I trust, be a faithful and valuable friend. . . .

I think sometimes that A. is all alone at Plymouth. There is a Friend, whose friendship, if she would secure it, would never leave her alone. Without his friendship she will soon be worse than alone. O the pleasure which a lively Christian must enjoy in communion with God! It is all one whether he is in a city or a desert, among relations or among savage foes, in the heat of the Indies or in the ice of Greenland; his infinite Friend is always at hand. He need not fear want,

* Rev. Gardner Spring, D. D., now of New York.

or sickness, or pain, for his best Friend does all things well. He need not fear Death, though he come in the most shocking form; for death is only a withdrawing of the veil which conceals his dearest Friend.

I enjoy good health. My eyes prevent studying in the evening, but are much better than they were. My constitution grows firm, and appears to be capable of enduring much. My prospects for life, though in a measure shaded with uncertainty, hardship, and danger, are very animating and bright. My prospects for another life, blessed be God, are still brighter. "This life's a dream, an empty show." O, if we could always realize this, and live above the world, — if we could tread on its trifling vanities, live far from its perplexing cares, and keep an eye fixed on our heavenly inheritance, — how comfortable and useful we might be! Bless the Lord, O our souls, that he allows us to hope for a better state.

A. Judson, Jr.

The communication to the General Association of Massachusetts, of which a copy is inserted in the preceding letter, was referred to a committee, consisting of the Rev. Dr. Spring and Rev. Messrs. Worcester and Hale.

On the subsequent day, the committee made the following report, which was unanimously adopted: —

The committee, to whom was referred the request of the young gentlemen, members of the Divinity College, for advice relative to missions to the heathen, beg leave to submit the following report: —

The object of missions to the heathen cannot but be regarded, by the friends of the Redeemer, as vastly interesting and important. It deserves the most serious attention of all who wish well to the best interests of mankind, and especially of those who devote themselves to the service of God, in the kingdom of his Son, under the impression of the special direction, "Go ye into all the world, and preach the gospel to every creature." The state of their minds, modestly expressed by the theological students who have presented themselves before this body, and the testimonies received respecting them, are such as deeply to impress the conviction that they ought not "to renounce the object of missions," but sacredly to cherish "their present views" in relation to that object: and it is submitted whether the peculiar and abiding impressions, by which they are influenced, ought not to be gratefully recognized as a divine intimation of something good and great in relation to the propagation of the gospel, and calling for correspondent attention and exertions.

Therefore, —

Voted, That there be instituted, by this General Association, a Board of Commissioners for Foreign Missions, for the purpose of devising ways and means, and adopting and prosecuting measures, for promoting the spread of the gospel in heathen lands.

Voted, That the said Board of Commissioners consist of nine members, all of them, in the first instance, chosen by this association; and afterwards, annually, five of them by this body, and four of them by the General Association of Connecticut. Provided, however, that, if the General Association of Connecticut do not choose to unite in this object, the annual election of all the commissioners shall be by this General Association.

It is understood that the Board of Commissioners, here contemplated, will adopt their own form of organization, and their own rules and regulations.

Voted, That, fervently commending them to the grace of God, we advise the young gentlemen, whose request is before us, in the way of earnest prayer and diligent attention to suitable studies and means of information, and putting themselves under the patronage and direction of the Board of Commissioners for Foreign Missions, humbly to wait the openings and guidance of Providence in respect to their great and excellent design.

Extract from a Letter of the Rev. S. Nott, Jr., of Wareham, Mass., to the Rev. Dr. Worcester.

Dr. S. M. Worcester. WAREHAM, July 18, 1851.

Rev. and dear Sir: In turning to some old papers, I find the first memorandum of earnest consideration as to my personal duty on the subject of missions to be October 17, 1808, which, and the other memoranda which follow, show the growth of the principle of my final decision and action, viz., as a question of obedience to command. I was then twenty years of age, alone, at my father's house, spending, in solitary study with my father, the year after my graduation. In November, 1809, I went to Andover.

My first memorandum on the subject at Andover was March 4, 1810, and on March 11th a reference is made to conversation with brethren Judson and Mills on that subject. Mr. Hall was not at Andover at all until late that spring.

It has never seemed to me of any consequence to settle the matter who was or who was not the leader of the movement, unless it were to show that, strictly speaking, no *man* was. . . . In my own mind, at least, the starting point and early progress, the essence of the whole, was without any knowledge of the existence even of those who were so soon to be my associates, and on such a principle as possessed a solemn and independent power. In the memoranda, I find Mr. Judson mentioned with every confidence in his sincere and earnest spirit.

On Sabbath, June, 1810, I preached for Dr. Spring. On Monday he came with me in the carriage to Andover, on his way to the General Association at Bradford; but I have no recollection except of general conversation on our missionary intentions. On Tuesday evening, by request of Dr. Griffin, myself and associates met Dr. Spring, Dr. Worcester, and several other ministers, at Mr. Stuart's, where our views were freely discussed, and "an opinion expressed in favor of our object," and a request made to Dr. G. to write to England immediately for information. "On Wednesday evening, we received a request from Dr. Spring and Mr. Worcester to present a petition for advice to the General Association." On Thursday the petition was presented, and resulted as has been uniformly stated. It might be that if I were to see your history of 1809 and 1810, other things might occur. The timely bequest of Mrs. Norris * as an encouragement, and yet the as timely delay to realize it, so that it might open, and not dry up, the public fountain, cannot have escaped your notice; nor the extremely limited supply February 6, 1812, and its gracious enlargement before February 18, in such ways as to interest two great sections of the country.

* Mrs. Norris died in March, 1811, having left a legacy of thirty thousand dollars to the Board of Commissioners.

CHAPTER III.

MISSION TO ENGLAND. — CAPTURE, AND DETENTION IN FRANCE — INTERVIEWS WITH THE DIRECTORS OF THE LONDON MISSIONARY SOCIETY. — RETURNS TO THE UNITED STATES. — APPOINTED A MISSIONARY OF THE AMERICAN BOARD OF COMMISSIONERS FOR FOREIGN MISSIONS. — MARRIAGE AND ORDINATION. — RELATIONS WITH THE BOARD.

1810-1812.

THE last chapter closed with an account of the meeting of the General Association at Bradford, and the appointment of the Board of Commissioners.

This board held its first meeting, September 5, 1810, at Farmington, Connecticut. Its organization was there completed, and its rules of proceeding adopted. The object of the board was declared to be "to devise, adopt, and prosecute ways and means for propagating the gospel among those who are destitute of the knowledge of Christianity." It was voted, "that the Prudential Committee and Corresponding Secretary be requested to obtain the best information in their power respecting the state of unevangelized nations on the western and eastern continents, and report at the next meeting of the board."

It was also voted, "that the board highly approve the readiness of the young gentlemen at Andover to enter upon a foreign mission, and that it is advisable for them to pursue their studies till further information relative to the missionary field be obtained, and the finances of the institution will justify the appointment."

The Prudential Committee elected at this meeting of the board consisted of William Bartlet, Esq., Rev.

Dr. Spring, and Rev. Samuel Worcester. Mr. Worcester was also appointed Corresponding Secretary.

The board also prepared an address to the public, and a form of subscription to be printed and circulated among the churches.

It will be seen from the above proceedings that, at this time, the board was prepared to take no other than incipient measures. They were in doubt whether the churches in this country were willing to incur the expenditure which missions to the East demanded. Their eyes were naturally directed to the London Missionary Society, which was already prosecuting this work with signal success. It seemed desirable to inquire whether we in this country could not unite with Christians in England, and carry on missions in concert.

Impressed with these considerations, the Prudential Committee thought it desirable to send Mr. Judson to England, in order to ascertain whether such an arrangement were practicable. The candidates were all examined by the committee, so that every proper assurance might be given to the directors of the London society; and Mr. Judson was directed to sail for London on the 1st of January, 1811.

The letter of instructions addressed to him by the Corresponding Secretary, and the letter of the secretary to the Rev. George Burder, are as follows: —

Letter of Instructions from the Prudential Committee to Mr. Judson.

MR. ADONIRAM JUDSON: As you and your brethren, Samuel Newell, Samuel Nott, and Gordon Hall, have professed to hold yourselves sacredly devoted to the service of Christ, in some part or parts of the heathen world, as in divine providence a door may be opened to you, and as, with reference to this important object, you have chosen to place yourselves under the superintendence and direction of the American Board of Commissioners for Foreign Missions, the Prudential Committee of the said board, after obtaining satisfaction in regard to your qualifications severally for the contemplated service, and seriously consulting on the subject at large, have judged it advisable to have a full and distinct understanding with the directors of the London Missionary Society, in relation to the general object. For this purpose they have determined on sending you, dear sir, to England, under the following instructions:—

Agreeably to arrangements made, you will sail for England in the ship Packet, and on your arrival at her port of destination, you will proceed, as soon as convenient, to London, and deliver your letter of introduction to the Rev. George Burder, secretary of the London Missionary Society. Mr. Burder, we doubt not, will receive you with Christian courtesy, and from him, and his brethren of the Board of Directors, you will receive such notices as will enable you to accomplish in the best manner the design now in view. A principal object of your attention will be to ascertain, as distinctly as possible, whether any and what arrangements can be made for a concert of measures, in relation to missions, between the American Board of Commissioners and the London Missionary Society; particularly whether, if circumstances should render it desirable, you and your brethren can be supported in missionary service for any time by the London funds, without committing yourselves wholly and finally to the direction of the London society; or whether it may be in any case consistent for the mission to be supported partly by them and partly by us; and if so, under whose direction it must be held. On these points you will possess yourself of the views of the directors of the London society, and receive their propositions for our consideration. You will also, during your stay in England, avail yourself of your opportunities and advantages for obtaining ample and correct information relating to missionary fields, the requisite preparations for missionary services, the most eligible methods of executing missions, and generally to whatever may be conducive to the missionary interest; and the most important parts of such information as you may obtain you will commit to writing for the use of the American Board.

As it is not expected that you will be at your own charge in this engagement, you will keep a full account of your expenditures, for adjustment on your return.

We commend you, dear brother, to the providence and the grace of God, with fervent prayers for your safety, your success, and your happiness. In behalf of the Prudential Committee of the American Board of Commissioners for Foreign Missions,

Yours, dear brother, with great affection,

SAMUEL WORCESTER.

From the Rev. Dr. Worcester, to the Rev. George Burder.

SALEM, January 3, 1811.

REV. AND DEAR SIR: Enclosed with this you will receive a printed paper, in which you will see in general what has recently been done in this country in relation to foreign missions. Four young gentlemen, Messrs. Adoniram Judson, Jr., Samuel Newell, and Samuel Nott, whose names you will find in the paper referred to, and Mr. Gordon Hall, have offered themselves as candidates for missions to the heathen, under a solemn profession that they have devoted themselves to God for this arduous service, wherever in his providence he may see fit to employ them. These beloved brethren have all passed through a course of collegial education, and received a collegial degree. Since leaving the universities, they have completed a course of studies at the theological institution in this vicinity, where they have acquitted themselves to the high satisfaction of their instructors and friends. According to our established order, they have been regularly licensed for the Christian ministry, and for a considerable time they have all preached in our churches to good acceptance. Their moral and Christian reputation is good, and their talents and attainments are respectable. Before the Prudential Committee of the American Board of Commissioners for Foreign Missions they have passed an examination in form, relative to their religious sentiments, their religious feelings, and their views in offering themselves for the missionary service; and their answers and declarations throughout were highly satisfactory. They profess their full belief in the articles of faith which are established in the theological institution, a copy of which you will receive; and the Prudential Committee have great confidence that they have received the truth in love; that they are persons of sincere and ardent piety; that they have offered themselves for the missionary service from the best motives; and, in a word, that they have qualifications for distinguished usefulness. The manner in which these young men have come forward, together with a similar disposition manifested by several others, has made, extensively, a deep impression, and excited a lively interest. It is gratefully hailed as an indication that the Lord is about to do something by his friends in this country, in furtherance of the great design in which their brethren in England have been so nobly and so exemplarily engaged.

On our own continent, indeed, there are many millions of men "sitting in darkness and in the region and shadow of death," and our brethren in England may wonder that, while such is the fact, we should turn our views to any other part of the world. But the attempts which have been made to evangelize the aboriginal tribes of the North American wilderness have been attended with so many discouragements, and South America is yet in so unpromising a state, that the opinion very generally prevalent is, that for the pagans on this continent but very little can immediately be done. Hence, though the hope is entertained, that the time is coming when the benevolent exertions of the Redeemer's friends here, for spreading the knowledge of his name, may be successfully employed nearer home, yet at present the eastern world is thought to offer a more promising field.

As yet, however, we have no adequate funds established for the support of distant and expensive missions. What may be done in the course of a short time we know not. It is the desire and the prayer of many, that American missionaries may have American support; and we are not without hope that He to whom the silver and the gold belong will open the hearts of the rich among us for this interesting purpose. Should this hope be realized, and missionary funds to any considerable amount be raised, they will probably be placed under such an arrangement as to be employed either in the East, or on our own continent, as divine Providence may direct.

Under existing circumstances, the American Board are desirous to open a communication with the London Missionary Society, whose knowledge of missionary concerns is ample, and the praise of whose liberality and persevering exertions is in all parts of the world. For this purpose, Mr. Judson, one of the missionary brethren, of whom you have already some knowledge, and who has been favored with a letter from you, has been appointed to go to London. To your courtesy and Christian attention he is most affectionately and respectfully recommended; and for the particular objects for which he is sent, I beg leave to refer you to his letter of instructions.

Besides the official testimonial contained in this letter, Mr. Judson will carry with him others, and particularly one from the faculty of the theological institution at Andover — an institution which, though young, is fast rising in importance, and in which, both on account of the principles on which it is founded, and the ability and piety with which it is conducted, great confidence is reposed. Should these testimonials be satisfactory, and should it in the event be thought best that our young brethren should be resigned to the patronage and direction of your society, your venerable and highly respected Board of Directors will judge, whether, after the course of studies through which they have passed, it will be expedient for them to spend any time at your school at Gosport, and whether, for any purpose, it will be necessary for the other three to go to England, before they shall be actually engaged in your service.

It may not be improper to state, that some of the young

men propose to take wives with them to the missionary field. If this meet the approbation of your board, as we are not unapprised of the laudable care which you take in regard to the character not only of your missionaries themselves, but also of their wives, we shall certainly consider it important that similar care be taken here.

With great personal consideration, and in behalf of the American Board of Commissioners for Foreign Missions, I tender to you, dear sir, and through you to your brethren of the Board of Directors, the most affectionate and respectful salutations.

SAMUEL WORCESTER, Cor. Sec.

Rev. George Burder, Sec. London Miss. Soc.

The following reminiscences of the voyage to England are derived from conversations of Dr. Judson: —

There were on the ship Packet two Spanish merchants; and these, I believe, were the only passengers beside Mr. Judson. When they were captured by L'Invincible Napoleon, these two gentlemen, being able to speak French, and most likely to furnish a bribe, were treated very civilly. Mr. Judson, however, was very young, with nothing distinctive in his outward appearance, and was, moreover, speechless, friendless, and comparatively moneyless. He was, without question or remonstrance, immediately placed in the hold, with the common sailors. This was the first hardship he had ever known, and it affected him accordingly. He shrank from the associations of the place, and the confined air seemed unendurable. Soon the weather roughened, and he, together with several of his more hardy companions, became excessively seasick. The doctor visited him every day, but he could not communicate with him, and the visit was nearly useless. Sick, sorrowful, and discouraged, his thoughts went back to his dear old Plymouth home, then to Bradford, and finally the Boston church — "the biggest church in Boston;" and he became alarmed at the strange feeling that crept over him. It was the first moment of misgiving he had known. As soon as he became aware of the feeling, he commenced praying against it, as a temptation of the adversary. It seemed to him that God had permitted this capture, and all his trouble, as a trial of his faith; and he resolved, in the strength of God, to bear it, as he might be called upon to bear similar trials hereafter. As soon as he had come to this resolution, he fumbled about in the gray twilight of his prison, till he succeeded in finding his Hebrew Bible. The light was very faint, but still he managed to see for a few moments at a time, and amused himself with translating mentally from the Hebrew to the Latin — a work which employed his thoughts, and saved his eyes. One day the doctor, observing the Bible on the pillow, took it up, stepped towards the gangway, and examined it; then returned, and addressed his patient in Latin. Through the medium of this language, Mr. Judson managed to explain who he was; and he was consequently admitted to a berth in the upper cabin, and a seat with his fellow-passengers, the Spaniards, at the captain's table.

His second day on deck was a somewhat exciting one. A sail was reported from the mast head; and while the stranger was yet a mere speck to the naked eye, many glasses were levelled curiously at her, and a general feeling of anxiety seemed to prevail among the officers. Of course, Mr. Judson was all excitement; for although he was now in comfortable circumstances, he dreaded the effect of this detention on his mission to England. Finally, the stranger loomed up against the sky, a beautiful brig under a full press of canvas. As they watched her, some anxiously and some admiringly, suddenly her fine proportions became blended in a dark mass; and it was evident to the most inexperienced landsman that she had changed her course. The two Spaniards interchanged significant glances. Mr. Judson felt very much like shouting for joy, but he suppressed the inclination; and the next moment the order came for the decks to be cleared, and he, with his companions, was sent below. The Spaniards informed him that they were pursued by a vessel much larger than their own; that the privateer had little to hope in an engagement, but she was the swifter sailer of the two, and the approaching darkness was in her favor. Mr. Judson passed a sleepless night, listening each moment for unusual sounds; but the next morning, when he carefully swept the horizon with the captain's glass, not a mote was visible.

The privateer touched at Le Passage, in Spain, and there permitted the two Spaniards to go on shore. From thence the prisoners were conveyed to Bayonne, in France; and Mr. Judson again, to his surprise and indignation, found himself marched through the streets in company with the crew of the Packet. He had as yet acquired only a few words of French, and of these he made as much use as possible, to the infinite amusement of the passers by. Finally it occurred to him that he was much more likely to meet some person, either a native or a foreigner, who understood English, than to make his broken French intelligible. Accordingly he commenced declaiming in the most violent manner possible against oppression in general, and this one act in particular. The guards threatened him by gestures, but did not proceed to violence; and of the passers by, some regarded him a moment carelessly, others showed a little interest or curiosity, while many laughed outright at his seemingly senseless clamors. Finally a stranger accosted him in English, advising him to lower his voice. "With the greatest pleasure possible," he answered, "if I have at last succeeded in making myself heard. I was only clamoring for a listener." "You might have got one you would have been glad to dismiss, if you had continued much longer," was the reply. In a few hurried words Judson explained his situation, and, in words as few, learned that the gentleman was an American from Philadelphia, and received his promise of assistance. "But you had better go on your way quietly now," added his new friend. "O, I will be a perfect lamb, since I have gained my object."

The prison was a gloomy-looking, massive structure, and the apartment into which they were conveyed was under ground, dark and dismal. In the centre was a sort of column, on which burned a solitary lamp, though without it was still broad day. Around the walls a quantity of straw had been spread, on which his companions soon made themselves at home; but Mr. Judson could not divest himself of the idea that the straw was probably not fresh, and busied his imagination with images of those who had last occupied it. The weather had seemed almost oppressively hot above ground; but now he shivered with the chilling dampness of the place, while the confined air and mouldy smell rendered him sick and giddy. He paced up and down the cell, he could not tell how long, but it seemed many hours, wondering if his new friend would really come; and again, if he did not, whether he could keep upon his feet all night; and in case of failure, which part of the straw he should select as the least loathsome. And then his thoughts would wander off again to Plymouth, and to Bradford, and to the "biggest church in Boston," but not with the feeling that he had before. On the contrary, he wondered that he ever could have been discouraged. He knew that at most his imprisonment could not last long. If he only had a chair, or the meanest stool, that was all he would ask. But he could not hope to walk or stand long.

While leaning against the column for a moment's rest, the door of the cell opened, and he instantly recognized the American he had seen in the street. He suppressed a cry of joy, and seeing that the stranger did not look at him, though he stood close by the lamp, tried himself to affect indifference. The American, making some remark in French, took up the lamp, and then adding, (or perhaps translating,) in English, "Let me see if I know any of these poor fellows," passed around the room, examining them carelessly. "No; no friend of mine," said he, replacing the lamp, and swinging his great military cloak around Mr. Judson, whose slight figure was almost lost in its ample folds. Comprehending the plan, Mr. Judson drew himself into as small a compass as possible, thinking that he would make the best of the affair, though having little confidence in the clumsy artifice. His protector, too, seemed to have his doubts, for as he passed out, he slid some money into the jailer's hand, and again, at the gate, made another disbursement, and as soon as they were outside, released his protégé, with the expressive words, "Now run!" Mr. Judson quite forgot his fatigue from walking in the cell, as he fleetly followed his tall conductor through the streets to the wharf, where he was placed on board an American merchantman for the night. The next evening his friend returned, informing him that his place of refuge had been only temporarily chosen, and as the papers necessary to his release could not be procured immediately, he would be much safer in the attic of a ship builder, who had kindly offered this place of concealment. Accordingly he removed to the attic, from which, after a few days, he was released on parole.

Mr. Judson passed about six weeks in Bayonne, boarding with an American lady who had spent most of her life in France. He told his landlady that he was a clergyman, and frequently held long religious conversations with her; but he did not permit his character to be known generally in the house, as he thought it would interfere with a plan he had of learning as much as possible of the real state of French society. He attended various places of amusement with his fellow-boarders, pleading his ignorance of the language and customs of the country as an excuse for acting the spectator merely; and in general giving such evasive replies as enabled him to act his part without attracting undue attention. It was not long, however, before his companions became pretty well aware that indifference formed no part of his real character. His shrewdness was at variance with his implied ignorance of the world, and his simplicity sometimes wore a solemn impressiveness, from the influence of which it was impossible to escape. The last place of amusement he visited was a masked ball; and here his strong feelings quite overcame his caution, and he burst forth in his real character. He declared to his somewhat startled companions that he did not believe the infernal regions could furnish more complete specimens of depravity than he there beheld. He spoke in English, and at first addressed himself to the two or three standing near him, who understood the language; but his earnestness of manner and warmth of expression soon drew around him a large circle, who listened curiously and with apparent respect. He spoke scornfully of the proud professions of the (so called) philosophy of the age, and pointed to the fearful exhibitions of that moment as illustrative of its effectiveness. He rapidly enumerated many of the evils which infidelity had brought upon France and upon the world, and then showed the only way of escape from those evils — the despised, but truly ennobling religion of Jesus Christ. Finally he sketched the character of man as it might have been in its original purity and nobleness, and then the wreck of soul and body to be ascribed to sin, and wound up all by a personal appeal to such as had not become too debased to think and feel. He had warmed as he proceeded with his subject, noting with pain and surprise the great number of those who seemed to understand the English language, and drawing from it an inference by no means favorable to his travelled countrymen. Most of the maskers evidently regarded the exhibition as part of the evening's entertainment; but those who understood his remarks seemed confounded by the boldness, and perhaps unexpectedness, of the attack, and when he had finished, stood aside, and allowed him to pass from the place without a word. This incident, I have been told, was reported by some person present on the occasion, and published in a Boston newspaper.

Mr. Judson, I do not recollect by what means, was introduced to some of the officers of Napoleon's suite, and travelled through the country in one of the emperor's carriages. At Paris, he spent most of his time in the society of these officers, and persons whom they introduced, and, in general, pursued the same course as at Bayonne. In view of the opportunity thus afforded for observation, and the store of practical knowledge really gathered, he always regarded his detention in France as a very important, and, indeed, necessary part of his preparation for the duties which afterwards devolved upon him.

In England he was received in a manner peculiarly flattering, and I think his appearance there must have created a very favorable impression. He was at this time small and exceedingly delicate in figure, with a round, rosy face, which gave him the appearance of extreme youthfulness. His hair and eyes were of a dark shade of brown, in his French passport described as "chestnut." His voice, however, was far from what would be expected of such a person, and usually took the listeners by surprise. An instance of this occurred in London. He sat in the pulpit with a clergyman somewhat distinguished for his eccentricity, and at the close of the sermon was requested to read a hymn. When he had finished, the clergyman arose, and introduced his young brother to the congregation as a person who purposed devoting himself to the conversion of the heathen, adding, "And if his faith is proportioned to his voice, he will drive the devil from all India."

Mr. Judson crossed the channel, and arrived at Dartmouth on the 3d of May, 1811. On the 6th of the same month he went up to London, and presented his credentials to the directors of the London Missionary Society. They received him with every mark of Christian kindness, and, as it will be seen, appointed him and his brethren missionaries to the heathen in their service. The following letters contain all the memorials which I have found relating to these events:—

Extracts from the Minutes of the Board of Directors of the London Missionary Society.

Meeting of the Directors, June 25, 1810.

Read a letter from Mr. Adoniram Judson, a student in the Divinity College at Andover, in America, dated April 23, 1810, saying that he wished to become a missionary to the heathen; requesting to be informed whether two or three young unmarried men, having received a liberal education, desirous of becoming missionaries, would be accepted on their arrival in England next spring, on probation, to be sent to Gosport, with a view to a mission to India or Tartary.

Resolved, That the secretary be desired to write immediately, requesting that testimonials be forwarded from Andover, as soon as possible, giving a full account of the religious views, &c., of these young men.

Meeting, May 20, 1811.

Read a letter, dated January 3, 1811, from Rev. S. Worcester, of Salem, secretary to the Board of Commissioners for Foreign Missions, requesting the coöperation of this society in sending out four young men as missionaries to the heathen.

Read also a letter from Rev. Messrs. Griffin, Woods, and Stuart, professors of Andover College recommending Messrs. A. Judson, S. Newell, S. Nott, and G. Hall, as having received a liberal education, and of good moral and religious characters, suitable for this purpose.

Read a letter of instructions to Mr. Judson, also a recommendatory letter from Rev. Mr. Codman, of Dorchester, dated December 19, 1810.

Resolved, That a committee be appointed, to consist of Messrs. Alers, Cowie, and Roberts, with the secretary, to consider what measures may be suitable to be adopted respecting the proposition made by the American brethren to this society, and report.

Meeting, May 27, 1811.

The committee to whom the proposals from the Commissioners for Foreign Missions, by Mr. Judson, were referred, reported.

The committee have to report, that it is the particular wish, as well of the commissioners as of the candidates themselves, that they should be employed in forming a new station for missionary exertions, rather than be separated from each other among the several stations already occupied by the society. This appears to be the chief, if not the only stipulation connected with the offer of service made by Mr. Judson, on his own part and that of his brethren. The precise station is stated by Mr. Judson to be entirely at the disposal of the Missionary Society, if he and his brethren can be accommodated by the Missionary Society in the respect just referred to.

That Mr. Judson wishes most explicitly to state, whatever may be the expressions of the instructions he has received, that they do not intend to require any engagement from the Missionary Society contrary to the established usage in the formation of its stations; and that he and his brethren are willing to consider themselves the missionaries of this society, in all respects the same as the other missionaries engaged by them.

That Mr. Judson is able to afford very little encouragement as to pecuniary assistance. The zeal for missionary efforts seems to have been excited chiefly, if not entirely, among those who have only their personal services to offer. The encouragement which this disposition has hitherto met with from those who are able to cherish such endeavors by pecuniary contributions is at present so limited, that no assurances can be given to the society of any efficient aid in that respect.

The committee think it right to state to the directors, that they have received very great satisfaction from the statements given by the candidates themselves of their religious experience and missionary views, and from the strong and unequivocal testimonies to their religious and moral character and ministerial qualifications, which have been transmitted by judicious and experienced ministers, who are personally acquainted with them.

The committee have peculiar pleasure in stating likewise, upon the information of Mr. Judson, that a lively zeal for the propagation of the blessed gospel among the heathen has manifested itself among the young students in the Divinity College of which he is a member, which is cherished by meetings of prayer and conversation relative to that object, and that in the event of the present offer from himself and his brethren receiving the countenance of the society, he has the fullest assurance that others of his junior brethren, now prosecuting their divinity studies, will, when prepared, be found ready to devote their lives and labors in the same line of active service.

The committee have, therefore, on the preceding grounds, great satisfaction in recommending to their brethren, the directors of the Missionary Society, that the proposals of Mr. Judson be received with the most friendly attention, and that the services of himself and brethren be accepted on such terms as the directors shall, on due consideration, judge most expedient.

Resolved, That the report of the committee be accepted.

Resolved, That Messrs. Adoniram Judson, Samuel Newell, Samuel Nott, and Gordon Hall be accepted as missionaries, to be employed by this society in India.

Resolved, That Mr. Alers be requested to write a letter of instructions for Mr. Judson and his brethren.

Mr. Judson subsequently visited the missionary seminary at Gosport, then under the care of the venerable Dr. Bogue, to confer with that pious and devoted friend of missions. There was nothing to detain him in England after he had accomplished his missionary purposes; and within about six weeks after his arrival, on the 18th of June, 1811, he embarked at Gravesend in the ship Augustus, bound to New York. He arrived in New York on the 17th of August following.

The Board of Commissioners held their second meeting at Worcester, Massachusetts, September 18, 1811. At this meeting Mr. Judson and Mr. Nott were present.

The Prudential Committee, in their annual report, after inserting the letter of instructions to Mr. Judson, their letter to Mr. Burder, and his answer, proceed to remark as follows: " The board will perceive that, though the London directors gave the most favorable reception to our messenger, and show'd the most Christian zeal towards the general object, yet in this letter of the Rev. Mr. Burder nothing is said in direct reference to the points on which Mr. Judson was instructed to confer with the directors, relating to a coöperation in the support and conduct of missions. Though the committee have not received any written communication from Mr. Judson, yet they have learned from him in general that the London directors are of opinion that a joint conduct of missions will not be practicable, and that, although they are ready to receive our young brethren under their patronage, and would gladly have aid from us in respect to their support, yet they do not think it consistent to admit this board to a participation with them in the direction of the mission."

The report then proceeds to state that one of two courses is plainly before the board — either to surrender these four young brethren to the London society, which had already appointed them, or undertake to support them themselves. They recommend the latter course, give their reasons for this recommendation, and suggest the manner in which funds may be raised. They direct the attention of the board to the various openings for missionary labor, and mention Burmah as a specially inviting field. This report is accompanied by the following vote: —

"*Voted*, That this board will retain under their care the young gentlemen who last year devoted themselves to the service of God for life, as missionaries in foreign parts."

This report of the Prudential Committee was accepted.

On the following day, it was voted, "That this

board do not advise Messrs. Adoniram Judson, Jr., and Samuel Nott, Jr., to place themselves at present under the direction of the London Missionary Society, but to wait the further intimations of Providence relative to our means of furnishing them with the requisite support in the proposed foreign mission."

"Messrs. Adoniram Judson, Jr., Samuel Nott, Jr., Samuel Newell, and Gordon Hall were appointed missionaries to labor under the direction of this board in Asia, either in the Burman empire, or in Surat, or in Prince of Wales Island, or elsewhere, as, in the view of the Prudential Committee, Providence shall open the most favorable door."

By a subsequent vote, the salary of a married and of an unmarried missionary was fixed, together with the sum that should be allowed for the outfit of each; and an appropriation of three hundred dollars was made for the purchase of books for missionaries.

The way was now open for these pioneers of American missions to proceed on their errand of mercy. At this time, however, intercourse with the East Indies was infrequent, and passages were not easily secured. The company were obliged to delay their departure until the following February. On the 3d of February, Mr. Judson took a final leave of his parents at Plymouth. On the 5th, he was married to Ann Hasseltine. On the 6th, he was ordained at Salem, in company with Messrs. Nott, Newell, Hall, and Rice. They expected to sail immediately, but their departure was delayed until the 18th and 19th, a part of the company embarking at Salem, and the remainder at Philadelphia. The account of these events which follows is from the Panoplist for February, 1812.

Ordained, on Thursday, the 6th instant, at the Tabernacle in Salem, the Rev. Messrs. Samuel Newell, Adoniram Judson, Samuel Nott, Gordon Hall, and Luther Rice, to the work of the gospel ministry, as missionaries to the heathen in Asia. The ordaining council was composed of the pastors of the North Congregational Church in Newburyport, the Congregational Church in Charlestown, and the Tabernacle church in Salem, and delegates from the same churches; and of the Rev. Dr. Griffin, pastor of Park Street Church, Boston, late professor at Andover, and the Rev. Dr. Woods, professor at Andover. The Rev. Professor Stuart was invited to attend, but was necessarily prevented.

The young gentlemen were examined with respect to their doctrinal views, their personal hopes of the divine favor, and their motives and prospects in offering themselves to this important service among the heathen.

The parts in the solemnities of the day were as follows: The Rev. Dr. Griffin made the introductory prayer; the Rev Dr. Woods preached the sermon, from Psalm lxvii.; the Rev. Dr. Morse made the consecrating prayer; the Rev. Dr. Spring delivered the charge; the Rev. Dr. Worcester presented the right hand of fellowship, and the Rev. Dr. Spring made the concluding prayer. The exercises were solemn and appropriate, and evidently made a deep impression on a crowded audience. The sermon, charge, and right hand of fellowship are printed. A very large impression is struck off, and the profits will be applied to the support of this mission.

This transaction may justly be considered as forming a new and important era in the annals of the American churches — the *era of foreign missions*. It would be natural to indulge in pleasing anticipations of the blessings, which, with the divine assistance, these missionaries may be the means of communicating to Asia. But, while we leave the issue of this benevolent enterprise to the disposal of infinite wisdom, the good effects of these missionary exertions among ourselves ought to be mentioned with devout gratitude. Christians feel more sensibly than ever the value of their holy religion, while devoting their money and their time to extend its blessings to the heathen. Christians of different denominations, *who love our Lord Jesus Christ in sincerity*, experience the blessedness of uniting in this great catholic labor of love.

Messrs. Newell and Judson, with their wives, sailed from Salem in the brig Caravan, Captain Heard, on Wednesday, the 19th instant, amidst the prayers and benedictions of multitudes, whose hearts go with them, and who will not cease to remember them at the throne of grace.

Messrs. Nott, Hall, and Rice, and the wife of Mr. Nott, sailed from Philadelphia in the ship Harmony, Captain Brown, on the 18th instant. They and their brethren from Salem probably lost sight of the shores of their native country about the same time. Though they never expect to return, they will not be forgotten; and, if they obtain grace to be faithful to their Lord and Master, their memories will be blessed.

Before closing this chapter, it seems necessary to advert to the reprimand said to have been administered to Mr. Judson, at the meeting of the board at Worcester, September 19, 1811. I regret that I am called to treat of this subject, since it has been supposed by many persons to present the character of good men in an unamiable light. With unfeigned pleasure, however, I am able to state, that I can discover nothing in the facts which tends in the least to diminish our love and esteem for any of the parties concerned.

The facts in the case are briefly as follows: —

1. The missionaries were all received, so far as it was known to the public, on the same terms of affectionate regard. No one supposed that either of them was, or ever had been, under censure. It would have been an act of unwarrantable rashness in the board to send out as missionary pioneers men in whom they had not entire confidence.

2. On the passage, Mr. Judson became convinced that the New Testament furnished no authority for infant baptism. Shortly after his arrival at Calcutta, he was baptized by immersion, and joined the Baptist church in that city. He afterwards published a sermon, in which he presented the reasons for the change in his opinions.

3. In due time, a reply to this sermon, by a much respected Congregational clergyman, appeared. In the introduction to the sermon, it was stated that Mr. Judson had been reprimanded by the board at Worcester; and it was understood to be intimated that the irritation caused by this censure had induced him to embrace the earliest opportunity for leaving their service. This intimation has, we believe, been long since withdrawn, and men of all denominations regret that it was ever made.

4. To this imputation Mr. Judson replied by a direct denial. He affirmed that no reprimand had ever been administered; he appealed to all the members of the board for confirmation of his testimony; and he showed conclusively that no such motives as had been suggested could possibly have affected his decisions.

5. Upon the receipt of this denial, it was, I believe, reasserted by the Corresponding Secretary of the board, that the reprimand had been administered.

6. Rev. Samuel Nott, Jr., the intimate friend of Mr. Judson, and formerly his missionary associate, published his "testimony in favor of Judson." He admits, however, that Mr. Judson's "proceedings previously to his leaving this country were in some respects unsatisfactory to the board and the committee, and that Mr Judson was informed of this formally and solemnly."

7. In 1830, Mr. Judson wrote a letter to Mr. Evarts, then Corresponding Secretary, (Dr. Worcester having died in 1821,) in which he acknowledges that many circumstances had convinced him that there was, at the time referred to, an expression of dissatisfaction which gave some just ground for the statements which had been made on the subject, and expressing sincere regret for the spirit of the letter which he had written to his father in relation to it.

Such are, I believe, all the prominent facts in the case. I beg leave to offer such suggestions in regard to them as have occurred to me.

In the first place, there can be no doubt that an admonition was addressed to Mr. Judson by Dr. Spring, by direction of the board. The reasons for such a measure are obvious. Mr. Judson had been sent to England to propose a union between the London society and the American board, to learn all in his power respecting missions, and make a written report to the board. He had made no written report, and the letter from Mr. Burder made no allusion to the points which he had been directed to present. Mr. Judson came back with an appointment from the London society, and thus left the board only the option of appointing the four missionaries at once, or of surrendering them to the London society. I can easily sympathize with the feelings of the board on this occasion. They were committing themselves to a great undertaking. It was of the utmost importance to all the parties concerned, that the relations in which they stood to each other should be well defined and clearly understood. They wished to mark the first instance of departure from the principles which should govern their intercourse with their missionaries. They might do, and they evidently did all this, without in the least abating their confidence in the individual. This very self-reliance, which had appeared somewhat in excess, was a quality of the highest value in the service to which he was appointed. This was precisely Dr. Spring's estimate of Judson, whom he loved as a son.

But Mr. Judson denied that a reprimand had ever been given. I think that this is susceptible of easy explanation. Mr. Judson was inflamed with a "passion for missions" in as high a degree as any person of whom I have ever read. He believed that God had called him to this service, and that, having called, God would sustain him in it. He preferred greatly to go out under the auspices of the American churches. If these failed, he would have gone out under the sanction of the London society. If this hope had failed, he would have begged his passage money from Christians at home, and taking a few hundred dollars, which he happened to possess, would have thrown himself, with no other aid, on the providence of God. He, however, believed that, if he and his brethren took such a step, it would effectually arouse the churches at home, and that thus all needed aid would be afforded.

With these views, he went to England, his whole mind being intent on finding some way of getting to the heathen. Every thing else seemed to him of little consequence; and the plan of uniting with the London society was found at first view to be impracticable. He returned with the means of going to the East for himself and his brethren. Still he wished to be sent by the American churches. With these views, and with his constitutional ardor of temperament, I presume that he pressed the board to a decision with a somewhat unceremonious earnestness. plainly intimating that, if they did not send him and his brethren, they would at once use the appointment of the London society.

This earnestness succeeded, and on the second day of the session the appointment was made. Still, the board were annoyed by his pertinacity, and plainly informed him that there were parts of his conduct of which they disapproved. This was, I doubt not, a recital of errors which Judson had often confessed in humiliation before God, over which he had wept, and against which he had labored and prayed times without number. He felt thankful to the fathers for their faithfulness, and resolved to strive the harder for Christian perfection. He had no idea that any serious displeasure was intended; and every other thought was immediately swallowed up in the consideration that he and his brethren were now appointed missionaries to the heathen, and appointed by their American brethren. In his letters at this period he speaks of this event as the consummation of all his wishes. The board afterwards, until the time of his embarkation, gave him no reason to suppose that he had been subject to any serious displeasure; and the whole thing passed entirely out of his mind. Hence, when, some years afterwards, it was asserted that he had been censured by the board, and censured so gravely as to occasion his profession of a change of sentiment in order to separate himself from them, he at once met it with a flat denial, and publicly called on every member of the board to vindicate his character.

Some years passed away. He could now more readily place himself in the position of the board, and understand their duties and responsibilities. He could see how his zealous pertinacity, even with the best motives, would affect men in their circumstances. He saw the *a priori* probability that some admonition would have been given. He remembered that Dr. Spring had addressed him. Mr. Nott, his friend and companion, admitted a "solemn and formal admonition." The members of the board all testified to the same fact. Under these circumstances, he could not but admit that something had taken place of a graver character than he had been at the time aware of. He no sooner came to this conclusion than he at once corrected his error, and resolved to do justice to the memory of Dr. Worcester, whom he had unintentionally injured. This he did in his letter from Prome, to which allusion has been made. Nothing that Dr. Judson has done through life presents his character in a more favorable light, or exhibits more clearly the controlling power of Christian integrity, than this transaction.

One other remark, and I have done. There was, in the year 1811, a strong feeling of sectarian antagonism between the Congregationalists and Baptists. The change of sentiment in Mr. Judson was considered by his former brethren a severe trial and a painful disappointment. Remembering the address of Dr. Spring to Judson through the medium of existing feeling, is it too much to suppose that it assumed a graver aspect than it wore at the moment of its delivery, or that a faithful paternal admonition, to an overzealous and too confident youth, assumed afterwards the lineaments of a grave reprimand or a decided censure? That any member of the board would, under these circumstances, have intentionally made the slightest deviation from the exact verity, I do not for a moment believe; but that they should, under such a trial, have been affected by the general laws of humanity, is surely not improbable.

To sum up the whole matter, then, I would say that Judson, in wholly untried circumstances, did not perceive distinctly his relations to the board, and, acting from the dictates of self-sacrificing zeal, did not sufficiently recognize their authority. On this subject they very properly admonished him, but with so much parental and Christian feeling, that, while he was melted to tears, it left on his mind no trace of displeasure. When it was intimated that he had been censured, and so censured that it incited him to leave the service of the board,—the most self-sacrificing act, as he always testified, of his whole life,—he met it with a prompt denial. In the course of years, when he reviewed the whole subject, recalled the whole series of events, and received the testimony of Mr. Nott and of the members of the board, he was satisfied that more had occurred than he at first recollected. He then, at once, as became a Christian and an honorable man, made all the reparation in his power by confessing his error. His letter should have been published at the time, according, I think, to his manifest intention.

The following letters, addressed, the one to Dr. Spring, of Newburyport, and the other to Jeremiah Evarts, Esq., indicate the views of Mr. Judson at the commencement and the close of this transaction.

RANGOON, June 30, 1819.

REV. AND DEAR SIR: I have been perfectly astonished to find it publicly asserted, that "a formal and solemn reprimand was administered to me in presence of the board," at the

Worcester session, in 1811. My best recollections assure me that this assertion is founded on a mistake.

I am induced to apply particularly to you, sir, by my recollecting a conversation which passed between us, in Madam Phillips's house, in Andover, some days after the session, in which you suggested a fear that I had alienated the minds of some of the members of the board, and instanced General Huntington, as having particularly disapproved of my proceedings. Now, it appears to me that this conversation would have been quite irrelevant, and, indeed, could not possibly have taken place, if we had both been conscious at the time that a formal reprimand had been given me by the board.

I am further induced to apply to you, from feeling that your opinion on that subject would tend more than that of any other person to relieve and satisfy my mind. Will you, therefore, please to inform me whether you think the charge correct or not?

I hope that my unfortunate apostasy will not be considered as depriving me of the privilege of receiving your kindness, in which it was my happiness to participate so largely in former days, and of which I shall ever retain a most grateful recollection. I remain, reverend and dear sir,

Your much obliged and obedient friend and servant,

A. JUDSON, JR.

Rev. Dr. Spring.*

PROME, June 13, 1830.

MY DEAR SIR: I have lately felt it my duty to confess my faults to all those whom I have in any way injured, whether wilfully or inadvertently; and were the late Dr. Worcester still living, I should desire to write him in the following manner: "Rev. Sir: When I read your public letter concerning the reprimand said to have been given me by the Board of Commissioners, I was perfectly astonished; and for many years I really thought that there was no ground whatever for your allegations. I am now, however, convinced from a number of

---

* Of Newburyport. Dr. S. was a member of the Prudential Committee. He had deceased previous to the arrival of this letter.

circumstances that I was mistaken, and that there was some expression of dissatisfaction on the part of the board, which, though it made so slight an impression on my mind as to be entirely forgotten for many years, furnished you with some just ground for a part of the statements in the said letter. There are other parts, concerning which I have nothing to say in addition to what I wrote at the time, except, in general, that I deeply regret and condemn the spirit with which I penned my reply in self-vindication, it being, as I now perceive, at variance with the spirit of the blessed Saviour, whose law requires us to resist not evil, but when smitten on the right cheek, to turn the other. I hope that I have humbly repented before God, and received his pardon; and I humbly beg your pardon also."

Such is the tenor of the letter I should be glad to address to Dr. Worcester; but it is now too late for me to do any thing more than to forward it to you, his successor in the Corresponding Secretary's office, and leave it for you to make what use of it you think proper.

I hope you will excuse my troubling you. I am aware that this communication will afford you no pleasure; nor should I make it if I consulted my credit with men. But I write to please One whom I desire to love supremely, and whose smiles I covet above all created good.

Yours, in Christian love,

A. JUDSON.

Jer. Evarts, Esq., Cor. Sec. A. B. C. F. M.

In a conversation on this subject, but a year or two before his death, Dr. Judson confirmed the view which I have taken above. He said that his first statement to Dr. Baldwin was made in perfect sincerity. He never considered himself reprimanded; he was ignorant of the passing of any vote on the subject, and was not aware of any serious displeasure on the part of the committee, though quite aware that they were annoyed (momentarily, as he supposed) at his pertinacity. When Nott's testimony was published, he was astonished to find so much admitted, though the formal reprimand was denied. In the course of years, however, circumstances came gradually to his recollection which made him think that Dr. Worcester's assertion had some just foundation, and that the board were more displeased at his zealous boldness than he was aware of at the time. He said, however, that he could not, on the whole, regret his course before the board at Worcester, and speculated at some length on what would have been the probable result if he and Nott had waited for "the further intimations of Providence." He also said that his letter from Prome, though written under peculiar influences, met the approval of his sober judgment, and he felt a satisfaction in having done his duty as soon as he became aware of it, however much the meaning of his honest communication might be perverted.

In another conversation, he alluded to the injudiciousness of calling up these long-forgotten incidents, and added, "When I grasp the hand of Dr. Worcester in heaven, I do not think we shall either of us feel called upon to settle any such differences."

I do not know how I can close this subject more appropriately than by adding the following letter from Dr. Judson to Dr. Anderson, the present secretary of the American Board, and the noble and beautiful reply of Dr. Anderson.

MAULMAIN, January 21, 1839.

REV. AND DEAR SIR: The Missionary Herald has been kindly sent to me gratis, through Messrs. Cockerell & Co., and by way of Rangoon, in parcels of several numbers at a time, by which means it does not reach me in good season. I beg leave to request that each number, as soon as published, may be sent, *with my name upon it*, to the Missionary Rooms of the Baptist Board, and then it will be forwarded, with other articles, by the earliest and most direct conveyance.

I am aware that it is not regular to trouble *you* with this business; but, to tell the truth, I have rather caught at it as giving me an occasion to drop you a line, and perhaps get one in return. Though I have been (as some may think) a wayward son of the American Board of Commissioners for Foreign Missions, I have always retained the warmest filial affection for that body, under whose auspices I first came out.

I was also afraid that, attempting to change the mode of conveyance, I should, by some accident, lose my *Herald* altogether, unless I wrote you, and begged you to secure me from such a misfortune.

There are not many, perhaps, now living, who can say, as I can, that they have read every number of the Herald, from the time it first commenced its existence, in the form of the Panoplist and Massachusetts Missionary Magazine, to the present time; and I hope to enjoy the privilege as long as I live. The Herald, in my view, contains more interesting missionary information, and a development of sounder missionary principles, than any other publication in the world.

I remain, reverend and dear sir,
Yours, most sincerely,
A. JUDSON.

Rev. Dr. Anderson, Cor. Sec. A. B. C. F. M.

MISSIONARY HOUSE, BOSTON, August 1, 1839.

REV. ADONIRAM JUDSON, Maulmain, India.

REV. AND DEAR SIR: A few days since I had the great pleasure of receiving your favor of January 21. If any thing was wanted, in addition to your long, devoted, and successful missionary life, to perfect the impression made by your letter to Mr. Evarts, dated June 13, 1830, (and which I replied to February 25, 1831,) it was such a letter as lies now before me. But I should not have said, nor am I aware, that any thing was necessary to give you a stronger hold upon our hearts than any other one of the brethren of your society can possibly have. We rejoice in the good, the very great good, which has grown out of your change of relation. We see the good hand of our God in this. We would not, therefore, have it otherwise. The old asperities of feeling have perished in the grave, or have been softened down by time and the grace of God. We love to think of you as intimately related to us — having a common missionary parentage. Hence we send you the Herald, and on this account we mean to send it to you as long as you continue a missionary of our Lord and Master.

I will give directions for sending the Herald monthly to the Baptist Missionary Rooms, with your name upon it, and will take all the pains I can to see that this is done from year to year. Still, while this method will insure its being sent to you without the long delays attendant on the other course, there is a liability, which I know not how to prevent, that it may *accidentally* stop at the *end* of almost any year. I would therefore request you, should there be any interruption in your receipt of the work, to attribute it to *accident in the publishing office*, and write immediately to me, or my successor, (for secretaries are apt to be a short-lived race,) state what numbers are wanting to complete the series, and remind us of our duty.

I send a small parcel of our recent publications to the Baptist Missionary Rooms for you, and may perhaps trouble you in this manner in time to come.

With great esteem and cordial affection, and with fervent desires for the continued prosperity of yourself and your fellow-laborers, I am, my dear brother, most truly yours,

R. ANDERSON,
Sec. of A. B. C. F. M.

CHAPTER IV.

EMBARKATION.—ARRIVAL IN INDIA.—CHANGE OF VIEWS ON BAPTISM.—COURSE OF THE EAST INDIA COMPANY.—ESCAPE TO THE ISLE OF FRANCE.—PASSAGES TO MADRAS AND RANGOON.—FORMATION OF THE BAPTIST GENERAL CONVENTION FOR FOREIGN MISSIONS.

1812-1813.

On the 19th of February, 1812, Mr. and Mrs. Judson and Mr. and Mrs. Newell embarked at Salem, in the brig Caravan, Captain Heard, bound for Calcutta. They had been some time waiting for a fair wind; and, on the 18th, the long-expected change in the weather took place, and the passengers were in haste summoned on board. The brig remained, however, at anchor during the night, and on the following morning set sail with a favorable breeze.

The embarkation was sudden, and but few of their friends were aware of the time of their departure. Every comfort which kindness could suggest had, however, been previously provided. The captain was an intelligent and amiable gentleman, and they commenced their voyage under the most auspicious circumstances. The passage was pleasant, and on the 17th of June they arrived in Calcutta. Messrs. Nott, Hall, and Rice, who sailed about the same time in the Harmony, from Philadelphia, did not arrive until the 8th of the following month.

A controversy has, unfortunately, been carried on, respecting the embarkation at Salem, to which it is necessary very briefly to advert.

When Dr. Judson returned to this country, after thirty-three years' absence, he was greatly surprised at the change which had taken place in public opinion on the subject of missions. When he left for India, devout men were beginning to be interested in it; a few others looked with admiration at the romantic self-sacrifice which it exhibited; but I think I do not err in asserting that it was by many good men considered a hopeless undertaking. From my own personal knowledge, I can testify that, as late as Mrs. Ann Judson's second embarkation, it was with some difficulty that passages were procured for missionaries to India. When Dr. Judson returned, he found the cause of missions to the heathen the favorite object of Christian benevolence. It had entirely silenced opposition, and multiplied without limit the number of its friends. He was filled with admiration at what he saw, and felt assured that his highest anticipations of the progress of the cause had been more than realized.

In speaking on this subject, he, on one or two occasions, contrasted the circumstances of the pioneers, when they left their native country, with those of their brethren who were at the present day following them. I am confident that, in these remarks, he had not the most remote idea of undervaluing the kindness of his friends in Salem. In all his letters, as well as those of Mrs. Judson, this subject is never alluded to but in terms of affectionate gratitude. A use was, however, made of these remarks, which gave pain to the family of the late Dr. Worcester, and some of his friends at Salem. This was as far as possible from his intention. The contrast struck him forcibly, and, in speaking of it, he alluded to circumstances which happened to occur to him. He did not suppose that they would give pain to any one; for, as they existed in his mind, there was nothing either wrong or unkind associated with them.

The only event on the passage which has become specially worthy of note is the fact that Mr. Judson availed himself of this period of leisure to investigate anew the scriptural authority for infant baptism. He was prompted to this course by two considerations. In the first place, he looked forward to the time when he should be surrounded by converts from heathenism. How should he treat their children and servants? Was he authorized to baptize them? and if so, what would be their relation to the Christian church afterwards? Besides this, he was going in the first instance to Serampore, to reside for a time with the Baptist missionaries. He felt the necessity for reëxamining the subject, as he expected to be called upon by them to defend his belief. In this latter respect, however, he found himself singularly disappointed; for the gentlemen at Serampore made it a matter of principle never to introduce the subject of their peculiar belief to any of their brethren of other denominations who happened to be their guests.

As it seems proper to allow Mr. Judson to explain the reasons for his change of sentiment, I shall here insert a large part of his letter to the Third Church in Plymouth, of which he had been until lately a member.

It was on board the vessel, in prospect of my future life among the heathen, that I was led to investigate this important subject. I was going forth to proclaim the glad news of salvation through Jesus Christ. I hoped that my ministrations would be blessed to the conversion of souls. In that case, I felt that I should have no hesitation concerning my duty to the converts, it being plainly commanded in Scripture that such are to be baptized, and received into church fellowship. But how, thought I, am I to treat the unconverted children and domestics of the converts? Are they to be considered members of the church of Christ by virtue of the conversion of the head of the family, or not? If they are, ought I not to treat them as such? After they are baptized, can I consistently set them aside, as aliens from the commonwealth of Israel, until they are readmitted? If they are not to be considered members of the church, can I consistently administer to them the initiating ordinance of the church?

If I adopt the Abrahamic covenant, and consider the Christian church a continuation of the Abrahamic or Jewish system, I must adopt the former part of the alternative. I must consider the children and domestics of professors as members of the church, and treat them accordingly. Abraham, according to the terms of the covenant which God made with him, circumcised not only his own sons, but all the males that were born in his house, or bought with money. His male descendants, in the line of Isaac and Jacob, were entitled to the same ordinance, by virtue of natural descent, and, together with their domestics, composed the ancient church, and were entitled to all its privileges. This is put beyond a doubt by the single fact, that, in the Abrahamic community, or the society of Israel, there was no separate party calling themselves, by way of distinction, *the church*, and saying to others, who were equally circumcised with themselves, Stand by ; touch not the passover; we are holier than you. No. All the members of the community or nation were of course members of the church. They were entitled to church membership by birth or purchase. Their church membership was recognized, or they were initiated into the church by circumcision; and in subsequent life they partook of the passover, which was the standing sacrament of the church, analogous to the Lord's supper, and enjoyed all the rights and privileges of the church, unless they were excommunicated, or, in scriptural language, " cut off from the people." *

---

* If any one should be inclined to doubt the right of circumcised children to the passover, let him consider the following : —

Witsius. "In those companies" (that partook of the passover) " men and women sat down together, old men and young, whole and

Now, let me be consistent. Since I am exhorted to walk in the steps of father Abraham, let me follow him with the same faithfulness which procured him eminent praise. Let me not adopt some parts of his covenant, and reject others, as suits my own convenience, or accords with the notions in which I have been educated. Nor let me complain for want of example and prescription. Behold the established church of England. She proves herself, in many respects, a worthy daughter of the Abrahamic or Jewish church. She receives into her charitable bosom all the descendants of professors, and all those who, though not of her seed, belong to the families of professors ; and these collectively come, in process of time, to comprise the whole nation. This is truly Abrahamic. This is the very system which the ancestors of the Jewish race, and their succeeding rulers and priests, uniformly maintained. And if I claim an interest in the Abrahamic covenant, and consider the Christian church a continuation of the Jewish, why should I hesitate to prove myself a true child of Abraham, and a consistent Christian, by adopting this system in all its parts, and introducing it among the heathen?

But I considered again : How does this system accord with the account of the church of Christ given in the New Testament? It appeared to me, from the manner in which this church commenced and was continued, from the character of

---

sick, masters and servants, in fine, every Jew that could eat a morsel of flesh, not excluding even young children." — *Œcon. Fœd.* l. iv. c. ix. § 14.

Dr. Scott. " Every person, in each household, including women and children, ate this first passover, none being excepted but uncircumcised males ; and afterwards all, who were not ceremonially unclean, partook of it. The women and children were not indeed commanded to go up to the tabernacle, where it was celebrated ; but when they did, they joined in this sacred feast." — *Note on Exodus* xii. 43-45.

After the tabernacle, where alone the passover could be eaten, was established at Jerusalem, young children, on account of distance, not on account of any personal disqualification, were seldom brought to partake of the passover. This neglect, however, was not allowed after they had attained the age of twelve years.

its members, and, in fine, from its whole economy, so far as detailed in the New Testament, that it was a company consisting of select individuals, men and women, who gave credible evidence of being disciples of Christ; and that it had no regard to natural descent, or accidental connection with the families of professors.

When I proceeded to consider certain passages, which are thought to favor the Pedobaptist system, I found nothing satisfactory.

The sanctification which St. Paul ascribes to the children of a believer, (1 Cor. vii. 14,) I found that he ascribed to the unbelieving parent also; and therefore, whatever be the meaning of the passage, it could have no respect to church membership, or a right to church ordinances.

The declaration of St. Peter, "The promise is unto you, and to your children, and to all that are afar off, even as many as the Lord our God shall call," (Acts ii. 39,) appeared not to bear at all on the point in hand, because the apostle does not command his hearers to have their children baptized, or acknowledged members of the church, but to repent and be baptized themselves. There is indeed a promise made to their children, and to all others that God shall call; but it does not follow that they were to procure the baptism of their children, or of those that were afar off, until they gave evidence that God had called them.

When Christ said, concerning little children, that "of such is the kingdom of heaven," (Matt. xix. 14,) it appeared to me that his comparison had respect, not to the age or size of little children, but to the humility and docility which distinguish them from adults. This seemed to be put beyond a doubt by his own explanation, in a similar passage, in which he says, "Except ye be converted, and become as little children, ye shall not enter into the kingdom of heaven." (Matt. xviii. 3.)

The baptism of households, which is mentioned in three instances, I could not consider as affording any evidence one way or the other, because in a household there may be infants and unbelieving domestics, and there may not. Besides, I discovered some circumstances in each of the cases which led me to conclude, that the members of the households were real believers. They are expressly said to be so in the case of the jailer, (Acts xvi. 34;) and the same is evidently implied in the case of Stephanas, when it is said that they addicted themselves to the ministry of the saints. (1 Cor. i. 16.)

In a word, I could not find a single intimation in the New Testament that the children and domestics of believers were members of the church, or entitled to any church ordinance, in consequence of the profession of the head of their family. Every thing discountenanced this idea. When baptism was spoken of, it was always in connection with believing. None but believers were commanded to be baptized; and it did not appear to my mind that any others were baptized.

Here, then, appeared a striking difference between the Abrahamic and the Christian systems. The one recognized the membership of children, domestics, and remote descendants of professors, and tended directly to the establishment of a national religion. The other appeared to be a selective system, acknowledging none as members of the church but such as gave credible evidence of believing in Christ.

This led me to suspect that these two systems, so evidently different, could not be one and the same. And now the light began to dawn. The more I read, and the more I meditated on the subject, the more clearly it appeared to me that all my errors and difficulties had originated in confounding these two systems. I began to see that since the very nature and constitution of the church of Christ excluded infants and unregenerate domestics, repentance and faith being always represented as necessary to constitute a disciple, we had no right to expect any directions for, or any examples of, the initiation of such unqualified persons into the church. To search for such directions and examples in the New Testament, would be as if the citizen of a republic should go to search his national code for laws concerning the royal family, which, by the very nature and constitution of a republic, is excluded. Suppose that such a citizen, disappointed in his search, should have recourse to the constitution and laws of a neighboring monarchy for the desired information. This, it appeared to me, would aptly represent the proceeding of those who, unable to find in the New Testament satisfactory proof of the right of infants, or unregenerate domestics, should have recourse to the Abrahamic and Jewish codes.

At length I adopted the following sentiments concerning the two churches, and the concern which we have at present with the old dispensation. The Abrahamic church was preparatory to, and typical of, the Christian. The constitution was radically different; but it was, nevertheless, wisely adapted to answer the ends which God had in view. Natural descent or purchase was sufficient to introduce a person into this church; but still it appears that in every age there were some who were truly pious; who embraced the gospel promise made to Abraham before the covenant of circumcision was instituted; who also looked beyond the literal meaning of the requirements and promises, contained in that covenant, to the glorious things typified thereby, and thus exercised true faith in the coming Messiah, and in a better country, that is, the heavenly. When the Messiah appeared, this preparatory and typical system, having answered its end, was destined to cease; and the Lord Jesus set up his kingdom on earth, the gospel church, composed of such only as repent and believe, or rather give credible evidence of these gracious exercises. The bar of separation between the Jews and the rest of the world was removed; thenceforth none were to plead that they had Abraham for their father; none were to rest in the covenant of circumcision, assured that, if they did, Christ would profit them nothing; but it was distinctly declared, that thenceforth there was neither Jew nor Greek, bond nor free, male nor female, but all were one in Christ. (Gal. iii. 28.)

But whereas the Abrahamic system was typical of the Christian, so the spiritual meaning of the requirements and promises still remains in force. Thus, by looking beyond the letter, and regarding the spiritual import, according to the example of the pious Jews, a great part of the Old Testament is still applicable to us, though the New Testament is emphatically the Christian's law book. The natural seed of Abraham typifies the spiritual seed. The land of Canaan typifies the heavenly land. External circumcision typifies the circumcision of the heart, a circumcision made without hands, that is, the putting off the body of the sins of the flesh, even the circumcision of Christ. (Col. ii. 11.) Believers, therefore, may embrace the promise of Canaan, in its spiritual application, as made to themselves, the spiritual seed, who have received the spiritual circumcision. Hence, also, all the devotional parts of the Old Testament, particularly the Psalms of David, the modern believer can make his own, adopting the language as the genuine expressions of his own devout feelings.

In the same way are to be explained all the New Testament allusions to the ancient dispensation. When, for instance, the apostle says, "If ye be Christ's, then are ye Abraham's seed, and heirs according to the promise," (Gal. iii. 29,) we are to understand, not Abraham's natural seed, surely, but his spiritual seed, those who by faith are assimilated to him, and thus become his children; not heirs of the land of Canaan, in the literal acceptation of the words, but heirs of the blessing of justification by faith, concerning which the apostle had been discoursing, and consequently of the spiritual Canaan, the city of the living God, the heavenly Jerusalem.

I cannot describe to you, dear brethren, the light and satisfaction which I obtained in taking this view of the matter, in considering the two churches distinct, and in classing my ideas of each in their proper place. I became possessed of a key that unlocked many a difficulty, which had long perplexed me; and the more I read the Bible, the more clearly I saw that this was the true system therein revealed.

But while I obtained light and satisfaction on one side, I was plunged in difficulty and distress on the other. If, thought I, this system is the true one; if the Christian church is not a continuation of the Jewish; if the covenant of circumcision is not precisely the covenant in which Christians now stand, the whole foundation of pedobaptism is gone; there is no remaining ground for the administration of any church ordinance to the children and domestics of professors; and it follows inevitably, that I, who was christened in infancy, on the faith of my parents, have never yet received Christian baptism. Must I, then, forsake my parents, the church with which I stand connected, the society under whose patronage I have come out, the companions of my missionary undertaking? Must I forfeit the good opinion of all my friends in my native land, occasioning grief to some, and provoking others to anger, and be regarded henceforth, by all my former dear acquaintances, as a weak, despicable Baptist, who has not sense enough to comprehend the connection between the Abrahamic and the Christian systems? All this was mortifying; it was hard to flesh and blood. But I thought again, it is better to be guided by the opinion of Christ, who is the truth, than by the opinion of men, however good, whom I know to be in an error. The praise of Christ is better than the praise of men. Let me cleave to Christ at all events, and prefer his favor above my chief joy.

There was another thing which greatly contributed, just at this time, to drive me to an extremity. I knew that I had been sprinkled in infancy, and that this had been deemed baptism. But throughout the whole New Testament I could find nothing that looked like sprinkling, in connection with the ordinance of baptism. It appeared to me, that if a plain person should, without any previous information on the subject, read through the New Testament, he would never get the idea, that baptism consisted in sprinkling. He would find that baptism, in all the cases particularly described, was administered in rivers, and that the parties are represented as going down into the water, and coming up out of the water, which they would not have been so foolish as to do for the purpose of sprinkling.

In regard to the word itself which is translated *baptism*, a very little search convinced me that its plain, appropriate meaning was immersion or dipping; and though I read extensively on the subject, I could not find that any learned

Pedobaptist had ever been able to produce an instance, from any Greek writer, in which it meant sprinkling, or any thing but immersion, except in some figurative applications, which could not be fairly brought into the question. The Rev. Professor Campbell, D. D., of Scotland, the most learned Greek scholar and biblical critic of modern times, has the candor to declare, (though he was no Baptist, and, therefore, not to be suspected of partiality to the Baptist system,) that the word was never, so far as he knew, employed in the sense of sprinkling, in any use, sacred or classical. (See his note on Matt. iii. 11.)

But as my limits will not permit me to enter further into detail on this part of the subject, I must beg leave to refer you to my sermon, a copy of which will accompany this letter. Suffice it to say, that whereas a consideration of the nature of the church convinced me, that I had never received Christian baptism, so a consideration of the nature of baptism convinced me, that I had never been baptized at all, nothing being baptism but immersion.

Reduced to this extremity, what, dear brethren, could I do? I saw that, in a double sense, I was unbaptized, and I felt the command of Christ press on my conscience. Now, if I quieted my conscience in regard to my own personal baptism, and concluded that, on account of my peculiar circumstances, it was best to consult my own convenience, rather than the command of Christ, still the question would return, with redoubled force, How am I to treat the children and domestics of converted heathen? This was the beginning of all my difficulties, and this, on Pedobaptist principles, I could not resolve by the Bible, or by any books that I consulted.

In order that you may feel the trying situation in which I was placed, I beg you to make the case your own, particularly in regard to this one point — the treatment of the families of believers. You may thus be brought to feel the gripe of this Gordian knot, as I have felt it. It is true you have not the prospect of converted heathen and their families to trouble you; yet permit me to submit the case of your own families

In what light do you consider and treat them? Do you strictly comply with the terms of the Abrahamic covenant? Does your conduct perfectly accord with the Abrahamic system? Do you baptize (if baptism is in the place of circumcision) your male children, and those only, on the eighth day after their birth? Do you baptize your male domestics? and if you had slaves, would you have them also baptized? Still further, Do you consider your baptized children and servants members of the church, as circumcised Jewish children and servants were members of the Jewish church? Do you acknowledge their right to the Lord's supper, as soon, at least, as they are capable? and do you feel your own obligations to require their attendance, and to discipline and exclude them if they do not attend? Circumcision was the initiating ordinance of the Abrahamic or Jewish church. Baptism has been regarded in every age, and by all parties, as the initiating ordinance of the Christian church. Baptized persons are, therefore, members of the church. And if so, is it not wrong and dangerous to treat them as if they were not? I need not inform you, that among yourselves, and among all the Congregational churches in New England, children and servants, who were baptized on account of the head of their family, are considered no more members of the church than before — no more members of the church than others that have not been baptized. They are, in fact, considered and treated as out of the church altogether, and as having no right to any further church privilege, until they give evidence of possessing religion, and make a personal public profession. Do you not hesitate, my brethren, at pursuing a course so anti-Abrahamic, so unscriptural? How can you plead the promises made to Abraham, when you so flagrantly violate the covenant in which they are contained, and depart from the course divinely prescribed in his family, and in subsequent generations? But, on the other hand, if you adopt and practise the Abrahamic system, you will inevitably confound the church and the world; you will receive into the church multitudes who are destitute of those qualifications which are represented in the New Testament as requisite to constitute a member of the kingdom which Christ set up; you will ultimately establish a national religion; and this will be as contrary to the system laid down in the New Testament as your present system is to the Abrahamic.

The extracts which follow from the letters of Mrs. Judson exhibit the manner in which she and Mr. Judson pursued their inquiries, and the loneliness into which their change of opinions by necessity plunged them.

From Mrs. Judson to a Friend.
September 7, 1812.

Can you, my dear Nancy, still love me, still desire to hear from me, when I tell you I have become a Baptist? If I judge from my own feelings, I answer, you will, and that my differing from you in those things which do not affect our salvation will not diminish your affection for me, or make you unconcerned for my welfare. You may, perhaps, think this change very sudden, as I have said nothing of it before; but, my dear girl, this alteration hath not been the work of an hour, a day, or a month. The subject has been maturely, candidly, and, I hope, prayerfully examined for months.

An examination of the subject of baptism commenced on board the Caravan. As Mr. Judson was continuing the translation of the New Testament, which he began in America, he had many doubts respecting the meaning of the word *baptize*. This, with the idea of meeting the Baptists at Serampore, when he would wish to defend his own sentiments, induced a more thorough examination of the foundation of the Pedobaptist system. The more he examined, the more his doubts increased; and, unwilling as he was to admit it, he was *afraid* the Baptists were right and he wrong. After we arrived at Calcutta, his attention was turned from this subject to the concerns of the mission, and the difficulties with government. But as his mind was still uneasy, he again renewed the subject. I felt afraid he would become a Baptist, and frequently urged the unhappy consequences if he should. But he said his duty compelled him to satisfy his own mind, and embrace those sentiments which appeared most concordant with Scripture. I always took the Pedobaptist side in reasoning with him, even after I was as doubtful of the truth of their system as he. We left Serampore to reside in Calcutta a week or two, before the arrival of our brethren; and as we had nothing in particular to occupy our attention, we confined it exclusively to this subject. We procured the best authors on both sides, compared them with the Scriptures, examined and reëxamined the sentiments of Baptists and Pedobaptists, and were finally compelled, from a conviction of truth, to embrace those of the former. Thus, my dear Nancy, we are confirmed Baptists, not because we wished to be, but because truth compelled us to be. We have endeavored to count the cost, and be prepared for the many severe trials resulting from this change of sentiment. We anticipate the loss of reputation, and of the affection and esteem of many of our American friends. But the most trying circumstance attending this change, and that which has caused most pain, is the separation which must take place between us and our dear missionary associates. Although we are attached to each other, and should doubtless live very happily together, yet the brethren do not think it best we should unite in one mission. These things, my dear Nancy, have caused us to weep and pour out our hearts in prayer to Him whose directions we so much wish and need. We feel that we are alone in the world, with no real friend but each other, no one on whom we can depend but God.

From Mrs. Judson to her Parents.

ISLE OF FRANCE, PORT LOUIS, February 14, 1813.

I will now, my dear parents and sisters, give you some account of our change of sentiment, relative to the subject of baptism. Mr. Judson's doubts commenced on our passage from America. While translating the New Testament, in which he was engaged, he used frequently to say that the Baptists were

CHANGE OF VIEWS ON BAPTISM. 107

right in their mode of administering the ordinance. Knowing he should meet the Baptists at Serampore, he felt it important to attend to it more closely, to be able to defend his sentiments. After our arrival at Serampore, his mind for two or three weeks was so much taken up with missionary inquiries and our difficulties with government, as to prevent his attending to the subject of baptism. But as we were waiting the arrival of our brethren, and having nothing in particular to attend to, he again took up the subject. I tried to have him give it up, and rest satisfied in his old sentiments, and frequently told him, if he became a Baptist, *I would not.* He, however, said he felt it his duty to examine closely a subject on which he had so many doubts. After we removed to Calcutta, he found in the library in our chamber many books on both sides, which he determined to read candidly and prayerfully, and to hold fast, or embrace the truth, however mortifying, however great the sacrifice. I now commenced reading on the subject, with all my prejudices on the Pedobaptist side. We had with us Dr. Worcester's, Dr. Austin's, Peter Edwards's, and other Pedobaptist writings. But after closely examining the subject for several weeks, we were constrained to acknowledge that the truth appeared to lie on the Baptists' side. It was extremely trying to reflect on the consequences of our becoming Baptists. We knew it would wound and grieve our dear Christian friends in America — that we should lose their approbation and esteem. We thought it probable the commissioners would refuse to support us; and, what was more distressing than any thing, we knew we must be separated from our missionary associates, and go alone to some heathen land. These things were very trying to us, and caused our hearts to bleed for anguish. We felt we had no home in this world, and no friend but each other. Our friends at Serampore were extremely surprised when we wrote them a letter requesting baptism, as they had known nothing of our having had any doubts on the subject. We were baptized on the 6th of September, in the Baptist chapel in Calcutta. Mr. J. preached a sermon at Calcutta, on this subject, soon after we were baptized, which, in compliance with the request of a number who heard it, he has been preparing for the press. Brother Rice was baptized several weeks after we were. It was a very great relief to our minds to have him join us, as we expected to be entirely alone in a mission.

The day after her baptism, she wrote to her parents a further account of the progress of their inquiries on the subject, and mentions some additional particulars.

Mr. Judson resolved to examine it candidly and prayerfully, let the result be what it would. No one in the mission family knew the state of his mind, as they never conversed with any of us on this subject. I was very fearful he would become a Baptist, and frequently suggested the unhappy consequences if he should. He always answered, that his duty compelled him to examine the subject, and he hoped he should have a disposition to embrace the truth, though he paid dear for it. I always took the Pedobaptists' side in reasoning with him, although I was as doubtful of the truth of their system as he. After we came to Calcutta, he devoted his whole time to reading on this subject, having obtained the best authors on both sides. After having examined and reëxamined the subject, in every way possible, and comparing the sentiments of both Baptists and Pedobaptists with the Scriptures, he was compelled, from a conviction of the truth, to embrace those of the former. I confined my attention almost entirely to the Scriptures, comparing the Old with the New Testament, and tried to find something to favor infant baptism, but was convinced it had no foundation there. I examined the covenant of circumcision, and could see no reason for concluding that baptism was to be administered to children because circumcision was. Thus, my dear parents and sisters, we are both confirmed Baptists, not because we wished to be, but because truth compelled us to be. A renunciation of our former sentiments has caused us more pain than any thing which ever happened to us through our lives.

As soon as Mr. Judson had come to the conclusion

indicated in the preceding letters, he of course informed the American Board of Commissioners for Foreign Missions of his change of sentiment on the subject of baptism. By the same conveyance, he also communicated a knowledge of the facts to some of the Baptist clergymen in Boston and Salem. The following letters refer to this portion of our narrative: —

To the Rev. Dr. Baldwin, of Boston.

CALCUTTA, August 31, 1812.

REV. AND DEAR SIR: I write you a line to express my grateful acknowledgments to you for the advantage I have derived from your publications on baptism; particularly from your "Series of Letters;" also to introduce the following copy of a letter which I forwarded last week to the Baptist missionaries at Serampore, and which you are at liberty to use as you think best.

I am, sir, with much affection and respect,
Your obliged friend and servant,
ADONIRAM JUDSON, JR.

CALCUTTA, August 27, 1812.

TO THE REV. MESSRS. CAREY, MARSHMAN, AND WARD.

As you have been ignorant of the late exercises of my mind on the subject of baptism, the communication which I am about to make may occasion you some surprise.

It is now about four months since I took the subject into serious and prayerful consideration. My inquiries commenced during my passage from America, and after much laborious research and painful trial, which I shall not now detail, have issued in entire conviction, that *the immersion of a professing believer is the only Christian baptism.*

In these exercises I have not been alone. Mrs. Judson has been engaged in a similar examination, and has come to the same conclusion. Feeling, therefore, that we are in an unbaptized state, we wish to profess our faith in Christ by being baptized in obedience to his sacred commands.

ADONIRAM JUDSON, JR.

CALCUTTA, September 1, 1812.

REV. SIR: After transmitting to the Rev. Dr. Worcester a copy of the above letter to the Baptist missionaries, I have, under date of this day, written him as follows: —

REV. AND DEAR SIR: My change of sentiments on the subject of baptism is considered by my missionary brethren as incompatible with my continuing their fellow-laborer in the mission which they contemplate on the Island of Madagascar; and it will, I presume, be considered by the Board of Commissioners as equally incompatible with my continuing their missionary. The board will, undoubtedly, feel as unwilling to support a Baptist missionary as I feel to comply with their instructions, which particularly direct us to baptize "*credible believers with their households.*"

The dissolution of my connection with the Board of Commissioners, and a separation from my dear missionary brethren, I consider most distressing consequences of my late change of sentiments, and indeed, the most distressing events which have ever befallen me I have now the prospect before me of going alone to some distant island, unconnected with any society at present existing, from which I might be furnished with assistant laborers or pecuniary support. Whether the Baptist churches in America will compassionate my situation, I know not. I hope, therefore, that while my friends condemn what they deem a departure from the truth, they will at least pity me and pray for me.

With the same sentiments of affection and respect as ever,

I am, sir, your friend and servant,

ADONIRAM JUDSON, JR.

Rev. Dr. Worcester, Corresponding Secretary of the American Board of Commissioners for Foreign Missions.

You will receive a letter from Dr. Marshman, accompanying this. Should there be formed, in accordance with the ideas suggested therein, a Baptist society for the support of a mission in these parts, *I shall be ready to consider myself their missionary;* and remain, dear sir,

Your obliged friend and servant,

ADONIRAM JUDSON, JR.

To the Rev. Dr. Bolles, Salem, Mass.

CALCUTTA, September 1, 1812.

REV. SIR: I recollect that, during a short interview I had with you in Salem, I suggested the formation of a society among the Baptists in America for the support of foreign missions, in imitation of the exertions of your English brethren. Little did I then expect to be personally concerned in such an attempt.

Within a few months, I have experienced an entire change of sentiments on the subject of baptism. My doubts concerning the correctness of my former system of belief commenced during my passage from America to this country; and after many painful trials, which none can know but those who are taught to relinquish a system in which they had been educated, I settled down in the full persuasion that the immersion of a professing believer in Christ is the only Christian baptism.

Mrs. Judson is united with me in this persuasion. We have signified our views and wishes to the Baptist missionaries at Serampore, and expect to be baptized in this city next Lord's day.

A separation from my missionary brethren, and a dissolution of my connection with the Board of Commissioners, seem to be necessary consequences. The missionaries at Serampore are exerted to the utmost of their ability in managing and supporting their extensive and complicated mission.

Under these circumstances I look to you. Alone, in this foreign heathen land, I make my appeal to those whom, with their permission, I will call *my Baptist brethren* in the United States.

With the advice of the brethren at Serampore, I am contemplating a mission on one of the eastern islands. They have lately sent their brother Chater to Ceylon, and their brother Robinson to Java. At present, Amboyna seems to present the most favorable opening. Fifty thousand souls are there perishing without the means of life; and the situation of the island is such that a mission there established might, with the blessing of God, be extended to the neighboring islands in those seas.

But should I go thither, it is a most painful reflection that I must go alone, and also uncertain of the means of support. But I will trust in God. He has frequently enabled me to praise his divine goodness, and will never forsake those who put their trust in him. I am, dear sir,

Yours, in the Lord Jesus,

ADONIRAM JUDSON, JR.

Extract from a Letter of Dr. Marshman, of Serampore, to the Rev. Dr. Baldwin, of Boston, dated September 1, 1812.

A note which brother Judson sent to brother Carey last Saturday has occasioned much reflection among us. In it he declares his belief that believers' baptism alone is the doctrine of the Scriptures, and requests to be baptized in the name of the Lord Jesus.

This unexpected circumstance seems to suggest many ideas. The change in the young man's mind, respecting this ordinance of Christ, seems quite the effect of divine truth operating on the mind. It began when no Baptist was near, (on board ship,) and when he, in the conscientious discharge of his duty, was examining the subject in order to maintain what he then deemed truth on his arrival in Bengal. And so carefully did he conceal the workings of his mind from us, on his arrival, that he scarcely gave us a hint respecting them before he sent this note to brother Carey. This was not indeed very difficult for him to do, as we make it a point to guard against obtruding on missionary brethren of different sentiments any conversation relative to baptism.

This change then, which I believe few who knew brother Judson will impute to whim, or to any thing besides sincere conviction, seems to point out something relative to the duty of our Baptist brethren with you, as it relates to the cause of missions. It can scarcely be expected that the Board of Commissioners will support a Baptist missionary, who cannot, of course, comply with their instructions, and baptize *whole households* on the parents' faith; and it is certain that the young man ought not to be left to perish for want, merely because he loved the truth more than father or mother; nor be compelled to give up missionary work for want of support therein. Now, though we should certainly interfere to prevent a circumstance like this happening, particularly as we have given our Pedobaptist brother Newell, gone to the Isle of France, an order to draw there upon us should he be in distress, yet, to say nothing of the missionary concerns already lying on us, and constantly enlarging, it seems as though Providence itself were raising up this young man, that you might at least partake of the zeal of our Congregational missionary brethren around you. I would wish, then, that you should share in the glorious work, by supporting him. Let us do whatsoever things are *becoming*, and whatsoever things are *lovely*, and leave the reverse of these for others. After God has thus given you a missionary of your own nation, faith, and order, without the help or knowledge of man, let me entreat you, and Dr. Messer, and brethren Bolles and Moriarty, humbly to accept the gift.

To you I am sure I need add no more than to beg you to give my cordial love to all our brethren around you.

I may probably write you again soon, and in the mean time remain yours, in the Lord,

JOSHUA MARSHMAN.

The preceding extracts exhibit the condition of Mr. and Mrs. Judson in Calcutta as by no means encouraging. At a great sacrifice of feeling, they had found themselves obliged to pursue a course which separated them as missionaries from the board on which they relied solely for support. They knew that no Baptist organization existed at home adequate to undertake a mission to the East; and, moreover, they were personally almost unknown to the Baptist community. The brethren at Serampore would, of course, supply their immediate necessities; but they were decidedly of opinion that the responsibility for their maintenance should be assumed by the Baptists in America. Besides, this change in their sentiments rendered it inexpedient for them and their fellow-missionaries to labor any longer together. Here, again, ties the most endearing must be sundered, and hopes the most cherished must be forever abandoned. One circumstance, however, tended to modify the loneliness of this last trial. Mr. Rice, who was ordained at the same time as Mr. Judson, had also become a Baptist, and was, of course, united with them in anxieties and hopes.

But this was only a part of their present trial. It is well known that, at this period, the East India Company were both theoretically and practically opposed to every effort for the evangelization of India. They professed to believe, and charity obliges us to suppose that they did believe, that the preaching of the gospel would excite the Hindoos to rebellion. It is beyond question that the company was deriving large revenues directly from the toleration, not to say the protection, which it extended to the idolatry of the Hindoos. Whatever may have been their reasons, they had determined, by all the means in their power, to resist the introduction of Christianity among the native subjects of the British crown in Bengal.

About ten days after the arrival of Messrs. Judson and Newell, they were summoned to Calcutta, and an order was read to them requiring them immediately to leave the country and return to America. Nothing could be more fatal to their most dearly cherished hopes than such a command. They petitioned for leave to reside in some other part of India, but were prohibited from settling in any part of the company's territory, or in any of its dependencies. They then asked leave to go to the Isle of France. This was granted; and Mr. and Mrs. Newell embarked for Port Louis about the 1st of August. The vessel could, however, carry but two passengers; and Mr. and Mrs. Judson and Mr. Rice were obliged to emain behind.

They had resided in Calcutta about two months, waiting for a passage, when they received a peremptory order to proceed to England in one of the company's ships. A petty officer accompanied Messrs. Judson and Rice to their place of residence, and requested them not to leave it without permission. Their names were inserted in the daily papers in a list of passengers of the ship in which they were ordered to sail. A vessel was then found about to proceed to the Isle of France; but they were forbidden to take passage in her. They communicated to the captain their circumstances, and asked if he would venture to take them without a pass. He replied that he would be neutral; there was his ship, and they might do as they pleased.

They succeeded in getting on board the ship without being discovered, and the vessel sailed. After they had proceeded down the river for two days, they were overtaken by a government despatch forbidding the pilot to go farther, as the vessel contained passengers who had been ordered to England.

They were thus obliged to leave the ship. Every effort was made to procure a remission of the order, but in vain. An attempt to procure a passage to Ceylon failed. After spending several days in fruitless attempts to escape the necessity of proceeding to England, when every hope had failed, a letter was put into Mr. Judson's hand containing a pass from the magistrate for a passage in the Creole, the vessel which they had left. To whose kindness they were indebted for this favor they never ascertained. It was three days since the Creole had left them; and there was every reason to suppose that she had gone to sea. They, however, immediately set out in pursuit of her. After twenty-four hours of rowing and sailing, they reached Saugur, where they found the Creole at anchor. They were taken on board; and thus ended their first experiences of the East India Company's government in India.*

I mention these facts because they form a part of the narrative which I have undertaken to write. I do it with pain, for it presents in an unamiable light distinguished men whose characters we are accustomed to look upon with respect and esteem. It is delightful, however, to record the change which has taken place in the administration of the government of India, and in the treatment of the missionaries of all nations by the officers of the British crown. Gentlemen of the army and the navy, civil residents, and ambassadors, have for many years extended to missionaries from this country every aid which their circumstances required, and have frequently ministered to them in sickness and affliction with a spirit of fraternal kindness which has brought tears of gratitude into the eyes of thousands of Christians in America. It was not many years after the events which I have recorded that Mr. Judson was employed in a confidential service by the British government in nego-

---

* A more detailed account of these painful occurences may be found in Knowles's Life of Mrs. Ann H. Judson.

tiating the treaty of Yandabo, and for his services received, I believe, the thanks of the governor general in council. No missionary of any denomination was more highly esteemed than he in Calcutta; in no other place did his death call forth more general lamentation; and nowhere else have such spontaneous and liberal offerings been made in behalf of his widow and orphans.

On the 30th of November, 1812, Mr. and Mrs. Judson and Mr. Rice, fleeing from the intolerance of the East India Company, embarked on board the Belle Creole, bound for Port Louis, in the Isle of France. The passage was long and tempestuous. There were four passengers besides the missionaries; but none of them manifested any interest in religion. On the 17th of January they arrived at Port Louis.

They here met with a heavy affliction. Mrs. Newell, the intimate friend and first missionary associate of Mrs. Judson, had finished her course on the 30th of the preceding November. This event affected the whole company very deeply, and taught them, more emphatically than their wandering loneliness, that here they had no continuing city.

Mr. Rice had already been severely attacked with disease of the liver, and his health had become quite precarious. The views of the Baptists in this country were unknown to the missionaries, and it seemed desirable that some direct intercourse might be commenced between the parties at present personally unknown to each other. It was probable, moreover, that the labors of Mr. Rice might be eminently useful in awaking a missionary spirit among the churches at home. With the hope of recovering his health, and at the same time accomplishing these objects, it was deemed wise for Mr. Rice to return to this country. He sailed March 15, 1813, for New York, by the way of St. Salvador.

Mr. and Mrs. Judson were now left alone in the Isle of France. After much deliberation they decided to attempt the establishment of a mission on Pulo Penang, or Prince of Wales Island. There was no opportunity of procuring a passage thither from the Isle of France. They therefore, after a residence of three months at Port Louis, determined to proceed to Madras, as the only course by which they might arrive at their destination.

May 7, 1813, they embarked in the Countess of Harcourt, for Madras, and arrived there on the 4th of June. They were hospitably entertained by Mr. and Mrs. Lovelace, English missionaries residing there, and received much kindness from other friends of Christ in that city. Their embarrassments, however, were by no means diminished. They were again under the jurisdiction of the East India Company, from which they had lately escaped. Their case was immediately reported to the governor general, and no doubt existed that the reply to the despatch would bring an order for their immediate transportation to England. No vessel for Penang was in the harbor. Their only means of escape was by a vessel bound to Rangoon. They therefore, on the 22d of June, embarked on board the Georgiana for that port.

The vessel was old and unseaworthy. Mrs. Judson's condition required the aid of a nurse. A female in this capacity was engaged by the friends in Madras. A few hours after the vessel sailed, this woman dropped dead on the deck, and Mrs. Judson was obliged to pursue the voyage without either female attendant or medical adviser; and the captain was the only individual on board who could speak English.

The passage was tempestuous, and Mrs. Judson became very ill. By a kind Providence, the vessel was driven into a narrow strait, near the Andaman Islands, out of the reach of the tempest. Dr. Judson always believed that, but for this merciful interposition, Mrs. Judson would never have survived the voyage They arrived at Rangoon on the 13th of July, 1813, and made their first home in Burmah in the Baptist mission house, occupied by Felix Carey. Mr. Judson's account of these events is found in the following extract of a letter written after his arrival in Rangoon : —

A slight sketch of our movements, particularly at the time of our coming to Rangoon, I now submit. After a mournful separation from brother Rice, at the Isle of France, in March, 1813, we remained there about two months, waiting for a passage to some of the eastern islands, not venturing at that time to think a mission to Burmah practicable. But there being no prospect of accomplishing our wishes directly, we concluded to take passage to Madras, and proceed thence as circumstances should direct. We arrived there in June, and were immediately informed of the renewed hostilities of the company's government towards missionaries, exhibited in their treatment of the brethren both at Serampore and Bombay. We were, of course, reported to the police, and an account of our arrival forwarded to the supreme government in Bengal. It became, therefore, a moral certainty that, as soon as an order could be received at Madras, we should be again arrested, and ordered to England. Our only safety appeared to consist in escaping from Madras before such order should arrive. It may easily be conceived with what feelings I inquired the destination of vessels in the Madras roads. I found none that would sail in season, but one bound to Rangoon. A mission to Rangoon we had been accustomed to regard with feelings of horror. But it was now brought to a point. We must either venture there or be sent to Europe. All other paths were shut up; and thus situated, though dissuaded by all our friends at Madras, we commended ourselves to the care of God, and embarked the 22d of June. It was a crazy old vessel. The captain was the only person on board that could speak our language, and we had no other apartment than what was made by canvas. Our passage was very tedious. Mrs. Judson was taken dangerously ill, and continued so until, at one period, I came to experience the awful sensation which necessarily resulted from the expectation of an immediate separation from my beloved wife, the only remaining companion of my wanderings. About the same time, the captain being unable to make the Nicobar Island, where it was intended to take in a cargo of cocoa nuts, we were driven into a dangerous strait, between the Little and Great Andamans, two savage coasts, where the captain had never been before, and where, if we had been cast ashore, we should, according to all accounts, have been killed and eaten by the natives. But as one evil is sometimes an antidote to another, so it happened with us. Our being driven into this dangerous but quiet channel brought immediate relief to the agitated and exhausted frame of Mrs. Judson, and conduced essentially to her recovery. And in the event, we were safely conducted over the black rocks which we sometimes saw in the gulf below, and on the eastern side of the islands found favorable winds, which gently wafted us forward to Rangoon. But on arriving here, other trials awaited us.

We had never before seen a place where European influence had not contributed to smooth and soften the rough features of uncultivated nature. The prospect of Rangoon, as we approached, was quite disheartening. I went on shore, just at night, to take a view of the place, and the mission house; but so dark, and cheerless, and unpromising did all things appear, that the evening of that day, after my return to the ship, we have marked as the most gloomy and distressing that we ever passed. Instead of rejoicing, as we ought to have done, in having found a heathen land from which we were not immediately driven away, such were our weaknesses that we felt we had no portion left here below, and found consolation only in looking beyond our pilgrimage, which we tried to flatter ourselves would be short, to that peaceful region where the wicked cease from troubling and the weary are at rest. But if ever we commended ourselves sincerely, and without reserve, to the disposal of our heavenly Father, it was on this evening. And after some recollection and prayer, we experienced something of the presence of Him who cleaveth closer than a brother; something of that peace which our Saviour bequeathed to his followers — a legacy which we know from this experience endures when the fleeting pleasures and unsubstantial riches of the world are passed away. The next day Mrs. Judson was carried into the town, being unable to walk; and we found a home at the mission house, though Mr. Carey was absent at Ava.

When information of these events was received in this country, it produced an impression which, at the present day, can hardly be realized. As I have remarked before, there was a general feeling in favor of missions throughout the Baptist denomination. The labors and successes of the missionaries at Serampore were well known among the churches. The names of Carey, Marshman, and Ward, in India, and of Fuller, Ryland, and Sutcliffe, in England, were familiar to us as household words. Sums of money were contributed occasionally by benevolent individuals. There, however, seemed no particular point to which our efforts could be directed. There was no union of design. There was no general organization. We were scattered in large numbers over the different states of the Union. Each separate locality had its association; but the associations had no bond of union with each other, except by casual correspondence. We knew nothing of our numbers, and were scarcely aware in all *points* of the doctrinal sentiments embraced by the churches in different parts of our country. Ignorant of our strength, and unaware of the reliance which we could place on each other, we were unprepared to attempt any important enterprise, for we knew not who could be relied on to carry it forward.

The change of sentiment in Messrs. Judson and Rice was just the event which was required to awaken the dormant energies of the Baptists in America, and concentrate them all, in every part of our country, upon one object, truly Christian in its essence, and yet denominational in its form. It was universally acknowledged, that in this matter the providence of God had left us no option. Not to enter at once and vigorously upon the work of missions, would be to belie our profession as Christians, and expose us to the merited scorn of the whole religious world.

These sentiments led to universal action. Societies in aid of foreign missions were immediately formed in all our principal cities, and liberal contributions were made to their treasuries. A society was formed in Boston, named the Society for Propagating the Gospel in India and other Foreign Parts, which at once assumed the charge of the support of Mr. and Mrs. Judson. But the same want of confidence in ourselves existed among us, as, a short time previously, had been manifested in our Congregational brethren. We clung to the English Baptists, and desired at first that our missionaries should be connected with the family at Serampore. Under date of May 6, 1813, Rev. Daniel Sharp, of Boston, wrote to Mr. Judson as follows: —

DEAR BROTHER: By the arrival of the Tartar, in January last, we received the intelligence of your change of views on the subject of Christian baptism, and also intimations of your readiness to embark in a mission under our patronage, should a society be formed among the Baptists in America for that purpose.

Your letters excited peculiar emotions. We considered it as the voice of God calling us to the formation of a missionary society. That we might not, however, be charged with acting prematurely, or be considered as interfering with the Board of Commissioners, we ascertained whether they intended to continue you in their service before we formally decided to engage you in ours.

Satisfied on inquiry what was our path of duty, we formed ourselves into a society for propagating the gospel in India and other foreign parts. At a meeting of the trustees, we unanimously agreed to employ you as our missionary, and to stand prepared to support you with all the pecuniary aid we can command.

By the arrival of another vessel, we have heard that the Rev. Mr. Rice entertains the same sentiments as yourself on the subject of baptism. This event gives us joy, because it must add much to your comfort in a foreign land to have a fellow-laborer in the gospel. The board have not met since Mr. Rice's letter was received, but I am confident that he will be taken under their care. We have not had time to mature our thoughts so as to say with decision whether it would be best for you to be connected with, or independent of, our brethren at Serampore.

At present it appears to us that a connection with them would most subserve the interests of the Redeemer's kingdom in India, and be most productive of happiness to yourselves. All the benefits which can be derived from union with men of integrity, disinterested benevolence, and a knowledge of the country, growing out of a twenty years' experience, would accrue to you from a relation with them. These considerations induced us in March last to write to Mr. Fuller, of Kettering, on the subject, expressing our wishes that you might be considered as belonging to the mission family at Serampore. Should it appear, from future events, more desirable that you should act alone, or as American missionaries, separately from the English brethren, then, no doubt, we shall be pleased to have it so; but our present sentiments are, that you had better act with and by their advice.

In behalf of the society,
Yours, affectionately,
DANIEL SHARP.

The letter to Andrew Fuller above referred to is as follows:—

BOSTON, March 5, 1813.

MY DEAR BROTHER: We have lately heard with peculiar pleasure of the arrival of your missionary brethren[*] at Serampore. The same vessel brought us the intelligence that Rev. Adoniram Judson, one of the American missionaries, together with his wife, had experienced a change of views on the subject of baptism, and had expressed a desire to be immersed in the name of the Lord Jesus.

This intelligence has made a deep impression on our minds. We cannot bear that our brother should be neglected, or left to suffer because of his attachment to the truth. He looks to us for aid, and we stand ready to support him. We have formed a society, as you will perceive by the accompanying circular, named "The Baptist Society for Propagating the Gospel in India and other Foreign Parts."

The brethren here, however, suppose that it would much more advance the cause of Christ, and that brother Judson would be much more useful and happy in the missionary service, if he were intimately connected with, and under the direction of, our beloved brethren at Serampore. Their acquaintance with the country, the manners, prejudices, and superstitions of the people, their knowledge of the missionary

---

[*] Messrs. Johns and Lawson, who sailed in the Harmony from Philadelphia.

efforts, likely, with the blessing of God, to be most efficient, a knowledge the result of twenty years' experience, their weight of years, their unshaken fortitude, intense zeal, and unquestionable integrity, and their disinterested course in so glorious a cause, render it very desirable that our brother should be considered as one of the mission family. I am therefore requested, in behalf of the newly-formed society in Boston, to solicit that Mr. Judson may be taken into the society of the Baptist brethren in India, and be under the direction of Messrs. Carey, Marshman, and Ward, and also be entitled to such privileges as would naturally arise from such a coalition.

We shall esteem it an honor and a pleasure to render him the pecuniary aid which from time to time he may need. Indeed, we expect that our exertions will not be limited to the support of our American brother, but that we shall be able to forward to Serampore a willing tribute for the promotion of the general cause.

Wishing you every blessing, I remain,
Dear sir, yours, very affectionately,
DANIEL SHARP.

Rev. Andrew Fuller, Sec. Baptist Mission in England.

The brethren in Serampore and in England, however, took a much wiser view of this subject. They, with every manifestation of kindness and respect, declined this coalition, and advised the Baptists in America to form a missionary organization, and establish missions for themselves. Indeed, had this course not been advised, it was already the only course which could have been pursued. Residence in Serampore was impossible. Dr. Sharp's letter to Mr. Judson was dated May 5. On the 13th of June following, Mr. Judson landed in Rangoon, and thus an American mission was already commenced.

I mentioned that missionary societies were rapidly formed in most of our cities and large towns. They were, however, destitute of any bond of connection. It became at once evident that some general organization, in which they all should unite, was absolutely necessary. Incipient steps towards the formation of such a society had been already taken, when Mr. Rice arrived from India. He was immediately requested to visit the various parts of the country, organize societies, and promote the formation of a general association. This object he performed with eminent success. Every where he was received almost with acclamation. Societies in aid of the cause were formed almost at his bidding. Contributions, in amounts unprecedented, were made to the object. Christians of all denominations in many cases extended liberal aid. It was thus soon ascertained that we were able not only to support Mr. Judson and his wife, but to carry on missions upon a somewhat liberal scale.

In obedience to the general wish, a convention was called at Philadelphia of delegates from the various missionary societies which had thus been formed. The delegates appointed for this purpose assembled on the 18th of May, 1814, in the First Baptist Church in that city. They there formed the " General Missionary Convention of the Baptist Denomination in the United States of America for Foreign Missions." Under this name the Baptist organization for foreign missions was known until the year 1845. At that time, the brethren in the Southern States having felt it to be their duty to withdraw, and afterwards to form a Southern Convention, it was found desirable to adopt a somewhat different organization. On the 20th of November, at a special meeting of the convention in the city of New York, a new constitution was unanimously adopted, and the organization assumed the name of the "American Baptist Missionary Union." The change has been found in practice to have been eminently beneficial, and every succeeding year has added to its efficiency, and given it a firmer hold upon the affections of Baptists in the United States.

Who can fail to observe in these events the wonder-working hand of omniscient wisdom? The change of sentiment of these two young men, in respect to the administration of one of the ordinances of the Christian church, was made the means of arousing to a conviction of their duty a large denomination of Christians; nay, more than this, it led directly to an organization in which all their efforts could be concentrated, so that their united power might be employed in labors to evangelize the world. The momentary irritation which the change occasioned rapidly passed away. Baptists and Pedobaptists delight to aid each other in these labors of love. Not unfrequently are they seen contributing to each other's treasury. At their monthly concerts they communicate the missionary intelligence from both societies, and rejoice with unfeigned joy at the successes of each other. Looking at the results which have taken place, Congregationalists are delighted to remember that brethren sent out by themselves have served in so remarkable a degree the cause of our common Lord. I am happy, moreover, to add, that when, after an absence of thirty-three years, Dr. Judson visited this country, he was received with universal kindness and respect by his Christian brethren of all denominations; and that the officers of the "American Board" especially delighted to greet him as a "brother beloved."

CHAPTER V.

THE BURMAN EMPIRE. — EXTENT. — RIVERS. — POPULATION. — RESOURCES. — GOVERNMENT. — RELIGION.

Mr. Judson and his wife had now arrived at the scene of their future labors. Before proceeding further, it may be proper to present a brief sketch of the country which was henceforth to be their home, and to delineate the character of the people to whose spiritual improvement their lives were to be so earnestly devoted.

The Burman empire occupies that extensive region of Eastern India, or India beyond the Ganges, which lies between the British possessions on the west and Siam and China on the east, being bounded by Thibet on the north, and the Bay of Bengal on the south. At the time of Mr. Judson's arrival, its extent was considerably greater than at present. Its sea coast then stretched from the southern limits of the province of Chittagong to Junk Ceylon, at the southern extremity of the Tenasserim provinces. It thus commanded more than a third part of the Bay of Bengal. Its length was about ten hundred and twenty miles, and its breadth about six hundred.

By the treaty of Yandabo, the Burmans ceded to Great Britain the larger part of their territory lying upon the sea coast. This included the province of Arracan from Chittagong to Cape Negrais on the east, and the Tenasserim provinces from the mouth of the Salwen River to Junk Ceylon. Their sea coast is now bounded by Cape Negrais on the west, and Martaban on the east, embracing the district occupied by the numerous mouths of the Irrawadi River.

Its length is now about seven hundred and twenty, and its breadth about four hundred miles. Its two principal seaports are Rangoon on the eastern, and Bassein on the western branch of the Irrawadi. Both are very favorably situated for commerce. Rangoon is said by English writers to possess the finest capabilities of any port in the Bay of Bengal.

The great river of Burmah is the Irrawadi, which, rising in the Chinese province of Yunan, with the exception of a flexure to the west, between Ava and Pugan, pursues a course almost directly south. The Kyen Dwen, a large tributary from the north, unites with it at Yandabo. A smaller stream from the east empties into it at Ava. The Salwen River, the eastern boundary of Burmah, communicates by numerous branches with the Irrawadi, watering the intermediate region, and opening facilities for internal navigation for the regions which occupy the central part of the empire.

The Irrawadi is one of the noblest rivers in India. In the rainy season, it is navigable for large vessels as far as Ava, about four hundred and fifty miles above Rangoon. Mr. Crawfurd, the British commissioner to negotiate the commercial treaty at the close of the war in 1826, proceeded to Ava in the steamer Diana, and found a depth of water sufficient for a much larger vessel. On his return, in the dry season, the steamer twice grounded on sand banks — a misfortune, however, which seems to have arisen mainly from the unskilfulness of the pilot. Above Ava, the river is navigable for large boats, but to what distance it is not possible to determine, as but little is known of the geography of the northern portions of the empire

A few miles from the town of Sarwa, the Irrawadi

divides into two branches, the one pursuing a south-eastern, the other a south-western, course to the Bay of Bengal. From each of these smaller branches proceed in every direction, uniting with each other and forming a perfect network of navigable waters, which covers the whole peninsula from the base of the Arracan Mountains to the banks of the Salwen River. These various streams, or natural canals, at last enter the Bay of Bengal by fourteen separate channels. Most of them are, however, rendered useless for foreign commerce by sand bars, which obstruct navigation.

From the sea coast to nearly the latitude of Prome, the country is a level, alluvial plain, intersected, as I have remarked, by innumerable watercourses. The soil is exceedingly productive, and is specially adapted to the cultivation of rice, the universal diet of the inhabitants of India. This is, therefore, the granary of the empire. Ascending the river, as you leave Prome, the face of the country changes. High ranges of mountains appear on the right hand and on the left, and the intermediate region becomes undulating and hilly. The mountains approach nearer and nearer to the river, until the banks become steep and precipitous. Above the latitude of Ava, the whole region is intersected by mountain ranges running north and south, and penetrating Asam on the west and the province of Yunan on the east.

The portions of Burmah ceded to the British at the close of the last war were the kingdom of Arracan and the Tenasserim provinces.* The former is gener-

---

* Since this paragraph was written, the Burman empire has been again dismembered, and the British have annexed to the possessions of the Hon. East India Company the kingdom of Pegu, which formed

ally hilly, with extensive alluvial flats near the sea, and along the numerous streams, fertile, and adapted to the cultivation of rice. Akyab, the principal port, has a secure and convenient harbor. Of the Tenasserim provinces, the principal rivers are the various branches of the Salwen, the Ataran, the Tavoy, and the Mergui rivers. Most of these streams are, for a short distance, navigable for vessels of considerable burden, and must, in time, become the homes of extensive commerce.

Respecting the population of Burmah, the difference of the estimates is quite remarkable. Colonel Symes, who visited the empire in the year 1795, supposed the number of inhabitants to be about seventeen millions. When the Baptist mission was first established in Rangoon, this computation was supposed to be correct, and it was frequently said that the population of Burmah equalled that of the United States. Later travellers have reduced it to eight millions. Crawfurd, after as careful a computation as he was able to form, does not believe that it exceeds four millions. Dr. Malcom believes that there may be three million Burmans, three million Shyans, and probably two millions of other tribes, subject to the Burman dominion. When estimates of this kind are made, the lowest is, I think, most likely to be correct. Travellers, in such a country as this, must, of necessity, pursue the most frequented routes, and follow the most navigable watercourses. These, being always the most thickly-peopled portions of a country, would naturally convey an exaggerated idea of its population. I am of the opinion that more

the whole lower portion of the country. The Burmans thus have lost the whole of their territory lying on the Bay of Bengal, their southern limit being to the north of Promo.

accurate investigation than is now possible will show that the population of the empire and its present dependencies does not exceed six or eight millions.*

A large portion of the soil of Burmah is fertile, and under a good government would be remarkably productive. The lower provinces, from the sea to the latitude of Prome, produce, as I have said, rice in great abundance. In the more elevated districts, cotton of a good quality, of a soft and silky texture, but of short staple, is every where cultivated. The teak tree, the best ship timber in the world, grows on the mountains. Maize, wheat, millet, and various kinds of pulses, with the usual variety of edible roots, and a multitude of tropical fruits, are produced with very little labor. The domestic animals are such as are common in India — the buffalo, braminy cattle, the horse, and the goat; and in the forests are found the elephant, the rhinoceros, the tiger, and several varieties of the deer.

The mineral wealth of Burmah is probably great. It possesses mines of iron, tin, silver, and gold, and produces sapphires, emeralds, and rubies, with amber in large quantities. Sulphur, arsenic, and antimony are found in abundance, and coal, both anthracite and bituminous, exists in various places, but has not yet been brought into use. On the banks of the Irrawadi, a short distance above Prome, petroleum is obtained in large quantities. The annual yield of the wells here is said by Dr. Malcom to be about eighty millions of pounds. Marble is found in various places, and some of the quarries yield a product which is said, for statuary purposes, to equal that from Carrara.

---

* The population has since been greatly reduced by the loss of the kingdom of Pegu within the present year.

The commerce of the empire is but limited. The Burmans are intelligent and industrious, and under a good government would probably soon excel in manufactures. Under the protection of English employers, they at one time became excellent ship builders at Rangoon. But manufactures require fixed capital, and when the possession of capital invites oppression and spoliation, they cannot exist. Hence the exports of Burmah are limited almost exclusively to the raw materials produced by their unskilful labor. The most important of them are teak wood, raw cotton, both white and yellow, precious stones, and lackered ware. Teak wood is sent to Calcutta, and is mostly used in the naval service of Great Britain. Cotton and precious stones, lackered ware, and edible birds' nests are sent to China. The English send, in return, cotton fabrics, hardware, cutlery, and old muskets. The Chinese bring principally raw silk, which is made into coarse goods by the Burmans, and the velvets which are worn on state occasions by the grandees of the empire. Rice, salt, and salt fish are carried from the southern provinces and the sea coast to the upper country, and exchanged for lackered ware, raw cotton, precious stones, metals, and petroleum.

The government of Burmah is an unmitigated despotism of the sternest character. The king is the acknowledged possessor of the soil, and the people are his slaves. He is lord of the life and property of all his subjects. No rank or office protects a citizen from the liability of being ordered to immediate execution, if such be the will of the monarch. Several of the commanders who were defeated in the last war with the British were beheaded within a few hours of their arrival at the capital. Mr. Crawfurd saw one of the chief officers of state, for some trifling offence, exposed to the meridian sun, lying on his back, with a weight on his chest, for several hours. When a man is put to death by the order of the king, his property reverts to the crown. Hence the possession of large wealth becomes a somewhat unenviable distinction.

The government of the empire is administered by a council of state, appointed by the king. This council is called collectively lut-d'hau, from the name of the hall in which its business is transacted. The councillors are four in number, unless, as it sometimes happens, on a special emergency, another member is added. These officers are called woon-gyees. All public matters are discussed in this council, and the decision is by the majority of voices. Every royal edict is by usage sanctioned by this council, and, in fact, appears in their name, rather than in that of the king. Their functions are legislative, judicial, and executive.

Each woon-gyee has a deputy, who is called a woondouk. The woon-douks, although they sit in council, neither deliberate nor vote. Whatever business they transact is in the name of their superiors.

The woon-douks have also their assistants, who are called sara-dau-gyee. They are from eight to ten in number. These are, in fact, the secretaries of the lut-d'hau, and their business is to record its proceedings. Their name signifies "great royal scribes."

A second council forms another branch of the government. This, like the other, consists of four members. Their title is atwen-woon, meaning "inside" ministers of state.* These officers constitute the private advisers of the king. Whatever emanates directly from him is first discussed in this privy council,

---

* Inside ministers, or privy councillors.

before it is transmitted to the lut-d'hau. It deliberates and votes like the superior council, and its members exercise also judicial functions. It is a matter of dispute at the court of Ava whether the rank of atwen-woon or of woon-douk be the higher.

Attached to the privy council are secretaries, commonly thirty in number. These are called than-dau-sens. They hold the same relation to the atwen-woons that the woon-douks hold to the woon-gyees. Their business is to record the proceedings of the council, to take minutes of the king's commands, and to read and report upon petitions. Attached to both of these councils are four or five officers, called nakandau, meaning "deputies of the royal star." Their business is, nominally, to convey messages between the two councils, but, really, to report to the king what is done in the lut-d'hau.

Such is the theory of the government. In practice, however, a council which may be degraded or executed at the word of the monarch must be useless as advisers. In the former war with Great Britain, they frequently did not dare to make known the facts to the king, or even offer their opinions upon the state of affairs. They are really the passive instruments for carrying into effect the will of the monarch. They are willing to live in constant apprehension of disgrace and death for the privilege of subjecting all below them to the same condition. Political life seems to be much the same in all countries.

The rank of every officer of government is determined by the tsalway, or golden chain, which passes over the left shoulder, and crosses the breast. In front, it is divided into several strands of chain work. Three common strands indicate the lowest grade of office; three of more elaborate workmanship the next above; then come those of six, nine, and twelve, which last number indicates the highest rank attainable by a subject. Princes of the blood most nearly related to the king wear eighteen. The monarch himself alone wears twenty-four.

The civil administration is organized as follows: The kingdom is divided into provinces, provinces into townships, townships into districts, and districts into villages or hamlets.

The governor of a province is called myo-woon, and is vested with the entire charge of the province, civil, judicial, military, and fiscal. Under him are collectors of customs, deputies, &c., who form his council, without whose assent no order of importance can be executed. The myo-woon has power of life and death.

The governor of a township is called myo-thoo-gyee. The governor, or head man, of a district or village is called thoo-gyee. These are all respectively subordinate to each other.

No public functionary receives any fixed salary. The principal officers of state are rewarded by assignments of certain districts, from the inhabitants of which they exact as much as they are able. Inferior officers are paid by fees, emoluments, perquisites, together with all that can be collected by extortion and bribery. Each of these officers exercises judicial functions within his own district, an appeal, however, lying to the next higher in office. Bribery is universal; and it rarely happens that a criminal is punished, if he is able to satisfy the rapacity of the officer before whom he is arraigned. The judges take bribes from both sides, and the decree, except in very palpable cases, will be in favor of him who pays the highest. ' On the 7th of February, 1817, seven persons found guilty of sacrilege were conveyed to the place of execution near Rangoon, and secured in the usual way to the stake. The first of them was fired at four successive times by a marksman without being hit. At every shot there was a loud peal of laughter from the spectators. The malefactor was taken down, declared to be invulnerable, pardoned, and taken into a confidential employment by the governor. He had paid a large bribe. The second culprit was shot, and the remaining five were decapitated " *

The various provinces of the kingdom are apportioned out to favorites of the court, or are made responsible for the support of some branch of the government. The individual to whom this cession is made becomes then the governor of that province, or, as the Burmans appropriately term him, its "eater," or consumer. By means of his subordinate agents, he taxes every family as much as it is supposed to be able to pay. Every subordinate officer takes his share of this tax, and the governor at last divides with the king the portion which he receives. The poor peasant is thus obliged to satisfy a succession of harpies, while but a small portion of what he pays ever reaches the public treasury. Besides these contributions paid to the lord of the land, the cultivators are from time to time, and according to the public exigency, called upon for contributions to the state. The amount of these is fixed by the lut-d'hau, or chief council. These contributions, being levied through the lords, or local officers, are made a pretext for additional exactions on their own account, often greater

* Crawfurd's Embassy, vol. ii.

than those taken for the government. The Burman officers are thus turned loose upon the country, to prey upon it like a swarm of locusts. The contributions paid into the public treasury are little better than a hoard to gratify the desires of the reigning prince; and the amount exacted from the people for this purpose depends entirely upon his personal character. His subordinate officers, from the highest to the lowest, follow the example of their chief; and every energy of the people is crushed under a savage, selfish, and relentless despotism.

The religion of Burmah is Buddhism. To present an extended view of this form of religion, which numbers among its believers a larger portion of the inhabitants of the earth than any other, would be foreign to the design of a memoir like the present. I can do nothing more than offer a brief statement of the Burman religious system, compiled from such sources as have been within my reach. I was happy to find, after a pretty extensive research, that Dr. Judson had furnished Mr. Crawfurd with an article on this subject, which is inserted in the fourth chapter of the second volume of his "Embassy." As I consider this of the highest authority, I transcribe it entire.

A life period, called A-yen-kat, is a revolution of time, during which the life of man gradually advances from ten years to an A-then-kye, and returns again to ten. Sixty-four life periods make one *intermediate period*, (An-ta-ra-kat;) sixty-four intermediate periods make one quarterly period, which may be so termed because four such periods make one grand period (Ma-ha-kat,) a complete revolution of nature. The revolutions of nature, as marked by the various periods, are eternal or infinite. Some grand periods are distinguished by the development of an extraordinary being called a

Budd'ha, who, though born of earthly parents, attains to the summit of omniscience.* The present grand period has been favored by four of these personages, whose names are Kan-kri-than, Gau-na-gong, Ka-tha-pa, and Gau-ta-ma. The fifth Budd'ha, or A-ri-mi-te-ya, is now reposing, according to the best authorities, in one of the lower celestial regions, and will develop himself in due time.

The communications of all Budd'has previously to Gau-ta-ma are now lost. His communications, made at first to his immediate disciples, and by them retained in memory during five centuries more, after his decease agreed upon in several successive general councils, (Then-ga-ya-na,) and finally reduced to writing on palm leaves, in the Island of Ceylon, in the ninety-fourth year before Christ, and the four hundred and fiftieth after Gau-ta-ma, form the present Buddhist scriptures, the only rule of faith and practice. They are comprised in three grand divisions, (Pe-ta-kat,) which are again subdivided into fifteen, and those into six hundred.

According to the Buddhist scriptures, the universe is composed of an infinite number of worlds, or Sakya systems. A Sakya system consists of one central Myen-mo, or mount, the surrounding seas and islands, the celestial regions, including the revolving luminaries and the infernal regions. The earth on which we live is the southernmost of the four grand islands which surround the mount, each of which is again surrounded by four hundred of smaller size.

The celestial regions consist of six inferior and twenty superior heavens. Of the six inferior heavens, the first occupies the middle, and the second the summit of the Myen-mo mount. The remaining arise above each other in regular gradation. The same remark applies to the superior heavens, which are again distinguished into the sixteen visible and four invisible. The inferior regions consist of eight hills, one above another, each being surrounded by sixteen smaller hills.

---

* "Omniscience" is, according to Buddhists, the principal attribute of Gautama.

The universe is replete with an infinity of souls, which have been transmigrating in different bodies from all eternity; ascent or descent in the scale of existence being at every change of state ascertained by the immutable "mysterious laws of fate," according to the merit or demerit of the individual. No being is exempt from sickness, old age, and death. Instability, pain, and change are the three grand characteristics of all existence.

"However highly exalted in the celestial regions, and whatever number of ages of happiness may roll on," say the Burmans, "the fatal symptom of a moisture under the armpits will at length display itself." The mortal being, when this presents itself, must be prepared to exchange the blandishments and dalliance of celestial beauties for the gridirons, pitchforks, mallets, and other instruments of torture of the infernal regions. The chief end of man, according to the Burmese, is to terminate the fatiguing course of transmigratory existence. This attainment Lord Gautama made in the eightieth year of his life, and all his immediate disciples have participated in the same happy fate. What remains to the present race of beings is to aim at passing their time in the regions of men and gods, until they shall come in contact with the next Budd'ha, the Lord Arimiteya, whom they may hope to accompany to the golden world of nigban, or annihilation. In order to this, it is necessary to keep the commands of the last Budd'ha, to worship the Budd'ha, his law and his priests; to refrain from taking life; from stealing; from adultery; from falsehood, and from drinking intoxicating liquors; to regard the images and temples of the Budd'ha the same as himself; to perform acts of worship, and listen to the instructions of religion on the days of the new moon, the full moon, and the quarters; to make offerings for the support of the priests, to assist at funerals, and, in general, to perform all charitable and religious duties.

In the year 930 after Gautama, A. D. 386, Budd'ha-gautha transcribed the Buddhist scriptures, with an iron pen of celestial workmanship, and brought them by sea to Pugan, the seat of supreme government. The time and manner in which the religion of Gautama was introduced into the country are not sufficiently ascertained. It subsequently underwent some modification, and was finally established in its present form by King Anan-ra-tha-men-sau, who began to reign in Pugan in the 1541st year after Gautama, the 359th of the present vulgar era, and A. D. 997.

To this brief statement, which contains by far the most intelligible account of the system of Buddhism that I have seen, I will add a few items of information, which I have been able to glean from a tolerably extensive reading on the subject.

It will be seen that the moral code of Buddhism is simple and pure. Its five precepts are, I. Thou shalt not take life. This precept is universal. The priests, in order to obey it, carry with them a brush, with which they sweep the seat on which they are about to sit down, lest they should inadvertently crush the smallest insect. II. Thou shalt not steal. III. Thou shalt not commit adultery. IV. Thou shalt not lie. V. Thou shalt drink no intoxicating liquors. It is by obedience to these that, at death, we enter by transmigration into a better condition than we occupy at present.

The rules more at large for the regulation of our conduct are contained in the institutions of Menu, an ascetic, who, ages ago, on account of his austerities, was favored with a remarkable degree of divine illumination. This work, entitled "The Damathat, or the Laws of Menu," * has been translated into Eng-

* For a copy of this work I am indebted to the kindness of my friend and former pupil, Rev. E. A. Stevens, of Maulmain. It is to be remembered that this is an entirely different work from the Brahminical institutes of Menu. Why they should both have the sam name, I am not able to discover.

lish by D. Richardson, Esq., principal assistant to the commissioner, Tenasserim provinces, and was published in Maulmain, at the American Baptist mission press, in 1847. It consists of fourteen books, each of which is generally devoted to a class of subjects in law and ethics. Each book commences with the following title: "I worship the God who is worthy of homage, who possesses an intuitive knowledge of good." I had intended to give a brief account of this work, but I find that my limits render it impracticable. In no instance is any general principle explained to which moral cases may be referred; but each book is made up of a multitude of supposed instances, and a decision is given applying to that instance. They exhibit much acuteness, and indicate, from their frequent complexity, that they must have been composed in an advanced period of civilization. Frequently the solution of the case is given in a parable or an allegory. They are generally of a description that would give large room for special pleading and chicanery. As no general principle is laid down, the party accused would find it easy in most cases to show that some difference exists between the case at issue and that mentioned in the books. In a note to the first book of the Institutes, I find the following remark by the translator, which, I think, throws some light upon the doctrines of Buddha: "Zan Mina. There are four states of Zan: 1. Thought or desire; 2. Reflection; 3. Joy or pleasure; 4. Happiness, bliss, and permanency or immutability; all of which enable the possessor to traverse different worlds." The illustration of this doctrine is as follows, and it presents so good a specimen of the manner in which such subjects are treated in the work that I insert it: "A man sleeping at the foot of a mango tree, with his cloth over his head, is in a state of unintelligence. A mango falls on him, and awakes him; he is then in the first state. He considers what this can be; he is then in the second state. He puts the cloth off his head, and, looking at the mango, approves of it, and is in the third state. He then takes it up, and eats it; it is sweet and pleasant; and he is then in the fourth state; or, having eaten it, he is in a state of great enjoyment, blissful repose — the fifth state."

The Buddhist priesthood is confined to no class, and indeed the doctrines of Gaudama allow of no hereditary caste; any man who complies with the required precepts may be admitted to the sacred order. He, however, is not obliged to remain in it for life, but may quit it at his pleasure, and, I think, without reproach. The priests are bound by the vows of celibacy and poverty. They are forbidden to hold property, and are supported by voluntary contributions of the people. They go out daily in the streets with their rice pots, and every one gives them what he pleases. They are forbidden, however, to take money, and they never ask for any thing. Travellers assure us that they are never seen to turn their heads, or even look upon the offering made to them. It were well if the ecclesiastics of many other countries derived instruction from their example.

The labors of the priests seem unlike those of any other religion. They seldom preach, nor do they generally seem to perform any specially religious service for the people. They are merely men sacredly devoted to pious observances and holy austerities. They reside altogether in monasteries which have been erected for them, and in some cases endowed by monarchs or governors — an appropriation of property held to be specially meritorious. They are forbidden to have any connection with the civil power, and they seem to have but very little. Their principal employment is that of instructing the young, to which they commonly devote themselves. The monasteries are, therefore, in general, the school houses of Burmah, and the priests are her schoolmasters. What they teach is very little; but it suffices to enable a large portion of the male population to read. In this respect the Buddhist priesthood compares very favorably with that of other false or perverted systems of religion.

The Buddhists have been commonly denominated atheists. Whatever may be the views which have subsequently obtained among the people at large, I doubt whether the *system* of Gaudama is chargeable with this error. Men are believed to exist after death, inhabiting other bodies; and the change which then takes place is determined by their conduct in the state which they occupy at the present. They may be changed from men into nats, and from nats in an inferior to those of a superior grade; thus gradually rising until they arrive at nigban. Or, on the other hand, they may be changed from men into animals, and, in successive transformations, from animals of a higher to those of a lower grade, until they reach hell, or a place of unmixed torment. In cases of atrocious crime, as the murder of a parent, or a priest, they pass through no intermediate transformations, but at once enter the place of torment. The doctrine of future rewards and punishments, as consequences of moral character in this life, is thus distinctly recognized. The peculiarity of their belief is, that this life is not considered as *the* state, but only *a* state of probation.

Probation extends to every state but nigban. Hence every living thing which we see is inhabited, for the time being, by a soul similar to our own; and we and it may, at any time, change places. From this idea is derived the prohibition to slay animals and every thing that has life.

This system of rewards and punishments is administered, according to the Buddhist belief, by the various grades of existence *superior* to men, and *inferior* to Buddh. An inquiry is instituted by these deities into the character of every individual, and, in obedience to their decision, each one either ascends or descends in the scale of being. The government of the universe is, therefore, carried on, not by the supreme divinity, who is, according to the notions of oriental happiness, exempt from all care, but by inferior beings, who are still themselves striving upwards in order to arrive at nigban.

As this is a subject on which I found great difficulty in arriving at any accurate information, I will, for the benefit of others, present a few extracts from such authorities as seem to me most worthy of confidence in illustration and confirmation of the statements above. The following extract is from Upham's History of Buddhism, chap. ix. p. 105, quarto, London, 1829: —

Immediately after death, the judgment is pronounced by Yame-rajah, the god of the heaven Wape-warty-rajah, upon such mortal beings as having inthralled their souls by a mixture of good and evil, yet entertain a hope to come into the Brama Loha; but the thoroughly wicked go to the hell unheard, and even without approaching the tribunal of the judge.

Before the gate of each hell sit judges, who condemn the guilty according to the weight of their evil deeds. These judges are selected from the Nat Apura, but their office does not exclude them from enjoying the pleasures of their happy companions. They have no occasion to examine into crimes of a very atrocious nature; the weight of them sinks the perpetrators at once into hell.

There are four states of misery appropriated to the punishment of atrocious crimes, among the most conspicuous of which is disrespect to the priesthood. In the lesser hells are punished those who do not honor their parents, the magistrates, or old age; who take wine and inebriating liquors; who corrupt wells, or destroy highways; who are fraudulent and deceitful; who speak angrily and roughly; who use personal violence; who pay little attention to the words of pious men; who afflict others; who propagate scandal; who chain, bind, or fetter their fellow-creatures; who admit forbidden things into their words, actions, or desires; and who do not solace the sick. All these will be punished according to the atrocity of the deed and the frequency of its repetition; and they will suffer also in another hell, compared in shape to a kettle of molten brass, where they are three thousand years in descending to the bottom, and three thousand years in ascending.

These various hells, and the crimes which they are intended to punish, are dwelt on in the Buddhist books with great particularity. I need go no further into detail. The above extracts are sufficient to show that Buddhism is not strictly atheism; that it acknowledges a moral government of the universe, and a most comprehensive and minute system of rewards and punishments.

The belief that it is a system of atheism has been derived from the idea of nigban, or, as it is translated, annihilation, which is the state in which the deity for the present period, always exists. So far as I can learn, the system of Gaudama does not represent nigban as annihilation. It is, rather, the precisely antagonist idea to that of transmigration, change, and painful vicissitude, to which the rest of the universe is ever subjected.

The most celebrated of the Burman priests at Ava, in reply to inquiries made by one of the Catholic missionaries, replied as follows: "When a person is no longer subject to any of the following miseries, namely, to weight, old age, disease, and death, then he is said to have obtained nigban. No thing, no place, can give us any adequate idea of nigban; we can only say that to be free from the four above-mentioned miseries, and to obtain salvation, is nigban. In the same manner as when any person laboring under a severe disease recovers by the assistance of medicine, we say he has obtained health; but if any person wishes to know the manner or cause of his thus obtaining health, it can only be answered, that to be restored to health signifies no more than to be removed from disease. In the same manner only can we speak of nigban, and after this manner Gaudama taught." *

Upham remarks that "the Pali doctrinal books speak of Nirvana (Nicban) as an exemption from old age, from decay, and from death; and as being also the acquirement of all bliss. . . . Even when the Buddha bestows the Nirvana, his votary *hears* his great voice, *beholds* the face, and *accepts* a state which enables him to see the succession of other Buddhas. Such is the clear import of the phrases, which cannot leave us to doubt of the system possessing an ulterior state of reward, combined with posi-

* Asiatic Researches, vol. vi. p. 266.

tive vitality. The Buddhist doctrine always treats life in the stage of human existence as a state of suffering and misfortune; regarding it as a situation of painful probation, growing out of its changes, which can be escaped from in no other way than by the acquirement of the unchangeable state of Nirvana. Every expression of illusion, disappointment, and pain is applied to life, and the opposite epithets of unruffled peace, repose, and profound tranquillity ascribed to the envied rewards of Nirvana — expressions carried even to the length of non-existence."

While, however, the system of Gaudama may not be strictly chargeable with theoretical atheism, inasmuch as it recognizes the existence of superior beings who govern this world, and reward and punish us for our actions, it is, I believe, the common opinion that nigban is non-existence, and that annihilation is the greatest good after which we can aspire. Nor is this the belief of the uneducated alone; the priests themselves teach this doctrine, and defend it on philosophical principles. They hold that divinity itself is not exempt from change, that it is base and grovelling to cling to existence, since a nat to-day may be a monkey to-morrow. Even a god (their gods attain to deityship in this world) is subject to sickness and death; and it is noble and philosophic, the mark of a superior mind, not in love with mean and paltry things, to choose *not to be*. The Brahminical idea of absorption in the deity is utterly unknown to the greater part of the Buddhists, and would be abhorrent to them, for their deity himself lays down his existence, and becomes a nonentity. Mr. Judson found that the minister of state, Moung Zah, had an indistinct notion of a deity who *ought to be* eternal, and said that he and the Prince Mekara came the nearest to deism of any pure Burmans he had ever met with. Mrs. Judson states, that her old teacher, a Christian, who had been a Buddhist priest in his youth, assured her that he had never heard nor imagined that nigban meant any thing but annihilation. This difference between the teachings of a religious system and the belief of those who profess it, is unfortunately a matter of very common occurrence.

Such, then, seems to be the system of Buddhism.* In its moral precepts it is remarkable for purity. So far as the relations between man and man are concerned, it is, in many respects, similar to the Mosaic law. The punishments which it denounces against sin are awful beyond conception; and the rewards of obedience are as great as the authors of the system could imagine. For the least aberration from rectitude the consequence is pain only less than infinite. It, however, in no case that I have seen, makes any allusion to repentance. After one sin, the being is forever helplessly under condemnation, unless he can attain to annihilation. It presents no way of escape for the sinner by means of an atonement. It is a pure system of law, with its rewards and punishments, without relenting, without pardon, and without hope for the guilty.

It remains to consider what has been the practical effect of this system upon the mind of man. It is a system, it will be remembered, devised to govern the moral conduct of a race of sinners. Hence the impossibility of avoiding its penalties is at once evident. Do what we will, conscience must convict us

---

* See Appendix A, for other views held by Dr. Judson.

of grievous moral imperfection, involving the necessity of ages of suffering, without the certainty of any eventual escape. Under such a system, the mind sinks down in utter helplessness. When there is no escape from punishment, the difference between ten millions and twenty millions of transmigrations is not capable of being appreciated. Virtue and vice, in our imperfect state, are, therefore, hardly capable of being distinguished from each other in their results. Thus the system which seems to have exhausted the human faculties in conceiving of terrors which should deter us from sin, is found practically to have created against it no barrier whatever.

The result was such as might have been expected. While the law of Gaudama forbids us to take the life of any animated being, the Burmans are bloodthirsty, cruel, and vindictive, beyond most of the nations of India. Murders are of very common occurrence, and the punishment by death is inflicted with every aggravation of cruelty. While licentiousness is absolutely forbidden, they are said to be universally profligate. While the law denounces covetousness, they are almost to a man dishonest, rapacious, prone to robbery, and to robbery ending in blood. The law forbids, on all occasions, treachery and deceit, and yet, from the highest to the lowest, they are a nation of liars. When detected in the grossest falsehood, they indicate no consciousness of shame, and even pride themselves upon successful deceit. An amusing instance of national want of faith occurred towards the close of the former Burman war. On the 3d of January, 1826, the Burman commander-in-chief and one of the high officers of the empire signed a treaty with Sir A. Campbell, and required fifteen days' truce, for the purpose of sending the articles to Ava for the sanction of the emperor The fifteen days elapsed, during which, in violation of the armistice, they were busily engaged in strengthening their defences; and the ratifications did not arrive. Hostilities were recommenced, and the Burman general was, in unexpected haste, driven from his head-quarters. When the British entered the fort, they found the English and Burman copies of the treaty in the state in which they had been signed, they never having been even transmitted to Ava. In the military chest were also found thirty thousand rupees in silver. Sir A. Campbell sent the copies of the treaty to the woon-gyee, with a note stating that he supposed he had merely forgotten them in the hurry of his departure from Maloun. The woon-gyee answered, with much coolness and good humor, "that in the same hurry he had also left behind him a large sum of money, which, he was confident, the British general only waited an opportunity of returning." *

Respecting the practical effect of this system, Mr. Upham observes: " The scheme is sustained by a system of morals of the most exemplary kind, such as may cause a blush of shame in many a Christian who feels his higher privileges, while he considers the inferiority of his practice; but this system is absolutely powerless to enforce or fasten its dictates upon the conscience, or to renovate the heart."† Mr. Upham sustains his view of the practical result of Buddhism by the following quotation from Mr. Judson, whom he describes as one who has had the best opportunity to

---

* Annual Register, anno 1826, p. 215.
† Upham's History of Buddhism, p. 102.

examine it, and whose coloring he declares to be strong, but faithful: "Let those who plead the native innocence and purity of heathen nations visit Burmah. The system of religion here has no power over the heart or restraint on the passions. Though it forbids, on pain of many years' suffering in hell, theft and falsehood, yet, I presume to say, there is not a single Burman in the country, who, if he had a good opportunity, without danger of detection, would hesitate to do either. Though the religion inculcates benevolence, tenderness, forgiveness of injuries, and love of enemies, — though it forbids sensuality, love of pleasure, and attachment to worldly objects, — yet it is destitute of power to produce the former, or to subdue the latter, in its votaries. In short, the Burman system of religion is like an alabaster image, perfect and beautiful in all its parts, but destitute of life. Besides being destitute of life, it provides no atonement for sin. Here also the gospel triumphs over this and every other religion in the world."

If, now, we revert to what we have stated above, we shall perceive that the Burman empire is large in extent, and that its soil is of unusually great and varied productiveness. It possesses a regular government, by which the decisions of the court are carried with effect to the remotest hamlet, through a succession of officers proceeding in regular gradation from the emperor to the magistrate of the smallest district. Its people are active, athletic, and as industrious as could be expected under a tyrannical and oppressive government. A large portion of the people is able to read. It possesses a well-defined system of religion, and a regularly-organized priesthood. But the whole people are destitute of any semblance either of piety to God or benevolence to man. They have no hope, and are living without God in the world. They have acknowledged that St. Paul's description of the heathen, in the first of Romans, delineates accurately the national character. Such is the nation which Mr. Judson went forth to convert to the religion of Jesus Christ.

CHAPTER VI.

ENTRANCE UPON MISSIONARY WORK. — HIS VIEWS OF THAT WORK. — ACQUISITION OF THE LANGUAGE. — PROGRESS OF THE MISSION. — VOYAGE TO MADRAS.

1813-1818.

MR. JUDSON having now arrived in Rangoon, the principal seaport of Burmah, that portion of the heathen world to which the labors of his future life were to be devoted, it may be worth while to pause for a moment, to consider definitely the object which so exclusively controlled every energy of his soul. His life was unique and consistent, bearing upon one point, and ever striving to realize a single conception. When we know the principles which he embraced, and the manner in which he felt obliged to carry them into practice, we are at once enabled to estimate his character, and take a just view of his services.

Mr. Judson believed that the race of man was created holy; that our first parents sinned; and that, in consequence of their sin, their whole posterity have become sinners. He believed that, in consequence of the sin of each individual, every descendant of Adam is deserving of eternal banishment from God in the life to come, and of his righteous displeasure in the life that now is. He thus conceived that all the miseries, individual and social, physical and moral, which we suffer in the present state, are the consequences of sin; of sin which, in all its infinite diversity, may be traced to the alienation of our moral affections from God.

If such be the fact, it is evident that, without a remedial dispensation, the race of man must be doomed to misery, temporal and eternal.

But Mr. Judson believed that a remedial dispensation had been devised. "God so loved the world that he gave his only-begotten Son, that whosoever believeth in him should not perish, but have everlasting life;" that in consequence of the incarnation, obedience, and sufferings of Christ, a free and full pardon is now offered to all the race of man, who, in sincere repentance for sin, commit themselves, in humble trust, to the mercy of God through the mediation of Jesus Christ. Thus the affections of the heart, by nature estranged from God, are restored to him again, and the radical moral evil of the soul being corrected, there will flow from it, by necessity, the fruits of justice and charity, and man, individual and social, transformed in the image of his mind, will awake to a life of righteousness.

But still further, Mr. Judson believed that God had promised that this work of Christ Jesus should not be in vain, but that the whole world should yet yield a cheerful and happy obedience to the Prince of peace; that the Holy Spirit should with irresistible energy accompany the proclamation of the message of salvation wherever the gospel shall be preached in simple and earnest faith: so that the means are amply provided for carrying forward the regeneration of our race. This provision having been made, Jesus Christ has imposed upon every one of his disciples the duty of making known the good news of salvation to his fellow men, with the promise that he will attend the delivery of this message with his ever-present aid. "Go ye," said he, "into all the world, and preach the gospel to every creature; and lo, I am with you alway even unto the end of the world."

Mr. Judson believed himself to be a disciple of Christ, saved from condemnation through the merits of the atonement; he acknowledged his personal obligation to obey this last command of his ascended Redeemer; nay, more, he was satisfied that he had been called to devote his life to this service. Holding such a belief, and acknowledging such obligations, he consecrated his whole being to the work, and with this consecration he allowed nothing else whatever to interfere.

The providence of God clearly directed him to the empire of Burmah. He felt assured that he was thus sent, as the herald of Christ, to preach the gospel of peace to this benighted people. There was not, at the time of his arrival at Rangoon, a single native who had embraced the religion of Jesus. He was aware of the oppression and cruelty of the rulers, and of the wickedness and misery of the people; he knew that they were steeped in an idolatry that had become venerable by antiquity; yet he believed that in the gospel there existed the sovereign remedy for all these evils. He doubted not that, when the gospel should be preached, the sinful nature of men would be transformed into the holy image of Christ; that every convert would become a centre of moral illumination, that thus, by its own inherent power of indefinite expansion, the gospel would spread on every side among the people, until the temples of Gaudama should be deserted, the moral character of men be renewed, and Burmah become a kingdom of our Lord and of his Christ.

His object, then, was to accomplish the most stupendous revolution of which we can conceive in this whole people; it was nothing less than an entire transformation of the moral character of every individual. The means by which this was to be accomplished was very simple. It was the announcement of the message from God to man, attended by the omnipotent power of the Spirit of God. He believed that this work would thus be accomplished simply because God had promised it.

The instrument on which he relied for success was the preaching of the gospel. But he knew not a word of the language in which he was to offer to men the blessings of eternal life. This language must first be acquired and thoroughly mastered. He must learn it as perfectly as his vernacular tongue, so that he might transfer into it, with exact accuracy, the lively oracles of God. The Burmans are a reading people. They have their religious books, and possess the teachings of Gaudama in their own language. They demanded our Scriptures, that they might read for themselves the doctrines which were delivered to them orally. Hence it was evident that the Bible must be placed in their hands as soon as the missionary was prepared to preach to them the unsearchable riches of Christ.

To the attainment of the language, therefore, Mr. Judson at once addressed himself, combining with his studies, at as early a period as possible, the work of translation. The aids which he could command were meagre. It is true that the English Baptists had established a mission in Rangoon as early as 1807, under the care of Messrs. Chater and Mardon. Mr. Mardon, after a few months, left the station, and Mr. Chater was joined by Mr. Felix Carey, the eldest son of Dr. Carey, of Serampore. Soon after, Messrs. Pritchett and Brain, of the London Missionary Society, arrived; but Mr. Brain soon died, and Mr. Pritchett, after a year's residence, removed to Vizagapatam. Mr. Chater remained four years, and made considerable progress in the language. He translated the Gospel by Matthew, which was revised by Mr. Carey, and published at Serampore. At length Mr. Chater relinquished the mission, and removed to Ceylon. Mr. Carey remained, and was joined by a young man from Calcutta, who soon quitted the station. When Mr. Judson arrived, Mr. Carey had gone to Ava, by order of the king. "Mrs. Carey, who was a native of the country, still resided at Rangoon, in the mission house, which Mr. Chater had erected in a pleasant rural spot, almost half a mile from the walls of the town."*

By these gentlemen some progress had been made in the language. Mr. Carey had printed a grammar; but its inaccuracies were such that I have seldom seen it even referred to by students of Burman. He and Mr. Chater had also translated the Gospel by Matthew; but the work was done so incorrectly that I believe it was never put into circulation. Mr. Carey, who at this time was in attendance at the court of Ava, soon entered the service of the king, was promoted, lost his rank, left the mission, and relinquished the ministry. The reliable helps, therefore, were few; and Mr. Judson was obliged to commence the work almost *de novo*, and, as he advanced, to prosecute it by his own unaided efforts.

* Knowles's Memoir of Mrs. Judson. The house, however, was by no means pleasantly situated. It was near the place of public execution, where all the offal of the city was thrown, and not far from the place for burning the dead. It was beyond the protection of the walls, exposed to wild beasts and almost as wild men. They afterwards removed into the city.

The attainments which he made in the language were considered in India to be of the very highest order. He wrote and spoke it with the familiarity of a native and the elegance of a cultivated scholar. At an early period of his study, he prepared a brief grammar of the language for the use of missionaries, and modestly entitled it "Grammatical Notices," which, twenty years afterwards, (in 1842,) was printed at the mission press at Maulmain. Of this work a late writer in the "Calcutta Review" speaks as follows: "He [Dr. Judson] published another work, a grammar of no pretensions, and of very small dimensions, yet a manual which indicated the genius of the man, perhaps, more strikingly than any thing else, except his Bible. He has managed, from a thorough knowledge of the language, to condense into a few short pages [only seventy-six] a most complete grammar of this difficult tongue; and, as the student grows in knowledge, *pari passu*, this little volume rises in his estimation; for its lucid, comprehensive conciseness becomes more and more manifest. In our limited acquaintance with languages, whether of the East or West, we have seen no work in any tongue which we should compare with it for brevity and completeness; yet we have, in our day, had to study and wade through some long and some would-be short grammars."

This thoroughness of knowledge of the language could, of course, be the result of nothing but a very extensive acquaintance with Burman literature. Yet he considered this knowledge, in his case, as valueless, except in so far as it enabled him the better to present a perfect transcript of the word of God in the Burman language. In the strictness with which he carried out his principles on this subject, there is much that is worthy of distinct remark. He had a natural facility for the acquisition of languages, and great fondness for linguistic researches; yet he acquired no language of the East, except the Burman. He was strongly attached to physical science, and his researches in this direction might have acquired for him great reputation, and, as many good men might believe, would have given to the mission a desirable standing with scientific men; yet he never published a line on these subjects, and he even discouraged a taste for such pursuits among his missionary brethren. He had become fully aware of the temptations to which missionaries are exposed when the treasures of a new language and of a peculiar form of literature are presented before them, and he therefore guarded himself with peculiar strictness. At one time, he had found the literature of Burmah exceedingly fascinating, especially its poetry; and he had sundry pleasant visions of enriching the world of English literature from its curious stores. He, for a moment, flattered himself that, by interesting the Christian world in Burmah through her literature, he should open the floodgates of sympathy so as to bring about her emancipation from pagan thraldom. But the dream was soon dispelled. He saw that such an appropriation of his time would lead him aside from the peculiar work to which God had called him; and, though perfectly familiar with more than a hundred Burman tales, and able to repeat Burman poetry by the hour, he never committed a line to paper. He was fond of searching into doubtful histories and mousing among half fabulous antiquities, and Burmah presented an alluring field for this sort of research; yet he not only resisted his own natural tendencies, but took care never to excite in the minds of others an interest in things of this sort. He admitted nothing into the library of native books (palm leaf books, selected by himself, but the property of the mission) which would cultivate a taste for these comparatively trivial things. He was revered and caressed by the best society in India, yet he religiously kept aloof from it; and not all the representations of his friends could induce him to turn from his work to relieve the spiritual wants of Englishmen, or preach before an English congregation.*

It will not, of course, be supposed, by any one who knew Dr. Judson, that he was deficient in love of the beautiful, or wanting in zeal for the diffusion of knowledge. He did not proscribe such studies as I have alluded to as sinful, nor would he make rules for missionaries stricter than those for other Christians. He believed that there were temptations to which missionaries in unexplored fields are exposed, which are utterly destructive of usefulness, and may not be tampered with even for a moment. He looked upon a missionary as consecrated to a peculiar work, a work of incomparably greater importance than any other on earth, and he believed that it can be successfully prosecuted only by consecrating to it exclusively the entire energies of the soul. As Howard, when he visited Rome, left unnoticed the impressive monuments of ancient grandeur, and spent his time wholly in dungeons and prisons, so Dr. Judson believed that he who has undertaken to deliver a nation from the thraldom of sin has objects in view more

---

* Manuscript notes.

important than the researches of antiquaries or the companionship of *savans*. It were well if this exclusive devotion to substantially the same object governed the lives of ministers at home as well as of missionaries abroad.

The following anecdote will place in a clear light Dr. Judson's views on this subject. Not long before his death, a gentleman of Calcutta, a member of a literary society in that city, proposed that Mrs. Judson should translate the Life of Gaudama into English, to be published by the society. Dr. Judson replied, that as Mrs. Judson's health was suffering from too severe study, he was not sure that a light work of this nature would be objectionable. As the proposal was intended to be, and it really was, both kind and complimentary, the gentleman seemed disconcerted, until Mrs. Judson remarked, that her husband considered many things perfectly proper, and even desirable, on the part of others, "objectionable" in a missionary. In fact, Mr. Judson disapproved of missionary contributions made either to literature or science, even as a recreation; for he insisted that they could not be made with safety, and that nothing reliable could be accomplished without a draught on those energies which should be devoted to higher objects. Illustrations of the truth of his views he found in the history of some modern missions. He believed in general that the ministry is from its nature a self-denying employment. He who expects to indulge in worldly amusement, or spend his time in cultivating literary tastes or secular science, had better seek some other profession. This is specially true of a missionary. His work is great, the laborers are few, the temptations are alluring, and every thing binds him to exclusive consecration to his work.

But while Mr. Judson felt that *his* appropriate field was Burmah, and nothing but Burmah, he gave to this field no peculiar preëminence. The whole heathen world was always in his view. He was ever suggesting to the board new fields of labor, and he was constantly bringing before the mercy seat, in his most retired hours of devotion, particular nations who had not yet attracted the attention of the friends of missions. Thus, at Maulmain, he was always urging his brethren, and specially those whom he most highly esteemed, and whose society he most enjoyed, to establish new missions in neighboring unevangelized countries. In no case, however, did he propose any labor to them which he was not willing to undertake himself. He desired that every one of them, as far as possible, should be a new centre of gospel light, and he wished such centres to be multiplied as widely as possible. If the station at Maulmain has been the means of diffusing the knowledge of salvation to other and distant regions of India, this result has been owing, I apprehend, more to Dr. Judson's counsels, labors, and prayers, than to those of any other individual.

The letters which follow will present a tolerably connected view of the establishment and progress of the mission from the arrival of Mr. Judson at Rangoon to his return from the voyage to Madras, August 2, 1818: —

Extract from Mrs. Judson's Journal, commencing, September, 1813.

Our home is in the mission house built by the English Baptist Society, on the first arrival of Messrs. Chater and Carey in this country. It is large and convenient, situated in a rural place, about half a mile from the walls of the town. We have gardens enclosed, containing about two acres of ground, full of fruit trees of various kinds. In the dry season our situation is very agreeable. We often enjoy a pleasant walk, within our own enclosure, or in some of the adjoining villages.

September 20. This is the first Sabbath that we have united in commemorating the dying love of Christ at his table. Though but two in number, we feel the command as binding, and the privilege as great, as if there were more, and we have indeed found it refreshing to our souls.

December 11. To-day, for the first time, I have visited the wife of the viceroy. I was introduced to her by a French lady, who has frequently visited her. When we first arrived at the government house, she was not up; consequently we had to wait some time. But the inferior wives of the viceroy diverted us much by their curiosity in minutely examining every thing we had on, and by trying on our gloves, bonnets, &c. At last her highness made her appearance, dressed richly in the Burman fashion, with a long silver pipe at her mouth, smoking. At her appearance, all the other wives took their seats at a respectful distance, and sat in a crouching posture, without speaking. She received me very politely, took me by the hand, seated me upon a mat, and herself by me. She excused herself for not coming in sooner, saying she was unwell. One of the women brought her a bunch of flowers, of which she took several, and ornamented her cap. She was very inquisitive whether I had a husband and children; whether I was my husband's first wife; meaning by this, whether I was the highest among them, supposing that my husband, like the Burmans, had many wives; and whether I intended tarrying long in the country.

When the viceroy came in, I really trembled, for I never before beheld such a savage-looking creature. His long robe and enormous spear not a little increased my dread. He spoke to me, however, very condescendingly, and asked if I would drink some rum or wine. When I arose to go, her highness again took my hand, told me she was happy to see me; that I must come to see her every day, for I was like a sister to her. She led me to the door, and I made my *salaam*, and departed. My only object in visiting her was, that, if we should get into any difficulty with the Burmans, I could have access to her, when perhaps it would not be possible for Mr. Judson to get access to the viceroy. One can obtain almost any favor from her by making a small present. We intend to have as little to do with government people as possible, as our usefulness will probably be among the common people. Mr. Judson lately visited the viceroy, when he scarcely deigned to look at him, as English *men* are no uncommon sight in this country; but an English female is quite a curiosity.

January 11, 1814. Yesterday we left the mission house, and moved into one in town, partly through fear of robbers, and partly for the sake of being more with the natives, and learning more of their habits and manners. We shall also be in a way of getting the language much quicker, as we shall hear it spoken much more frequently than we could in the other house.

From Mrs. Judson to the Rev. Samuel Newell.

RANGOON, April 23, 1814.

MY DEAR BROTHER NEWELL: As Mr. Judson will not have time to write you by this opportunity, I will endeavor to give you some idea of our situation here, and of our plans and prospects. We have found the country, as we expected, in a most deplorable state, full of darkness, idolatry, and cruelty — full of commotion and uncertainty. We daily feel that the existence and perpetuity of this mission, still in an infant state, depend in a peculiar manner on the interposing hand of Providence; and from this impression alone we are encouraged still to remain. As it respects our temporal privations, use has made them familiar, and easy to be borne; they are of short duration, and when brought in competition with the worth of immortal souls, sink into nothing. We have no society, no dear Christian friends, and with the exception of two or three sea captains, who now and then call on us, we never see a European face. But then we are still happy in each other; still find that our own home is our best, our dearest friend. When we feel a disposition to sigh for the enjoyments of our native country, we turn our eyes on the miserable objects around. We behold some of them laboring hard for a scanty subsistence, oppressed by an avaricious government, which is ever ready to seize what industry had hardly earned; we behold others sick and diseased, daily begging the few grains of rice which, when obtained, are scarcely sufficient to protract their wretched existence, and with no other habitation to screen them from the burning sun, or chilly rains, than what a small piece of cloth raised on four bamboos under a tree can afford. While we behold these scenes, we feel that we have all the comforts, and, in comparison, even the luxuries, of life. We feel that our temporal cup of blessings is full, and runneth over. But is our temporal lot so much superior to theirs? O, how infinitely superior our spiritual blessings! While they vainly imagine to purchase promotion in another state of existence by strictly worshipping their idols and building pagodas, our hopes of future happiness are fixed on the Lamb of God who taketh away the sin of the world. When we have a realizing sense of these things, my dear brother, we forget our native country and former enjoyments, feel contented and happy with our lot, with but one wish remaining — that of being instrumental of leading these Burmans to partake of the same source of happiness with ourselves.

Respecting our plans, we have at present but one — that of applying ourselves closely to the acquirement of the language, and to have as little to do with government as possible. Brother Carey has never yet preached in Burman, but has made considerable progress towards the completion of a grammar and dictionary, which are a great help to us. At present, however, his time is entirely taken up with government affairs. It is now almost a year since he was ordered up to

Ava, which time has been wholly occupied in the king's business. He has just returned from Bengal, and is now making preparations for Ava, where he expects to found a new mission station. His family go with him; consequently we shall be alone until the arrival of brother Rice, who, we hope, will arrive in six or seven months.

Our progress in the language is slow, as it is peculiarly hard of acquisition. We can, however, read, write, and converse with tolerable ease, and frequently spend whole evenings very pleasantly in conversing with our Burman friends. We have been very fortunate in procuring good teachers. Mr. Judson's teacher is a very learned man, was formerly a priest, and resided at court. He has a thorough knowledge of the grammatical construction of the language, likewise of the Pali, the learned language of the Burmans.

Mr. Judson to the Rev. Mr. Emerson.

RANGOON, January 7, 1814.

DEAR BROTHER EMERSON: It is nearly a year since I wrote to America, my last being forwarded by brother Rice. I have had no opportunity of conveyance since that time, nor have I any at present. I intend to send this to England, hoping that on its arrival the war may have terminated, or that it may find a conveyance in a despatch vessel. We have been here about six months; have been living in the mission house, with brother F. Carey's family, but expect within a few days to take a house within the walls of the town, on account of the bands of robbers which infest all the country, and which have lately been very numerous and daring. Our situation is much more comfortable than we expected it would be in such a country. We enjoy good health, and though deprived of all congenial Christian society, we are very happy in each other, and think we frequently enjoy his presence whose smile can turn the darkest night to day, and whose favor is the fountain of all happiness. " Peace I leave with you — my peace I give unto you." There has yet been but very little effected in this country to any real missionary purpose. Brother Carey's time is greatly occupied in government matters. The emperor has given him a title, and requires him to reside in the capital. He is just now going to Bengal on his majesty's business, and expects, after his return, to reside at Ava. Not a single Burman has yet been brought to a knowledge of the truth, or even to serious inquiry. In all the affairs of this government, despotism and rapine are the order of the day. The present viceroy of this province is a savage man. Life and death depend on his nod. He is very large in stature, and when he stalks about with his long spear, every body shrinks from before him. I called on him once, but he scarcely looked at me. Ann waited on her highness, and was much better received. This man is about to be recalled to Ava, and it is doubtful whether he will return. During the interim we expect all things will be in confusion, and this is one reason why we desire to get within the walls of the city.

My only object at present is to prosecute, in a still, quiet manner, the study of the language, trusting that for all the future "God will provide." We have this consolation, that it was the evident dispensation of God which brought us to this country; and still further, that if the world was all before us, where to choose our place of rest, we should not desire to leave Burmah. Our chief anxiety is that brother Rice may not be able to join us again; but even this we desire to leave in his hands who doeth all things well.

Your affectionate brother in the Lord Jesus,

A. JUDSON, JR.

Mrs. Judson had not been long in Rangoon before her health began to suffer from the effects of the climate. In January, 1815, her symptoms became alarming, and on the 25th of that month she sailed to Madras for medical advice. She was received by the residents of that city, and especially by the English missionaries, with the kindest hospitality. Her health was soon restored, under the skilful care of the medical gentlemen there, and she returned to Rangoon on the 13th of April. During her absence, Mr. Judson wrote the following letter to a friend: —

There is not an individual in the country that I can pray with, and not a single soul with whom I can have the least religious communion. I keep myself as busy as possible all day long, from sunrise till late in the evening, in reading Burman, and conversing with the natives. I have been here a year and a half, and so extremely difficult is the language — perhaps the most difficult to a foreigner of any on the face of the earth, next to the Chinese — that I find myself very inadequate to communicate divine truth intelligibly. I have, in some instances, been so happy as to secure the attention, and in some degree to interest the feelings, of those who heard me; but I am not acquainted with a single instance in which any permanent impression has been produced. No Burman has, I believe, ever felt the grace of God; and what can a solitary, feeble individual or two expect to be the means of effecting in such a land as this, amid the triumphs of Satan, the darkness of death? The Lord is all powerful, wise, and good; and this consideration alone always affords me unfailing consolation and support. Adieu, &c. A. JUDSON, JR.

Additional Extracts from Mrs. Judson's Journal.

April 16, 1815. Mr. Carey has lately returned from Calcutta, and much refreshed our minds with letters and intelligence from our friends there. We are so much debarred from all social intercourse with the rest of the Christian world, that the least intelligence we receive from our friends is a great luxury. We feel more and more convinced that the gospel must be introduced into this country through many trials and difficulties, through much self-denial and earnest prayer. The strong prejudices of the Burmans, their foolish conceit of superiority over other nations, the wickedness of their lives, together with the plausibility of their own religious tenets, make a formidable appearance in the way of their receiving the strict requirements of the gospel of Jesus. But all things are possible with God, and he is our only hope and confidence. He can make mountains become valleys, and dry places streams of water.

August 20. To-day Mr. Carey, wife, and family left us for Ava, where they expect to live. We are now alone in this great house, and almost alone as it respects the whole world. We are daily expecting dear brother and sister Hough, when we hope our lonely hours will be more than repaid with their society. If it were not that Burmah presents such an unbounded field for missionary exertions, we would not be contented to stay in this miserable land. But we are convinced that we are in the very situation in which our heavenly Father would have us to be; and if we were to leave it for the sake of enjoying a few more temporal comforts, we should have no reason to expect his blessing on our exertions. We frequently receive letters from our Christian friends in this part of the world, begging us to leave a field so entirely rough and uncultivated, the soil of which is so unpromising, and enter one which presents a more plentiful harvest. God grant that we may live and die among the Burmans, though we should never do any thing more than smooth the way for others.

September 3. Heard the dreadful intelligence of the loss of Mr. Carey's vessel, his wife, and children, and all his property. He barely escaped with his life. How soon are all his hopes blasted! He set out to go to Ava in a brig which belonged to the Burman government; had got his furniture, medicine, wearing apparel, &c., on board. The brig had been in the river about ten days, when she upset, and immediately went down. Mrs. Carey, two children, all the women servants, and some of the men servants, who could not swim, were lost. Mr. Carey endeavored to save his little boy, three years old; but finding himself going down, was obliged to give up the child. Thus far from my journal.

As it respects ourselves, we are busily employed all day long, and I can assure you that we find much pleasure in our employment. Could you look into a large open room, which we call a veranda, you would see Mr. Judson bent over his table, covered with Burman books, with his teacher at his side, a venerable-looking man, in his sixtieth year, with a cloth wrapped round his middle, and a handkerchief round his head. They talk and chatter all day long with hardly any cessation.

My mornings are busily employed in giving directions to the servants, providing food for the family, &c. At ten my teacher comes; when, were you present, you might see me in an inner room, at one side of my study table, and my teacher the other, reading Burman, writing, talking, &c. I have many more interruptions than Mr. Judson, as I have the entire management of the family. This I took on myself for the sake of Mr. Judson's attending more closely to the study of the language; yet I have found by a year's experience that it was the most direct way I could have taken to acquire the language, as I am frequently obliged to talk Burman all day. I can talk and understand others better than Mr. Judson, though he knows really much more about the nature and construction of the language than I do.

This climate is one of the most healthy in the world. There are only two months in the year when it is severely hot. We doubt not but you pray much for us in this miserable land, deprived of all Christian society. We need much, very much grace, that we may be faithful, and bear a faithful testimony to the religion of Jesus.

The following extract, giving an account of an attempt of Mr. Judson to convey religious knowledge to his teacher, presents a view of the notions of intelligent Burmans on this subject.

September 30, 1815. Had the following conversation with my teacher, as nearly as I can recollect it. This man has been with me about three months, and is the most sensible, learned, and candid man that I have ever found among the Burmans. He is forty-seven years of age, and his name is Oo Oungmen. I began by saying, Mr. J—— is dead. *Oo.* I have heard so. *J.* His soul is lost, I think. *Oo.* Why so? *J.* He was not a disciple of Christ. *Oo.* How do you know that? You could not see his soul. *J.* How do you know whether the root of that mango tree is good? You cannot see it; but you can judge by the fruit on its branches. Thus I know that Mr. J. was not a disciple of Christ, because his words and actions were not such as indicate a disciple. *Oo.* And so all who are not disciples of Christ are lost? *J.* Yes, all, whether Burmans or foreigners. *Oo.* This is hard. *J.* Yes, it is hard indeed; otherwise I should not have come all this way, and left parents and all, to tell you of Christ. He seemed to feel the force of this, and after stopping a little he said, How is it that the disciples of Christ are so fortunate above all men? *J.* Are not all men sinners, and deserving of punishment in a future state? *Oo.* Yes, all must suffer in some future state for the sins they commit. The punishment follows the crime as surely as the wheel of the cart follows the footsteps of the ox. *J.* Now, according to the Burman system, there is no escape. According to the Christian system, there is. Jesus Christ has died in the place of sinners, has borne their sins; and now those who believe on him, and become his disciples, are released from the punishment they deserve. At death, they are received into heaven, and are happy forever. *Oo.* That I will never believe. My mind is very stiff on this one point, namely, that all existence involves in itself principles of misery and destruction. The whole universe is only destruction and reproduction. It therefore becomes a wise man to raise his desires above all things that exist, and aspire to *nigban*, the state where there is no existence. *J.* Teacher, there are two evil futurities, and one good. A miserable future existence is evil, and annihilation, or nigban, is an evil, a fearful evil. A happy future existence is alone good. *Oo.* I admit that is best, if it could be perpetual; but it cannot be. Whatever is is liable to change, and misery, and destruction. Nigban is the only permanent good, and that good has been attained by Gaudama, the last deity. *J.* If there be no eternal being, you cannot account for any thing. Whence this world, and all that we see? *Oo.* Fate. *J.* Fate! The cause must always be equal to the effect. See, I raise this table. See also that ant under it. Suppose I were invisible, would a wise man say the ant raised it? Now, fate is not even an ant. Fate is a word; that is all. It is not an agent; not a thing. What is fate? *Oo.* The fate of creatures is the influence which their good or bad deeds have on their future existence. *J.* If influence be exerted, there must be an exerter. If there be a determination, there must be a determiner. *Oo.* No, there is no determiner. There cannot be an eternal being. *J.* Consider this point. It is a main point of true wisdom. Whenever there is an execution of a purpose, there must be an agent. *Oo.* (After a little thought.) I must say that my mind is very decided and hard, and unless you tell me something more to the purpose, I shall never believe. *J.* Well, teacher, I wish you to believe, not for my profit, but for yours. I daily pray the true God to give you light that you may believe. Whether you will ever believe in this world, I do not know; but when you die, I know you will believe what I now say. You will then appear before the God that you now deny. *Oo.* I don't know that. *J.* I have heard that one Burman, many years ago, embraced the Portuguese religion, and that he was your relation. *Oo.* He was a brother of my grandfather. *J.* At Ava, or here? *Oo.* At Ava he became a Portuguese; afterwards went to a ship country with a ship priest, and returned to Ava. *J.* I have heard he was put to death for his religion. *Oo.* No, he was imprisoned and tortured by order of the emperor. At last he escaped from their hands, fled to Rangoon, and afterwards to Bengal, where they say he died. *J.* Did any of his family join him? *Oo.* None; all forsook him; and he wandered about, despised and rejected by all. *J.* Do you think that he was a decided Christian, and had got a new mind?

Oo. I think so; for whet. he was tortured hard, he held out. *J.* Did he ever talk with you about religion? *Oo.* Yes. *J.* Why did you not listen to him? *Oo.* I did not listen. *J.* Did you ever know any other Burman that changed his own for a foreign religion? *Oo.* I have heard that there is one now in Rangoon, who became a Portuguese; but he keeps himself concealed, and I have never seen him.

January 1, 1816. The greater part of my time, for the last six months, has been occupied in studying and transcribing, in alphabetical arrangement, the Pali Abigdan, or dictionary of the Pali language, affixing to the Pali terms the interpretation in Burman, and again transferring the Burman words to a dictionary, Burman and English. With the close of the year, I have brought this tedious work to a close, and find that the number of Pali words collected amounts to about four thousand. It has grieved me to spend so much time on the Pali, but the constant occurrence of Pali terms in every Burman book made it absolutely necessary.

The two languages are entirely distinct. The Burman is a language *sui generis* — peculiar to itself. It is true, we cannot know what affinity it has to some of the Indo-Chinese languages that are yet uninvestigated; but it is essentially different from the Sanscrit, the parent of almost all the languages in India proper, and, indeed, from every language that has yet come under the cognizance of Europeans.

The Pali, on the other hand, is a dialect of the Sanscrit, and was introduced into this country with the religion of Boodh. This personage, whose proper name is Gaudama, appeared in Hindostan about two thousand three hundred years ago, and gave a new form and dress to the old transmigration system, which, in some shape or other, has existed from time immemorial. The Brahmans, in the mean time, dressed up the system after their fashion; and these two modifications, Brahmanism and Boodhism, struggled for the ascendency. At length the family of Gaudama, which has held the sovereignty of India, was dethroned, his religion was denounced, and his disciples took refuge in Ceylon and the neighboring countries. In that island, about five hundred years after the decease and supposed annihilation of their teacher or deity, they composed their sacred writings, in that dialect of the Sanscrit whch had obtained in Ceylon; thence they were conveyed, by sea, to the Indo-Chinese nations. Boodhism, however, had gained footing in Burmah before the arrival of the sacred books from Ceylon. It is commonly maintained that it was introduced by the emissaries of Gaudama before his death.

It is obvious that the introduction of a new religion and new sacred writings must have great effect on the language of a people. And, accordingly, (not to speak of the influence which the Pali has had on the general construction of the Burman language,) a considerable number of words in common use, and a very great proportion of theological terms, are of Pali origin. Thus, though the Pali is now a dead language, cultivated by the learned only, some knowledge of it is indispensable to one who would acquire a perfect knowledge of the Burman, and especially to a missionary, who intends to translate the Scriptures, and who ought, therefore, above all others, to be perfectly acquainted with the terms he employs.

With these views, I was desirous of laying a little foundation for such further improvements in the language as necessity should require and leisure permit. And having done this, having a vocabulary for daily reference, correction, and enlargement, I now propose to devote my whole time again to the Burman.

On the 11th of September, their loneliness was cheered by the birth of a son, whom, in honor of the apostle of religious liberty, they named Roger Williams. The blessing was, however, short lived, for on the 4th of May, 1816, they were called upon to consign him to an early grave.

To the Rev. Dr. Bolles.

RANGOON, January 16, 1816.

DEAR BROTHER: Yours of March, 815, I lately received, and read with real satisfaction. Neither brother Rice nor any of the others that you mention have yet been heard of in these parts. May they not be far distant. Whenever they shall arrive, I hope to be of some real service to them in their preparatory studies, and to be able to give them, in a short time, information on many points which it has cost me months to acquire. I just now begin to see my way forward in this language, and hope that two or three years more will make it somewhat familiar; but I have met with difficulties that I had no idea of before I entered on the work. For a European or American to acquire a *living* oriental language, root and branch, and make it his own, is quite a different thing from his acquiring a cognate language of the West, or any of the dead languages, as they are studied in the schools. One circumstance may serve to illustrate this. I once had occasion to devote about two months to the study of the French. I have now been above two years engaged on the Burman; but if I were to choose between a Burman and French book to be examined in, without previous study, I should, without the least hesitation, choose the French. When we take up a western language, the similarity in the characters, in very many terms, in many modes of expression, and in the general structure of sentences, its being in fair print, (a circumstance we hardly think of,) and the assistance of grammars, dictionaries, and instructors, render the work comparatively easy. But when we take up a language spoken by a people on the other side of the earth, whose very thoughts run in channels diverse from ours, and whose modes of expression are consequently all new and uncouth; when we find the letters and words all totally destitute of the least resemblance to any language we had ever met with, and these words not fairly divided and distinguished, as in western writing, by breaks, and points, and capitals, but run together in one continuous line, a sentence or paragraph seeming to the eye but one long word; when, instead of clear characters on paper, we find only obscure scratches on dried palm leaves strung together and called a book; when we have no dictionary, and no interpreter to explain a single word, and must get something of the language before we can avail ourselves of the assistance of a native teacher, —

"Hoc opus, hic labor est."

I had hoped, before I came here, that it would not be my lot to have to go on alone, without any guide in an unexplored path, especially as missionaries had been here before. But Mr. Chater had left the country, and Mr. Carey was with me but very little, before he left the mission and the missionary work altogether.

I long to write something more interesting and encouraging to the friends of the mission; but it must not yet be expected. It unavoidably takes several years to acquire such a language, in order to converse and write intelligibly on the great truths of the gospel. Dr. Carey once told me, that after he had been some years in Bengal, and thought he was doing very well in conversing and preaching to the natives, they (as he was afterwards convinced) knew not what he was about. A young missionary who expects to pick up the language in a year or two will probably find that he has not counted the cost. If he should be so fortunate as to find a good interpreter, he may be useful by that means. But he will find, especially if he is in a new place, where the way is not prepared, and no previous ideas communicated, that to qualify himself to communicate divine truth intelligibly by his own voice or pen, is not the work of a year. However, notwithstanding my present incompetency, I am beginning to translate the New Testament, being extremely anxious to get some parts of Scripture, at least, into an intelligible shape, if for no other purpose than to read, as occasion offers, to the Burmans I meet with.

My paper allows me to add nothing more but to beg your prayers, that while I am much occupied in words and phrases, and destitute of those gospel privileges you so richly enjoy, in the midst of your dear church and people, I may not lose the life of religion in my soul.

I remain, dear brother,
Yours very affectionately,
A. JUDSON, JR.

To the Rev. Dr. Staughton.

I am sometimes a little dispirited, when I reflect that, for two or three years past, I have been drilling at A, B, C, and grammar. But I consider again that the gift of tongues is not granted in these times; that some one must acquire this language by dint of application; must translate the Scriptures, and must preach the gospel to the people in their own tongue, or how can they be saved? My views of the missionary object are, indeed, different from what they were, when I was first set on fire by Buchanan's "Star in the East," six years ago. But it does not always happen that a closer acquaintance with an object diminishes our attachment and preference. We sometimes discover beauties, as well as deformities, which were overlooked on a superficial view; when some attractions lose their force, others more permanent are exerted; and when the glitter in which novelty invested the object has passed away, more substantial excellences have room to disclose their influence: and so it has been with me, I hope, in regard to the work of missions.

I remain, reverend and dear sir,
Yours affectionately in the Lord,
A. JUDSON, JR.

To the Rev. Luther Rice.

RANGOON, August 3, 1816.

MY DEAR BROTHER RICE: I have completed a grammar of the Burman language, which I hope will be useful to you; also a tract, which I hope to get printed as soon as Mr. Hough arrives.

If any ask what success I meet with among the natives, tell them to look at Otaheite, where the missionaries labored nearly twenty years, and, not meeting with the slightest success, began to be neglected by all the Christian world, and the very name of Otaheite began to be a shame to the cause of missions; and now the blessing begins to come. Tell them to look at Bengal also, where Dr. Thomas had been laboring seventeen years (that is, from 1783 to 1800) before the first convert, Krishna, was baptized. When a few converts are once made, things move on; but it requires a much longer time than I have been here to make a first impression on a heathen people. If they ask again, What prospect of ultimate success is there? tell them, As much as that there is an almighty and faithful God, who will perform his promises, and no more. If this does not satisfy them, beg them to let me stay and try it, and to let you come, and to give us our *bread;* or, if they are unwilling to risk their bread on such a forlorn hope as has nothing but the WORD OF GOD to sustain it, beg of them, at least, not to prevent others from giving us bread; and, if we live some twenty or thirty years, they may hear from us again.

This climate is good — better than in any other part of the East. But it is a most filthy, wretched place. Missionaries must not calculate on the least comfort, but what they find in one another and their work. However, if a ship was lying in the river, ready to convey me to any part of the world I should choose, and that, too, with the entire approbation of all my Christian friends, I would prefer dying to embarking. This is an immense field, and, since the Serampore missionaries have left it, it is wholly thrown on the hands of the American Baptists. If we desert it, the blood of the Burmans will be required of us.

Yours ever,
A. JUDSON, JR.

To the Rev. Dr. Baldwin.

RANGOON, August 5, 1816.

REV. AND DEAR SIR: It is about seven months since I wrote to America. The first three months of this time I was employed on the Burman language in a more interesting manner than I had ever been. I began to enter into my studies with such pleasure and spirit, and to make such rapid progress, as encouraged me to hope that the time was not far distant when I should be able to commence missionary operations. I was going forward in a course of most valuable Burman reading, and, at the same time, had begun to translate one of the Gospels, and to write a View of the Christian Religion in Burman, which, in imagination, were already finished and circulating among the natives, when, all of a sudden, in the midst of the hot season, which, in this country, is most severe during the months of March and April, I was seized with a distressing weakness and pain in my eyes and head, which put a stop to all my delightful pursuits, and reduced me to a pitiable state indeed. Since that time, excepting at some intervals, I have been unable to read, or write, or make any exertion whatever. Sometimes I have almost given up the hope that I should ever be of any more service; sometimes I have been on the point of trying a short voyage at sea. This last was my intention, when I heard of brother Hough's arrival in Bengal, and concluded to wait until he should be settled here, when I could leave more conveniently. But, thanks be to God, it is now ten days since I have experienced a turn of severe pain, though I still feel great weakness in my head, and, indeed, throughout my whole nervous system. I begin now to hope that I shall gradually recover, though I fear I never shall be as I formerly was.

During my illness, when able to do any thing, I have employed myself in collecting what knowledge I have hitherto acquired of the language, and putting it together in the shape of a grammar, that it might not be wholly lost to others. My tract also is at length ready for the press, and I send a copy by this conveyance to Philadelphia, which may be some gratification to the board. I would send a copy of the grammar also if I was able, but it is too bulky to be transcribed, in my present state.

I expect it will not be long before I shall be ordered up to Ava. The press also, which has just arrived from Bengal, will not probably be allowed to stop long in Rangoon. This will open a wide field, and make it necessary to support two stations. I beg, therefore, that the board will endeavor to send out one or two men with brother Rice, or as soon after as possible. The sooner they are on the ground, learning the language, the sooner they will be fit for service. I have never before thought it prudent to write for more men in addition to those I knew were already destined to the place. But some favorable prospects lately begin to open, and the more I become acquainted with the state of things, the less reason I have to fear that the government of the country will, at present, oppose the work.

We know not the designs of God in regard to this country; but I cannot but have raised expectations. It is true we may have to labor and wait many years before the blessing comes. But we see what God is doing in other heathen lands, after trying the faith and sincerity of his servants some fifteen or twenty years. Look at Otaheite, Bengal, Africa. And is Burmah to remain a solitary instance of the inefficacy of prayer, of the forgetfulness of a merciful and faithful God? Is it nothing that an attempt is begun to be made; that, in one instance, the language is considerably acquired; that a tract is ready for publication, which is intelligible and perspicuous, and will give the Burmans their *first ideas* of a Saviour and the way of salvation; that a press and types have now arrived, and a printer is on the way; that a grammar is finished, to facilitate the studies of others, and a dictionary of the language is in a very forward state; and that the way is now prepared, as soon as health permits, to proceed slowly in the translation of the New Testament? Is it nothing that, just at this time, the monarch of the country has taken a violent hate to the priests of his own religion, and is endeavoring, with all his power, to extirpate the whole order, at the same time professing to be an inquirer after the true religion? Is all this to be set down a mere cipher? It is true that we may desire much more. But let us use what we have, and God will give us more. However, men and money must be forthcoming.

Work cannot be done without men, and men cannot work without bread; nor can we expect the ravens to feed them in ordinary cases. I do not say several hundred missionaries are needed here. This, though true, would be idle talk. My request I think modest. Five men, allowing two or three to each of the stations, is the smallest number that will possibly answer.

I have received one letter only from Dr. Baldwin; Mrs. Judson has also received one. I hope that brother Hough is the bearer of others. We expect him by the first opportunity.

With the greatest respect, yours, &c.,

A. JUDSON, JR.

From Messrs. Judson and Hough to the Corresponding Secretary, Rev. Dr. Staughton.

RANGOON, November 7, 1816.

REV. AND DEAR SIR: It is with peculiar satisfaction that we are, at length, able to address a letter to the board, in our joint capacity. We had a joyful meeting in this place the 15th ult. Mr. Hough has settled in one part of the mission house; and we are now united, both as a church of Christ and as a mission society. Our regulations on the latter point we here submit to the board. It will be evident, at first sight, that these regulations have a prospective view, and are framed somewhat differently from what they would have been had we not expected that our society would soon be enlarged. But we hope that the time is not far distant when they will receive the signature of brother Rice also. Indeed, we hope for more than this; we hope that one or two others will be found to accompany Mr. Rice.

It is true that one of us remained about three years in this place without uttering any Macedonian cries. But we apprehend that the time is now come, when it is consistent with the strictest prudence to lift up our voice and say, Come over the ocean and help us. By a residence of three years in this country, many doubts, which at first occurred, are removed; and many points concerning the practicability of a mission, and the prospect of success, are ascertained. We cannot now enter much into detail; but we desire to say, that we consider the mission established in this land. We unite in opinion, that a wide door is set open for the introduction of the religion of Jesus into this great empire. We have at present no governmental interdict to encounter, and no greater obstacles than such as oppose the progress of missionaries in every heathen land. It appears to us (and may it so appear to our fathers and brethren) that God, in removing the English mission from this place, and substituting in their stead an American mission, is emphatically calling on the American churches to compassionate the poor Burmans, and to send their silver, and their gold, and their young men, to this eastern part of the world, to the help of the Lord against the mighty.

It is with great pleasure that we announce the valuable present of a press and Burman types, made to us by the Serampore brethren. We are now closing in a room for a temporary printing office, and hope very soon to issue a gospel tract, which has been in readiness some time, and which is intended to give the heathen around us some idea of the way of salvation through the Lord Jesus. But we cannot move one step in the way of printing without money. Though favored with the press, in the first instance, gratis, we have already expended, in paper, freight, and sundries, about four hundred rupees. We therefore beg an immediate appropriation, not only to liquidate the expenses already incurred, but to enable us to proceed in this all-important part of our work. The accounts of the mission press we propose to keep distinct; and they shall be submitted together with the accounts of the mission.

We know not how long the press will be permitted to remain in Rangoon; we do not, however, deprecate its removal to Ava. Such a measure would doubtless tend to the furtherance of the cause, and to the introduction of religion into the very heart of the empire, where Satan's seat is. But in this case, more men and more money would be imperatively demanded; and we trust that the patronage of the board will not fail us in these necessary points. We desire humbly to repeat to the board what the first missionaries from the Baptist society in England said to their friends, when on the point of embarkation in the great work which seems destined to illumine Western India with the light of the gospel. "We are," said they, "like men going down into a well; you stand at the top and hold the ropes. Do not let us fall." Hold us up, brethren and fathers; and if health and life be spared to us, we hope, through the grace of God, to see Eastern India also beginning to participate in the same glorious light. Many years may intervene, in the latter as well as in the former case; many difficulties and disappointments may try your faith and ours. But let patience have her perfect work; let us not be weary of well-doing; for in due time we shall reap, *if we faint not.*

Your servants in the Lord Jesus,

A. JUDSON, JR.
GEORGE H. HOUGH.

Articles of Agreement.

In order more effectually, under the blessing of our Lord and Master, to accomplish the important work for which we have come into this heathen land, we, the undersigned, form a union on the following principles, namely: —

1. We give ourselves to the Lord Jesus Christ, and to one another by the will of God.

2. We agree to be kindly affectioned one towards another with brotherly love, in honor preferring one another; feeling that we have one Master, even Christ, and that all we are brethren.

3. We agree in the opinion that our sole object on earth is to introduce the religion of Jesus Christ into the empire of Burmah; and that the means by which we hope to effect this are, translating, printing, and distributing the Holy Scriptures, preaching the gospel, circulating religious tracts, and promoting the instruction of native children.

4. We therefore agree to engage in no secular business for the purpose of individual emolument; and not at all, unless, in the opinion of the brethren, the great object of the mission can be best promoted thereby.

5. We agree to relinquish all private right to remittances from America, avails of labor, and compensation for service; in a word, to place all money and property, from whatever quarter accruing, in the mission fund: provided, that nothing in this article be construed to affect our private right to inheritances, or personal favors, not made in compensation of service.

6. We agree that all the members of the mission family have claims on the mission fund for equal support, in similar circumstances; the claims of widows and orphans not to be in the least affected by the death of the head of their family. But it is to be understood, that no one shall have a right to adopt a child into the mission family, so as to entitle it to the claims secured in this article, but by consent of the brethren.

7. We agree to educate our children with a particular reference to the object of the mission; and if any expense be necessary or expedient for this purpose, it shall be defrayed from the mission fund.

8. All appropriations from the mission fund shall be made by a majority of the missionary brethren united in this compact; subject, however, to the inspection of our patrons, the board.

A. JUDSON, JR.
GEORGE H. HOUGH.

To the Rev. Luther Rice.

RANGOON, November 14, 1816.

MY BELOVED BROTHER RICE: In encouraging other young men to come out as missionaries, do use the greatest caution. One wrong-headed, conscientiously obstinate fellow would ruin us. Humble, quiet, persevering men; men of sound, sterling talents, (though, perhaps, not brilliant,) of decent accomplishments, and some natural aptitude to acquire a language; men of an amiable, yielding temper, willing to take the lowest place, to be the least of all and the servants of all; men who enjoy much closet religion, who live near to God, and are willing to suffer all things for Christ's sake, without being proud of it, these are the men, &c. But O, how unlike to this description is the writer of it! Still, however, I am, with never-ceasing affection,

Your most affectionate brother in the Lord,
A. JUDSON, JR.

To the Rev. Dr. Baldwin.

RANGOON, February 10, 1817.

REV. AND DEAR SIR: Have just heard that a person whom we have some time calculated on as a letter carrier to Bengal is unexpectedly going off in the course of an hour. Have, therefore, time only to accompany the enclosed tracts with a line or two.

We have just begun to circulate these publications, and are praying that they may produce some inquiry among the natives. And here comes a man, this moment, to talk about religion. What shall I do? I will give him a tract, to keep him occupied a few moments while I finish this. "Here, my friend, sit down, and read something that will carry you to heaven, if you believe and receive the glorious Saviour therein exhibited."

We are just entering on a small edition of Matthew, the translation of which I lately commenced. But we are in great want of men and money. Our hands are full from morning till night. I cannot, for my life, translate as fast as brother Hough will print. He has to do all the hard work in the printing office, without a single assistant, and cannot, therefore, apply himself to the study of the language, as is desirable. As for me, I have not an hour to converse with the natives, or go out and make proclamation of the glorious gospel. In regard to money, we have drawn more from Bengal than has been remitted from America; so that now, if not for their truly brotherly kindness in honoring our bills on credit, we should actually starve. Moreover, an edition of five thousand of the New Testament will cost us nearly five thousand dollars. And what are five thousand among a population of seventeen millions, five millions of whom can read? O that all the members of the Baptist convention could live in Rangoon one month! Will the Christian world ever awake? Will means ever be used adequate to the necessities of the heathen world? O Lord, send help. Our waiting eyes are unto thee!

Your brother in the Lord,

A. JUDSON, JR.

To the Corresponding Secretary.

RANGOON, March 7, 1817.

REV. AND DEAR SIR: Since the beginning of this year, we have printed two tracts, the one a view of the Christian religion, seven pages, one thousand copies; the other a catechism of six pages, 12mo., three thousand copies. After which, finding that we had paper sufficient for an edition of eight hundred of Matthew, we concluded to undertake this one Gospel, by way of trial, and as introductory to a larger edition of the whole New Testament. I am now translating the eleventh chapter, and in the printing room the third half sheet is setting up. Having premised thus much concerning the present posture of our affairs, I proceed to mention the circumstance which induced me to take up my pen at this time. I have this day been visited by the first inquirer after religion that I have ever seen in Burmah. For, although in the course of the last two years I have preached the gospel to many, and though some have visited me several times, and conversed on the subject of religion, yet I have never had much reason to believe that their visits originated in a spirit of sincere inquiry. Conversations on religion have always been of my proposing, and, though I have sometimes been encouraged to hope that truth had made some impression, never, till to-day, have I met with one who was fairly entitled to the epithet of *inquirer*.

As I was sitting with my teacher, as usual, a Burman of

respectable appearance, and followed by a servant, came up the steps, and sat down by me. I asked him the usual question, where he came from, to which he gave no explicit reply, and I began to suspect that he had come from the government house, to enforce a trifling request which in the morning we had declined. He soon, however, undeceived and astonished me, by asking, "How long time will it take me to learn the religion of Jesus?" I replied that such a question could not be answered. If God gave light and wisdom, the religion of Jesus was soon learned; but, without God, a man might study all his life long, and make no proficiency. "But how," continued I, "came you to know any thing of Jesus? Have you ever been here before?" "No." "Have you seen any writing concerning Jesus?" "I have seen two little books." "Who is Jesus?" "He is the Son of God, who, pitying creatures, came into this world, and suffered death in their stead." "Who is God?" "He is a being without beginning or end, who is not subject to old age and death, but always is." I cannot tell how I felt at this moment. This was the first acknowledgment of an eternal God that I had ever heard from the lips of a Burman. I handed him a tract and catechism, both which he instantly recognized, and read here and there, making occasional remarks to his follower, such as, "This is the true God; this is the right way," &c. I now tried to tell him some things about God and Christ, and himself, but he did not listen with much attention, and seemed anxious only to get another book. I had already told him two or three times that I had finished no other book, but that in two or three months I would give him a larger one, which I was now daily employed in translating. "But," replied he, "have you not a little of that book done, which you will graciously give me now?" And I, beginning to think that God's time is better than man's, folded and gave him the first two half sheets, which contain the first five chapters of Matthew, on which he instantly rose, as if his business was all done, and, having received an invitation to come again, took leave.

Throughout his short stay, he appeared different from any

Burmans I have yet met with. He asked no questions about customs and manners, with which the Burmans tease us exceedingly. He had no curiosity, and no desire for any thing, but "MORE OF THIS SORT OF WRITING." In fine, his conduct proved that he had something on his mind, and I cannot but hope that I shall have to write about him again.

March 24. We have not yet seen our inquirer; but to-day we met with one of his acquaintance, who says that he reads our books all the day, and shows them to all that call upon him. We told him to ask his friend to come and see us again.

March 26. An opportunity occurs of sending to Bengal. I am sorry that I cannot send home more interesting letters. But I am not yet in the way of collecting interesting matter. I have found that I could not preach publicly to any advantage, without being able, at the same time, to put something into the hands of the hearers. And in order to qualify myself to do this, I have found it absolutely necessary to keep at home, and confine myself to close study for three or four years. I hope, however, after Matthew is finished, to make a more public entrance on my work than has yet been done. But many difficulties lie in the way. Our present house is situated in the woods, away from any neighbors, and at a distance from any road. In this situation we have no visitors, and no passing travellers, whom we could invite to stop and hear of Christ. My attempts to go out and find auditors have always occasioned such a waste of time, and interruption of study, as could not often be indulged in or justified. We are very desirous of building a small house near town, on some public road, but do not venture to incur the expense. We wish further instructions, and further explanations of the views and intentions of the board. The approaching triennial convention, also, we contemplate with the deepest interest. May God give abundant wisdom, and zeal, and holy spirit.

Permit me to close with a word in behalf of eastern missions. Great Britain and the United States appear to be the only countries which can at present take a very active part in missionary concerns. The British are fully occupied with India, Africa, and the South Sea islands. East of the British possessions in India are Burmah, Siam, several other Indo-Chinese nations, the great empire of China, Japan, thence north indefinitely, and southward the numerous Malayan Isles. With all these countries the British are no more connected than the Americans. The British are under no greater obligations to evangelize them than the Americans. They are no nearer the English, in point of transportation, than the Americans. And furthermore, throughout all these countries the British are suspected and feared; but not the Americans.

The idea that the western continent belongs to the Americans, and the eastern continent to the British, however plausible at first sight, cannot bear a moment's examination. I apprehend that all the north-western Indians, and the inhabitants of those parts of South America which are accessible, will scarcely outnumber the inhabitants of this single empire of Burmah. And on what principle can the Americans, who are perhaps half as numerous as the British, be let off with one twentieth or one thirtieth part of the work? But when we apply the case to the Baptists, it is still more decisive. There are about five hundred Baptist churches in Great Britain, which average one hundred members each. There are two thousand in America, which average about the same. Behold Ireland, also, almost as destitute as South America. And suppose the British should say, This is the proper province of our missionary exertions; let us leave Asia and Africa to the Americans, and "not send our young men to the antipodes."

Yours, respectfully,

A. JUDSON, JR.

To the Rev. Dr. Baldwin.

RANGOON, August 26, 1817.

REV. AND DEAR SIR: I am at present wholly absorbed in the dictionary. I hope to have it finished by the time that brother Rice arrives. The rains make it difficult for me to go out much; and for the same reason, we have not many Burman visitors in our insulated situation. Even those who have visited us frequently, and acquired some knowledge of our religion, and manifested some spirit of inquiry, are deterred from prosecuting their inquiries by fear of persecution. The two most hopeful persons suddenly discontinued their visits two months ago, and we have not seen them since. We suppose, from the circumstances, that they became fearful of being suspected. Sometimes persons who have been conversing with me on religion have been surprised by others, on which I have observed that they were disconcerted, remained silent, and got off as soon as possible. They all tell me that it would ruin a Burman to adopt the new religion. My teacher was lately threatened in public for having assisted a foreigner in making books subversive of the religion of the country. He replied that he merely taught me the language, and had no concern in the publication. In view of these difficulties, our first thought is, God can give to the inquirers that love to Jesus, and that resolution to profess his religion, which will overcome their fears. Our second thought is this: We are not under a free government, where every one is his own master, but under an absolute monarchy, where all are the property of one man. Is it not regular and prudent to say something to the master of this great family of slaves, before we take such measures as may be considered trespassing on his rights, and occasion our being deprived of any further opportunity of prosecuting those measures? With these views, I concluded, a few months ago, to distribute the tracts and Gospel which we have published, but with caution and discrimination, to converse on religion with all that I met, but to direct my labors chiefly to preparing what will be invaluable to future missionaries, and thus spend the rest of this year, until we shall have further assistance and advice from home. Then it may be thought best for one of us to go up to Ava, and introduce the matter gradually and gently to the knowledge of the emperor. I am fully persuaded that he has never yet got the idea that an attempt is making to introduce a new religion among his slaves. How the idea will strike him is impossible to foresee. He may be enraged, and order off the heads of all concerned. The urbanity, however, with which he treats all foreigners, and his known hatred of the present order of Boodhist priests, render such a supposition improbable. And if he should only be indifferent, should discover no hostility, especially if he should treat the missionaries with complacency, it would be a great point gained. No local government would dare to persecute the espousers of a new religion if it was known that they had friends at court. I do not mean to imply that all persecution is to be dreaded, but that persecution which would effectually prevent the use of the means of grace certainly is. It is true that God will call those whom he has chosen; but since he has made means necessary to the end, since it is by the gospel of his Son that he calls his people, it is certainly as much the duty of his servants to endeavor to avert such persecution as would effectually prevent the use of means as it is to use any means at all; and we may reasonably conclude that, when God has a people whom he is about to call, he will direct his servants in such a course.

I have no doubt that God is preparing the way for the conversion of Burmah to his Son. Nor have I any doubt that we who are now here are, in some little degree, contributing to this glorious event. This thought fills me with joy. I know not that I shall live to see a single convert; but, notwithstanding, I feel that I would not leave my present situation to be made a king.

I remain, dear sir,
Your servant in the Lord,
A. JUDSON, JR.

To the Corresponding Secretary.

MADRAS, May 28, 1818.

In former letters I have stated my circumstances at the close of last year, and the reasons which induced me to leave Rangoon on a visit to Chittagong; particularly the prospect of a direct passage, and speedy return in the same ship — an opportunity of very rare occurrence in Rangoon.

Since that time a series of unexpected providences have befallen me, which, though uninteresting in detail, must be briefly mentioned, in order to account for my present situation.

When we left Rangoon, December 25, we expected a passage of ten or twelve days. At the expiration of a month, however, by reason of contrary winds, and the unmanageableness of the ship in the difficult navigation along the coast, we found ourselves still at a great distance from port; and the season being so far advanced as to deprive us of the hope of more favorable winds, the captain and supercargo agreed on a change of the ship's destination, and made sail for Madras.

Previous to leaving the coast, we put into Cheduba, a place under Burman government, for a supply of provisions. I was unable to go ashore, but took the opportunity of sending a tract by the boat. It happened to be conveyed directly to the governor, and he ordered it read in his presence. Soon after, when our captain had an audience, the governor inquired after the writer of the tract, who he was, and how long he had been in the country. The captain evaded some questions, for fear of detention, I suppose, and merely stated that the writer was a foreigner, who had resided in Rangoon about four years. "No," replied the governor, " that is not to be credited. You cannot make me believe that a foreigner, in so short a time, has learned to write the language so well. It must have been written by some other person." The captain related this to me on his return. I felt particularly gratified by this testimony to the perspicuity of the style, and thought it not unworthy of mentioning, because it could not be suspected, as others which had been made to me personally, of having been a mere compliment.

The ship's destination was changed on the 26th of January. We retraced our course for a few days, and then stood to the westward. It was with the most bitter feelings that I witnessed the entire failure of my undertaking, and saw the summits of the mountains of Arracan, the last indexes cf my country, sinking in the horizon, and the ship stretching away to a distant part of India, which I had no wish to visit, and where I had no object to obtain. It was, however, some mitigation of my disappointment, that I should, in all probability, be able to return to Rangoon, and resume my missionary business much earlier than if I had visited Chittagong. But even the consolation of this hope was not long allowed me. We had, indeed, a quick passage across the bay; but on drawing near the Coromandel coast the wind and current combined to prevent our further progress, and at the expiration of another month, having for a long time subsisted on nothing scarcely but rice and water, and being now reduced to very short allowance, we concluded to make sail for Masulipatam, a port north of Madras, which we doubted not we should be able to reach in a very few days. In this, again, we were disappointed, and through the unmanageableness of the ship, or the mismanagement of the captain, were detained at sea nearly another month. During this period we were sometimes in great distress, deeming ourselves very fortunate when able to get a bag of rice, or a few buckets of water, from any native vessel which happened to pass. Once we sent the long boat to the shore, and obtained a considerable supply of water, which was a great relief. But of rice we could obtain no sufficient supply, and all other articles of provision were quite out of the question.

The low state to which I was at length reduced occasioned a partial return of the disorder of my head and eyes, to which I was subject two years ago. This, with other circumstances united, left me no other source of consolation but resignation to the will of God, and an unreserved surrender of all to his care; and praised be his name, I found more consolation and happiness in communion with God, and in the enjoyments of religion, than I had ever found in more prosperous circumstances.

Finally we did reach Masulipatam, and I left the ship on the 18th of March, twelve weeks after embarking at Rangoon.

I waited at Masulipatam a few days, until it was ascertained that the ship would unlade her cargo, and remain several months. And as there was no prospect that season of reaching Madras by sea, the only port on the coast where I could hope to find a vessel bound to Rangoon, I was under the necessity of taking a journey by land — distance about three hundred miles. I accordingly hired a palanquin and bearers, and arrived here the 8th of April. My first aim was, of course, the beach, and my first inquiry a vessel bound to Rangoon. But my chapter of disappointments was not yet finished. No vessel had sailed for Rangoon this year, and such, it was understood, was the unsettled state of the Burman country, that none would probably venture for some time to come.

Here I have remained ever since, under very trying circumstances. Have scarcely heard from Rangoon since I left, or been able to transmit any intelligence thither by a conveyance to be depended on. The weakness of my eyes prevents my application to study, or attempt at any exertion. I am making no progress in missionary work; I am distressed by the appalling recollection of the various business which was pressing on me at Rangoon, and made me very reluctant to leave home for the shortest time. Now, I have been detained twice as long as I anticipated, and have, withal, wholly failed in my undertaking. Where, my rebellious heart is ready to cry, where is the wisdom of all this? But it is wise, though blindness cannot apprehend. It is best, though unbelief is disposed to murmur. Be still, my soul, and know that He is GOD.

To the Corresponding Secretary.

RANGOON, October 9, 1818.

My last was dated Madras, May 28, 1818. At that place I remained, waiting for a conveyance to Rangoon, until the 20th of July, when I took passage on an English vessel, at one hundred and sixty-seven rupees. During my stay in Madras, I experienced great kindness and hospitality in the families of the Rev. Mr. Thompson, chaplain, and the Rev.

Mr. Loveless, missionary; and received such proofs of Christian affection from many dear friends, as rendered parting with them very painful, though my detention in Madras had, in other respects, been almost insupportable. We anchored at the mouth of Rangoon River, on the 2nd of August. The next morning, when the pilot came on board, I was overwhelmed with the intelligence that, on account of the dangerous situation of affairs, the mission had been broken up, and that Mr. Hough and family, and Mrs. Judson, had taken passage for Bengal. To my great relief, however, it was added, that, before the ship left the river, Mrs. Judson's reluctance to leave the place had so increased as to force her back to the mission house alone; and further, that the ship, being found unfit for sea, was still detained. On my arrival, I found that brother Hough was inclined to pursue his original plan. His reasons he will doubtless communicate to the board. It is expected that the vessel will be ready for sea in about a fortnight.

The brethren, Colman and Wheelock, and their wives, arrived the 19th of September, about six weeks after my return. We had, I can truly say, a most joyful meeting. You have never seen them, or it would be unnecessary to add, that they are four *lovely* persons, in every sense of the word, and appear to have much of a humble, prayerful spirit. Such being their interesting appearance, we regret more deeply to find that the health of the brethren is so feeble. They have both had a slight return of bleeding at the lungs, an old complaint, to which they were subject in America. May the Lord graciously restore and preserve them.

A few days after their arrival, I introduced them into the presence of the viceroy. He received us with marked attention, which, however, must be ascribed to the influence of a handsome present, which went before us. Though surrounded with many officers, he suspended all business for a time, examined the present, and condescended to make several inquiries. On being told that the new teachers desired to take refuge in his glory, and remain in Rangoon, he replied,

"Let them stay, let them stay; and let your wife bring their wives, that I may see them all." We then made our obeisance, and retired.

The examination which brother Hough sustained during my absence, and the persecution of the Roman Catholic padres, have made us feel more deeply than ever the precarious situation of this mission, and the necessity of proceeding with the utmost caution. It was only through the favor of the viceroy that the padres were allowed to remain here, when they arrived from Ava, under sentence of banishment. And it is only through his mediation, and the influence of large presents made to the king, that the order of banishment is reversed, if indeed it be reversed — a report not yet confirmed. One malicious intimation to the king would occasion our banishment; and banishment, as the Burmans tell us, is no small thing, being attended with confiscation of all property, and such various abuses as would make us deem ourselves happy to escape with our lives.

Such a situation may appear somewhat alarming to a person accustomed to the liberty and safety of a free government. But let us remember that it has been the lot of the greater part of mankind to live under a despotic government, devoid of all security for life or property a single moment. Let us remember that the Son of God chose to become incarnate under the most unprincipled and cruel despot that ever reigned. And shall any disciple of Christ refuse to do a little service for his Saviour, under a government where his Saviour would not have refused to live and die for his soul? God forbid. Yet faith is sometimes weak — flesh and blood sometimes repine. O for grace to strengthen faith, to animate hope, to elevate affection, to embolden the soul, to enable us to look danger and death in the face; still more, to behold, without repining, those most dear to us suffering fears and pains, which we would gladly have redoubled on ourselves, if it would exonerate them.

We feel encouraged by the thought that many of the dear children of God remember us at the mercy seat. To your prayers I desire once more to commend myself — the weakest, the most unqualified, the most unworthy, and the most unsuccessful of all missionaries.

Mr. Judson's sufferings during this voyage were far greater than he, in his letter, made known to his correspondent. They had sailed for Chittagong, a passage which should have been made in ten or twelve days, at farthest. He had, therefore, prepared himself for only a few weeks' absence from home. When the vessel put in at Cheduba, the nervous affection of his head and eyes, occasioned at first by low diet, had so much increased by exhaustion and lack of food, that he was unable to go on shore. When they approached the Coromandel coast, and again encountered contrary winds, they were reduced to almost the last extremity, and the constitution of Mr. Judson sank under these accumulated hardships. The mouldy, broken rice, which they picked up from native vessels, and this in small quantities, with a limited supply of water, was their sole sustenance for three or four weeks. He was accustomed to look back on his sufferings at this time with a feeling of horror scarcely equalled by his reminiscences of Ava. Here he was alone, in a state of passive, monotonous suffering, with no one to share his sympathies, and nothing to arouse his energies. His scanty wardrobe, prepared for a trip of ten or twelve days, had been long since exhausted, and what with starvation, filth, pain, and discouragement, he became unable to leave his berth. At last he was attacked by a slow fever, and turning in disgust from his little mess of dirty rice, he begged continually for water! water! water! without ever obtaining enough to quench, even for a moment, his devouring thirst.

At length the little vessel came to anchor in the mud of Masulipatam, some two or three miles from the low, uninviting beach, and the captain came to inquire if he would be taken on shore. The fact that they were near land seemed to him an incredible thing, a kind of dreamy illusion too fanciful to interest him. After some urging, however, he became sufficiently roused to pencil a note, which he addressed to " any English resident of Masulipatam," begging only for a place on shore to die. After a little while, one of the men came below, to tell him that a boat was approaching from the shore. He now succeeded in crawling to the window of his cabin, from which he plainly distinguished, in the rapidly moving boat, both the red coat of the military and the white jacket of the civilian. In the first thrill of joyful surprise, the sudden awakening of hope and pleasure, he threw himself on his knees and wept. Before his new friends were fairly on board, he had succeeded in gaining some little self-control; but he added, his voice faltering and his eyes filling with tears as he related the incident to Mrs. Judson, " The white face of an Englishman never looked to me so beautiful, so like my conception of what angel faces are, as when these strangers entered my cabin." They were very much shocked at his visible wretchedness: he was haggard, unshaven, dirty, and so weak that he could with difficulty support his own weight. Their earnest cordiality was peculiarly grateful to him. One of the officers took him to his own house, supplied him from his own wardrobe, procured a nurse, whom, however, he had occasion to employ but a short time, and displayed throughout a generous hospitality which Dr. Judson never forgot.*

* Mrs. Judson's reminiscences.

During Mr. Judson's absence, the mission at Rangoon was reduced to the last extremity, and would have been wholly abandoned but for the conduct of that heroic woman, whose name will ever be associated with the introduction of Christianity into Burmah. After Mr. Judson had been absent for three months, a native boat arrived from Chittagong, bringing the intelligence that neither he nor the vessel had been heard of at that port. After this, several months passed away before any tidings arrived concerning him. While the mission family remained in this state of anxious suspense, Mr. Hough received an order, couched in the most menacing language, to appear immediately at the court house, and give an account of himself. This order spread terror among all their domestics and adherents. As the hour was late, Mr. Hough was merely ordered to give security for his appearance at an early hour on the following day.

The viceroy, who had always been their friend, had been recalled to Ava, and the present viceroy having left his family at the capital, this latter circumstance rendered it inconsistent with etiquette for a female to appear at *his* court. Mr. Hough was not sufficiently well acquainted with the language to make his appeal in person. On the following days, Friday and Saturday, Mr. Hough was detained, under every conceivable annoyance, at the court house, and it was apparently the object of the officers to harass and distress him as much as possible.

On the next day, Sunday, another order for Mr. Hough's appearance arrived. Mrs. Judson now determined to bring the matter to a crisis, by appealing at once to the viceroy. Her teacher drew up a petition, stating their grievances their summons to appear in public on their *sacred day*, and equesting that these molestations should cease. Mr. Hough accompanied her to the government house. On her arrival, she was immediately recognized by the viceroy, who called her in the kindest manner to come in and make known her request. As soon as he had heard the petition, he inquired of the very officer who had been foremost in molesting them, why the examination of this foreign teacher had been thus prolonged. He at once gave an order that Mr. Hough should be no more called upon on his sacred day, and that he should be molested no more. This trouble thus passed away, but its consequences remained. Mrs. Judson had succeeded in assembling some thirty or more females for religious instruction; but after this examination of Mr. Hough, the number at once diminished to ten or twelve.

Besides this, the cholera now began to rage among the native population, and the beating of the death drum sounded all the day long. The missionaries felt themselves exposed to its ravages; but, through a merciful Providence, not an individual on their premises suffered. Nor was this all. Reports were in circulation that Burmah was on the eve of a war with Great Britain. Arrivals from British India were becoming rare, and vessels in the port of Rangoon were making all haste to depart before the war should be declared. At last, but one English vessel remained in the river. Six months had elapsed, and not a syllable had been heard of Mr. Judson. It was probable that the vessel had foundered, and all on board had perished. The natives were becoming afraid of intercourse with the missionaries. Should war be declared, they would be shut out from all communication with the civilized world, exposed to the tender mercies of a despotic authority.

Under these circumstances, Mr. Hough thought it desirable to remove the mission and its effects from Rangoon, while removal was practicable. Mrs. Judson was long in favor of remaining. At last, however, on the 5th of July, she consented to accompany Mr. and Mrs. Hough, and took passage in the last vessel that was to sail for Calcutta. It happened that the vessel was detained several days in the river. During this period she had time for calmer reflection, and determined to leave the ship, return to Rangoon, and remain there at least until she heard from her husband. "Accordingly," she writes, " I immediately resolved on giving up the voyage, and returning to town. The captain sent up a boat with me, and engaged to forward my baggage the next day. I reached town in the evening, spent the night at the house of the only Englishman remaining in the place, and to-day have come out to the mission house, to the great joy of all the Burmans left on our premises. Mr. Hough and family will proceed, and they kindly and affectionately urged my return. I know I am surrounded by dangers on every hand, and expect to feel much anxiety and distress; but, at present, I am tranquil, intend to make an effort to pursue my studies as formerly, and leave the event with God."

On the 16th of July, the first glimmering of hope broke upon the darkness. The vessel in which Mr. Judson had sailed for Chittagong arrived in the harbor. Mrs. Judson then learned that the ship had landed him at Masulipatam, and that he had proceeded to Madras in search of a passage to Rangoon. It also appeared that the prospect of immediate hostilities between Great Britain and Burmah was less imminent than had been supposed. On the 25th of

July, Mr. and Mrs. Hough returned to the mission house, the ship in which they embarked not being able to proceed for some weeks, so that Mrs. Judson was no longer entirely alone. "I have again," she adds, "commenced my studies, and keep myself closely engaged until two o'clock. This I find the best method to avoid dejection; besides, my conscience will not permit me to sit idly down and yield to those desponding feelings in which a Christian should not indulge." Her anxieties in regard to her husband were, however, soon to cease. Under date of August 2, 1818, she thus wrote to her parents: "How will you rejoice with me, my dear parents, when I tell you that I have this moment heard that Mr. Judson has arrived at the mouth of the river! This joyful intelligence more than compensates for the months of dejection and distress which his long absence has occasioned. Now I feel ashamed of my repinings, my want of confidence in God and resignation to his will. I have foolishly thought, because my trials were protracted, they would never end, or, rather, that they would terminate in some dreadful event, which would destroy all hope of the final success of the mission. But now I trust our prospects will again brighten, and cause us to forget this night of affliction, or to remember it as having been the means of preparing us for the reception of that greatest of blessings — the conversion of some of the Burmans." *

* Mrs. Judson's Mission to Burmah, pp. 106-107.

CHAPTER VII.

CONFIDENCE IN GOD. — VIEWS OF THE IMPORTANCE OF PREACHING THE GOSPEL. — THAT WORK COMMENCED. — OPENING OF THE ZAYAT. — FIRST CONVERTS TO THE CHRISTIAN RELIGION. — PREPARATIONS FOR VISITING AVA.

1818-1819.

WE have now arrived at a most interesting period in the history of the mission. Mr. Judson had made himself, in a remarkable degree, familiar with the language. He had published and circulated a tract, in which the doctrines and duties of the Christian religion were briefly but clearly exhibited. Some portions of the Scriptures were also translated, and in the hands of the people. These writings, so unlike any thing which they had ever before seen, began to attract the attention of the natives. Although Mr. Hough and his family returned to Calcutta, where, for a while, the Burman printing was executed, yet the mission had been strengthened by the arrival of Messrs. Colman and Wheelock, young men of ardent piety and great promise of usefulness. They, with their wives, arrived in Rangoon, September 19, 1818, and entered upon their work with a simple-hearted Christian earnestness which has embalmed their names in the memory of every friend of missions.*

---

* The career of these interesting young men was, however, destined to be but short. Mr. Wheelock, soon after his arrival at Rangoon, was attacked by bleeding from the lungs, which soon terminated in pulmonary consumption. It was that form of this malady which, in its last stages, alternates with disease of the brain, producing mental derangement. After suffering for some time in Rangoon, he deter-

During these long years of preparation, surrounded by heathen, not one of whom had ever received a single Christian idea, and, for the greater part of the time, destitute of any religious associations, except what they found in each other, Mr. and Mrs. Judson were never for a moment harassed with a doubt of ultimate success. It never entered into their minds that it might be desirable to find a more promising field. If the idea had once arrested their attention, he could not, he said, tell what the result might have been; but God preserved them from being tempted with it. They never felt a single regret or misgiving, and hence their letters never even allude to it, except it be to encourage their friends at home, who, they feared, might despond, in consequence of their want of success. They always enjoyed the most entire certainty as to the result of their labors, though occasionally doubting whether they should live to witness it. Their confidence rested firmly and exclu-

---

mined to sail for Calcutta, in the hope of deriving benefit from the voyage. On the passage, in a fit of insanity, he threw himself overboard, and was drowned. His widow was subsequently married in Calcutta, where she has since resided. Mr. Colman was also threatened, at the beginning of his residence in India, with pulmonary disease. From this he recovered, and was a beloved co-worker with Mr. Judson until their return from the first visit to Ava. It was then deemed important to establish another mission station on the confines of Burmah, to which, in case of intolerable persecution, the missionaries and the converts might resort, and from which the gospel might penetrate into the empire. Chittagong was selected for this purpose, and Mr. Colman proceeded to occupy it. He found, however, that Cox's Bazaar, a native but unhealthy village in the neighborhood, was better adapted to missionary objects; and here he fixed his residence. Incessant labor soon brought on the fever of the country, and he died July 4, 1822. This was the severest blow which the mission had yet received. His widow is now the wife of the Rev. A. Sutton, D. D., of the Orissa mission.

sively on the word of God. They believed that he had promised; they, doing, as they believed, his will, accepted the promise as addressed to themselves personally. Their daily work was a transaction between God and their own souls. It never seemed possible to them that God could be false to his promises. Their confidence was the offspring of that faith which is the substance of things hoped for, the evidence of things not seen. By it they went forth, not knowing whither they went. By faith, through many long years of discouragement, they endured, as seeing Him who is invisible; relying not at all on what they could do, but wholly on what God had promised to do for them.

I am well aware that all missions, whose object it is radically to renew and render meet for heaven the heart of man, must be sustained by the same confidence in God. Nothing could be more absurd than the attempt, by human power, to create or to sustain in the human soul that holiness without which no man shall see the Lord. Paul may plant, Apollos may water, but God giveth the increase. The faith through which we are saved is the gift of God. But while all this is generally acknowledged, there are differences, both in the simplicity with which it is received, and the boldness with which it is carried into practice. The belief that the conversion of men is the work of the Spirit, and the reliance on the promise of God that he will make the message of the gospel effectual to the salvation of men, wherever it is delivered in faith and love, seem I think, to have stood out in bolder relief in the planting of this mission, than in many others with which I am acquainted.

This peculiarity gave rise to several others. As

Mr. Judson believed that this was the work of God, one thing seemed to him just as easy as another. Nothing is difficult to omnipotence. "He spake and it was done, he commanded and it stood fast." The direct way of securing the aid of almighty power, is to follow in the path marked out by omniscient wisdom. Mr. Judson therefore endeavored, first of all, to ascertain the manner in which Christ and his apostles labored to extend Christianity. This seems plainly exemplified in the New Testament. It is by the action of individual mind on individual mind. It is by embracing every opportunity, which our intercourse with men presents, to tell them of the love of Christ, of their danger and their duty, and to urge them, in Christ's stead, to be reconciled to God. Thus did Christ, and thus did his apostles labor. They had no plan, no sapping and mining, no preparatory work, extending over half a generation before they should be ready for direct and energetic effort. As the apostles opened their commission, they saw that it commanded them to preach the gospel to every creature. They obeyed the commandment, and God wrought with them by signs, and wonders, and mighty deeds. Mr. Judson followed these examples, and his labors were attended with signal success.

Hence it will be perceived that he addressed himself at once to adults, to those who denied the existence of an eternal God; and the Holy Spirit carried the message directly to their hearts. Missionaries have sometimes said that we could scarcely expect men grown old in heathenism ever to be converted, since they were beyond the reach, at least, of our immediate efforts. We must therefore begin with children. We must establish schools, by our superior knowledge gain influence over the young, and with their daily lessons instil into their minds a knowledge of Christianity. And more than this: as the religious systems of the heathen are indissolubly associated with false views of astronomy, geography, and physical science generally, if we can correct these errors, the religion resting upon them must by necessity be swept away. As these views have been carried into practice, a change has naturally come over missionary stations. Ministers of the gospel to the heathen have become schoolmasters. Instead of proclaiming the great salvation, they have occupied themselves in teaching reading, spelling, geography, arithmetic, and astronomy. While some are thus engaged as teachers, others are employed as book makers for the schools. Thus it sometimes comes to pass, that of the men sent out for the express purpose of preaching the gospel, a large portion do not preach the gospel at all.

Mr. Judson, as I have remarked, took a different view of the work to which he considered himself set apart. He saw men all around him perishing, and he at once offered to them the only remedy which God had provided. He believed that there is a Holy Ghost, and that to him the hearts of all men are open. The apostles were not sent to be schoolmasters, but to be heralds and ambassadors. He aimed to follow closely in their footsteps, and hence I think that the narrative of his labors resembles more nearly that in the Acts of the Apostles than most others with which I am familiar.

And in all this I cannot but believe that the "foolishness of God is wiser than men." The gospel is always to be preached to parents, rather than to children; and specially so in the first planting of Christianity. The first profession of the religion of Jesus must, by necessity, expose the disciple to obloquy, reproach, and persecution. No one can suppose it to be the will of God that all these are first to be borne by little children. It never was, and it never will be, done. Besides, the influence of the heathen parent will be more powerful over his child than that of the Christian school teacher. Hence, while schools diffuse knowledge, improve the intellect, hasten the progress of civilization, and are, therefore, benevolent and philanthropic, they are not, as it seems to me, the missionary work which Christ committed to his disciples. That they have done good who can doubt? But, as a means for converting men, that they have fallen very far below the simple preaching of the gospel, is, I think, beyond a question. The preaching of Mr. Abbott and his assistants, in Arracan, has, I believe, been the instrument of more conversions than all the school teaching of Protestant missions for the last thirty years.

And here it may be worth while to observe the object which Mr. Judson always kept steadily in view, to the exclusion of every other. It was not to teach men a creed, or to train them to the performance of certain rites, or to persuade them to belong to a particular church, but first of all to produce in them a radical and universal change of moral character, to lead them to repent of and forsake all sin, to love God with an affection that should transcend in power every other motive, and to rely for salvation wholly on the merits of that atonement which has been made for man by our Lord and Savior Jesus Christ. It pleased God to crown his labors with success. It will be seen that, as the fruit of his labors, this type of character, so peculiar to the New Testament, was created in the souls of ignorant, licentious, and atheistic Buddhists. These disciples talk, and act, and feel in the very spirit of Christ and his apostles. Never, until this temper of heart was exhibited, were they admitted to the ordinance of baptism, and received as members of the Christian church. At the same time, the persecutions to which they would be exposed were plainly set before them. They were told that unless they loved Christ better than houses, or lands, or brethren, or their own lives, they could not be his disciples. No one who could not bear this test was encouraged to hope that he was a child of God. And yet, in view of all this, many earnestly desired permission to profess themselves the disciples of Jesus. Such, and such only, formed the church at Rangoon. He believed himself authorized to admit to the fellowship of saints none but those on whom this great moral change had passed. Hence we find in his journals no account of children who were baptized on the faith of their parents. He believed religion to be a personal matter between God and the soul of man; and hence, where there could be no evidence of a renewal of the moral nature of man, there could be no reason for admitting an individual, whether young or old, to the ordinances of a spiritual church. It is in this respect mainly that Christians of the Baptist persuasion differ from their brethren who hold with them the other great doctrines of the reformation.

A few events alluded to in the following journals and letters may properly be inserted here, in chronological order.

April 4, 1819. Public worship was commenced in the Burman language.

April 25. The zayat was opened for public instruction in religion.

June 27. Moung Nau, the first Burman convert, was baptized.

July 29. A revision and enlargement of tract number one, and tract number two, with a catechism in Burman by Mrs. Judson, were completed.

August 7. Mr. and Mrs. Wheelock sailed for Bengal.

Extract from a Letter to a Friend.

RANGOON, October 9, 1818.

REV. AND DEAR SIR: Yours of March 12 and 18, 1817, arrived here during my absence, or I should have replied long ago. Yours of the following November was brought by the brethren, who arrived here the 19th of last month — about six weeks after my return.

In regard to the education necessary for missionaries, it appears to me that whatever of mental improvement, or of literary and scientific attainment, is desirable in a minister at home, is desirable in a missionary. I think I could illustrate this in a variety of particulars; but the limits of a letter do not allow. I feel, however, more and more, the inadequacy and comparative insignificance of all human accomplishments, whether in a minister or a missionary, and the unspeakable, overwhelming importance of spiritual graces, — humility, patience, meekness, love, — the habitual enjoyment of closet religion, a soul abstracted from this world, and much occupied in the contemplation of heavenly glories. Here I cannot help digressing from the subject to myself. You know not, my dear sir, you cannot conceive, how utterly unfit I am for the work in which I am engaged. I am, indeed, a worm, and no man. It is a wonder that I am allowed to live as a missionary among the heathen, and receive an undeserved support from the dear people of God — from many who are poor in this world, but rich in faith. Yet I feel necessity laid on me to remain here, and try to do a little something.

In regard to an interview with the king, I have long thought it desirable, but have never felt that the time had come. I would rather that God should open the way than attempt to open it myself.

To the Corresponding Secretary.

RANGOON, February 20, 1819.

REV. AND DEAR SIR: The prospect of the speedy departure of a vessel for Bengal reminds us of our unanswered letters. Brother Colman has nearly recovered his health, which suffered much on his first arrival. But brother Wheelock still remains in a low, and, I fear, declining state.

My time, for the last few months, has been divided between reading Burman, writing some portions of Scripture, and other things preparatory to public worship, holding conversations on religion, and superintending the erection of a zayat, (as the Burmans call it,) or place of public resort, where we intend to spend much of our time, and where we hope to have stated worship, or, at least, to try the practicability of such an attempt under this government.

The peculiarly retired situation of the mission house has long rendered the erection of such a building, or a change of residence, a very desirable measure. After much hesitation and perplexity about our duty, we were so fortunate as to procure, at a very moderate price, a piece of ground which is contiguous to the mission premises, and at the same time opens on a public road. The building is now going up, with such scanty materials and means as we can afford, or, rather, as we think you can afford. The whole concern will cost about two hundred dollars. And should this zayat prove to be a Christian meeting house, the first erected in this land of atheists, for the worship of God — a house where Burmans who now deny the very existence of Deity shall assemble to adore the majesty of heaven, and to sing with hearts of devotion the praises of the incarnate Saviour —— But the thought seems too great to be realized. Can *this* darkness be removed? Can *these* dry bones live? On thee, Jesus, all our hopes depend. In thee all power is vested, even power to make sinful creatures instrumental of enlightening the heathen.

You want to hear of some poor benighted Burman brought to taste that the Lord is gracious; but O, not more than I want to speak f it. I hope, I do hope, my dear sir, that we shall both one day be gratified.

I remain, with much affection and respect,

Yours, &c.,

A. JUDSON, JR.

Mr. Judson's Journal, addressed to the Corresponding Secretary.

April 4, 1819. My close application to the Burman dictionary during the year 1817, and my subsequent loss of nearly a year in the unsuccessful attempt to visit Chittagong, have occasioned a long interruption in my journal. Since my return to Rangoon, the little I have to say I have communicated in letters. With this day, a new, and I hope important era in the mission, I resume the journal.

To-day, the building of the zayat being sufficiently advanced for the purpose, I called together a few people that live around us, and commenced public worship in the Burman language. I say *commenced*, for, though I have frequently read and discoursed to the natives, I have never before conducted a course of exercises which deserved the name of *public* worship, according to the usual acceptation of that phrase among Christians; and though I began to preach the gospel as soon as I could speak intelligibly, I have thought it hardly becoming to apply the term *preaching*, since it has acquired an appropriate meaning in modern use, to my imperfect, desultory exhortations and conversations. But I hope, though with fear and trembling, that I have now commenced a course of public worship and regular preaching. This would have taken place just a year ago, had I returned to Rangoon, as I expected, and still earlier, had I not been under a government where I thought it prudent to gain a considerable acquaintance with the language before commencing public operations, lest I should be unable properly to vindicate my conduct when called to a judicial account.

The congregation to-day consisted of fifteen persons only, besides children. Much disorder and inattention prevailed, most of them not having been accustomed to attend Burman worship. May the Lord grant his blessing on attempts made in great weakness and under great disadvantages; and all the glory will be his.

April 6. This evening I went, for the second time, to hear a popular Burman preacher. On our arrival, we found a zayat, in the precincts of one of the most celebrated pagodas, lighted up, and the floor spread with mats. In the centre was a frame raised about eighteen inches from the ground, where the preacher, on his arrival, seated himself. He appeared to be about forty-five years old, of very pleasant countenance and harmonious speech. He was once a priest, but is now a layman. The people, as they came in, seated themselves on the mats, the men on one side of the house, and the women on the other. It was an undistinguished day, and the congregation was very small, not more than one hundred. When we entered, some said, "There come some wild foreigners." But when we sat down properly, and took off our shoes, they began to say, "No, they are not wild; they are civilized." Some recognized me, and said to one another, "It is the English teacher" — a name by which I am commonly known. The preacher soon took notice of us, entered into some conversation, invited us to visit him, and so on; but on learning that I was a missionary, or, in their idiom, a religion-making teacher, his countenance fell, and he said no more. The people being now convened, one appointed for the purpose called three times for silence and attention. Each one then took the flowers and leaves which had been previously distributed, and placing them between his fingers, raised them to his head, and in that respectful posture remained motionless until the service was closed. This ceremony we of course declined. When all things were properly adjusted, the preacher closed his eyes, and commenced the exercise, which consisted in repeating a portion from their sacred writings. His subject was the conversion of the two prime disciples of Gaudama, and their subsequent promotion and glory. His oratory I found to be entirely different from all that we call oratory. At first he seems dull and monotonous; but presently his soft, mellifluent tones win their way into the heart, and lull the soul into that state of calmness and serenity which to a Burman mind somewhat resembles the boasted perfection of their saints of old. His discourse continued about half an hour; and, at the close, the whole assembly burst out into a short prayer, after which all rose and retired. This man exhibits twice every evening, in different places. Indeed, he is the only popular lay preacher in the place. As for the priests, they preach on special occasions only, when they are drawn from their seclusion and inactivity by the solicitations of their adherents.

April 28. Nothing interesting through the day. At night, encountered a bitter opposer; he had visited Bengal, and some foe to missions had poisoned his mind; he manifested a most virulent spirit. I felt that he would most gladly be foremost in destroying us. But through divine grace, I was enabled to treat him with meekness and gentleness, and he finally left me politely. He appeared to be rich, and had several followers. In the evening, there were some hopeful appearances in Mrs. Judson's female meeting — a meeting which she has recommenced since public worship has been set up in the zayat.

April 29. A precious case has just occurred. A young man of twenty-four, by name Moung Koo, happened to stroll in last Sunday, and was present at worship. He appeared to be rather wild and noisy, though his manners were respectful. He took a tract, and went away. This morning he made his appearance again, and has been with me about two hours. I have been enabled, through divine assistance, to give him a great deal of truth, and especially to expatiate with some feeling on the love and sufferings of the Saviour. The truth seems to have taken hold of his mind. And though he is quick and sensible, and has some savage fire in his eye, he is very docile, and ready to drink in the truth, without the numberless cavils and objections which are so common among the Burmans. He engaged to come next Sunday, promised to pray constantly, and gave me his name, that I might pray for him, that he might be a disciple of Christ, and be delivered from hell. I feel considerable attachment to this young man, and my heart goes forth to the mercy seat in behalf of his precious soul.

April 30. I was agreeably surprised in the morning to see the young man of yesterday come again so soon. He staid all the forenoon, and seemed desirous of hearing as much as possible about religion. Several others came and went. A very busy day; hardly time to prepare these minutes to be forwarded by a vessel which leaves this port for Bengal early to-morrow morning.

May 1, 1819. Burman day of worship; of course many visitors; among the rest, Moung Nau, a man who was with me several hours yesterday; but, from his silence and reserve, excited little attention or hope. To-day, however, I begin to think better of him. Moung Koo came again at night, and appeared pretty well. These two men, with the two persons from Kambet, of the 27th, I call the fruits of the week. But let us see who of them will remember the day of worship.

May 2, Lord's day. About three o'clock, the quiet and modest Moung Nau came in and took his usual place. For the others we looked in vain. About thirty present at worship. Very few paid much attention, or probably received any benefit.

May 3. Among the vistors of to-day was a respectable man, formerly an officer, now a merchant, resident at Little Bridge, a village contiguous to Kambet. After long and various conversation, in which he paid close and respectful attention, he said that he was a person not a little versed in Burman literature, but that he now saw he had erred in all; he regretted that he had lived two years in the neighborhood without knowing me; to-day was an auspicious day; he wished to become my disciple, would read my writings with attention, and come as often as possible.

May 5. Moung Nau has been with me several hours. I

begin to think that the grace of God has reached his heart. He expresses sentiments of repentance for his sins, and faith in the Saviour. The substance of his profession is, that from the darknesses, and uncleannesses, and sins of his whole life, he has found no other Saviour but Jesus Christ; nowhere else can he look for salvation; and therefore he proposes to adhere to Christ, and worship him all his life long.

It seems almost too much to believe that God has begun to manifest his grace to the Burmans; but this day I could not resist the delightful conviction that this is really the case. PRAISE AND GLORY BE TO HIS NAME FOREVERMORE. Amen.

May 6. Moung Nau was again with me a great part of the day. He appears to be slowly growing in religious knowledge, and manifests a teachable, humble spirit, ready to believe all that Christ has said, and obey all that he has commanded. He is thirty-five years old; no family, middling abilities, quite poor, obliged to work for his living, and therefore his coming, day after day, to hear the truth affords stronger evidence that it has taken hold of his mind. May the Lord graciously lead his dark mind into all the truth, and cause him to cleave inviolably to the blessed Saviour.

May 8. Burman day of worship. Thronged with visitors through the day. Had more or less company, without intermission, for about eight hours. Several heard much of the gospel, and engaged to come again. Moung Nau was with me a great part of the day, and assisted me much in explaining things to new comers. Towards night a man came in, by name Moung Shwaa Oo, whom I think it time to mention particularly, as he has visited me several times; and though, like Moung Nau, apparently backward at first, he appears to be really thoughtful. He is a young man of twenty-seven, of very pleasant exterior, and evidently in good circumstances. Poor Moung Koo, who appeared so forward at first, alas! too forward! has quite discontinued his visits. No news yet from the villagers of Kambet and Little Bridge.

May 9, Lord's day. Moung Shwaa Oo came in the

morning, and staid through the whole day. Only two or three of all I conversed with yesterday came again. Had, however, an assembly of thirty. After worship, some warm disputation. I begin to feel that the Burmans cannot stand before the truth. In the course of the conversation, Moung Nau declared himself a disciple of Christ, in presence of a considerable number; and even Moung Shwaa Oo appeared to incline the same way.

May 10. Early in the morning, Moung Nau came to take leave, being obliged to go to a distance after timber, his usual occupation. I took him alone and prayed with him, and gave him a written prayer to help him in his private devotion. He received my parting instructions with great attention and solemnity; said he felt that he was a disciple of Christ; hoped that he should be kept from falling; desired the prayers of us all; expressed a wish that, if he held out some time after his return, we would allow him to profess Christ in baptism; and so he departed. The Lord Jesus go with him and bless him. He is poor. I felt a great desire to give him something, but thought it safer to put no temptation in his way. If, on his return, he still cleaves to Christ, his profession will be more satisfactory than it would be if he had any expectations from us.

May 11. Had more or less company, from morning till night; among the rest, Moung Shwaa Oo, and two or three others, who appear to be pretty well satisfied that the Buddhist religion has no foundation. Conversation was very animated, and somewhat encouraging; but I wanted to see more seriousness, and more anxiety to be saved from sin.

Heard much, to-day, of the danger of introducing a new religion. All agreed in opinion that the king would cut off all who embraced it, being a king who could not bear that his subjects should differ in sentiment from himself; and who has, for a long time, persecuted the friends of the established religion of the empire, because they would not sanction all his innovations. Those who seemed most favorably disposed whispered me that I had better not stay in Rangoon and talk to common people, but go directly to the "*lord of life and death.*" If he approved of the religion, it would spread rapidly; but, in the present state of things, nobody would dare to prosecute their inquiries, with the fear of the king before their eyes. They brought forward the case of the Kolans, a sect of Burmans who have been proscribed and put to death under several reigns. I tried to set them right in some points, and encourage them to trust in the care of an almighty Saviour; but they speak low and look around fearfully when they mention the name of the "*owner of the sword.*"

May 13. Had company all day, without intermission. About noon, Moung Nau came in, having given up his journey on account of the unfaithfulness of his employer. His behavior and conversation were very satisfactory. He regrets the want of a believing associate, but declares his determination of adhering to Christ, though no Burman should ever join him.

Moung Shwaa Doan, a man who has attended two Sundays and made some occasional visits, was with me several hours. He professes to have felt the truth of this religion ever since he first heard about it, and now desires to be a disciple of Christ. He has obtained, I find, considerable knowledge of the Christian system, but does not appear to have much sense of his own sins. May the Spirit teach him what man cannot.

May 15. Moung Nau has been with me all day, as well as yesterday. He is anxious to be received into our company, and thinks it a great privilege to be the first among the Burmans in professing the religion of Jesus Christ. He has been told plainly that he has nothing to expect in this world but persecution, and perhaps death; but he thinks it better to die for Christ, and be happy hereafter, than to live a few days and be forever wretched. All the members of the mission have, at different times, conversed with him, and are satisfied that a work of grace is begun in his heart.

May 16, Lord's day. In the forenoon, a man came in from Kyaikasan, a neighboring village, and listened with more apparent sincerity than is commonly manifested the first visit. He had received a tract about a year ago, and had thought considerably on the subject.

About the usual number was present at worship, but a larger proportion than common were strangers. A lawyer belonging to the viceroy, and some other respectable persons, were present, and gave me much trouble, without, I fear, receiving any benefit. Moung Shwaa Doan was present, and appeared pretty well after worship. Moung Shwaa Oo has, I suppose, returned to Henthadah, the next city above Rangoon. He took no leave of me; yet I cannot give up all hope of him. The last visit, he said he should constantly read my writings, and pray to the eternal God.

May 17. Moung Nau has received an advantageous offer to go to Ava, in the employ of a boat owner. We were afraid to dissuade him from accepting, as he has no way of getting a living, and equally unwilling to have him absent several months. At length we advised him not to go, and he at once acquiesced.

May 21. Had several attentive hearers; among the rest Moung A, who says that the good news has taken hold of his mind. I have been so frequently disappointed in visitors who appeared promising the first time, but never came again, that I have lost all credit in early professions; yet I cannot but hope well of this man, especially as Moung Nau appeared to like him better than any other inquirer.

May 22. We have taken Moung Nau to live with us, intending to employ him in copying some small things for distribution, which we cannot get printed at present, and allow him ten ticals a month. Our principal object, however, is to keep him in the way of instruction, hoping that he will ultimately be useful to his countrymen.

At night, Moung A came the second time, and appeared anxious to know the way of salvation. But I am grieved to find that he is going away on business to-morrow morning, and will be absent a long time.

May 23, Lord's day. The Kyaikasan villager Moung Nyo, mentioned last Sunday, came again, with three companions.

He staid the whole day, and appears to be in the same state of mind as Moung A. Both say they are convinced that there is an eternal God; that having denied him all their lives, and of course lived contrary to his commands, their sins are great; and that the news of salvation, through the death of the Son of God, is good news. Thus far they venture. But whether the Spirit has given, or will give, them true love to the Saviour, and thus enable them to trust in him, we must leave for time to ascertain.

June 6, Lord's day. Had two interesting visitors. They were present at worship, and staid till dark — certain they should come again — but will they?

After partaking of the Lord's supper in the evening, we read and considered the following letter of Moung Nau, which he wrote of his own accord: —

"I, Moung Nau, the constant recipient of your excellent favor, approach your feet. Whereas my Lord's three have come to the country of Burmah, — not for the purposes of trade, but to preach the religion of Jesus Christ, the Son of the eternal God, — I, having heard and understood, am, with a joyful mind, filled with love.

"I believe that the divine Son, Jesus Christ, suffered death, in the place of men, to atone for their sins. Like a heavy-laden man, I feel my sins are very many. The punishment of my sins I deserve to suffer. Since it is so, do you, sirs, consider that I, taking refuge in the merits of the Lord Jesus Christ, and receiving baptism, in order to become his disciple, shall dwell one with yourselves, a band of brothers, in the happiness of heaven, and therefore grant me the ordinance of baptism.* It is through the grace of Jesus Christ that you, sirs, have come by ship from one country and continent to another, and that we have met together. I pray my Lord's

---

* At the time of writing this, not having heard much of baptism, he seems to have ascribed an undue efficacy to the ordinance. He has since corrected his error; but the translator thinks it the most fair and impartial to give the letter just as it was written at first.

three that a suitable day may be appointed, and that I may receive the ordinance of baptism.

"Moreover, as it is only since I have met with you, sirs, that I have known about the eternal God, I venture to pray that you will still unfold to me the religion of God, that my old disposition may be destroyed, and my new disposition improved."

We have all, for some time, been satisfied concerning the reality of his religion, and therefore voted to receive him into church fellowship, on his being baptized, and proposed next Sunday for administering the ordinance.

June 20, Lord's day. For the last fortnight, have had but little company at the zayat, owing probably to the rains which have now fully set in. The town has also been in great confusion, in prospect of the viceroy's departure for Ava. We have been called on to pay another tax of fifteen ticals — got off with paying half. Have had several other molestations from petty officers of government. Concluded to postpone Moung Nau's baptism till the viceroy be fairly off. He left Rangoon yesterday, and has arrived at the next village, which is a kind of rendezvous to the vast multitude of boats that accompany him.

To-day, Moung Shwaa Doan appeared again, after an absence of several weeks, and a little revived our hopes concerning him. Several, whom I have particularly mentioned, have discontinued their visits, though I am satisfied that they are convinced of the falsity of the Burman religion, and of the truth of the Christian. I cannot possibly penetrate their motives. Whether, after several visits, they meet with some threatening suggestion, that awakens their fears of persecution, or whether, at a certain stage in their inquiries, they get such an insight into the gospel as rouses the enmity of the carnal heart, I am not able, from my experience hitherto, to ascertain.

June 21 The town is in the utmost anxiety and alarm. Order after order has reached our viceroy, to hasten his return to Ava, with all the troops under arms. Great news are whispered. Some say there is a rebellion; some say the king is sick, some that he is dead. But none dare to say this plainly. It would be a crime of the first magnitude; for the "*lord of land and water*" is called immortal. The eldest son of his eldest son (his father being dead) has long been declared the heir of the crown; but he has two very powerful uncles, who, it is supposed, will contest his right; and in all probability the whole country will soon be a scene of anarchy and civil war.

June 22. Out all the morning, listening for news, uncertain whether a day or an hour will not plunge us into the greatest distress. The whole place is sitting in sullen silence, expecting an explosion. About 10 o'clock, a royal despatch boat pulls up to the shore. An imperial mandate is produced. The crowds make way for the sacred messengers, and follow them to the high court, where the authorities of the place are assembled. Listen ye: The immortal king, wearied, it would seem, with the fatigues of royalty, has gone up to amuse himself in the celestial regions. His grandson, the heir apparent, is seated on the throne. The young monarch enjoins on all to remain quiet, and wait his imperial orders.

It appears that the Prince of Toung Oo, one of his uncles, has been executed, with his family and adherents, and the Prince of Pyee placed in confinement. There has probably been bloody work; but it seems, from what has transpired, that the business has been settled so expeditiously that the distant provinces will not feel the shock.

June 23. Had some encouraging conversation with Moung Thahlah, a young man who has been living in our yard several months. He has lately made me several visits at the zayat, and appeared very thoughtful and teachable. To-day, on being asked the state of his mind, he replied, with some feeling, that he and all men were sinners, and exposed to future punishment; that according to the Buddhist system, there was no way of pardon; but that according to the religion which I taught, there was not only a way of pardon, but a way of enjoying endless happiness in heaven; and that, therefore, he wanted to believe in Christ. I stated to him, as usual, that he must think much on the love of Christ, and pray to God for an enlightened and loving heart, and then gave him a form of prayer suited to his case.

In the female evening meeting, his sister, Ma Baik, whose husband also lives in our yard, manifested considerable feeling, especially when Mrs. Judson prayed with her alone, and expressed strong desire to obtain an interest in the Saviour.

June 27, Lord's day. There were several strangers present at worship. After the usual course, I called Moung Nau before me, read and commented on an appropriate portion of Scripture, asked him several questions concerning his *faith*, *hope*, and *love*, and made the baptismal prayer, having concluded to have all the preparatory exercises done in the zayat. We then proceeded to a large pond in the vicinity, the bank of which is graced with an enormous image of Gaudama, and there administered baptism to the first Burman convert. O, may it prove the beginning of a series of baptisms in the Burman empire which shall continue in uninterrupted succession to the end of time!

July 4, Lord's day. We have had the pleasure of sitting down, for the first time, to the Lord's table with a converted Burman; and it was my privilege — a privilege to which I have been looking forward with desire for many years — to administer the Lord's supper in two languages. And now let me, in haste, close my journal for transmission to the board.

Letter from Mrs. Judson.

RANGOON MISSION HOUSE, June 2, 1819.

In my last, I mentioned Mr. Judson's commencing public preaching in a building which we had erected for that purpose, and which you will in future know by the name *zayat*. Little did I think, when I last wrote, that I should so soon have the joyful intelligence to communicate, that one Burman has embraced the Christian religion, and given good evidence of being a true disciple of the dear Redeemer. This event, this single trophy of victorious grace, has filled our hearts with sensations hardly to be conceived by Christians in Christian countries. This event has convinced us that God can and does operate on the minds of the most dark and ignorant, and that he makes his own truths, his own word, the instrument of operation. It serves also to encourage us to hope that the Lord has other chosen ones in this place. As Mr. Judson has given some account of the first impressions of this man, and as I have had him particularly under my instruction since his conversion, I will give you some of his remarks in his own words, with which you will be much interested. " Besides Jesus Christ, I see no way of salvation. He is the Son of the God who has no beginning, no end. He so loved and pitied men that he suffered death in their stead. My mind is sore on account of the sins I have committed during the whole of my life, particularly in worshipping a false god. Our religion, pure as it may be, does not purify the minds of those who believe it; it cannot restrain from sin. But the religion of Jesus Christ makes the mind pure. His disciples desire not to grieve him by sinning. In our religion there is no way to escape the punishment due to sin; but, according to the religion of Christ, he himself has died in order to deliver his disciples. I wish all the Burmans would become his disciples; then we should meet together as you do in your country; then we should all be happy together in heaven. How great are my thanks to Jesus Christ for sending teachers to this country, and how great are my thanks to the teachers for coming! Had they never come and built that zayat, I should never have heard of Christ and the true God. I mourn that so much of my life passed away before I heard of this religion. How much I have lost!" It is peculiarly interesting to see with what eagerness he drinks in the truths from the Scriptures. A few days ago, I was reading with him Christ's Sermon on the Mount. He was deeply impressed and unusually solemn. "These words," said he, "take hold on my very liver; they make me tremble. Here God commands us to do every thing that is good in secret, not to be seen of men. How unlike our religion is this! When Burmans make offerings to the pagodas, they make a great noise with drums and musical instruments, that others may see how good they are. But this religion makes the mind fear God; it makes it, of its own accord, fear sin." When I read this passage, "Lay not up for yourselves treasures," &c., he said, "What words are these! It does not mean that we shall take the silver and gold from this world, and carry them to heaven; but that, by becoming the disciples of Jesus, we shall live in such a manner as to enjoy heaven when we die." We have taken him into our employ for the present, as a copyist, though our primary object was to have him near us, that we might have a better opportunity of knowing more of him before he received baptism, and of imparting to him more instruction than occasional visits might afford. Mornings and evenings he spends in reading the Scriptures, and when we all meet in the hall for family worship, he comes and sits with us; though he cannot understand, he says he can think of God in his heart.

Journal continued.

Rangoon, July 6, 1819. First day of Burman Lent. All the members of government went to the great pagoda, and took the oath of allegiance to the new king. At night a large company came in, all disposed to condemn, and ridicule, and persecute, influenced by one very virulent opposer, who has been here before. When the storm was gathering, Moung Nau withdrew. A most trying time, chiefly rendered so by its being an indication of the spirit which generally prevails among this people, though commonly restrained by politeness, and which, we fear, may issue in something worse and more to be dreaded than our own personal inconvenience and persecution.

Heard, at the same time, that several of the people who live about us, and commonly attend worship, had privately gone to the pagoda and made an offering. All these circumstances conspire to make us feel desolate, and to put our trust in God alone.

July 10. Some pleasant conversation with Moung Thahlah. Seldom a day passes in which he does not spend an hour or two with me or Moung Nau. This man is rather superior to the common Burmans in point of abilities, and, though not very learned, he has read much more than the generality. He is much superior to any one resident on our premises, and, if converted, would be a valuable acquisition to the mission.

July 12. Considerable company all day. Moung E, whose name I have not yet mentioned, though he has made several visits, broke through his usual reserve, and acknowledged his love for this religion, and thought he should become a disciple, and not return to Tavoy, whence he lately came on some government business. Moung Thahlah appears to be really earnest in his desires to become a disciple of Christ. His sister, Ma Baik, who was lately drawn into a high quarrel with a neighbor, expresses much sorrow, and says that the circumstance has convinced her more than ever of the evil of her heart, and the necessity of getting a new nature before she can be a disciple.

Much encouraged by the events of the day. The Lord can bless the feeblest means, the most unworthy instruments. Praised be his name.

July 13. The sixth anniversary of the commencement of the mission.

July 18, Lord's day. Discoursed on Matt. vii. 13, concerning the broad way to destruction and the narrow way to life; the hearers considerably attentive. To-day our viceroy has returned to Rangoon, being forbidden to proceed to Ava before taking the oath of allegiance to the new king.

July 19. Had some particular conversation with Moung Thahlah on his spiritual state. He says that the more he reads and hears of the Christian religion, the more inclined he becomes to believe and embrace it, but fears that his weakness and sinfulness incapacitate him for keeping his holy precepts as it becomes a professing disciple.

July 29. Finished revising the tract for a new edition.

have considerably enlarged it, particularly by adding several prayers; so that it now stands, "A View of the Christian Religion, in four Parts, Historical, Practical, Preceptive, and Devotional." We intend sending the manuscript to Serampore, with a request to brother Hough that he will get it printed in a large edition of five thousand copies. The first edition, of one thousand, is nearly exhausted. Such, indeed, is the demand for it since the opening of the zayat, that we should have given away all the copies long ago, had we not been doubtful about a fresh supply.

July 30. Had several attentive visitors; one of them staid two hours, and appeared very unwilling to leave. His mild manners and apparent openness of heart tended to heighten my desires and stimulate my prayers for the salvation of his precious soul.

August 1, Lord's day. Several respectable and wealthy people present at worship. One of them visited me several months ago, and received a tract. Since then he has thought much, and has conversed with some of his friends about the new religion. Yesterday he sent word that he was coming up to worship, with several others. He was rather reserved today, and said but little, yet sufficient to show that he has imbibed some new notions, which, whether they issue in conversion or not, will, I trust, prevent his ever settling down in his old system. His name is Oo Yah.

August 2. The family of the old gentleman of yesterday came to see Mrs. Judson, saying that their father had sent them to listen to the instructions of the female teacher. They appear to be one of the most civilized families we have met with, behaved with much politeness and respect, and begged leave to come again.

August 3. Several neighbors of Oo Yah spent some time at the zayat, and listened attentively.

August 7. Brother Wheelock embarked for Bengal, but in so low a state that we fear the voyage, instead of being beneficial, will tend to shorten his life.

August 8, Lord's day. Several strangers present at worship; a larger assembly than usual.

August 19. Had more company than for a fortnight past. Very little intermission through the day. Just at night, three strangers came in, and listened with remarkable attention. They appeared to be particularly impressed with the value of a happy immortality, as far superior to any thing which the Burman system can offer, and also with the love of Christ, as far surpassing all other love.

August 20. Several Mahometans came in, having heard, as they said, that I denounced all religions but the Christian. We had a long debate on the divine Sonship of Jesus Christ. At first it was very offensive to them; but when the doctrine of the Trinity was explained to them, they had no other objection to make than that the Koran denied that God had a Son. They appeared to be somewhat desirous of knowing what is truth; said they should come again, and must either convert me to Mahometanism or themselves become converted to Christianity. I discovered afterwards that one of them was a priest; but he kept in the background, and said nothing.

August 21. Have not lately mentioned Moung Thahlah, though he has continued to visit me regularly. To-day I had a conversation with him, that almost settled my mind that he is really a renewed man. He, however, thinks he is not, because he finds his heart so depraved that he cannot perfectly keep the pure commands of Christ.

August 22, Lord's day. Two of the adherents of the Mangen teacher, the popular preacher that I mentioned some time ago, were present at worship. I had much conversation with them, in the course of which I so clearly refuted their system, in two or three instances, that they could not refrain from an involuntary expression of assent and approbation. They directly said, however, that it was impossible for them to think of embracing a new religion. I never saw more clearly the truth of our Saviour's words, "Ye *will not* come unto me."

After worship, had another conversation with Moung Thahlah. He hopes that he is a disciple of Jesus Christ in heart, but wants to know whether a profession of religion is indispensable to salvation. He fears the persecution that may hereafter come on those who forsake the established religion of the empire. I gave him such explanation as I thought suitable, and left him with the solemn consideration, that unless he loved Christ above his own life, he did not love him sincerely, and ought not to hope that he is interested in his redemption.

His sister, Ma Baik, is in a very similar state. She has been particularly attentive and solemn in her appearance for some time past. In such cases it is a great consolation to reflect that the tender, compassionate Saviour will not break the bruised reed, or quench the smoking taper. He will strengthen and restore the one, and the other he will light up with his own celestial fire.

August 24. Another conversation with Moung Thahlah, which at length forces me to admit the conviction that he is a real convert; and I venture to set him down the second disciple of Christ among the Burmans. He appears to have all the characteristics of a new-born soul, and though rather timid in regard to an open profession, has, I feel satisfied, that love to Christ which will increase and bring him forward in due time.

August 26th. Was visited by Moung Shwa-gnong, a teacher of considerable distinction. He appears to be half deist and half sceptic, the first of the sort I have met with among the Burmans. He, however, worships at the pagodas, and conforms to all the prevailing customs. We had a very interesting debate, in which we cleared up some preliminaries, preparatory, I hope, to future discussions.

Just at night, the viceroy, returning from an excursion of pleasure, passed by our road, for the first time since the zayat was built. He was seated on a huge elephant, attended by his guards and numerous suite, and, as he passed, eyed us very narrowly. Several Burmans were sitting round me and Mrs. Judson.

After he had passed some time, two of his private secretaries came in with a viceregal order, signifying his highness's desire to see the manner in which printing is executed. I replied, that the teacher who understood printing had gone to Bengal, taking the types with him, and that it was impossible to comply with the order. They departed with evident dissatisfaction.

August 27. In order to obviate the bad effects of the report of the officers of yesterday, I went to the government house, intending to have a personal interview with the viceroy. After waiting two hours in the levee hall, he made his appearance, and on recognizing me, immediately inquired about the press and types. I told him my story, and when he understood that I was ignorant of the art of printing, he appeared satisfied to let the matter rest. In the course of the few words which passed between us, he said that he wished to get several Burman books printed. He seemed to be more kindly disposed towards me than formerly; but it seems impossible to introduce the subject of religion in his presence, surrounded, as he always is, with a crowd of courtiers and secretaries, petitioners and lawyers.

Had but just returned home, when the teacher Moung Shwa-gnong came again, and staid from noon till quite dark. We conversed incessantly the whole time; but I fear that no real impression is made on his proud, sceptical heart. He, however, promised to pray to the eternal God, through Jesus Christ, and appeared, at times, to be in deep thought. He is a man of very superior argumentative powers. His conversion would probably shake the faith of many.

August 28. A great deal of company all day long. Quite worn out with incessant toil. At night, the viceroy again passed, as the day before yesterday; and the same secretaries came in, saying, that it was the viceroy's desire that I should translate and get printed, if possible, some historical writings of my country. I told them I would take the first opportunity of calling on his highness.

August 31. A man, by name Moung Ing, has visited the zayat five or six days in succession. At first, a variety of other company prevented my attending much to him, and he conversed chiefly with Moung Nau, and employed himself in reading Matthew. He once told Moung Nau that he had long been looking after the true religion, and was ready to wish that he had been born a brute, rather than to die in delusion, and go to hell. Sunday I conversed with him largely, and his attention, during worship, was very close and solemn. To-day he has made me half inclined to believe that a work of grace is begun in his soul. He says that he formerly had some idea of an eternal God from his mother, who was christened a Roman Catholic, in consequence of her connection with a foreigner; but that the idea was never rooted in his mind until he fell in with the zayat. Within a few days, he has begun to pray to this God. He is quite sensible of his sins, and of the utter inefficacy of the Boodhist religion, but is yet in the dark concerning the way of salvation, and says that he wants to know more of Christ, that he may love him more. Lord Jesus, give him the saving knowledge of thine adorable self!

September 1. Moung Thahlah continues to express similar sentiments to those already noted; is still afraid of persecution and death, but professes to be laboring to obtain that love to Christ, and faith in him, which will raise him above the fear of man; and particularly requests us to pray that he may obtain these graces.

September 3. A great crowd of company through the whole day, the teacher Moung Shwa-gnong, from ten o'clock till quite dark, with several of his adherents. He is a complete Proteus in religion, and I never know where to find him. We went over a vast deal of ground, and ended where we began, in apparent incredulity. After his adherents, however, were all gone, he conversed with some feeling; owned that he knew nothing, and wished me to instruct him; and when he departed, he prostrated himself, and performed the *sheeko* — an act of homage which a Burman never performs but to an acknowledged superior.

After he was gone, Moung Ing, who has been listening all day, followed me home to the house, being invited to stay with Moung Nau through the night. We conversed all the evening, and his expressions have satisfied us all that he is one of

God's chosen people. His exercises have been of a much stronger character than those of the others, and he expresses himself in the most decided manner. He desires to become a disciple in profession, as well as to be in Christ, and declares his readiness to suffer persecution and death for the love of Christ. When I stated the danger to which he was exposing himself, and asked him whether he loved Christ better than his own life, he replied, very deliberately and solemnly, " When I meditate on this religion, I know not what it is to love my own life." Thus the poor fisherman Moung Ing is taken, while the learned teacher Moung Shwa-gnong is left.

September 5, Lord's day. A very dull day — not one stranger present at worship. In the evening Moung Thahlah was a spectator of our partaking of the Lord's supper. Moung Ing could not be present. He lives at some distance, and is getting ready to go to sea, pursuant to his purpose before he became acquainted with us. We have endeavored to dissuade him from going, and to keep him near us ; but we are afraid that his circumstances will not allow him to comply with our advice and his own inclinations.

September 6. Spent the evening in conversing with Moung Byaa, a man who, with his family, has lived near us for some time, a regular attendant on worship, an indefatigable scholar in the evening school, where he has learned to read, though fifty years old, and a remarkably moral character. In my last conversation, some time ago, he appeared to be a thorough legalist, relying solely on his good works, but yet sincerely desirous of knowing and embracing the truth. The greater part of the evening was spent in discussing his erroneous views; his mind seemed so dark and dull of apprehension, that I was almost discouraged. Towards the close, however, he seemed to obtain some evangelical discoveries, and to receive the humbling truths of the gospel in a manner which encourages us to hope that the Spirit of God has begun to teach him. The occasion of this conversation was my hearing that he said that he intended to become a Christian, and be baptized with Moung Thahlah. He accordingly professes a full belief in the eternal God, and his Son Jesus Christ.

September 7. Am grieved that Moung Ing comes no more. Presume he has gone off, contrary to our advice, and was reluctant to take leave of us under such circumstances.

September 10. Surprised by a visit from Moung Ing. It appears that he has been confined at work on board the vessel in which he is engaged, and has not been ashore for several days. As the vessel is certainly going to-morrow, he got leave of absence for a short time, and improved it in running out to the zayat. I was exceedingly glad, as it afforded me an opportunity of giving him some parting instructions, and praying with him alone. He appears very well indeed. He is quite distressed that he has so far engaged himself, and appears desirous of getting off, and returning to us, if possible; but I have very little hope of his succeeding. I believe, however, that he is a real Christian, and that, whenever he dies, his immortal soul will be safe, and that he will praise God forever for his transient acquaintance with us. The Lord go with him and keep him.

September 11. Moung Shwa-gnong has been with me all day. It appears that he accidentally obtained the idea of an eternal Being about eight years ago; and it has been floating about in his mind, and disturbing his Boodhistic ideas ever since. When he heard of us, which was through one of his adherents, to whom I had given a tract, this idea received considerable confirmation; and to-day he has fully admitted the truth of this first grand principle. The latter part of the day we were chiefly employed in discussing the possibility and necessity of a divine revelation, and the evidence which proves that the writings of the apostles of Jesus contain that revelation; and I think I may say that he is half inclined to admit all this. He is certainly a most interesting case. The way seems to be prepared in his mind for the special operation of divine grace. Come, Holy Spirit, heavenly Dove!

His conversion seems peculiarly desirable, on account of his superior talents and extensive acquaintance with Burmese and Pali literature. He is the most powerful reasoner I have yet met with in this country, excepting my old teacher, Oo Oungmen, (now dead,) and he is not at all inferior to him.

September 15. Moung Thahlah spent the evening with me in asking several questions on difficult passages in Matthew. At the close I asked him whether he yet loved Christ more than his own life; he understood my meaning, and replied that he purposed to profess the Christian religion, and began to think seriously of being baptized. His sister, Ma Baik, appears to have lost her religious impressions.

September 16. After having lately made two unsuccessful attempts to get an interview with the viceroy, I this day succeeded. He inquired about the historical writings. I told him I was not so well acquainted with that style of writing in Burman as with the religious style, and then presented him with a tract, as a specimen of what I could do. He delivered it to a secretary, and on hearing the first sentence, remarked that it was the same with a writing he had already heard, and *that he did not want that kind of writing.* I suppose that one of the secretaries, to whom I had formerly given a tract, presented it without my knowledge.

September 18. Moung Shwa-gnong has been with me a few hours; had spent the greater part of the day with Oo Yah, the merchant that I mentioned some time ago, conversing on religion. Our interview chiefly passed in discussing his metaphysical cavils.

September 19, Lord's day. The teacher and Oo Yah came to worship, according to their agreement of yesterday, accompanied with part of the family of the latter, and several respectable men of their acquaintance, so that the assembly consisted of about fifty. Some paid profound attention, and some none at all. After the exercises, Oo Yah seemed afraid to have it appear that he had any acquaintance with me, and kept at a distance. They finally all dropped away but the teacher, who staid, as usual, till quite dark. He is, in many respects, a perfect enigma; but just before he left, a slight hope began to spring up in our minds that his proud heart was yielding to the cross. He confessed that he was constrained to give up all dependence on his own merits and his literary attainments; that he had sinned against God all his life long, and that, therefore, he deserved to suffer hell. And then he asked, with some feeling, how he could obtain an interest in the merits and salvation of Jesus Christ. He appears to have a considerable share of that serious solemnity which I have observed to characterize the few who persevere in their religious inquiries, and which has been wanting in every instance of mere temporary promise. O that he may be brought in, if it is not too great a favor for this infant mission to receive.

September 20. One of the three visitors of the 19th of August came again, and, though a long interval has elapsed, his appearance is quite encouraging. He says, feelingly, that he knows nothing, is distressed at the thought of dying in his present ignorance and uncertainty, and wants to find some kind of salvation.

September 26, Lord's day. Moung Shwa-gnong came, with several adherents. Some warm conversation before worship, but nothing personal. During worship, discoursed from, "Fear not them that kill the body," &c. My discourse was chiefly intended for Moung Thahlah and Moung Byaa; but the latter was absent, on account of sickness. After worship, the teacher immediately departed with his people, without even saying a word. Fear he has taken some offence.

October 5. Received a visit from the teacher. My hopes of his conversion are very low. He is settling down in Deism, and evidently avoids all conversation of a personal nature.

October 6. Conversation with Moung Thahlah and Moung Byaa, which revives my hopes of their coming forward before long. They are both growing in religious knowledge, and give evidence of being in the exercise of gracious feelings.

October 7. Was rejoiced, in the morning, to see the teacher Moung Shwa-gnong come again so soon. We spent the whole day together, uninterrupted by other company. In the forenoon, he was as crabbed as possible; sometimes a Berkeïeian, sometimes a Humeite or complete sceptic. But in the afternoon he got to be more reasonable, and before he left he obtained a more complete idea of the atonement than I have commonly been able to communicate to a Burman. He exclaimed, "That is suitable; that is as it should be," &c. But whether this conviction resulted from a mere philosophic view of the propriety and adaptedness of the way of salvation through Jesus Christ, or from the gracious operations of the Holy Spirit, time must discover. I hardly venture to hope the latter. O Lord, the work is thine! O come, Holy Spirit!

October 23. Have for some days been wondering at the long absence of the teacher. To-day heard a report that he has been summoned by the viceroy to give an account of his heretical sentiments.

At night Moung Thahlah and Moung Byaa presented a paper, professing their faith in Jesus Christ, and requesting to be baptized, but in private. We spent some time with them. They appear to have experienced divine grace; but we advised them, as they had so little love to Christ as not to dare to die for his cause, to wait and reconsider the matter.

October 29. The teacher came again, after an interval of three weeks; but he appears to be quite another man. He has not been personally summoned, as we heard; but, through the instigation of the Mangen teacher, he was mentioned before the viceroy as having renounced the religion of the country. The viceroy gave no decisive order, but merely said, "Inquire further about him." This reached the ears of Moung Shwa-gnong; and he directly went to the Mangen teacher, and, I suppose, apologized, and explained, and flattered. He denies that he really recanted, and I hope he did not; but he is evidently falling off from the investigation of the Christian religion. He made but a short visit, and took leave as soon as he could decently.

November 1. One of the greatest festivals in the year. The crowds are truly immense and overwhelming. We vacated the zayat, as we have several days of late, beginning to query whether it is prudent to go on boldly in proclaiming a new religion, at the hazard of incensing the government, and drawing down such persecution as may deter all who know us from any inquiry.

November 2. This is the birthday and the coronation day of the new king. All the grandees of the empire have, for some time past, been assembling at Ava, to be present at the august celebration.

November 6. The two candidates for baptism again presented their urgent petition that they might be baptized, not absolutely in private, but about sunset, away from public observation. We spent some hours in again discussing the subject with them and with one another. We felt satisfied that they were humble disciples of Jesus, and were desirous of receiving this ordinance purely out of regard to his command and their own spiritual welfare; we felt that we were all equally exposed to danger, and needed a spirit of mutual candor, and forbearance, and sympathy; we were convinced that they were influenced rather by desires of avoiding unnecessary exposure than by that sinful fear which would plunge them into apostasy in the hour of trial; and when they assured us that, if actually brought before government, they could not think of denying their Saviour, we could not conscientiously refuse their request, and therefore agreed to have them baptized to-morrow at sunset. The following is a literal translation of the paper presented this evening:—

"Moung Byaa and Moung Thahlah venture to address the two teachers: Though the country of Burmah is very far distant from the country of America, yet the teachers, coming by ship the long way of six months, have arrived at this far distant country of Burmah, and town of Rangoon, and proclaimed the propitious news by means of which we, having become acquainted with the religion, know that there is an eternal God in heaven, and that there is a divine Son, the Lord Jesus Christ, deserving of the highest love; and we know that the Lord Jesus Christ, the divine Son, endured, on account of all his disciples, sufferings and death, even severe sufferings on a cross, in their stead. On account of our sins, we were like persons laden with a very heavy burden. On account of our many sins, we found no deliverance, no place of refuge, and our minds were distressed. In this state remaining, the two teachers produced the sacred system from the Scriptures, and we became informed of the existence of the one God, and of the facts that the divine Son, the Lord Jesus Christ, redeemed with his sacred life all who love and trust in him, and, in order to save his disciples from hell, suffered death in their stead. Now we know that we have sinned against the sacred One, and we know, assuredly, that if we become disciples of the divine Son, the Lord Jesus Christ, we shall be saved from the hell which we deserve. We desire to become disciples, and with the two teachers, like children born of the same mother, to worship the true God, and observe the true religion.

"On searching in the Scriptures for ancient rules and customs it does not appear that John and other baptizers administered baptism on any particular time, or day, or hour. We, therefore, venture to beg of the two teachers, that they will grant that on the 6th day of the wane of the Tanzoungmong moon, (November 7,) at six o'clock at night, we may this once receive baptism at their hands."

November 7, Lord's day. We had worship as usual, and the people dispersed. About half an hour before sunset, the two candidates came to the zayat, accompanied by three or four of their friends; and after a short prayer, we proceeded to the spot where Moung Nau was formerly baptized. The sun was not allowed to look upon the humble, timid profession. No wondering crowd crowned the overshadowing hill. No hymn of praise expressed the exultant feelings of joyous hearts. Stillness and solemnity pervaded the scene. We felt, on the banks of the water, as a little, feeble, solitary band. But perhaps some hovering angels took note of the event with more interest than they witnessed the late coronation; perhaps Jesus looked down on us, pitied and forgave our weaknesses, and marked us for his own; perhaps, if we deny him not, he will acknowledge us, another day, more publicly than we venture at present to acknowledge him.

In the evening we all united in commemorating the dying love of our Redeemer; and I trust we enjoyed a little of his gracious presence in the midst of us.

November 10. This evening is to be marked as the date of the first Burman prayer meeting that was ever held. None present but myself and the three converts. Two of them made a little beginning — such as must be expected from the first essay of converted heathens. We agreed to meet for this purpose every Tuesday and Friday evening, immediately after family worship, which in the evening has for some time been conducted in Burman and English, and which these people, and occasionally some others, have attended.

November 14, Lord's day. Have been much gratified to find that this evening the THREE CONVERTS REPAIRED TO THE ZAYAT, AND HELD A PRAYER MEETING OF THEIR OWN ACCORD.

November 26. On taking our usual ride this morning, to bathe in the mineral tank, we were accosted, on one of the pagoda roads, by the Mangen teacher, and peremptorily forbidden to ride there in future on pain of being beaten. On our return we inquired into the affair, and find that the viceroy has really issued an order, at the instigation of this teacher, that henceforth no person wearing a hat, shoes, or umbrella, or mounted on a horse, shall approach within the sacred ground belonging to the great pagoda, which ground extends on some sides half a mile, and comprises all the principal roads; so that in future we must take a circuitous route in the woods, if we wish to visit our usual place of resort. This consideration, however, is very trifling, compared with another. The viceroy's order is quite unprecedented in Rangoon, and indicates a state of feeling on the subject of religion very unfavorable to our missionary designs. Since the death of the old king, who was known to be in heart hostile to religion, people have been more engaged than ever in building pagodas, making sacred offerings, and performing the public duties of their religion. They are just now engaged in new gilding the great pagoda, called Shwaa Dagón, which is considered the most sacred in the country, on account of its containing six or eight hairs of Gaudama.

Ever since the affair of Moung Shwa-gnong, there has been an entire falling off at the zayat. I sometimes sit there whole days without a single visitor, though it is the finest part of the year, and many are constantly passing. We and our object are now well known throughout Rangoon. None wish to call, as formerly, out of curiosity, and none dare to call from a principle of religious inquiry. And were not the leaders in ecclesiastical affairs confident that we shall never succeed in making converts, I have no doubt we should meet with direct persecution and banishment.

Our business must be fairly laid before the emperor. If he frown upon us, all missionary attempts within his dominions will be out of the question. If he favor us, none of our enemies, during the continuance of his favor, can touch a hair of our heads. But there is a greater than the emperor, before whose throne we desire daily and constantly to lay this business. O Lord Jesus, look upon us in our low estate, and guide us in our dangerous course!

November 21. Moung Shwa-gnong has been with us the greater part of the day, and a little revived our hopes concerning him.

November 27. This day brother Colman and myself came to a final decision to proceed to Ava without delay, and lay our business before the emperor.

November 29. Letters from Bengal and America, the first for six months. Learned the particulars of the melancholy end of our lamented brother Wheelock. The news of his death reached us some time ago. Learned also that brother Hough intends staying in Bengal. The tract which we forwarded is not yet printed — a circumstance which occasions us much regret, as we hoped to have obtained some copies to carry up to Ava.

December 4. Another visit from Moung Shwa-gnong. After several hours spent in metaphysical cavils, he owned that he did not believe any thing he had said, and had only been trying me and the religion, being determined to embrace nothing but what he found unobjectionable and impregnable. "What," said he, "do you think that I would pay you the least attention if I found you could not answer all my questions, and solve all my difficulties?" He then proceeded to say, that he really believed in God, his Son Jesus Christ, the atonement, &c. Said I, knowing his deistical weakness, "Do you believe all that is contained in the book of Matthew, that I have given you? In particular, do you believe that the Son of God died on a cross?" "Ah," replied he, "you have caught me now. I believe that he suffered death, but I cannot admit that he suffered the shameful death of the cross." "Therefore," said I, "you are not a disciple of Christ. A true disciple inquires not whether a fact is agreeable to his own reason, but whether it is in the book. His pride has yielded to the divine testimony. Teacher, your pride is still unbroken. Break down your pride, and yield to the word of God." He stopped and thought. "As you utter those words," said he, "I see my error. I have been trusting in my own reason, not in the word of God." Some interruption now occurred. When we were again alone, he said, "This day is different from all the days on which I have visited you. I see my error in trusting in my own reason; and I now believe the crucifixion of Christ, because it is contained in the Scripture." Some time after, speaking of the uncertainty of life, he said he thought he should not be lost, though he died suddenly. Why? "Because I love Jesus Christ." "Do you really love him?" "No one that really knows him can help loving him." And so he departed.

December 10. A few days ago, we succeeded in purchasing a boat for the journey to Ava, after having spent a whole week in the search. Have since been employing workmen to cover it and put it in order.

Yesterday we applied to the viceroy for a pass to go up to the golden feet, and lift up our eyes to the golden face. He granted our request in very polite terms.

I must now close up my journal, to be sent on board ship

to-morrow morning. We expect to leave Rangoon in about a week. My next will probably contain some account of our journey up the river, and our reception at court. O Lord, send *now* prosperity; yet not my will, but thine, be done.

To the Corresponding Secretary.

RANGOON, December 8, 1819.

REV. AND DEAR SIR: Being about to leave Rangoon, on a visit to the court of Ava, we feel it our duty briefly to state to the board the reasons of our procedure.

From the opening of the zayat, last spring, till within a month or two ago, our affairs appeared to be in a prosperous state. Many daily heard the gospel; cases of hopeful inquiry frequently occurred; no serious opposition appeared; and during the little interval of quiet, four precious souls, the first fruits of Burmah, gave evidence of having obtained the grace of God, three of whom have been baptized.

Some time, however, before the baptism of the last two, the death of the emperor, and the succession of the heir apparent to the crown, operated to give a new aspect to the religious affairs of this country. The former emperor was known to be, in heart, hostile to the priests of Boodh; and he frequently manifested his sentiments in such acts of persecution as kept the religion in a low and declining state. On his death, the hopes of the priests and their adherents began to revive; and every discovery of the new emperor's friendly disposition has tended to restore the religious establishment of the country to its former privileges and rank. The change effected even in Rangoon, under our own eyes, is very remarkable.

Soon after these events began to transpire, and probably in consequence of them, our fifth inquirer, a teacher of learning and influence, was accused, before the viceroy, of having embraced heretical sentiments. The viceroy gave no decisive order, but directed further inquiry to be made. Upon this our friend went to the principal informant, who is at the head of ecclesiastical affairs in Rangoon, made his peace with him, and discontinued his visits to the zayat. This circumstance spread an alarm among all our acquaintance, and combining with the general state of things, and the prevailing expectation that our attempts would shortly be proscribed, occasioned a complete falling off at the zayat; and with the exception of the teacher above named, who has lately visited us in private, and those who have already joined us, we are deserted.

Under these circumstances, it appears to us that there remains but one course of proceeding — to go directly into the imperial presence, lay our missionary designs before the throne, and solicit toleration for the Christian religion. By this proceeding, we hope to discover the real feelings and sentiments of the emperor. We hope to ascertain, as distinctly as possible, whether he is devoted to Boodhism, or has imbibed in any degree the opinions of his grandfather, and disguises them at present, from motives of policy merely. If the former be the case, he will prohibit our missionary work, and we shall be under the necessity of leaving his dominions. If the latter be the case, and he be, in any measure, pleased with the Christian system, he will, we hope, give us at least such private encouragement as will enable us to prosecute our work without incurring the charge of rashness and enthusiasm.

In approaching the throne, we desire to have a simple dependence on the presence and power of our Saviour, and a single eye to his glory. We have indeed no other ground of hope; we ought to have no other view. We trust that, if the set time to favor Burmah is come, He who is wonderful in counsel, and excellent in working, will open a wide and effectual door for the promulgation of divine truth. But if the Lord has other purposes, it becomes us meekly to acquiesce, and willingly to sacrifice our dearest hopes to the divine will. We rest assured, that, in either case, the perfections of God will be displayed, and desire to be thankful that we are allowed to be in any way instrumental in contributing to that display.

We commend ourselves and the mission, in the present solemn crisis, to the sympathies and prayers of our fathers and brethren, and the Christian public, and remain,

    Rev. and dear sir,

        Your devoted servants in the Lord,

                A. JUDSON, JR.,
                J. COLMAN.

CHAPTER VIII.

FIRST VISIT TO AVA. — RETURN TO RANGOON. — PROGRESS OF THE GOSPEL. — NEW STATION AT CHITTAGONG. — FAILURE OF MRS. JUDSON'S HEALTH. — VOYAGE TO BENGAL.

1819-1820.

THE following chapter contains the journal of Mr. Judson during his first visit to Ava, and his account of the gradual progress of the gospel at Rangoon. It will be perceived that the religion of Christ extended itself, as at the beginning, by transforming into its own image one individual after another, and that in all cases the moral feelings of the converts were essentially the same. They acknowledged the attributes of God, and their relations and obligations to him; they became deeply conscious of their sin against him, and of their desert of his endless displeasure; they fled for refuge from deserved wrath to the cross of Christ, and, humbly penitent for their past sins, they hoped for pardon in consequence of the great atonement; and the proof that all this was real was found in the fact that from these moral exercises there sprang up an entirely new life — a life of piety to God and charity to man. This is precisely what we all witness every day among ourselves, wherever the gospel is preached in simplicity and godly sincerity, or communicated by private conversation, and carried directly to the consciences of men.

If we would bear these facts in mind, we should discover that the work of converting men is essentially the same whether it be attempted in a heathen or in a civilized country. The means and the manner of employing them are in both cases identical. The means consist in proclaiming the message of salvation, and the manner is proclaiming it publicly, and from house to house. Nor is this labor, in either case, to be confined to ministers of the gospel, though they must undoubtedly devote themselves to it more exclusively, since it is their appropriate, daily calling. It is the duty of every disciple to make disciples. " Let every one that heareth say, Come." And I think that, whenever this great duty is neglected, piety decays, men are not converted, and the profession of Christianity soon becomes a name rather than a reality. The Acts of the Apostles teach us the manner in which the gospel was promulgated in the earliest age of the church. It were well if Christians at home and abroad were guided more implicitly by the examples of those who spake as they were moved by the Holy Ghost. We are never commanded to use indirect means for the conversion of men. No dispensation is granted to any class of men by which they are permitted to perform this duty by deputy. Every disciple of Christ is commanded meekly and lovingly to urge the claims of the gospel upon his brethren immediately around him. If he would labor for the next generation, he must labor for them by converting the generation now living. God has appointed but one way for the reformation of men. It is the inculcation of moral truth upon others by those who have already felt its influence on themselves.

The object of Mr. Judson's first visit to Ava was, to present to the king a petition in favor of religious liberty, or, in other words, to ask a ruler to permit his subjects to worship God. It has always seemed to me worth while to inquire whether a course of this kind should be pursued by missionaries of the gospel.

In the first place, I observe that the first Christian preachers never adopted such a measure. They made known to every one "the things which they had seen and heard." When arrested, they declared that they acted under a higher than human authority — an authority which they durst not, and would not, disobey. When driven from one city, they fled to another, every where preaching, but never asking permission to preach.

Again: if we strip this question of all accessories, it resolves itself simply into this: Can we properly ask one man to permit another man to obey God? Can the refusal of one man to grant this permission discharge another man from the obligation to worship his Creator? I think that but one answer can be given to these questions, and that this answer must preclude us from submitting a matter of this kind to the jurisdiction of man. By asking such a permission, we seem to admit the authority of a ruler to grant or to refuse it, and hence, in some sort, promise to be governed by his decision. This we have no right to do; and hence I think it doubtful whether the permission should ever be sought.

It may be urged that the case is modified when the government is a despotism, and life and property depend upon the caprice of a single man. I do not see that this alters the case in any essential particular. Under such a government, the permission would be specially worthless; for what was granted to-day might be withdrawn to-morrow. And again: when we have taught our converts to ask permission to obey God, what should we tell them to do when this permission is withdrawn? In the present instance, however, this contingency did not arise. The wisdom of God had decreed that the seed of a Christian church in Burmah should be sown amid persecution almost unto death. In this soil it took root, and bore fruit, and its fruit has remained. The appeals to the government were unheeded; but the jungles of Burmah and its adjoining provinces have resounded with the praises of God and of his Christ. A type of piety has been created which could scarcely have existed under the fostering care of government. It is my opinion that Dr. Judson, in the later years of his life, would have looked upon this subject in the light in which I have now presented it.

Journal.

December 21. After having made arrangements for our wives' residence in town during our absence, brother Colman and myself embarked. Our boat is six feet wide in the middle, and forty feet long. A temporary deck of bamboos is laid throughout, and on the hinder part of the boat the sides are raised with thin boards, and a covering of thatch, and mats tied on, so as to form two low rooms, in which we can just sit and lie down. Our company consists of sixteen besides ourselves: ten rowmen, a steersman, a head man,— whose name is inserted in our passport, and who, therefore, derives a little authority from government, — a steward or cook for the company,— which place is filled by our trusty Moung Nau,— our own cook, a Hindoo washerman, and an Englishman, who, having been unfortunate all his life, wishes to try the service of his Burman majesty; and this last personage may be called our gunner, he having charge of several guns and blunderbusses, which are indispensable on account of the robbers that infest the river.

We have been much perplexed in fixing on a present for the emperor, without which no person unauthorized can appear in his presence. Our funds were evidently inadequate to the purchase of articles which would be valuable to him in a pecuniary point of view: when we considered, also, that there ought to be a congruity between the present and our character, we selected that book which we hope to be allowed to translate under his patronage, the BIBLE, in six volumes, covered with gold leaf, in Burman style, and each volume enclosed in a rich wrapper. For presents to other members of government, we have taken several pieces of fine cloth and other articles.

Thus manned and furnished, we pushed off from the shores of Rangoon. The teacher Moung Shwa-gnong had not been to see us for several days, ashamed, probably, of having declined accompanying us; but just as we were pushing off, we saw his tall form standing on the wharf. He raised his hand to his head, and bade us adieu, and continued looking after the boat until a projecting point shut Rangoon and all its scenes from our view. When shall we redouble this little point? Through what shall we pass ere the scene now snatched away be re-presented? The expedition on which we have entered, however it may terminate, is unavoidably fraught with consequences momentous and solemn beyond all conception. We are penetrating into the heart of one of the great kingdoms of the world, to make a formal offer of the gospel to a despotic monarch, and through him to the millions of his subjects. May the Lord accompany us, and crown our attempt with the desired success, if it be consistent with his wise and holy will.

At night we moored by the banks of Kyee-myen-daing. It was near this place that, a few days ago, one of the boats belonging to Mr. G., late collector of Rangoon, was attacked by robbers, and the steersman and another man killed at a single shot. We felt unwilling to remain at this village, but found it necessary.

On the 30th reached Kah-noung, a considerable town, about ninety miles from Rangoon. Here we met a special officer from Bassein, with a detachment of men, sent in pursuit of a band of robbers who lately made a daring attack on a large boat, wounded and beat off the people, and took plunder to the amount of fifteen hundred ticals. The commander offered us an escort for the journey of to-morrow, which lies through a dangerous tract of country; but we declined accepting, as we should have been obliged to give the people presents, without deriving any substantial assistance in the hour of danger. Strict watch all night.

January 17, 1820. Reached Pugan, a city celebrated in Burman history, being, like Pyee, the seat of a former dynasty. It is about two hundred and sixty miles from Rangoon.

January 18. Took a survey of the splendid pagodas and extensive ruins in the environs of this once famous city. Ascended as far as possible some of the highest edifices, and, at the height of one hundred feet, perhaps, beheld all the country round, covered with temples and monuments of every sort and size; some in utter ruin, some fast decaying, and some exhibiting marks of recent attention and repair. The remains of the ancient wall of the city stretched beneath us. The pillars of the gates, and many a grotesque, decapitated relic of antiquity, checkered the motley scene. All conspired to suggest those elevated and mournful ideas which are attendant on a view of the decaying remains of ancient grandeur; and, though not comparable to such ruins as those of Palmyra and Balbec, (as they are represented,) still deeply interesting to the antiquary, and more deeply interesting to the Christian missionary. Here, about eight hundred years ago, the religion of Boodh was first publicly recognized and established as the religion of the empire. Here, then, Ah-rah-han, the first Boodhist apostle of Burmah, under the patronage of King Anan-ra-tha-men-zan, disseminated the doctrines of atheism, and taught his disciples to pant after annihilation, as the supreme good. Some of the ruins before our eyes were probably the remains of pagodas designed by himself. We looked back on the centuries of darkness that are past. We looked forward, and Christian hope would fain brighten the prospect. Perhaps we stand on the dividing line of the empires of darkness and light. O shade of Ah-rah-han, weep over thy falling fanes; retire from the scenes of thy past greatness. But thou smilest at my feeble voice. Linger, then, thy little remaining day. A voice mightier than mine, a still small voice, will ere long sweep away every vestige of thy dominion. The churches of Jesus will soon supplant these idolatrous monuments, and the chanting of the devotees of Boodh will die away before the Christian hymn of praise.

January 25. Passed Old Ava, the seat of the dynasty immediately preceding the present, and Tsah-gaing, a place of some note, distinguished for its innumerable pagodas, and the residence of one or two late emperors, and about noon drew up to O-ding-man, the lower landing-place of New Ava, or Amarapoora, about three hundred and fifty miles from Rangoon. At our present distance of nearly four miles from the city, (and we cannot get nearer this season,) it appears to the worst advantage. We can hardly distinguish the golden steeple of the palace amid the glittering pagodas, whose summits just suffice to mark the spot of our ultimate destination.

January 26. We set out early in the morning, called on Mr. G., late collector of Rangoon, and on Mr. R., who was formerly collector, but is now out of favor. Thence we entered the city, passed the palace, and repaired to the house of Mya-day-men, former viceroy of Rangoon, now one of the public ministers of state, (woon-gyee.) We gave him a valuable present, and another of less value to his wife, the lady who formerly treated Mr. G. with so much politeness. They both received us very kindly, and appeared to interest themselves in our success. We, however, did not disclose our precise object, but only petitioned leave to behold the golden face. Upon this, his highness committed our business to Moung Yo, one of his favorite officers, and directed him to introduce us to Moung Zah, one of the private ministers of state, (a-twen-woon,) with the necessary orders. This particular favor of Mya-day-men prevents the necessity of our petitioning and feeing all the public ministers of state, and procuring formal permission from the high court of the empire.

In the evening, Moung Yo, who lives near our boat, called on us to say that he would conduct us to-morrow. We lie down in sleepless anxiety. To-morrow's dawn will usher in the most eventful day of our lives. To-morrow's eve will close on the bloom or the blight of our fondest hopes. Yet it is consoling to commit this business into the hands of our heavenly Father — to feel that the work is his, not ours; that the heart of the monarch before whom we are to appear is under the control of Omnipotence; and that the event will be ordered in the manner most conducive to the divine glory and the greatest good. God may, for the wisest purposes, suffer our hopes to be disappointed; and if so, why should short-sighted, mortal man repine? Thy will, O God, be ever done; for thy will is inevitably the wisest and the best.

January 27. We left the boat, and put ourselves under the conduct of Moung Yo. He carried us first to Mya-day-men, as a matter of form; and there we learned that the emperor had been privately apprised of our arrival, and said, " Let them be introduced." We therefore proceeded to the palace. At the outer gate, we were detained a long time, until the various officers were satisfied that we had a right to enter, after which we deposited a present for the private minister of state, Moung Zah, and were ushered into his apartments in the palace yard. He received us very pleasantly, and ordered us to sit before several governors and petty kings, who were waiting at his levee. We here, for the first time, disclosed our character and object — told him that we were missionaries, or " propagators of religion;" that we wished to appear before the emperor, and present our sacred books, accompanied with a petition. He took the petition into his hand, looked over about half of it, and then familiarly asked several questions about our God and our religion, to which we replied. Just at this crisis, some one announced that the golden foot was about to advance; on which the minister hastily rose up, and put on his robes of state, saying that he must seize the moment to present us to the emperor. We now found that we had unwittingly fallen on an unpropitious time, it being the day of the celebration of the late victory over the Kathays, and the very hour when his majesty was coming forth to witness the display made on the occasion. When the minister was dressed, he just said, "How can you propagate religion in this empire? But come along." Our hearts sank at these inauspicious words. He conducted us through various splendor and parade, until we ascended a flight of stairs, and entered a most magnificent hall. He directed us where to sit, and took his place on one side; the present was placed on the other; and Moung Yo and another officer of Mya-day-men sat a little behind. The scene to which we were now introduced really surpassed our expectation. The spacious extent of the hall, the number and magnitude of the pillars, the height of the dome, the whole completely covered with gold, presented a most grand and imposing spectacle. Very few were present, and those evidently great officers of state. Our situation prevented us from seeing the farther avenue of the hall; but the end where we sat opened into the parade which the emperor was about to inspect. We remained about five minutes, when every one put himself into the most respectful attitude, and Moung Yo whispered that his majesty had entered. We looked through the hall as far as the pillars would allow, and presently caught sight of this modern Ahasuerus. He came forward unattended, — in solitary grandeur, — exhibiting the proud gait and majesty of an eastern monarch. His dress was rich, but not distinctive; and he carried in his hand the gold-sheathed sword, which seems to have taken the place of the sceptre of ancient times. But it was his high aspect and commanding eye that chiefly riveted our attention. He strided on. Every head excepting ours was now in the dust. We remained kneeling, our hands folded, our eyes fixed on the monarch. When he drew near, we caught his attention. He stopped, partly turned towards us — "Who are these?" "The teachers, great king," I replied. "What, you speak Burman — the priests that I heard of last night?" "When did you arrive?" "Are you teachers of religion?" "Are you like the Portuguese priest?" "Are you married?" "Why do you dress so?" These and some other similar questions we answered, when he appeared to be pleased with us, and sat down on an elevated seat, his hand resting on the hilt of his sword, and his eyes intently fixed on us. Moung Zah now began to read the petition; and it ran thus:—

"The American teachers present themselves to receive the favor of the excellent king, the sovereign of land and sea. Hearing that, on account of the greatness of the royal power, the royal country was in a quiet and prosperous state, we arrived at the town of Rangoon, within the royal dominions, and having obtained leave of the governor of that town to come up and behold the golden face, we have ascended and reached the bottom of the golden feet. In the great country of America, we sustain the character of teachers and explainers of the contents of the sacred Scriptures of our religion. And since it is contained in those Scriptures, that, if we pass to other countries, and preach and propagate religion, great good will result, and both those who teach and those who receive the religion will be freed from future punishment, and enjoy, without decay or death, the eternal felicity of heaven, — that royal permission be given, that we, taking refuge in the royal power, may preach our religion in these dominions, and that those who are pleased with our preaching, and wish to listen to and be guided by it, whether foreigners or Burmans, may be exempt from government molestation, they present themselves to receive the favor of the excellent king, tne sovereign of land and sea."

The emperor heard this petition, and stretched out his hand. Moung Zah crawled forward and presented it. His majesty began at the top, and deliberately read it through. In the mean time, I gave Moung Zah an abridged copy of the tract, in which every offensive sentence was corrected, and the whole put into the handsomest style and dress possible. After the emperor had perused the petition, he handed it back without saying a word, and took the tract. Our hearts now rose to God for a display of his grace. " O, have mercy on

Burmah! Have mercy on her king!" But, alas! the time was not yet come. He held the tract long enough to read the first two sentences, which assert that there is one eternal God, who is independent of the incidents of mortality, and that beside him, there is no God; and then, with an air of indifference, perhaps disdain, he dashed it down to the ground. Moung Zah stooped forward, picked it up, and handed it to us. Moung Yo made a slight attempt to save us by unfolding one of the volumes, which composed our present, and displaying its beauty; but his majesty took no notice. Our fate was decided. After a few moments, Moung Zah interpreted his royal master's will, in the following terms: "Why do you ask for such permission? Have not the Portuguese, the English, the Mussulmans, and people of all other religions, full liberty to practise and worship according to their own customs? In regard to the objects of your petition, his majesty gives no order. In regard to your sacred books, his majesty has no use for them: take them away."

Something was now said about brother Colman's skill in medicine; upon which the emperor once more opened his mouth, and said, "Let them proceed to the residence of my physician, the Portuguese priest; let him examine whether they can be useful to me in that line, and report accordingly. He then rose from his seat, strided on to the end of the hall, and there, after having dashed to the ground the first intelligence that he had ever received of the eternal God, his Maker, his Preserver, his Judge, he threw himself down on a cushion, and lay listening to the music, and gazing at the parade spread out before him.

As for us and our present, we were huddled up and hurried away, without much ceremony. We passed out of the palace gates with much more facility than we entered, and were conducted first to the house of Mya-day-men. There his officer reported our reception, but in as favorable terms as possible; and as his highness was not apprised of our precise object, our repulse appeared probably to him not so decisive as we knew it to be. We were next conducted two miles through the heat of the sun and dust of the streets of Ava to the residence of the Portuguese priest. He very speedily ascertained that we were in possession of no wonderful secret, which would secure the emperor from all disease, and make him live forever; and we were accordingly allowed to take leave of the reverend inquisitor, and retreat to our boat.

At this stage of the business, notwithstanding the decided repulse we had received, we still cherished some hope of ultimately gaining our point. We regretted that a sudden interruption had prevented our explaining our objects to Moung Zah in that familiar and confidential manner which we had intended; and we determined, therefore, to make another attempt upon him in private.

January 28. Early in the morning we had the pleasure of seeing our friend Mr. G. coming to our boat. It may not be amiss to mention that he is the collector who was chiefly instrumental in relieving us from the exorbitant demand which, a few months ago, was made upon us in Rangoon. He now told us that he had heard of our repulse, but would not have us give up all hope; that he was particularly acquainted with Moung Zah, and would accompany us to his house, a little before sunset, at an hour when he was accessible. This precisely accorded with our intentions.

In the afternoon, therefore, we called on Mr. G., and he went with us into the city. On the way we paid a visit to the wife of the present viceroy of Rangoon, whose eldest son is married to the only daughter of the present emperor. We carried a present, and were, of course, kindly received.

Thence we went to the house of Moung Zah, some way beyond the palace. He received us with great coldness and reserve. The conversation, which we carried on chiefly through Mr. G., it is unnecessary to detail. Suffice it to say, that we ascertained beyond a doubt, that the policy of the Burman government, in regard to the toleration of any foreign religion, is precisely the same with the Chinese; that it is quite out of the question, whether any of the subjects of the emperor, who embrace a religion different from his own, will be exempt from punishment; and that we, in presenting a petition to that effect, had been guilty of a most egregious blunder, an unpardonable offence. Mr. G. urged every argument that we suggested, and some others. He finally stated that, if we obtained the royal favor, other foreigners would come and settle in the empire, and trade would be greatly benefited. This argument alone seemed to have any effect on the mind of the minister, and looking out from the cloud which covered his face, he vouchsafed to say, that if we would wait some time, he would endeavor to speak to his majesty about us. From this remark it was impossible to derive any encouragement; and having nothing further to urge, we left Mr. G., and bowing down to the ground, took leave of this great minister of state, who, under the emperor, guides the movements of the whole empire.

It was now evening. We had four miles to walk by moonlight. Two of our disciples only followed us. They had ventured as near as they durst to the door of the hall of audience, and listened to words which sealed the extinction of their hope and ours. For some time we spoke not.

> "Some natural tears we dropped, but wiped them soon;
> The world was all before us, where to choose
> Our place of rest, and Providence our guide."

And, as our first parents took their solitary way through Eden, hand in hand, so we took our way through this great city, which, to our late imagination, seemed another Eden, but now, through the magic touch of disappointment, seemed blasted and withered, as if smitten by the fatal influence of the cherubic sword.

Arrived at the boat, we threw ourselves down, completely exhausted in body and mind. For three days we had walked eight miles a day, the most of the way in the heat of the sun, which, even at this season, in the interior of these countries, is exceedingly oppressive, and the result of our travels and toils has been — the wisest and best possible; a result which, if we could see the end from the beginning, would call forth our highest praise. O, slow of heart to believe and trust in the constant presence and overruling agency of our own almighty Saviour.

January 29. We again rose early, and, having considered the last words of Moung Zah, wrote down our request in the most concise and moderate terms, and sent it to Mr. G., with a message that he would once more see Moung Zah, lay the paper before him, and ascertain unequivocally whether there was any possibility of gaining our point by waiting several months.

The rest of the day, and the next, being Lord's day, we remained in the boat.

January 31, Monday. Mr. G. called upon us, with our little paper in his hand. "I have shown your paper to Moung Zah, and begged him not to deceive you, but to say distinctly what hopes you might be allowed to entertain. He replied, 'Tell them that there is not the least possibility of obtaining the object stated in this paper, should they wait ever so long; therefore let them go about their business.'"

I now thought of one more expedient; and, taking out the manuscript tract the emperor threw down, I handed it to Mr. G. "This is a brief view of the Christian religion. Do you present it, in our name, to Moung Zah, and persuade him to read it, or hear it read. We have indeed no hope of its efficacy; but it is our last resort, and God may help us in the extremity." He took it with some feeling, and promised to do his best.

Before leaving us, he communicated the important intelligence that the emperor, flushed with his late victory over the Kathays, had determined on war with Siam, and intended next fall to march in person to Pegu, and there establish his head quarters.

After Mr. G. left us, we went to visit Mr. R. We were formerly acquainted with him in Rangoon, and he would now have assisted us had he not been out of the favor of the new emperor. We related all our proceedings, and the disappointment of our hopes. "I knew it would be so," replied he, "when you first called on me; but I was not willing to discourage you from making trial for yourselves." He then related the following story, with the substance of which we were previously acquainted: —

"About fifteen years ago, the Roman Catholic priests converted to their faith a Burman teacher of talents and distinction. They took great pains to indoctrinate him thoroughly in their religion, and entertained great hope of his usefulness in their cause. After his return from Rome, whither they had sent him to complete his Christian education, he was accused by his nephew, a clerk in the high court of the empire, of having renounced the established religion. The emperor, who, it must be remembered, was far from approving the religion of Boodh, ordered that he should be compelled to recant. The nephew seized his uncle, cast him into prison and fetters, caused him to be beaten and tortured continually, and at length had recourse to the torture of the iron mall. With this instrument he was gradually beaten, from the ends of his feet up to his breast, until his body was little else but one livid wound. Mr. R. was one of those that stood by and gave money to the executioners, to induce them to strike gently. At every blow, the sufferer pronounced the name of Christ, and declared afterwards that he felt little or no pain. When he was at the point of death, under the hands of his tormentors, some persons who pitied his case went to the emperor with a statement that he was a madman, and knew not what he was about; on which the emperor gave orders for his release. The Portuguese took him away, concealed him until he was able to move, then sent him privately in a boat to Rangoon, and thence by ship to Bengal, where he finished his days. Since then, the Roman priests, of whom there are four only in the country, have done nothing in the way of proselyting, but confined their labors to their own flocks, which are composed of the descendants of foreigners. The man who accused his uncle is now the very first of the private ministers of state, taking rank before Moung Zah. Furthermore, the present chief queen, who has great influence with his majesty, is, and ever has been, particularly attached to the religion and the priests of Boodh." Mr. R. also confirmed the information we had received of approaching war with Siam.

Our case could not be more desperate. We directly returned to the boat, and ordered our people to sell off all unnecessary articles, and be ready to start as soon as our passport could be obtained.

February 1. Went to Mya-day-men, and applied for a passport to Rangoon. He appeared willing to oblige us, but said we must make formal application to Moung Zah.

February 2. Went to various places, and made various inquiries and applications for a passport. Ascertained that it was absolutely necessary, in our case, to procure a special one from the high court of the empire.

February 3. Sent our head man and some of our people with a petition to Moung Zah. After they had gone off, we called on Mr. G. He informed us that the tract had been presented to Moung Zah, and read in his presence. After listening to the whole of it, instead of throwing it down, or even returning it, he committed it to one of his people to keep, saying to Mr. G., "The doctrines and commands are very good; but it will be a long time before Burmans can be convinced that there is a God and Saviour." After this interview with Moung Zah, Mr. G. was summoned before the emperor. His majesty, among other things, inquired about the foreign teachers. Mr. G. told him our country, our character, and our object. The emperor observed that the Portuguese priest had told him very different things, particularly that we were a sect of Zandees, (a race very obnoxious to former emperors.) Mr. G. endeavored to vindicate our character, but the emperor appeared quite averse to hearing any thing in our favor. "What," said he, laughing, "they have come presuming to convert us to their religion. Let them leave our capital. We have no desire to receive their instructions. Perhaps they may find some of their countrymen in Rangoon who may be willing to listen to them."

Mr. G. now advised us to obtain a royal order protecting us personally from molestation, while we should remain in the country. "Otherwise," said he, "as it will be notorious that you have solicited royal patronage, and been refused, you will lie at the mercy of every ill-disposed person."

This suggestion of Mr. G. occupied our thoughts the rest of the day. We finally concluded that, as such an order would cost several hundred ticals, we would prefer trusting in the Lord to keep us and our poor disciples.

At night our people returned. They had found Moung Zah, and presented the petition for a passport, to which he made no other reply but, " Come to-morrow."

February 4. Sent the people, early in the morning, with a handsome present to Moung Zah. They returned late at night. He accepted the present, and assured them he would do our business to-morrow.

February 5. Sent the people as usual, our trusty Moung Nau accompanying them, with a quantity of silver. This did the business. Late in the evening I had the pleasure of taking into my hand the pointed palm leaf. It has cost us the value of thirty dollars.

February 6. Pushed off from the beach of O-ding-man. I could moralize half an hour on the apt resemblance, the beautiful congruity, between the desolate state of our feelings and the sandy, barren surface of this miserable beach. But "'tis idle all." Let the beach and our sorrow go together. Something better will turn up to-morrow.

February 12. Reached Pyee, two hundred and thirty miles from Ava; our descent on the river being, of course, much more rapid than our ascent. Here, to our great surprise, we met with the teacher Moung Shwa-gnong. He had come up from Rangoon, a few days ago, to visit an old acquaintance, who was dangerously ill; expects to return shortly; would gladly go with us, if we could wait a day or two. We stated to him all our adventures at court, the distressing result of the expedition, and the present danger of propagating or professing the religion of Christ, and wound off with the story of the iron mall. He appeared to be less affected and intimidated by the relation than we could have expected. Indeed, his language was rather too high for the occasion. I therefore told him that it was not for him that we were concerned, but for those who had become disciples of Christ. When they were accused and persecuted, they could not worship at the pagodas, or recant before the Mangen teacher. He felt the force of the reflection, and tried to explain his past conduct. "Say nothing," said I; "one thing you know to be true — that, when formerly accused, if you had not, in some way or other, satisfied the mind of the Mangen teacher, your life would not now be remaining in your body." "Then," said he, "if I must die, I shall die in a good cause. I know it is the cause of truth." He then repeated, with considerable emphasis, the most prominent points of his present faith, as follows: "*I believe in the eternal God, in his Son Jesus Christ, in the atonement which Christ has made, and in the writings of the apostles, as the true and only word of God.* Perhaps," continued he, "you may not remember that, during one of my last visits, you told me, that I was trusting in my own understanding, rather than the divine word. From that time I have seen my error, and endeavored to renounce it. You explained to me also the evil of worshipping at pagodas, though I told you that my heart did not partake in the worship. Since you left Rangoon, I have not lifted up my folded hands before a pagoda. It is true, I sometimes follow the crowd, on days of worship, in order to avoid persecution; but I walk up one side of the pagoda, and walk down the other. Now, you say that I am not a disciple. What lack I yet?" I was now satisfied that he had made a little advance, since our last interview, which required a corresponding advance on my side. I replied, therefore, "Teacher, you may be a disciple of Christ in heart, but you are not a full disciple. You have not faith and resolution enough to keep all the commands of Christ, particularly that which requires you to be baptized, though in the face of persecution and death. Consider the words of Jesus, just before he returned to heaven, 'He that believeth and is baptized shall be saved.'" He received this communication in profound silence, and with that air which I have observed to come upon him when he takes a thing into serious consideration. Soon after, I hinted our intention of leaving Rangoon, since the emperor had virtually prohibited the propagation of the Christian religion, and no Burman, under such circumstances, would dare to investigate, much less to embrace it. This intelligence evidently roused him, and showed us that we had more interest in his heart than we thought. "Say not so," said he; "there are some who will investigate, notwithstanding; and rather than have you quit Rangoon, I will go myself to the Mangen teacher, and have a public dispute. I know I can silence him. I know the truth is on my side." "Ah," said I, " you may have a tongue to silence him, but he has a pair of fetters and an iron mall to tame you. Remember that." This was the substance of our conversation, though much more prolix; and he left us about nine o'clock at night.

This interview furnished matter for conversation till past midnight, and kept us awake much of the remainder of the night. Perhaps, on arriving in Rangoon, we shall find the disciples firm, and some others seriously inquiring. Perhaps we shall discover some appearances of a movement of the divine Spirit. Perhaps the Lord Jesus has a few chosen ones, whom he intends to call in, under the most unpropitious and forbidding circumstances. Perhaps he intends to show that it is not by might, nor by power, but by his Spirit. In a word, perhaps, in the last extremity, God will help us. Ought we, then, hastily to forsake the place? Ought we to desert those of the disciples that we cannot take with us, and some others, for whom perhaps Christ died, in such an interesting crisis of their fate? Would it be rashness to endeavor to trust in God, and maintain the post, though disallowed by government, and exposed to persecution? But again: can we bear to see our dear disciples in prison, in fetters, under torture? Can we stand by them, and encourage them to bear patiently the rage of their persecutors? Are we willing to participate with them? Though the spirit may be sometimes almost willing, is not the flesh too weak?

Pondering on such topics as these, a little ray of hope seemed to shine out of the darkness of our despair. But it was not like the soft beam of the moon, which kindly shines on the path of the benighted pilgrim, and guides him to a place of shelter. It was rather like the angry gleam of lightning, which, while for a moment it illumines the landscape around, discloses the black magazines of heaven's artillery, and threatens death to the unwary gazer.

February 18. Arrived in Rangoon.

February 20, Lord's day. In the evening I called the three disciples together, and gave them a connected account of the affair at Ava, that they might have a full understanding of the dangers of their present condition, and the reasons of our intended departure from Rangoon. We expected that, after being destitute of all the means of grace for some time, and after seeing their teachers driven away from the presence of their monarch in disgrace, they would become cold in their affections, and have but little remaining zeal for a cause thus proscribed and exposed to persecution. We thought that, if one out of the three remained firm, it was as much as we could reasonably hope for. But how delightfully were we disappointed! They all, to a man, appeared immovably the same; yea, rather advanced in zeal and energy. They vied with each other in trying to explain away difficulties, and to convince us that the cause was not yet quite desperate. But whither are the teachers going? was, of course, an anxious inquiry. We told them that it was our intention never to desert Burmah; but that, since the emperor had refused to tolerate our religion, we thought it necessary to leave for a time those parts of the empire which are immediately under his dominion; that there is a tract of country lying between Bengal and Arracan, which, though under the government of Bengal, is chiefly inhabited by Arracanese, who speak a language similar to the Burman, the district being really a part of Arracan, one component part of the present Burman empire; that formerly a teacher from Bengal (De Bruyn) lived at Chittagong, the principal town in that district, and baptized several converts, who, at his death, were left destitute of all instruction to the present time; and that, in view of these considerations, it was our purpose to proceed thither, in hope of finding that toleration which was denied us in Rangoon. We then asked them, severally, what they would do. Moung Nau had previously told us that he would follow us to any part of the world. He was only afraid that he should be a burden to us; for, not being acquainted with another language, he might not be able to get his living in a strange land. "As for me," said Moung Thahlah, "I go where preaching is to be had." Moung Bya was silent and thoughtful. At last he said that, as no Burman woman is allowed to leave the country, he could not, on account of his wife, follow the teachers. "But," continued he, with some pathos, "if I must be left here alone, I shall remain performing the duties of Jesus Christ's religion; no other shall I think of." This interview with the disciples rejoiced our hearts, and caused us to praise God for the grace which he has manifested to them.

February 24. We have spent three or four days in inquiring about Chittagong, and the prospect of getting a passage directly thither, or by the way of Bengal.

This evening Moung Bya came up with his brother-in-law, Moung Myat-yah, who has lived in our yard several months, and formerly attended worship in the zayat. "I have come," said Moung Bya, "to petition that you will not leave Rangoon at present." "I think," replied I, "that it is useless to remain under present circumstances. We cannot open the zayat; we cannot have public worship; no Burman will dare to examine this religion; and if none examine, none can be expected to embrace it." "Teacher," said he, "my mind is distressed; I can neither eat nor sleep, since I find you are going away. I have been around among those who live near us, and I find some who are even now examining the new religion. Brother Myat-yah is one of them, and he unites with me in my petitions." Here Myat-yah assented that it was so. "Do stay with us a few months. Do stay till there are eight or ten disciples; then appoint one to be the teacher of the rest; I shall not be concerned about the event; though you should leave the country, the religion will spread of itself; the emperor himself cannot stop it. But if you go now, and take the two disciples that can follow, I shall be left alone. I cannot baptize those who may wish to embrace this religion. What can I do?" Moung Nau came in, and expressed himself in a similar way. He thought that several would yet become disciples, in spite of all opposition, and that it was best for us to stay a while. We could not restrain our tears at hearing all this; and we told them that as we lived only for the promotion of the cause of Christ among the Burmans, if there was any prospect of success in Rangoon, we had no desire to go to another place, and would, therefore, reconsider the matter.

February 26. Moung Shwa-boo, a sedate and pleasant man, who came to live in our yard, just before we went to Ava, accompanied Moung Myat-yah to the usual evening worship. When we were about breaking up, Moung Thahlah began conversation, by saying, "Teacher, your intention of going away has filled us all with trouble. Is it good to forsake us thus? Notwithstanding present difficulties and dangers, it is to be remembered that this work is not yours or ours, but the work of God. If he give light, the religion will spread. Nothing can impede it." After conversing some time, I found that Moung Louk, another inhabitant of the yard, had been listening without. Accordingly, he was invited to take his seat with the inquirers. Moung Bya now began to be in earnest; his arm was elevated, and his eyes brightened. "Let us all," said he, "make an effort. As for me, I will pray. Only leave a little church of ten, with a teacher set over them, and I shall be fully satisfied." Moung Nau took a very active part in the conversation. The three new ones said nothing, except that they were desirous of considering the religion of Christ. None of them, however, was willing to admit that, as yet, he believed any thing.

We felt that it was impossible for us *all* to leave these people, in these interesting circumstances; and, at the same time, we felt it very important that Chittagong should not be neglected. Under these circumstances, we came to the conclusion that brother Colman should proceed immediately to Chittagong, collect the Arracanese converts, and form a station to which new missionaries from the board may at first repair, and to which I may ultimately flee, with those of the disciples that can leave the country, when we find that persecution is so violent as to suppress all further inquiry, and render it useless and rash to remain; that I should remain in Rangoon until the state of things becomes thus desperate, and then endeavor to join brother Colman in Chittagong; but that if, contrary to our expectation, the Rangoon station should, after a lapse of several months, appear to be tenable, and that for an indefinite time, and some work be evidently going on, brother Colman, after settling one or two missionaries in Chittagong, to keep that place, should rejoin me in Rangoon.

February 27, Lord's day. Had private worship in the zayat — the front doors closed — none present but the disciples and inquirers.

February 28. A visit from Moung Shwa-gnong. He had considered, he said, my last words — that one must believe and be baptized in order to be a full disciple. It was his desire to be such, and he wanted to know what outward rules in particular he must observe in case he should become a professor. I told him that the disciples of Christ, after baptism, were associated together; that they assembled every Lord's day for worship, and that from time to time they received the sacrament of bread and wine. I then warned him of the danger of self-deception, and of the persecution to which disciples were exposed in this country, and advised him to reconsider the matter most thoroughly, before he made a definite request for baptism.

After he had gone, Oo Yan (mentioned December 19) came in — was disappointed in not finding Moung Shwa-gnong, having agreed to meet him at the mission house. We had a long conversation on doctrinal points, in which he discovered a very acute, discriminating mind.

March 2. Another visit from Oo Yan. Venture to

CONFERENCE WITH THE DISCIPLES. 269

indulge a little hope that truth is beginning to operate on his mind.

March 5, Lord's day. Private worship, as last Lord's day. In the evening received the sacrament of bread and wine. Moung Nau was not present, having gone on a visit to Bau-lay, his native place. Had a refreshing and happy season with the two other disciples. Two of the inquirers were spectators.

March 8. In the evening had a very pleasant and instructive conference with the disciples and inquirers. Moung Thahlah appeared to great advantage. Took the lead in explaining truth to the new ones, and quoted Scripture with singular facility and aptness. He has most evidently very correct views of the doctrines of grace. Moung Myat-yah appears to begin to discern the excellence of the Christian system, and to have some right feelings towards the Saviour.

March 10. Moung Shwa-gnong and Oo Yan have been with me several hours, but the interview has afforded very little encouragement. The former said but little on his own account, appearing chiefly desirous of convincing and persuading his friend, that he might gain, as I secretly suspected, some companion of his own rank in life, before he embraced the new religion. The latter acted on the defensive, and spent all his time in raising objections. He was ready to admit that the atheistic system of the Boodhists was not tenable, but endeavored to fortify himself on a middle system between that and the Christian — the very system in which Moung Shwa-gnong formerly rested, and which, for distinction's sake, may be fitly termed the semi-atheistic. Its fundamental doctrine is, that divine wisdom, not concentrated in any existing spirit, or embodied in any form, but diffused throughout the universe, and partaken in different degrees by various intelligences, and in a very high degree by the Boodhs, is the true and only God. This poor system, which is evidently guilty of suicide, Oo Yan made every possible effort to keep alive; but I really think that in his own mind he felt the case to be hopeless. His mode of reasoning is, however, soft, insinuating, and acute, and so adroitly did he act his part, that Moung Shwa-gnong, with his strong arm, and I with the strength of truth, were scarcely able to keep him down.

March 13. The teacher and Oo Yan, with two of their friends, came and spent several hours. The former staid later than the others, and attended evening worship. I asked him whether there was any point in the Christian system on which he had not obtained satisfaction. He replied that he was not yet satisfied as to the propriety of God's appointing one particular day in the week for assembling together, in distinction from all other days. I saw at once why he has always been so remiss in attending worship on the Lord's day; and I therefore proceeded to state the nature of positive commands, and their peculiar excellence, as the best test of obedience; that it was evidently beneficial for the disciples of Christ to assemble sometimes; that God, in appointing that such an assembly should be held at least one day in seven, must be supposed to be guided by wisdom infinitely transcending that of man; that, if the disciples of Christ are to meet once at least in seven days, it is evidently best to have the day of meeting designated, in order to secure their general union and concert; and that the first day of the week had at least this claim to preference, that it is the day on which our Saviour rose from the dead. I descanted on these points to his apparent satisfaction; but let us see whether he will come next Lord's day.

Later in the evening had an instructive conference with Moung Myat-yah and Moung Shwa Boo. They both appear to have obtained some of that light, which, like the dawn of morning, shineth more and more unto perfect day.

March 15. Another visit from the teacher, accompanied with his wife and child. Again discussed the necessity of assembling on the Lord's day. Found that the sacraments of baptism and the supper are, in his mind, liable to similar objections. Forsook, therefore, all human reasoning, and rested the merits of the case on the bare authority of Christ. "Ye are my friends if ye do whatsoever I command you." Notwithstanding the remains of his deistical spirit, however, I obtained, during this visit, more satisfactory evidence of his real conversion than ever before. He said that he knew nothing of an eternally existing God before he met with me; that, on hearing that doctrine, he instantly believed it, but that it was a long time before he closed with Christ. "Can you recollect the time?" said I. "Not precisely," he replied, "but it was during a visit, when you discoursed concerning the Trinity, the divine worship of Jesus, and the great sufferings which he, though truly God, endured for his disciples." He afterwards spoke, with much Christian feeling, on the preciousness of the last part of the sixth chapter of Matthew, which he heard me read, day before yesterday, at evening worship.

March 19, Lord's day. Looked in vain for the teacher and his acquaintances.

March 21. Moung Thahlah introduced one of his relations, by name Moung Shwa-ba, as desirous of considering the Christian religion. Spent an hour or two in conversing with him. He was afterwards present at evening worship, and staid to converse after the rest had retired.

March 22. Another conversation with Moung Shwa-ba. He appears to be under deep religious impressions. His language and his looks evince an uncommon solemnity of spirit — an earnest desire to be saved from the wrath to come. After praying with him, I left him in company with Moung Thahlah.

March 23. In the morning, Moung Thahlah informed me that he and his friend had sat up the greater part of the night in the zayat, reading, and conversing, and praying. In the afternoon, Moung Shwa-ba came in himself. His expressions are very strong; but I have no reason to doubt his sincerity. It only seems strange to us that a work of grace should be carried on so rapidly in the soul of an ignorant heathen. He presented a writing, containing a statement of his faith, and an urgent request to be baptized next Lord's day.

March 24. Spent all the evening with Moung Shwa-ba. Feel satisfied that he has experienced a work of divine grace, but think it advisable to defer his baptism till Sunday after next, in order to allow him full time to reëxamine the religion, and the foundation of his hopes.

March 26, Lord's day. Three women present at worship — acquaintances of Moung Shwa-gnong. They have visited Mrs. Judson once or twice before. The principal of them renounced Gaudama some years ago, and adopted the semi-atheistic system, but without obtaining any real satisfaction. Two years ago, she met with a copy of the tract, which gave her an idea of an eternally-existing God; but she knew not whence the paper came. At length, Moung Shwa-gnong told her that he had found the true wisdom, and directed her to us. Her case appears very hopeful.

In the evening, after worship, had a protracted conversation with the disciples and inquirers, on account of brother Colman's intended departure to-morrow. Moung Shwa-ba appeared very well indeed. Moung Myat-yah said, "Set me down for a disciple. I have fully made up my mind in regard to this religion. I love Jesus Christ; but I am not yet quite ready for baptism." After we dismissed them, *they went over to the zayat of their own accord, and held a prayer meeting.*

And here I must close my journal. We have spent the last evening with our very dear brother and sister Colman. They expect to embark to-morrow morning. Our parting is mournful; for happy, uncommonly happy has been our past intercourse. Nothing but a sense of duty could force the present separation. We hope that it will be of short duration, and that we shall soon reunite our labors in Chittagong or Rangoon.

On their departure, Mrs. Judson and myself will again be left to our former "loneliness of lot." In this situation, we renewedly commend ourselves to the remembrance and prayers of the board.

March 27. Brother and sister Colman took leave of us, and embarked for Bengal.

April 1. In the evening we had a final conversation with

Moung Shwa-ba, and became fully satisfied with the evidences of his conversion. We therefore expressed our willingness to receive him into church fellowship, and I announced to him my intention of baptizing him to-morrow, on which he expressed his gratitude and joy.

April 2, Lord's day. At night, after dark, we went privately to the accustomed pond, and baptized the new disciple. Afterwards sat down at the table of the Lord — two foreign and four native communicants. Three inquirers were admitted to be spectators.

April 11. A visit from Oo Yan, accompanied by two of his friends who have been here before. Long conversation on topics of the Christian religion.

April 14. The women mentioned March 26 spent most of the day with Mrs. Judson. They regularly visit her about once a week. I mention the visit of to-day, because it has afforded pretty satisfactory evidence that the principal one of the company, by name Mah Men-la, has experienced divine grace. Her husband is one of the visitors, who came with Oo Yan, on the 11th.

April 15. Moung Shwa-ba has for some days been talking of a visit to Shwa-doung, his native place, to communicate the treasure which he has found to his numerous relations and friends. This evening, after expressing his desires, he said it had occurred to him that it might be proper to ask permission or license so to do. Not that he aspired to set up as a teacher; far from that; but he wanted to feel that, in communicating the gospel, he was proceeding in a regular authorized manner. He thought that, if two or three disciples could be raised up in each of the large towns, it would much facilitate our operations. He was sure that at least one in ten of his relations and friends, on hearing his story, could not help embracing the new religion. I secretly exulted at hearing his proposal, so evidently the result of Christian principle, and exhorted him to constant self-examination and prayer, as the means of discovering his own duty and the divine will.

April 16, Lord's day. Early in the morning the teacher

Moung Shwa-gnong came in, after an absence of just a month. He was soon followed by Oo Yan and his two friends. They spent the whole day with me. All appear hopeful. The teacher remained, as usual, after the others had left, and thereby afforded me an opportunity for private conversation. He admitted that all his objections to positive commands were removed, and that it was his desire to be a full disciple; but, when urged closely on the subject, he intimated that his wife and friends were opposed to his taking any decided step, and that, if he did, he was, moreover, exposed to imminent danger of persecution and death. He mentioned these things with so much feeling, and such evident consciousness of simple weakness, as completely disarmed me. My heart was wrung with pity. I sincerely sympathized with him in his evident mental trials. I could not deny the truth of what he said, but gently hinted, as thy day is, thy strength shall be, and proposed the example of the apostles and martyrs, the glory of suffering for Christ, &c. But the thought of the iron mall, and a secret suspicion that, if I was in his circumstances, I should perhaps have no more courage, restrained my tongue. We parted with much solemnity, understanding one another better than ever before. I shall not probably see him again very soon; for it is too dangerous for a man of his distinction to be seen coming frequently to the mission house.

April 20. Mah Men-la and her friends have been with Mrs. Judson all day. She gives increasing evidence of being a real disciple, but is extremely timid, through fear of persecution. One of her remarks deserves notice, as a natural expression of true Christian feeling. "I am surprised," said she, "to find this religion has such an effect on my mind as to make me love the disciples of Christ more than my dearest natural relations." She is a woman of very superior discernment and mental energy. One of the women, who has frequently accompanied her in her visits, met with a tract at Old Pegu about six weeks ago, and came all the way to Rangoon, chiefly, she says, on that account.

This day I have finished the translation of the Epistle to the Ephesians, begun before I went to Ava, but intermitted on account of the weakness of my eyes. It is with real joy that I put this precious writing into the hands of the disciples. It is a great accession to their scanty stock of Scripture; for they have had nothing hitherto but Matthew. Intend to give them Acts as fast as my eyes will allow.

April 30, Lord's day. One of the busiest days I have ever spent. Not a multitude of visitants, as formerly. That we cannot expect in present circumstances. But, besides the usual evening assembly, there were eight or ten present at worship, some of whom were with me from nine in the morning till ten at night. Mah Men-la and her company were with Mrs. Judson, who, by the way, has had a serious attack of the liver complaint for a fortnight past, and is now in a course of salivation.

Oo Yan, after having searched out all the difficult points of religion, came to-day to the *ne plus ultra* — How are sin and eternal misery reconcilable with the character of an infinitely holy, wise, and powerful God? He at length obtained such satisfaction that he could not restrain laughing, from pure mental delight, and kept recurring to the subject, and repeating my remarks to those around him. He was accompanied, as usual, by his two friends, Moung Thah-a and Moung Myat-lah, husband of Mah Men-la. With these came also one Moung Yo, a disciple of Moung Shwa-gnong, a poor man, but a sharp reasoner. He was, or pretended to be, on the semi-atheistic plan. (See March 10.) After ascertaining his precise ground, I used an argument which, in a late combat with Oo Yan, I found quite invincible. It is simply this: "No mind, no wisdom; temporary mind, temporary wisdom; eternal mind, eternal wisdom." Now, as all the semi-atheists firmly believe in eternal wisdom, this concise statement sweeps with irresistible sway through the very joints and marrow of their system. And, though it may seem rather simple and inconclusive to one unacquainted with Burman reasoning, its effect is uniformly decisive. No sooner is this short sentence uttered than one significantly nods his head, as if to say,

"There you have it." Another cries out to the opponent, "You are undone, destroyed." Another says, "Talk about wisdom! where else will you find it?" The disputant himself, who was perhaps preparing a learned speech about the excellence, and efficacy, and eternity of wisdom, quite disconcerted by this unexpected onset, sits looking at the wreck of his system, and wondering at the simple means which has spread such ruin around him; presently he looks up, (for the Burmans are frequently candid,) and says, "Your words are very appropriate;" and perhaps his next question is, "How can I become a disciple of the God you worship?" All the visitors to-day, and, indeed, all the semi-atheists, are despisers of Gaudama and the established religion of the land. Moung Shwa-gnong has disseminated this heresy in Rangoon for several years; but since he has become acquainted with us, he frequently tells his adherents, "I know nothing; if you want true wisdom, go to the foreign teacher, and there you will find it." I have reason to believe that this heresy is not confined to Rangoon, but is taking root in various parts of the country, and preparing the way for the Christian religion. O for toleration — a little toleration! We will be content to baptize in the night, and hold worship in private; but we do pray that we may not be utterly banished from the land; that we may not be cut up, root and branch. O that these poor souls, who are groping in the dark, feeling after the truth, may have time and opportunities to find the precious treasure which will enrich them forevermore! We are all looking with anxiety towards the golden feet. Our viceroy, Moung Shwa-thah, has gone thither on a visit; and it is doubtful whether he will return, or his rival, Mya-day-men. If the latter, there is some reason to hope that we shall keep footing in Rangoon, at least during his administration.

May 5. Another visit from Moung Myat-lah and his wife, which has afforded us good reason to hope that he also has become a true believer. His wife appears the same as usual. They are both gaining courage in regard to an open profession of the Christian religion, and begin to wonder at the backwardness of their former oracle, Moung Shwa-gnong.

May 8. Moung Thah-a, the friend of Moung Myat-lah, has spent most of the day with me, and given equally good evidence of being a true disciple. He was formerly an officer under government, and amassed considerable property, which he mostly spent in building pagodas and making offerings. But he obtained no satisfaction, found no resting-place for his soul, until he became acquainted with the religion of Jesus. He now rests in this religion, with conscious security; believes and loves all that he hears of it, and prays that he may become fully a true disciple of the Saviour.

Both of these men are respectable householders, rather above the middling class. They live in a little village called Nan-dau-gong, about half a mile from the mission house. Moung Myat-lah has a large family; but Moung Thah-a has none, and were it not for an aged mother who depends on him, he would follow me, he says, throughout the world.

May 12. The three visitors from Nan-dau-gong have been with us part of the day. One characteristic trait in these people is a particular love for the Scriptures. They almost quarrel with one another for the only copy of the Ephesians which I have given them, and I therefore determine to spare them another as soon as it is done. They say that the translation of this Epistle is plainer, and more easily understood, than that of Matthew, which is very encouraging to me, as I made it without the assistance of any person, not even a Burman teacher. My old teacher went to Ava some months ago, and I am now afraid to employ another, lest he should become too well acquainted with the disciples and inquirers, and betray them to government.

May 14, Lord's day. A very busy day with the Nan-dau-gong visitors, and the usual evening assembly.

May 18. Mah Myat-lah and Mah Doke, who have frequently accompanied their relation Mah Men-la, came to-day by themselves. They appear to be under solemn religious impressions, sensible of their sin and danger, and anxious to obtain an interest in the Saviour, but are yet unenlightened in regard to the way. Mah Baik, also, sister of Moung

Thahlah, who formerly afforded us some encouragement, but afterwards fell off, has recommenced visiting us. We hope that during several months' confinement she has not in vain meditated on the truths she formerly heard. She says that her mind is changed, that she loves the Saviour, and trusts in him alone for salvation from sin and hell, and desires to become his disciple in full by receiving baptism. Her husband, Moung Nyo-dwa, and Moung Thah-yah, another resident in our yard, whom I think I have not yet mentioned, are constant attendants on evening worship, and seem to be making slow advances in the knowledge and love of divine truth. Moung Shwa-ba, the last baptized, begins to appear to great advantage; has very correct ideas of the gospel system, and communicates truth to the inquirers with much feeling and animation. In zeal for the extension of the Redeemer's kingdom, he surpasses the older disciples. This is the man who, from not knowing that there was such a being in the universe as a God, became a speculative believer, a penitent, a hopeful recipient of grace, and a candidate for baptism, all in the space of three days. Some of the above mentioned have, on the contrary, been several months in making similar attainments, and are yet found wanting. Thus diverse are the operations of the Holy Spirit.

June 16. Received letters from Bengal. News from Bombay that a Mahometan has professed the gospel, and from Java that brother Robinson has baptized the first Chinese convert. Thus there seems to be a beginning in several very important stations. May the little one become a thousand. Rejoiced to hear that brother Colman had safely arrived at Bengal, and embarked on a boat for Chittagong, and that thus far he had not met with any molestation or interruption from the police. May he get a footing in Chittagong, for every thing here, in regard to toleration, grows darker.

June 27. Mrs. Judson, after having been through two courses of salivation for the liver complaint, at length despairs of recovering without some proper medical assistance. For a few days we have hoped that she would get some relief from the various applications which are made, though at the expense of an almost total exhaustion of strength; but this morning, to our utter disappointment, the disorder has returned with increased violence, and her constitution appears to be rapidly failing. I have intended, for some time past, to send her alone to Bengal; but she has become too weak, and the present circumstances of the complaint are too alarming, to allow such a measure, and I have therefore, though with great reluctance and much conflict of mind, concluded to accompany her to Bengal. We have a special inducement to embrace the opportunity afforded us by the ship which lately brought our letters, since, if we reject this, we shall have to wait several months for another opportunity, during which time Mrs. J. will, in all probability, be placed beyond the reach of medical assistance.

July 9, Lord's day. Moung Nyo-dwa and Moung Gway request baptism. We have had a good hope of the former for some time. With the latter we are very slightly acquainted, though he has been a constant attendant on evening worship for nearly two months. This application, however, is approved by some of the most discerning in the church. The Nan-dau-gong people hope that they shall get grace and courage enough to profess the Christian religion by the time I return from Bengal.

July 15. Have been very busy all the past week in getting ready for the voyage. In procuring a governmental passport, received essential assistance from Mr. Lanciego, a Spaniard, the present collector of the port, and one of the chief magistrates of the place during the absence of the viceroy. He has also promised to protect the people whom we leave on the mission premises.

July 16, Lord's day. A few days ago we concluded to receive the two new applicants for baptism; but I thought it most prudent, partly by way of trying their sincerity, to send them a message, suggesting that, since I was greatly occupied in getting ready for sea, and since one of them was not so well acquainted with the doctrines of religion as was desirable, it might be better to defer their baptism till my return.

This morning they came up in much trouble. They stated that, as they had fully embraced the Christian religion in their hearts, they could not remain easy without being baptized, according to the command of Christ; that no man could tell whether I should ever return or not, and that it was their earnest petition, that if I could possibly find time, and thought them worthy of the ordinance, I would administer it to them before I went away. They did not wish me to go out to the usual place, as that was at some distance, but would be baptized in a small pond near the mission house. Moung Gway said that, though he was very ignorant, he knew enough of this religion to love it sincerely, and to trust in Christ for salvation from all his sins. I reëxamined them both, stated to them the great danger of professing a foreign religion, &c., and, on their urging their request, told them I would baptize them in the evening.

Was obliged to be out all the afternoon, getting our things aboard the ship, as we expect to move down the river to-morrow morning. At night baptized the two new disciples, after which we all partook of the Lord's supper for the last time.

July 17. Ship to be detained two days. In the forenoon, the teacher Moung Shwa-gnong came in. I received him with some reserve, but soon found that he had not staid away so long from choice, having been ill with a fever for some time, and occupied also with the illness of his family and adherents. He gradually wore away my reserve; and we had not been together two hours, before I felt more satisfied than ever, from his account of his mental trials, his struggles with sin, his strivings to be holy, his penitence, his faith, his exercises in secret prayer, that he is a subject of the special operations of the Holy Spirit, that he is indeed a true disciple. He staid all day. In the afternoon, the five Nan-dau-gong visitors, the doctor Oo Yan, and several others came together, and we had much interesting conversation. Towards the close, Moung Shwa-gnong, as if to bring things to a crisis, addressed me thus : " My lord teacher, there are now several of us present who have long considered this religion. I hope that we are all believers in Jesus Christ." " I am afraid," replied I, " to say that; however, it is easily ascertained; and let me begin with you, teacher. I have heretofore thought that you fully believed in the eternal God; but I have had some doubt whether you fully believed in the Son of God, and the atonement which he has made." " I assure you," he replied, " that I am as fully persuaded of the latter as of the former." " Do you believe, then," I continued, " that none but the disciples of Christ will be saved from sin and hell?" " None but his disciples." " How, then, can you remain without taking the oath of allegiance to Jesus Christ, and becoming his full disciple in body and soul?" " It is my earnest desire to do so, by receiving baptism; and for the very purpose of expressing that desire, I have come here to-day." " You say you are desirous of receiving baptism: may I ask *when* you desire to receive it?" " At any time you will please to give it. Now — this moment, if you please." " Do you wish to receive baptism in public or in private?" " I will receive it at any time, and in any circumstances, that you please to direct." I then said, " Teacher, I am satisfied from your conversation this forenoon, that you are a true disciple, and I reply, therefore, that I am as desirous of giving you baptism as you are of receiving it." This conversation had a great effect on all present. The disciples rejoiced; the rest were astonished; for though they have long thought that he believed the Christian religion, they could not think that such a man could easily be brought to profess it, and suffer himself to be put under the water by a foreigner. I then turned to Moung Thah-a, one of the Nan-dau-gong people, who, I hope, is a true believer. " Are you willing to take the oath of allegiance to Jesus Christ?" " If the teacher Moung Shwa-gnong consents," said he, " why should I hesitate?" " And if he does not consent, what then?" " I must wait a little longer." " Stand by," said I; " you trust in Moung Shwa-gnong, rather than in Jesus Christ. You are not worthy of being baptized." Moung Myat-lah, on being similarly interrogated, wished to consider a little longer. Oo Yan was still further from committing himself. Of the women present, I interrogated Mah Men-la only. She had evidently a considerable struggle in her mind, probably on account of her husband's having just declined. At length she said that, if I thought it suitable for her to be baptized, she was desirous of receiving the ordinance. I told her that her reply was not satisfactory. I could not consent to baptize any one who could possibly remain easy without being baptized, and then I related the story of the two last disciples; after which the party broke up.

In the evening, I laid the case of Moung Shwa-gnong before the church, and we joyfully agreed to receive him to communion, on his being baptized.

July 18. In the morning, the teacher again made his appearance. I again asked him whether he preferred being baptized in the day or in the evening, and he again left it to my decision; on which I advised him to wait till night. He appeared very well through the day, his deportment solemn, his conversation spiritual. Just at night, I called in two or three of the disciples, read the account of the baptism of the eunuch, made the baptismal prayer, and then proceeded with the teacher to the accustomed place, went down into the water, and baptized him.

On my return, I found that Mah Men-la, whom I had left with Mrs. Judson, had gone away. As soon as she saw that the teacher had actually gone to be baptized, she exclaimed, "Ah, he has now gone to obey the command of Jesus Christ, while I remain without obeying. I shall not be able to sleep this night. I must go home, and consult my husband, and return." In the evening, we again partook of the Lord's supper, in consequence of the admission of the teacher, and my expected departure on the morrow. We had just finished, when, about nine o'clock, Mah Men-la returned, accompanied by the two other women from her village. She immediately requested to be baptized. The disciples present assented without hesitation. I told her that I rejoiced to baptize her, having been long satisfied that she had received the grace of Christ; and, it being very late, I led her out to the pond near the house by lantern light, and thus baptized the tenth Burman convert, and the first woman. Mah Men-la is fifty-one years old, of most extensive acquaintance through the place, of much strength of mind, decision of character, and consequent influence over others. She is, indeed, among women what Moung Shwa-gnong is among men.

On returning to the house, she said, "Now I have taken the oath of allegiance to Jesus Christ, and I have nothing to do but to commit myself, soul and body, into the hands of my Lord, assured that he will never suffer me to fall away." Several visitors spent the night at the mission house.

July 19. In the morning, we all met for worship. After I had prayed, Moung Thah-lah and Moung Shwa-ba both prayed, with much propriety and feeling. In the course of the forenoon, Mah Men-la's husband, and Moung Thah-a, and the doctor, and several others, came in, so that we had quite a house full. At noon, we set out for the river, followed by near a hundred people, the women crying aloud in the Burman manner, and almost all deeply affected. When we entered the boat, I called the teacher, and Mah Men-la, and a few others, to go with us to the ship, which lay at some distance in the river. The rest remained on the wharf, bidding us farewell, telling us to come back soon, &c. Thus we left the shores of Rangoon. Those who accompanied us to the ship staid an hour or two, and returned. We stood as long on the quarter deck looking at them as the others had stood on the wharf looking at us.*

July 20. The ship having been unable to move yesterday,

---

* One of these female disciples was found at Rangoon, by the missionaries, in August, 1852, having attained the age of eighty years. From the time of her baptism until now, for thirty years, she has maintained, in the midst of heathenism, a consistent Christian profession. She remembered well Mr. Judson, and "the Mamma" Judson, and was in daily expectation of meeting them again in heaven.

on account of the anchor's being foul, the teacher Moung Shwa-gnong espied the masts from his village, and came off in a boat, with his wife and another woman. Soon after, most of the Nan-dau-gong people came to the mission house, and, finding that the ship had not dropped down, came off, accompanied by several of our own people. We were much gratified by this fresh proof of their attachment; but the ship got under way immediately, and they were obliged to leave us for the last time.

Extract from a Letter of the Rev. James Colman, dated Rangoon, March 25, 1820.

Perhaps some will begin to think that, as there are so many difficulties attending the Burman mission, it is best to relinquish it altogether. But while Burmans are willing, in prospect of persecution and death, to examine and embrace the gospel, let not Christians at home be discouraged from sending it to them. Is it a suitable time to leave a people when the Holy Spirit is operating on their minds, and creating in them ardent desires to know the way which leads to eternal life? True, the number of our inquirers is small; but if there is only one, his soul is worth more than the wealth of the world, nor should it perish for want of Christian instruction. I freely confess that nothing would tempt me to leave the station in Rangoon, were it not for the advice of my senior in the mission, and for the purpose of preparing a place of refuge, in case of imminent danger, from the Burman government.

The Burmans who have joined us continue to give increasing evidence of being real Christians. Their attachment to us, and to the gospel, has not in the least diminished by our disappointment at Ava. Indeed, this event has awakened their zeal. It is owing, in a great measure, to their exertions and entreaties, that the mission is continued in Rangoon. They are not insensible of the danger to which their conduct exposes them; but they act like men who are convinced of the rectitude of their proceedings, and of the important truth that it is better to suffer for Christ in this world than to endure the pains of hell in the world to come. We cannot, indeed, determine how they would conduct in the fire of persecution; but from their present deportment there is reason to hope that they have a claim to the divine promises, and would, in the day of trial, experience their supporting influence. Commending these sheep, literally placed among wolves, and the Burman mission, to your prayers, I remain yours in gospel bonds, &c.

The following letter, sent by the converts in Rangoon to their Christian brethren in America, illustrates the nature of that character which had been formed in them by the preaching of the gospel:—

Brethren all, who live in America! The brethren who live in Burmah address you.

We inform you, brethren, that, trusting in the grace of the eternal God, the divine Spirit, and the excellent Son, the Lord Jesus Christ, we remain happy; and seeing our real state and circumstances, we have repentance of soul, and an anticipation of the happiness of heaven.

God, the sum of all perfection, without beginning and without end, subsists through successive ages; and this world, the earth and sky, and all things therein, which he has created, are according as he created them.

God, the Creator, is replete with goodness and purity, and is exempt from old age, sickness, death, and annihilation; and thus there is none that can compare with him.

It is contained in the Scriptures, that God, in his own nature, unites three, the Father, the Son, and the Holy Spirit, and is [yet] mysteriously one God; that he is in all places, but dwells in heaven, by the clearer manifestation of his glory; that his power and wisdom are unrivalled; and that he enjoys happiness incomprehensible to creatures.

But the Burmans know not the true God; they know not

the true religion; they worship a false god; they practise a false religion; and [thus] they transgress the divine law, and sin against the most estimable Benefactor, and therefore they neither expiate their sins nor acquire merit. And by excessively loving themselves and the filth of this world, they love not nor worship the eternal God, nor believe in the Lord Jesus Christ, but regard the good things of this world merely.

That the Burmans, who know not the way to eternal happiness, might become acquainted with it; that they might be renewed; and that they might escape everlasting punishment, the American teacher Judson and wife have both come to Burmah, and proclaimed the gospel of the divine Son, the Lord Jesus Christ; on which some Burmans have become disciples. And on these accounts, the disciple Moung Shwa-ba says that your favor is very great, [or he gives you very many thanks.]

Those who love divine grace, who believe, who hear and consider the gospel, who trust in the Lord Jesus Christ, who repent of their sins, attain the state of disciples. And that this religion may spread every where, Moung Shwa-ba is making endeavors, and constantly praying, to proclaim the gospel. And he prays thus: O eternal God, graciously grant the favor which I desire. Graciously grant that I may have regard to thy divine will, and be conformed thereto. Be pleased to take notice of my supplications, O God. I desire not to seek my own profit; I desire constantly to seek the profit of others. Thou art the Creator of all things; and if thou art pleased to be gracious, O, grant that I may be enabled to promote the good of others. Open thou the eyes of my mind, and give me light. And when I shall preach in various places, evermore send forth the divine Spirit, that multitudes may become disciples. That thou wilt grant these things, I beseech thee, O God.

The disciple Moung Shwa-ba has composed this writing, and committed it to the hand of the teacher; [even] in the Burman year 1182, on the 7th of the waxing of the moon Wah-goung, he has written this, and delivered it to the teacher and his wife.

P. S. Brethren, there are in the country of Burmah nine persons who have become disciples.

The above is a literal translation of a letter in Burman, which Moung Shwa-ba wrote of his own accord, and handed to me, to be translated and forwarded to America. The postscript seems to have been written in the interval between the baptism of the teacher Moung Shwa-gnong, and that of Mah Men-la, on the 18th of July last, just before my departure from Rangoon.

A. JUDSON, JR.

On Passage to Bengal, August 9, 1820.

CHAPTER IX.

RETURN TO RANGOON. — GROWTH OF THE CHURCH. — INCREASED ILLNESS OF MRS. JUDSON. — SAILS FOR THE UNITED STATES. — THE MISSION REËNFORCED. — SECOND VISIT TO AVA. — TRANSLATION OF THE NEW TESTAMENT COMPLETED.

1820-1823.

At the close of the last chapter we left Mr. and Mrs. Judson embarking for Calcutta, on the 19th of July, 1820. They arrived there on the 18th of the following August. The voyage was attended with important benefit to the health of Mrs. Judson, and she was so far improved in the course of a few months that her medical advisers deemed it safe for her to return to Rangoon. They sailed from Calcutta November 23, 1820, and arrived in Rangoon January 5, 1821. The following extracts from Mr. Judson's journal present a delightful view of the progress of the gospel until August 21 of the same year, when alarming illness made it necessary for Mrs. Judson to embark for Calcutta, and to proceed thence to England and the United States.

Journal.

January 5, 1821. As we drew near the town, we strained our eyes to distinguish the countenances of our friends amid the crowd that we saw assembled on the wharf. The first that we recognized was the teacher Moung Shwa-gnong, with his hands raised to his head as he discerned us on the deck; and on landing we met successively with Mah Men-la, and Moung Thah-lah, and several others, men, women, and children, who, after our usual examination at the custom office, accompanied us to the mission house. Soon after, Moung

Nau, and others came in, who had not, at first, heard of our arrival. In the evening I took my usual seat among the disciples, and when we bowed down in prayer, the hearts of us all flowed forth in gratitude and praise.

January 7, Lord's day. Had worship, and administered the Lord's supper. Most of the disciples present; but some of them unavoidably detained in consequence of the distress which presses upon all ranks of people, occasioned by the expedition to Siam.

January 13. Have spent the past week in getting our things in order, and receiving visits from the disciples and inquirers. Yesterday, Moung Gway, the only one of the baptized whom we had not seen, returned from the woods, on hearing of our arrival; and I am now able to record (and I do it with the most heartfelt satisfaction and grateful praise to the preserving Saviour) that, though they have, for the space of six months, been almost destitute of the means of grace, and those who lived in our yard have been dispersed, and forced, through fear of heavy extortion and oppression from petty officers of government, to flee into the woods, or take refuge under some government person who could protect them, yet not one of them has dishonored his profession, but all remain firm in their faith and attachment to the cause. I do not, however, perceive that any of them have made the least advance in any respect whatever; nor was this to be expected, as they have not even enjoyed the privilege of meeting for worship.

The same remarks are to be made concerning the four Nan-dau-gong people, companions of Mah Men-la, who appeared to be hopefully pious before we left. The doctor, Oo Yan, with whom we did not feel so well satisfied, has been with me repeatedly, and, in the last interview, gave good reason to hope that he also is a true convert. He seems at length to have obtained light and satisfaction on the two difficult points which have so long perplexed him; namely, the doctrine of vicarious atonement, and the possibility of being a disciple of Christ, by keeping the two commands of grace,

Repent and believe, without perfectly keeping the two immutable commands of merit, Love God entirely, and love others as yourself. O, how interesting it is to see (you can almost see it with your eyes) the light of truth dawning upon a precious soul hitherto groping in darkness! If Oo Yan prove a true convert, he will be a most precious acquisition to our cause, next to Moung Shwa-gnong. He is a man of talents and respectability. His words are as smooth as oil, as sweet as honey, and as sharp as a razor.

In respect to Mah Bike, she has given way to her violent temper, and involved her husband in debt; and though she now professes to repent and desire baptism, and though we have some hope that she is not destitute of grace, we feel obliged at present to put her away from us, as a wicked person.

The most important event (and that relates of course to Moung Shwa-gnong) remains to be mentioned. It will be remembered that he was accused, before the former viceroy, of being a heretic, and that the simple reply, " Inquire further,' spread dismay amongst us all, and was one occasion of our visit to Ava. Soon after Mya-day-men assumed the government of this province, all the priests and officers of the village where Moung Shwa-gnong lives entered into a conspiracy to destroy him. They held daily consultations, and assumed a tone of triumph; while poor Moung Shwa-gnong's courage began to flag, and, though he does not like to own it, he thought he must flee for his life. At length, one of the conspiracy, a member of the supreme court, went into the presence of the viceroy, and in order to sound his disposition, complained that the teacher Moung Shwa-gnong was making every endeavor to turn the priests' rice pot bottom upwards. " *What consequence?* " said the viceroy. " *Let the priests turn it back again.*" This sentence was enough; the hopes of the conspiracy were blasted, and all the disciples felt that they were sure of toleration under Mya-day-men. But his administration will not probably continue many months.

January 20. This afternoon Mrs. Judson went to the village of the Nan-dau-gong people, to fix on a spot for the erection of a small school house. Mah Men-la has, *of her own accord*, proposed to open a school in the precincts of her house, to teach the girls and boys of the village to read; in consequence of which, the latter will not be under the necessity of going to the Burman priests for education, as usual. When we found that she had really made a beginning, we told her that some of the Christian females in America would, doubtless, defray the expenses of the undertaking, and make some compensation to the instructress. We fear the school will not succeed in the present state of the country; but we regard the voluntary attempt of Mah Men-la as illustrative of the efficiency of evangelical faith.

On Tuesday evening we recommenced our usual Tuesday and Friday evening prayer meetings; but we expect to have very few present, as most of the disciples who formerly lived around us are afraid to return, on account of the present general distress, from which we are unable to protect them.

January 21, Lord's day. All the disciples but one, and all the hopeful inquirers, were present at worship; who, together with some others, made up an assembly of about twenty-five adults, all paying respectful and devout attention; the most interesting assembly, all things considered, that I have yet seen. How impossible it seemed, two years ago, that such a precious assembly could ever be raised up out of the Egyptian darkness, the atheistic superstition of this heathen land! After worship, two of the Nan-dau-gong people had some particular conversation with Moung Thah-lah about baptism. Much encouraged by the general appearance of things this day. Why art thou ever cast down, O my soul? and why art thou disquieted within me? Hope thou in God — the God of the Burmans, as well as David's God; for I shall yet praise him for the help of his countenance, revealed in the salvation of thousands of these immortal souls.

January 25. Received a visit from a young priest and a novitiate, who reside in a neighboring kyoung, (a house inhabited by priests.) They staid with me above an hour, and paid more candid attention to divine truth than I have ever been able to obtain from any gentleman of the yellow cloth. On pressing the question whether they did not sometimes doubt the correctness of their religion, they confessed in the affirmative, and finally condescended to accept a tract; but it will be torn to pieces as soon as it reaches the hands of their superiors.

January 31. Received a visit from the teacher Oo Oung-let, of the village of Kambet. He has disseminated the semi-atheistic doctrine for several years, and formed a small party among his neighbors, who pay no respect to the priest and the religion of Gaudama. We had a most interesting conversation of about two hours, in the presence of a large company, most of whom came with him. He successively gave up every point that he attempted to maintain, and appeared to lay open his mind to the grand truths of an eternal God, eternal happiness, &c. Moung Shwa-gnong seconded me, and discoursed in a truly impressive manner, until the attention of the old man was so completely fixed that his friends with difficulty persuaded him to take leave.

February 4. Oo Oung-det repeated his visit. He acknowledges himself convinced of the existence of an eternal God, and appears to be desirous of knowing the whole truth; but business prevented his staying long.

February 12. Had a long conversation with Oo Oung-det, in which I at length endeavored to unfold to his view the whole mystery of the gospel, the way of salvation through the atonement of the Son of God, to which our previous conversations have been little more than preparatory. But his proud heart evidently repelled the humiliating doctrine; so true it is that the cross of Christ is the sure touchstone of the human heart. His nephew, however, Moung Oung-hmat, listened with the air of an awakened man. During a temporary suspense of conversation, I was much gratified by hearing him whisper to his uncle, "Ask him more about Jesus Christ." He received a form of prayer with eagerness, and listened to my parting instruction with some feeling.

February 16. Moung Ing has returned. He is the second Burman whose heart was touched by divine grace. We rejoiced to see his face again, notwithstanding his rough and unprepossessing appearance, occasioned by the hardships through which he has passed since he left us. On his arrival at Bike, a town far below Rangoon, he showed his copy of Matthew to the Roman Catholic priest stationed there, who directly committed it to the flames; and gave, instead of it, a writing of his own device. But, through divine grace, our poor friend retained his integrity, and remained steadfast in the sentiments which he formerly embraced.

February 19. Spent several pleasant hours with Moung Ing. During his residence at Bike, he was not satisfied with being a solitary disciple, but undertook to dispute with both Portuguese and Burmans, and found two or three who were disposed to listen to him. He is to return thither within a fortnight, but wishes to be baptized previously.

February 20. This is the second evening in which Mrs. Judson and myself have had an interview with the viceroy and his lady, in their inner apartment. Her highness gave us some very encouraging hints on the subject of religious toleration, and promised to introduce us to the emperor, on his visiting Rangoon next fall, in prosecution of the war with Siam.

February 25, Lord's day. Moung Ing presented his petition for baptism and admission into the church; and we unhesitatingly agreed to grant his request next Lord's day. Not one of the disciples has given more decided evidence of being a sincere and hearty believer in the Lord Jesus. The manner of his first acquaintance with the truth is somewhat noticeable. I had conversed with two men who visited the zayat the preceding evening, and given them a tract. On their way home they called at the house of the Tsah-len teacher, where Moung Ing resided, said a few things about the eternal God and the new religion, by way of disapproval, and concluded that the tract was good for nothing but to tear up and make cigars of. But the truth which they despised fell like a flash of lightning on the benighted soul of Moung Ing. The next morning, before sunrise, he was in the porch of the zayat, and, on opening the doors, we found the poor man standing without. He will not, I trust, meet with any such detention at the doors of heaven.

March 4, Lord's day. Moung Ing received baptism immediately after worship in the afternoon. Several of the hopeful inquirers witnessed the administration.

March 11, Lord's day. We partook of the Lord's supper in the evening, pursuant to a resolution of the church to celebrate this ordinance on the second Sunday after the change of the moon, in order to avail ourselves uniformly of light evenings.

After the ordinance, Moung Ing immediately took leave, for the purpose of returning to Bike. He is laden with various writings, in Burman and Portuguese, for distribution among the people of that place.

May 4. Several days have passed without any encouraging occurrence. The zayat never attracted less company, and I began to fear that the good old times of 1819 would never again return. A case, however, has just occurred, which reminds me of those times. I never before met with an instance of such openness of mind, and readiness to receive the truth, on first communication. The man is a regular bred Boodhist, without the least tincture of semi-atheism; and yet, strange to say, he listened to the truth with unprecedented candor, and apparent eagerness, for above two hours. I am sure I shall see him again. But yet, what have I found more fallacious than first appearances?

May 6, Lord's day. From various causes, there were only three of the baptized present at worship, and yet we had an assembly of above twenty adults, in all the various stages of religious inquiry; some almost ready to profess religion, and some just beginning to open their eyes to the wonders of redeeming love. Among the rest were two aged men, devout worshippers of Gaudama, and constant attendants on the lectures of the Mangen teacher. They listened with fixed attention to a long discourse from the parable of the pharisee and publican; and one of them declared himself pleased with the doctrine. There was also present, for the first time, a relation of Moung Shwa-ba, from the upper part of the country, who has received considerable information from his cousin. He was so much delighted with some things which he heard, that, in the midst of the discourse, he broke out into audible expressions of approbation.

After worship, we heard that the former viceroy, Moung Shwa-thah, has incurred the displeasure of the emperor, and been degraded from all his titles and emoluments; so that he will not, probably, be again allowed to supersede Mya-day-men, in the viceroyship of Rangoon.

May 12, Saturday. Have had several attentive listeners during the past week. Some of my old visitors from Kambet and other villages begin to find that the doors of the zayat are again open.

May 14. A succession of company through the day. A priest of some note listened with much apparent candor, and some expressions of approval.

May 15. Despatched the manuscript of Ephesians, and the first part of Acts, to Serampore, requesting brother Hough to procure an edition of six hundred of each, at the expense of the board.

At night, received a visit from Moung Gwa, brother-in-law to Moung Shwa-ba. He was accompanied by one Moung Thah-ee, an intractable, furious creature, noted for browbeating and silencing every antagonist. He professes to be a strict Boodhist, without the least doubt on the subject of religion; but having heard of my object in coming to this country, wishes to give me an opportunity of making him doubt. I found him extremely difficult to manage, and finally told him that he must get a humble mind, and pray to the true God, or he would never attain true wisdom. This threw him into a passion. He said he would have me to know that he was no common man. He could dispute with governors and kings, &c. I then gave him a tract, which he affected to disdain, but finally received it and went away.

May 16. Moung Gwa called to apologize for his companion's conduct. He said that, from being always victorious in disputation, he had become insolent and overbearing, but that he was really inquiring after the truth, and had been reading the tract attentively. Moung Gwa himself seems to be favorably disposed to the Christian religion.

May 17. Moung Thah-ee spent the whole evening with me. I find that he has a strong mind, capable of grasping the most difficult subject. He listened to the truth with much more attention and patience than at first.

May 18. Moung Thah-ee came again, accompanied by several of his admirers. At first he behaved with some propriety, and allowed conversation to proceed in a regular manner. But soon he descended into his own native element, and stormed and raged. When I found that he would be utterly unreasonable, and not permit me even to finish a sentence, I remained silent, and suffered him to display himself. When he was quite exhausted, I took an opportunity to exhibit a brief view of the reasons which convinced me that the religion of Gaudama is false, and the Boodhist scriptures fictitious, and then challenged him to refute my statement. But he declined, saying that we were both tired, and he would finish the debate some other time.

May 19. A succession of company all the day. At night, Moung Thah-ee came alone, intending to have some private conversation; but no opportunity offered.

May 20, Lord's day. Encountered another new character, one Moung Long, from the neighborhood of Shwa-doung, a disciple of the great Toung-dwen teacher, the acknowledged head of all the semi-atheists in the country. Like the rest of the sect, Moung Long is, in reality, a complete sceptic, scarcely believing his own existence. They say he is always quarrelling with his wife on some metaphysical point. For instance, if she says, "The rice is ready," he will reply, "Rice! what is rice? Is it matter or spirit? Is it an idea, or is it nonentity?" Perhaps she will say, "It is matter;" and he will reply, "Well, wife, and what is matter? Are you sure there is such a thing in existence, or are you merely subject to a delusion of the senses?"*

When he first came in, I thought him an ordinary man. He has only one good eye; but I soon discovered that that one eye has as "great a quantity of being" as half a dozen common eyes. In his manners he is just the reverse of Moung Thah-ee — all suavity, and humility, and respect. He professed to be an inquirer after the truth; and I accordingly opened to him some parts of the gospel. He listened with great seriousness, and when I ceased speaking, remained so thoughtful, and apparently impressed with the truth, that I began to hope he would come to some good, and therefore invited him to ask some question, relative to what he had heard. "Your servant," said he, "has not much to inquire of your lordship. In your lordship's sacred speech, however, there are one or two words that your servant does not understand. Your lordship says, that in the beginning God created one man and one woman. I do not understand (I beg your lordship's pardon) what a man is, and why he is called a man." My eyes were now opened in an instant to his real character; and I had the happiness to be enabled, for about twenty minutes, to lay blow after blow upon his sceptical head, with such effect that he kept falling and falling; and though he made several desperate efforts to get up, he found himself, at last, prostrate on the ground, unable to stir. Moung Shwa-gnong, who had been an attentive listener, was extremely delighted to see his enemy so well punished; for this Moung Long has sorely harassed him in time past. The poor man was not, however, in the least angry at his discomfiture, but, in the true spirit of his school, said that, though he had heard much of me, the reality far exceeded the report. Afterwards he joined us in worship, and listened with great attention, as did also his wife.

May 21. Moung Thah-ee came again, with several others;

* The doctrines of idealism and nihilism were fully and ably discussed by the Brahmins and Boodhists centuries before the time of Berkeley and Hume.

but he was so outrageous, and vulgar, and abusive, that I found it impossible to hold any rational conversation with him; and he finally went away in a great passion, saying that he had been sent by some men in authority to spy us out, and that by to-morrow he would bring us into trouble. Such threatenings tend to sink our spirits, and make us realize our truly helpless, destitute condition, as sheep in the midst of wolves. "Lord, behold their threatenings," &c.

May 27, Lord's day. A very busy day. Had scarcely dismissed the few Europeans who attend English worship in the morning, when the Burman visitors began to come in; and, though many of the disciples were absent, we finally had an assembly of thirty persons, who paid most earnest and uninterrupted attention to a discourse of about half an hour, from the text, "By one man's disobedience, many were made sinners." A few who visited the zayat during the past week were present for the first time. One of them, by name Moung Hla, may be claimed among the hopeful inquirers. Moung Long was again present, and another disciple of the Toungdwen teacher, of equal powers of mind; but these keen metaphysicians are, I fear, far from the kingdom of heaven.

June 3, Lord's day. A new acquaintance of last week, of Siamese extraction, and Moung Hla and Moung Long were present with the usual assembly. Mah Myat-lah, sister of Mah Men-la, appears to be resolved, at length, to profess religion.

June 4. Moung Long spent two or three hours with me, in which I endeavored to lay before him all the evidences of the truth of the Christian religion. His wife proves to be as sharp as himself, and has been harassing Mrs. Judson with all sorts of questions about the possibility of sin's finding entrance into a pure mind, or of its being permitted under the government of a holy sovereign.

I have this day taken Moung Shwa-ba into the service of the mission. He bids fairer than any other member of the church to be qualified, in due time, for the ministry. For, though inferior to Moung Thah-lah in fluency of speech, and to Moung Shwa-gnong in genius and address, he is superior to the former in consistency of character and gravity of deportment, and to the latter in experimental acquaintance with divine things and devotedness to the cause. But the principal trait of character which distinguishes him from the rest, and affords considerable evidence that he is called by higher authority than that of man to the Christian ministry, is his *humble* and *persevering* desire for that office — a desire which sprang up in his heart soon after his conversion, and has been growing ever since. I intend to employ him, at present, as an assistant in the zayat, on a small allowance of seven or eight rupees a month, which I hope the board will approve of. In that situation he will have an opportunity of improving in those qualifications which are requisite to fit him to be a teacher of religion among his fellow-countrymen.

June 8. The Siamese spent several hours with me. His mind is just on the poise between Boodhism and Christianity.

June 10, Lord's day. Moung Long again present — all eye and ear. Mrs. Judson pronounces his wife superior in point of intellect, to any woman that she has ever met with in Burmah.

After evening worship, Mah Myat-lah presented her petition for admission into the church, which was granted, and next Sunday appointed for her baptism. The evidences of her piety are of the most satisfactory kind. We esteem her quite as highly as her sister, Mah Men-la, though she is far inferior in external qualifications.

June 11. Moung Long and wife spent most of the day with us. Their minds are in a truly hopeful state, though still greatly governed by the maxims of the Toung-dwen school. Their main inquiry to-day was, how they could obtain faith in Christ. May the Holy Spirit solve their difficulties, by giving them an experimental acquaintance with that saving grace!

June 14. An intimate friend of the Woon-gyee-gah-dau told Mrs. Judson to-day, in presence of her highness, who by silence assented to the correctness of the remark, that when the emperor and others in government said that all might believe and worship as they please, the toleration extended merely to foreigners resident in the empire, and by no means to native Burmans, who, being slaves of the emperor, would not be allowed with impunity to renounce the religion of their master. This remark accords with all that we have heard at Ava, and may be depended on, (notwithstanding some private encouragement we have received from the viceroy and his wife,) as affording a correct view of the state of religious toleration in this country. It is a fact that, except in our own private circle, it is not known that a single individual has actually renounced Boodhism, and been initiated into the Christian religion.

Mah Myat-lah informs us that the news of her intended baptism has been rumored among her neighbors, and excited a great uproar. She is not, however, disheartened, but rather wishes that her baptism may not be deferred till Sunday, lest some measures be taken to prevent it. I expect that she will present herself for baptism to-morrow evening, but am obliged to close up this number, as the vessel by which it is conveyed is just going down the river.

Pray for us and our little church.

June 15. According to the purpose mentioned under the last date, Mah Myat-lah received baptism, about sunset, at the usual place.

July 3. Moung Thah-lah was married to a woman resident in our yard, a usual attendant on public worship — the event somewhat noticeable, as being probably the first Christian marriage ever performed between persons of pure Burman extraction.

July 14. The first day of Burmese Lent. The Woongyee-gah-dau, notwithstanding all she has heard from Mrs. Judson, set out most zealously in her course of religious performances, and the whole town seems to be following her example.

Many cases of hopeful inquiry, and interesting religious conversation, have occurred within the last month; but they passed away without much apparent fruit, and are therefore not worthy of notice. Moung Long and his wife are the most promising at present; and I begin to indulge some slight hope that they will obtain divine grace.

In the interval of receiving company, I have lately been employed in translating; have finished the Gospel and Epistles of John, those exquisitely sweet and precious portions of the New Testament, and am now employed on the latter part of Acts. I find Moung Shwa-ba a most valuable assistant in all parts of missionary work. Moung Shwa-gnong also begins "to be dissatisfied with being a mere disciple, and hopes that he shall some time be thought worthy of being a teacher of the Christian religion." These two, with Mah Men-la, are, at present, the flower of our little church. I have no reason, however, to complain of the conduct of any, considering the great disadvantages under which they all labor. Some have grown comparatively cold, but none have forgotten their first love. Praise forever be to Him

> "Who is faithful to his promises,
> And faithful to his Son."

August 4. Am just recovering from the second fit of sickness which I have had this season. The first was the cholera morbus; the present has been a fever. The second day after I was taken, Mrs. Judson was taken with the same; and for several days we lay side by side, unable to help one another. Through divine mercy, however, we contrived to get our medicines from time to time, and are now in a convalescent state, so far as the fever is concerned. Mrs. Judson, however, is suffering severely under the liver complaint, which, notwithstanding continual salivations, is making such rapid and alarming advances as to preclude all hope of her recovery in this part of the world.

August 6. Came to a final conclusion to send Mrs. Judson to America, for the reasons assigned in a letter to the corresponding secretary, accompanying this number.

August 21. Mrs. Judson embarked for Bengal.

On the occasion of Mrs. Judson's sailing for Calcutta, and probably for America, Mr. Judson wrote as follows to Mr. Hough, under date of August 13, 1821: —

My dear Brother Hough: I send you herewith Mrs. Judson, and all that remains of the blue pills and senna, and beg you will see the articles all well packed and shipped for America by the earliest safe opportunity. Whatever expenses may be incurred be so good as to defray from your own funds, and transmit your bill to me.

It is said that man is prone to jest in the depth of misery; and the bon-mots of the scaffold have been collected: you may add the above specimen to the list if you like. I feel as if I was on the scaffold, and signing, as it were, my own death warrant. However, two years will pass away at last. Time and tide wait for no man, heedless alike of our joys and sorrows.

When I last wrote, I was in the latter part of Acts; since that time, I have done nothing at all. For ten days or a fortnight we were laid by with fever, unable to help one another, and no living soul to depend on but Emily; and since we became convalescent, I have been occupied in making up my mind to have my right arm amputated, and my right eye extracted, which the doctors say are necessary in order to prevent a decay and mortification of the whole body conjugal.

To Mrs. Judson.

I wish I could always feel as I did last evening, and have this morning. At first, on hearing Moung Shwa-gnong's story, I felt much disheartened, and thought how pleasant it would be if we could find some quiet resting-place on earth, where we might spend the rest of our days together in peace, and perform the ordinary services of religion. But I fled to Jesus, and all such thoughts soon passed away. Life is short. Happiness consists not in outward circumstances. Millions of

Burmans are perishing. I am almost the only person on earth who has attained their language to such a degree as to be able to communicate the way of salvation. How great are my obligations to spend and be spent for Christ! What a privilege to be allowed to serve him in such interesting circumstances, and to suffer for him! The heavenly glory is at hand. O, let me travel through this country, and bear testimony to the truth all the way from Rangoon to Ava, and show the path to that glory which I am anticipating. O, if Christ will only sanctify me and strengthen me, I feel that I can do all things. But in myself I am absolute nothingness; and when through grace I get a glimpse of divine things, I tremble lest the next moment will snatch it quite away.

Let us pray especially for one another's growth in grace. Let me pray that the trials which we respectively are called to endure may wean us from the world, and rivet our hearts on things above. Soon we shall be in heaven. O, let us live as we shall then wish we had done. Let us be humble, unaspiring, indifferent equally to worldly comfort and the applause of men, absorbed in Christ, the uncreated Fountain of all excellence and glory.

Mrs. Judson took passage at Calcutta for London, and arrived there in greatly improved health. In Great Britain she was received by Christians of all persuasions with every mark of affectionate and respectful attention. She was domesticated for some time in the family of Mr. Butterworth, member of Parliament, who, referring to the fact, at a public meeting, remarked, that her visit reminded him of the apostolic admonition: "Be not forgetful to entertain strangers, for thereby some have entertained angels unawares." From England she proceeded to this country, where she arrived September 25, 1822. On the 22d of June, 1823, she sailed for Calcutta in the ship Edward Newton, accompanied by the Rev. Jonathan Wade and his wife, Mrs. Deborah Wade, who had recently been appointed missionaries to Burmah. The company arrived at Calcutta on the 19th of October, and reached Rangoon on the 5th of December, 1823.

It was my good fortune to become intimately acquainted with Mrs. Judson during this visit to the United States. I do not remember ever to have met a more remarkable woman. To great clearness of intellect, large powers of comprehension, and intuitive female sagacity, ripened by the constant necessity of independent action, she added that heroic disinterestedness which naturally loses all consciousness of self in the prosecution of a great object. These elements, however, were all held in reserve, and were hidden from public view by a veil of unusual feminine delicacy. To an ordinary observer, she would have appeared simply a self-possessed, well-bred, and very intelligent gentlewoman. A more intimate acquaintance would soon discover her to be a person of profound religious feeling, which was ever manifesting itself in efforts to impress upon others the importance of personal piety. The resources of her nature were never unfolded until some occasion occurred which demanded delicate tact, unflinching courage, and a power of resolute endurance even unto death. When I saw her, her complexion bore that sallow hue which commonly follows residence in the East Indies. Her countenance at first seemed, when in repose, deficient in expression. As she found herself among friends who were interested in the Burman mission, her reserve melted away, her eye kindled, every feature was lighted up with enthusiasm, and she was every where acknowledged to be one of the most fascinating of women.

After the departure of Mrs. Judson, Mr. Judson was left for a while entirely alone in the mission. He devoted himself with redoubled energy to the translation of the New Testament, and the labors of the zayat. When the vigilance of persecution relaxed, and the opportunities for preaching were more favorable, the greater part of his time was employed in imparting religious instruction. When some untoward expression of the Burman magistrates intimidated inquirers, he turned with the greater earnestness to the work of translation.

On the 13th of December, 1821, Rev. Jonathan Price, M. D., a missionary physician recently appointed by the board, arrived with his family at Rangoon. On the 20th of January, 1822, Mr. Hough and his family joined them from Calcutta, to unite again in missionary labors.

At this period of the mission, all the appearances were exceedingly encouraging. The knowledge of the Christian religion was silently insinuating itself among the people of Rangoon and the surrounding villages, and it was producing its legitimate effect — the turning of men from idols to the living God. Before the close of the summer, eighteen native Burmans in the whole had been baptized into the name of the Father, and the Son, and the Holy Ghost; and all but two had maintained an irreproachable Christian profession. It seemed that nothing was needed but toleration to enable true religion to spread throughout the empire.

Dr. Price immediately commenced the practice of his profession in Rangoon. His success in several operations, specially on the eyes of those suffering from cataract, was made known in Ava; and on the

20th of July, only seven months after his arrival, an order was received from the king, summoning him to the capital, on account of his medical skill. Mr. Judson was of course obliged to accompany him, though the step was most repugnant to his feelings. He had proceeded in his translation of the New Testament, as far as the Epistle to the Romans; and being the only person then living capable of completing the work, aware of the uncertainty of life, he earnestly desired to proceed in it without delay. The path of duty, however, seemed to be plainly marked out, and, on the 28th of August, 1822, the two missionaries left Rangoon in a boat furnished at the government expense, and arrived at Ava on the 27th of September.

The following extracts from Mr. Judson's journal relate the most important incidents of this second visit to the capital of the empire.

Journal.

After much tedious detention, resulting from our connection with government, brother Price and myself set out from Rangoon on the 28th of August, in a boat furnished at the public expense, and on the 27th of September reached Ava, the present capital, a few miles below A-ma-ra-poo-ra. We were immediately introduced to the king, who received brother Price very graciously, and made many inquiries about his medical skill, but took no notice of me, except as interpreter. The a-twen-woon Moung Zah, however, immediately recognized me, made a few inquiries about my welfare, in presence of the king, and, after his majesty had withdrawn, conversed a little on religious subjects, and gave me some private encouragement to remain at the capital.

October 1. To-day the king noticed me for the first time, though I have appeared before him nearly every day since our arrival. After making some inquiries, as usual, about brother

Price, he added, "And you in black, what are you? A medical man, too?" "Not a medical man, but a teacher of religion, your majesty." He proceeded to make a few inquiries about my religion, and then put the alarming question whether any had embraced it. I evaded, by saying, "Not here." He persisted. "Are there any in Rangoon?" "There are a few." "Are they foreigners?" I trembled for the consequences of an answer, which might involve the little church in ruin; but the truth must be sacrificed, or the consequences hazarded, and I therefore replied, "There are some foreigners, and some Burmans." He remained silent a few moments, but presently showed that he was not displeased, by asking a great variety of questions on religion, and geography, and astronomy, some of which were answered in such a satisfactory manner as to occasion a general expression of approbation in all the court present. After his majesty retired, a than-dau-sen (a royal secretary) entered into conversation, and allowed me to expatiate on several topics of the Christian religion, in my usual way. And all this took place in the hearing of the very man, now an a-twen-woon, who, many years ago, caused his uncle to be tortured almost to death under the iron mall, for renouncing Boodhism, and embracing the Roman Catholic religion; but I knew it not at the time, though, from his age, a slight suspicion of the truth passed across my mind. Thanks to God for the encouragement of this day! The monarch of the empire has distinctly understood that some of his subjects have embraced the Christian religion, and his wrath has been restrained. Let us, then, hope that, as he becomes more acquainted with the excellence of the religion, he will be more and more willing that his subjects should embrace it.

October 3. Left the boat, and moved into the house ordered to be erected for us by the king. A mere temporary shed, however, it proves to be, scarcely sufficient to screen us from the gaze of people without, or from the rain above. It is situated near the present palace, and joins the enclosure of Prince M., eldest half brother of the king.

October 4. On our return from the palace, whither we go

every morning after breakfast, Prince M. sent for me. I had seen him once before, in company with brother Price, whom he called for medical advice. To-day he wished to converse on science and religion. He is a fine young man of twenty-eight, but greatly disfigured by a paralytic affection of the arms and legs. Being cut off from the usual sources of amusement, and having associated a little with the Portuguese padres who have lived at Ava, he has acquired a strong taste for foreign science. My communications interested him very much, and I found it difficult to get away, until brother Price sent expressly for me to go again to the palace.

October 15. For ten days past, have been confined with the fever and ague. To-day, just able to go to the palace, and have a little conversation with some of the court officers. Afterwards visited Prince M.

October 16. Had a very interesting conversation, in the palace, with two of the a-twen-woons and several officers, on the being of God, and other topics of the Christian religion. Some of them manifested a spirit of candor and free inquiry, which greatly encouraged me.

October 21. Visited the a-twen-woon Moung Zah, and had a long conversation on the religion and customs of foreigners, in which I endeavored to communicate as much as possible of the gospel. Upon the whole, he appeared to be rather favorably disposed, and, on my taking leave, invited me respectfully to visit him occasionally. Thence I proceeded to the palace, but met with nothing noticeable, and thence to the house of Prince M., with whom I had an hour's uninterrupted conversation. But I am sorry to find that he is rather amused with the information I give him, than disposed to consider it a matter of personal concern. I presented him with a tract, which he received as a favor; and finally I ventured to ask him whether Burman subjects who should consider and embrace the Christian religion would be liable to persecution. He replied, "Not under the reign of my brother. He has a good heart, and wishes all to believe and worship as they please."

October 22. Brother Price went to A-ma-ra-poo-ra, to meet a gentleman just arrived from Rangoon, who, we hope, may have letters for us. Made an introductory visit to Prince T., second own brother of the king. He received me with the affability which characterizes his intercourse with foreigners. At night brother Price returned, with a large parcel of letters, and magazines, and newspapers from our beloved, far-distant native land, and, what was still more interesting to me, eight sheets from Mrs. Judson, on her passage towards England — the first direct intelligence I have received from her since she left Madras roads. The divine blessing appears to have crowned her efforts, and those of the pious captain of the ship, to the hopeful conversion of several souls, and, among others, the ladies of a family of rank, her fellow-passengers. At the last date, April 24, she was under the line, in the Atlantic, and experienced a slight return of her complaint, after having long indulged the hope that it was completely removed. A single line from Bengal informs me of the death of our dear brother Colman, but leaves me ignorant of all the particulars. May our bereaved sister be supported under this heaviest of all afflictions; and may the severe loss which the mission has sustained be sanctified to us all.

October 23. Had some pleasant conversation with Moung Zah in the palace, partly in the hearing of the king. At length his majesty came forward, and honored me with some personal notice for the second time, inquired much about my country, and authorized me to invite American ships to his dominions, assuring them of protection, and offering every facility for the purposes of trade.

October 24. Visited Moung Zah at his house. He treated me with great reserve, and repelled all attempts at conversation. Afterwards called on Prince M., and spent a long time with him and the officers in waiting. The whole tract was read before them by one of the secretaries. In the afternoon, went out of town, to visit Moung Shwa-thah, former viceroy of Rangoon. During our absence, Prince M. sent to our house to call me, saying that a learned pundit was in attendance, with whom he wished to hear me converse. I mention the circumstance as somewhat indicative of the prince's mind.

October 26. While I lay ill with the fever and ague, some days ago, a young man, brother of an officer of Prince M., visited me, and listened to a considerable exposition of gospel truth. Since then he has occasionally called, and manifested a desire to hear and know more. This evening he came to attend our evening worship, and remained conversing till nine o'clock. I hope that light is dawning on his mind. He desires to know the truth, appears to be, in some degree, sensible of his sins, and has some slight apprehension of the love and grace of the Lord Jesus Christ.

October 28. Spent the forenoon with Prince M. He obtained, for the first time, (though I have explained it to him many times,) some view of the nature of the atonement, and cried out, "Good! good!" He then proposed a number of objections, which I removed to his apparent satisfaction. Our subsequent conversation turned, as usual, on points of geography and astronomy. He candidly acknowledged that he could not resist my arguments in favor of the Copernican system, and that, if he admitted them, he must also admit that the Boodhist system was overthrown. In the afternoon, visited Prince T. A hopeless case.

October 29. Made an introductory visit to the Great Prince, so called by way of eminence, being the only brother of the queen, and sustaining the rank of chief a-twen-woon. Have frequently met him at the palace, where he has treated me rather uncourteously; and my reception to-day was such as I had too much reason to expect.

October 30. Spent part of the forenoon with Prince M. and his wife, the Princess of S., own sister of the king. Gave her a copy of Mrs. Judson's Burman catechism, with which she was much pleased. They both appear to be somewhat attached to me, and say, "Do not return to Rangoon, but, when your wife arrives, call her to Ava. The king will give you a piece of ground on which to build a kyoung" — a house appropriated to the residence of sacred characters. In the evening, they sent for me again, chiefly on account of an officer of government, to whom they wished to introduce me.

October 31. Visited the a-twen-woon Moung K., whom I have frequently met at the palace, who has treated me with distinguished candor. He received me very politely, and, laying aside his official dignity, entered into a most spirited dispute on various points of religion. He pretended to maintain his ground without the shadow of doubt; but I am inclined to think that he has serious doubts. We parted in a very friendly manner, and he invited me to visit him occasionally.

November 12. Spent the whole forenoon with Prince M. and his wife. Made a fuller disclosure than ever before of the nature of the Christian religion, the object of Christians in sending me to this country, my former repulse at court and the reason of it, our exposure to persecution in Rangoon, the affair of Moung Shwa-gnong, &c., &c. They entered into my views and feelings with considerable interest; but both said, decidedly, that, though the king would not himself persecute any one on account of religion, he would not give any order exempting from persecution, but would leave his subjects, throughout the empire, to the regular administration of the local authorities.

After giving the prince a succinct account of my religious experience, I ventured to warn him of his danger, and urge him to make the Christian religion his immediate personal concern. He appeared, for a moment, to feel the force of what I said, but soon replied, "I am yet young — only twenty-eight. I am desirous of studying all the foreign arts and sciences. My mind will then be enlarged, and I shall be capable of judging whether the Christian religion be true or not." "But suppose your highness changes worlds in the mean time." His countenance again fell. "It is true," said he, "I know not when I shall die." I suggested that it would be well to pray to God for light, which, if obtained, would enable him at once to distinguish between truth and falsehood; and so we parted. O Fountain of Light, shed down one ray into the mind of this amiable prince, that he may become a patron of thine infant cause, and inherit an eternal crown.

November 14. Another interview with Prince M. He seemed, at one time, almost ready to give up the religion of Gaudama, and listened with much eagerness and pleasure to the evidences of the Christian religion. But presently two Burman teachers came in, with whom he immediately joined, and contradicted all I said.

November 18. Visited the Princess of T., at her particular request. She is the eldest own sister of the king, and therefore, according to Burman laws, consigned to perpetual celibacy. She had heard of me from her brother-in-law Prince M., and wished to converse on science and religion. Her chief officer and the mayor of the city were present; and we carried on a desultory conversation, such as necessarily takes place on the first interview. Her highness treated me with uncommon affability and respect, and invited me to call frequently.

November 26. Have been confined since the 21st with a third attack of the fever and ague. To-day, went to the palace, and presented a petition for a certain piece of ground within the walls of the town, "to build a kyoung on." The king granted it, on condition that the ground should be found unoccupied.

November 28. Spent the whole day at the palace, in endeavoring to secure the ground petitioned for. At night, the land measurer general's secretary accompanied me to ascertain the premises, and make out a plan of the place.

November 29. The land measurer general reported to the a-twen-woons that the ground was not actually occupied, but, having been the site of a kyoung when formerly the city was the seat of government, must be considered sacred and unalienable; in which opinion nearly all the a-twen-woons coincided, notwithstanding the king's decision to the contrary.

Had an interesting interview with Prince M., and presented him with a copy of the three last chapters of Matthew, in compliance with his wish to have an account of the death and resurrection of Jesus Christ. He appeared concerned for our failure to-day in the privy council, but still maintained that, though the ground was sacred, it might with propriety be given to a priest, though not a priest of Gaudama, and advised me to make another application to the king.

December 25. I have had nothing scarcely of a missionary nature to notice since the last date, having been employed, most of the time, (that is, in the intervals of two more attacks of fever and ague,) in endeavoring to procure a piece of ground within the city, but have been defeated at every point. At one time, I had received the king's positive order for the place above mentioned, and, at considerable expense, passed it through the privy council and the supreme court as far as the chief woon-gyee; but, as soon as he saw it, he disputed its propriety; and at the next morning levee, which he summoned me to attend, he civilly told his majesty that the ground was sacred, and ought not to be given away. Three of the a-twen-woons joined him. The king at first remained silent, but at length said, "Well, give him some vacant spot." And thus was the order cancelled. As for the vacant spot, if we are debarred all sacred ground, I believe it will be impossible to find it within the walls either of the inner or the outer city, such is the immense demand for places, occasioned by the perpetual emigration from the old city.

In prosecuting this business, I had one noticeable interview with the king. Brother Price and two English gentlemen were present. The king appeared to be attracted by our number, and came towards us; but his conversation was directed chiefly to me. He again inquired about the Burmans who had embraced my religion. "Are they real Burmans? Do they dress like other Burmans?" &c. I had occasion to remark that I preached every Sunday. "What! in Burman?" "Yes." "Let us hear how you preach." I hesitated. An a-twen-woon repeated the order. I began with a form of worship which first ascribes glory to God, and then declares the commands of the law of the gospel; after which I stopped. "Go on," said another a-twen-woon. The whole court was profoundly silent. I proceeded with a few sentences, declarative of the perfections of God, when his majesty's curiosity was satisfied, and he interrupted me. In the course of subsequent conversation, he asked what I had to say of Gaudama. I replied, that we all knew he was the son of King Thog-dau-dah-nah; that we regarded him as a wise man and a great teacher, but did not call him God. "That is right," said Moung K. N., an a-twen-woon who has not hitherto appeared very friendly to me. And he proceeded to relate the substance of a long communication which I lately made to him, in the privy council room, about God and Christ, &c. And this he did in a very clear and satisfactory manner, so that I had scarcely a single correction to make in his statement. Moung Zah, encouraged by all this, really began to take the side of God before his majesty, and said, "Nearly all the world, your majesty, believe in an eternal God, all, except Burmah and Siam, these little spots!" His majesty remained silent, and after some other desultory inquiries, he abruptly arose, and retired.

January 2, 1823. To-day I informed the king that it was my intention to return to Rangoon. "Will you proceed thence to your own country?" "Only to Rangoon." His majesty gave an acquiescing nod. The a-twen-woon, Moung Zah, inquired, "Will you both go, or will the doctor remain?" I said that he would remain. Brother Price made some remark on the approaching hot season, and the inconvenience of our present situation; on which Moung Zah, inferring that it was on account of the climate that I was about leaving, turned to me, saying, "Then you will return here, after the hot season." I looked at the king, and said that if it was convenient, I would return; which his majesty again sanctioned by an acquiescing nod and smile, and in reply to brother Price, said, "Let a place be given him." Brother Price, however, thinks of retaining the small place on which we now live for medical purposes, and getting a place at Chagaing, on the opposite side of the river, for his permanent residence.

In the evening, had a long conversation with Moung Zah on

religion. He believes that there is an eternal God, and that Gaudama, and Christ, and Mahomet, and others are great teachers, who communicated as much truth respectively as they could, but that their communications are not the word of God. I pressed my arguments as far as I dared; but he seemed to have reflected much on the subject, and to have become quite settled and inflexible in his conclusions. He may be called a deistic Boodhist, the first that I have met in the country. On parting, however, he remarked, " This is a deep and difficult subject. Do you, teacher, consider further, and I also will consider."

January 7. Among the many places which I endeavored in vain to procure was a small one, sufficient for one family only, pleasantly situated on the banks of the river, just without the walls of the town, and about a mile from the palace. But it had been appropriated by the chief woon-gyee, and partly fenced in, with the intention of building a temporary zayat for his recreation and refreshment, when accompanying the king in that quarter of the city, and was, therefore, placed beyond any reasonable hope of attainment. Among other desperate attempts, however, I wrote a short petition, asking for that place, and begging leave to express my gratitude, by presenting a certain sum of money. It was necessary to put this into his own hand; and I was, therefore, obliged to follow him about, and watch his movements, for two or three days, until a favorable opportunity occurred, when he was apart from all his retinue. I seized the moment, presented myself before him, and held up the paper. He read it, and smiled, " You are indefatigable in your search after a place. But you cannot have that. It is for my own use. Nor, if otherwise, could you get it for money. Search further." I now concluded to return to Rangoon for the present, and wait until the town should be settled, when, as all inform me, I shall be able to accommodate myself better. I accordingly informed the king of my purpose, as mentioned above, and began to look about for a boat. In the mean time, it occurred to me to make a " seventh attempt to fix the thread," and I sought another interview with the chief woon-gyee, a being who is really more difficult of access than the king himself. This evening I was so fortunate as to find him at his house, lying down, surrounded by forty or fifty of his people. I pressed forward into the foremost rank, and placed myself in a proper attitude. After a while, his eye fell upon me, and I held up a small bottle of *eau de luce*, and desired to present it. One of his officers carried it to him. He happened to be much pleased with it, and sat upright. " What kind of a house do you intend to build?" I told him, but added, "I have no place to build on, my lord." He remained in a meditating attitude a few moments, and then suddenly replied, " *If you want the little enclosure, take it!* " I expressed my gratitude. He began to take more notice of me, inquired about my character and profession, and then entered, with considerable spirit, on the subject of religion. After some conversation, he desired a specimen of my mode of worship and preaching; and I was obliged to repeat much more than I did before the king; for whenever I desisted, he ordered me to go on. When his curiosity was satisfied, he lay down, and I quietly retired.

January 8. After taking the best advice, Burman and foreign, I weighed out the sum of money mentioned in the private petition, together with the estimated expense of fencing the place given me by the woon-gyee, and in the evening, carried it to his house, where I was again fortunate in finding him in the same position as yesterday evening. A few noblemen and their attendants were present, which prevented me from immediately producing the money. His excellency soon took notice of me, and from seven o'clock till nine, the time was chiefly occupied in conversation on religious subjects. I found opportunity to bring forward some of my favorite arguments, one of which, in particular, seemed to carry conviction to the minds of all present, and extorted from the great man an expression of praise; such praise, however, as is indicative of surprise rather than approbation. When the company retired, my people at the outer door overheard one say to another, "Is it not pleasant to hear this foreign teacher converse on religion?" "Ay," said the other, "but his doctrines are derogatory to the honor of Lord Gaudama." When they were gone, I presented the money, saying that I wished to defray the expense of fencing the ground, which had been graciously given me. His excellency was pleased with the offer, but gently declined accepting any thing. He then looked steadily at me, as if to penetrate into the motives of my conduct, and recollecting the manœuvres of the first English settlers in Bengal, thought he had discovered something. "Understand, teacher, that we do not give you the entire owning of this ground. We take no recompense, *lest it become American territory.* We give it to you for your present residence only, and, when you go away, shall take it again." "When I go away, my lord, those at whose expense the house is to be built, will desire to place another teacher in my stead." "Very well, let him also occupy the place; but when he dies, or when there is no teacher, we will take it." "In that case, my lord, take it."

January 10. Spent the whole of yesterday and to-day with various secretaries and officers of government, in getting actual possession of the ground given me.

January 13. Built a small house, and stationed one of the disciples and family to keep the place during my absence.

January 18. Removed to Chagaing, into a house which Prince M. has allowed brother Price to build on his ground, in expectation that a change of air and residence would relieve me from the fever and ague, under which I suffer nearly every other day. It is my intention, however, to return immediately to Rangoon, the time being nearly expired which I at first proposed to spend in Ava, and the ends for which I came up being sufficiently gained.

January 22. Took leave of Prince M. He desired me to return soon, and bring with me all the Christian Scriptures, and translate them into Burman. "For," said he, "I wish to read them all."

January 24. Went to take leave of the king, in company

with Mr. L., collector of the port of Rangoon, who arrived last evening. We sat a few moments conversing together. "What are you talking about?" said his majesty. "He is speaking of his return to Rangoon," replied Mr. L. "What does he return for? Let him not return. Let them both [that is, brother Price and myself] stay together. If one goes away, the other must remain alone, and will be unhappy." "He wishes to go for a short time only," replied Mr. L., to bring his wife, the female teacher, and his goods, not having brought any thing with him this time; and he will return soon." His majesty looked at me. "Will you, then, come again?" I replied in the affirmative. "When you come again, is it your intention to remain permanently, or will you go back and forth, as foreigners commonly do?" "When I come again, it is my intention to remain permanently." "Very well," said his majesty, and withdrew into his inner apartment.

Heard to-day of the death of Mah Myat-lah, sister of Mah Men-la, one of the most steadfast of the church in Rangoon.

January 25. Embarked on a small boat, intending to go day and night, and touch nowhere, in order to avoid the robbers, of which we have lately had alarming accounts.

February 2, Lord's day. At one o'clock in the morning reached Rangoon, seven days from Ava.

The Nan-dau-gong disciples soon came over from Dah-lah, on the opposite side of the river, whither they and the Pah-tsooan-doung disciples and inquirers have taken refuge, to escape the heavy taxations and the illegal harassments of every kind, allowed under the new viceroy of Rangoon. Others of the disciples have fled elsewhere, so that there is not a single one remaining in Rangoon, except three or four with us. The Nan-dau-gong disciples' house has been demolished, and their place taken by government, at the instigation of their neighbors, who hate them on account of religion. Mah Myat-la died before the removal. Her sister gave me the particulars of her death. Some of her last expressions were, "I put my trust in Jesus Christ; I love to pray to him;

am not afraid of death ; shall soon be with Christ in heaven."

A letter from Mrs. Judson, in England, informs me that she is going to America, and will not be here under several months. I propose, therefore, waiting her return, and occupying the interval in finishing the translation of the New Testament.

The following letter from Moung Shwa-ba to the Rev. Dr. Baldwin furnishes delightful evidence of the progress which the converts had already made in the knowledge of the gospel and the practice of piety: —

Translation of a Letter from Moung Shwa-ba to the Rev. Dr. Baldwin.

Moung Shwa-ba, an inhabitant of Rangoon, a town of Burmah, one who adheres to the religion of Christ, and has been baptized ; who meditates on the immeasurable, incalculable nature of the divine splendor and glory of the Invisible, even the Lord Jesus Christ and God the Father, and takes refuge in the wisdom, and power, and glory of God, affectionately addresses the great teacher Baldwin, a superintendent of missionary affairs in the city of Boston, of America.

BELOVED ELDER BROTHER : Though in the present state the places of our residence are very far apart, and we have never met, yet, by means of letters, and of the words of Yüda-than, who has told me of you, I love you, and wish to send you this letter. When the time arrives in which we shall wholly put on Christ, — him in loving whom we cannot tire, and in praising whom we can find no end, — and shall be adorned with those ornaments which the Lord will dispense to us out of the heavenly treasure house that he has prepared, then we shall love one another more perfectly than we do now.

Formerly I was in the habit of concealing my sins, that they might not appear ; but I am now convinced that I cannot conceal my sins from the Lord, who sees and knows all things, and that I cannot atone for them, nor obtain atonement from my former objects of worship. And, accordingly, I count myself to have lost all, under the elements of the world, and through the grace of the faith of Christ only to have gained the spiritual graces and rewards pertaining to eternity, which cannot be lost. Therefore I have no ground for boasting, pride, and self-exaltation. And, without desiring the praise of men, or seeking my own will, I wish to do the will of God the Father. The members of the body, dead in trespasses and sins, displeasing to God, I desire to make instruments of righteousness, not following the will of the flesh. Worldly desire and heavenly desire being contrary the one to the other, and the desire of visible things counteracting the desire of invisible things, I am as a dead man. However, he quickens the dead, he awakens those that sleep, he lifts up those that fall, he opens blind eyes, he perforates deaf ears, he lights a lamp in the great house of darkness, he relieves the wretched, he feeds the hungry. The words of such a Benefactor if we reject, we must die forever, and come to everlasting destruction. Which circumstance considering, and meditating also on sickness, old age, and death, incident to the present state of mutability, I kneel and prostrate myself, and pray before God, the Father of the Lord Jesus Christ, who has made atonement for our sins, that he may have mercy on me, and pardon my sins, and make me holy, and give me a repenting, believing, and loving mind.

Formerly I trusted in my own merits; but now, through the preaching and instruction of teacher Yüdathan, I trust in the merit of the Lord Jesus Christ. The teacher, therefore, is the tree; we are the blossoms and fruit. He has labored to partake of the fruit, and now the tree begins to bear. The bread of life he has given, and we eat. The water from the brook which flows from the top of Mount Calvary, for the cleansing of all filth, he has brought, and made us bathe and drink. The bread of which we eat will yet ferment and rise. The water which we drink and bathe in, is the water of an unfailing spring; and many will yet drink and bathe therein. Then all things will be regenerated and changed. Now we are strangers and pilgrims; and it is my desire, without adhering to the things of this world, but longing for my native abode, to consider and inquire how long I must labor here, to whom I ought to show the light I have obtained, when I ought to put it up, and when disclose it.

The inhabitants of this country of Burmah, being in the evil practice of forbidden lust, erroneous worship, and false speech, deride the religion of Christ. However, that we may bear patiently derision, and persecution, and death, for the sake of the Lord Jesus Christ, pray for us. I do thus pray. For, elder brother, I have to bear the threatening of my own brother, and my brother-in-law, who say, "We will beat, and bruise, and pound you; we will bring you into great difficulty; you associate with false people; you keep a false religion; and you speak false words." However, their false religion is the religion of death. The doctrine of the cross is the religion of life, of love, of faith. I am a servant of faith. Formerly I was a servant of Satan. Now I am a servant of Christ. And a good servant cannot but follow his master. Moreover, the divine promises must be accomplished.

In this country of Burmah are many strayed sheep. Teacher Yoodthan, pitying them, has come to gather them together, and to feed them in love. Some will not listen, but run away. Some do listen, and adhere to him; and that our numbers may increase, we meet together, and pray to the great Proprietor of the sheep.

Thus I, Moung Shwa-ba, a disciple of teacher Yüdathan, in Rangoon, write and send this letter to the great teacher Baldwin, who lives in Boston, America.

N. B. Translated from the Burmese original, September 23, 1823.

A. JUDSON, JR.

The rules of living which follow are copied from a paper in the handwriting of Dr. Judson. They are inserted here for the sake of illustrating the earnestness with which he strove after personal holiness, whilst engrossed with the labors of his missionary calling. He well knew that no external services could purify the heart; that this work could be done in no other way than by practically subjecting the whole soul to the commandments of Christ.

Rules adopted on Sunday, April 4, 1819, the era of commencing public ministrations among the Burmans; revised and re-adopted on Saturday, December 9, 1820, and on Wednesday, April 25, 1821.

1. Be diligent in secret prayer, every morning and evening.
2. Never spend a moment in mere idleness.
3. Restrain natural appetites within the bounds of temperance and purity. "Keep thyself pure."
4. Suppress every emotion of anger and ill will.
5. Undertake nothing from motives of ambition, or love of fame.
6. Never do that which, at the moment, appears to be displeasing to God.
7. Seek opportunities of making some sacrifice for the good of others, especially of believers, provided the sacrifice is not inconsistent with some duty.
8. Endeavor to rejoice in every loss and suffering incurred for Christ's sake and the gospel's, remembering that though, like death, they are not to be wilfully incurred, yet, like death, they are great gain.

Re-adopted the above rules, particularly *the 4th, on Sunday, August* 31, 1823.

Re-adopted the above rules, particularly *the 1st, on Sunday, October* 29, 1826, and adopted the following minor rules:—

1. Rise with the sun.
2. Read a certain portion of Burman every day, Sundays excepted.
3. Have the Scriptures and some devotional book in constant reading.

4. Read no book in English that has not a devotional tendency.

5. Suppress every unclean *thought* and *look.*

Revised and re-adopted all the above rules, particularly the second of the first class, on Sunday, March 11, 1827.

God grant me grace to keep the above rules, and ever live to his glory, for Jesus Christ's sake.

A. JUDSON

To the Rev. Dr. Baldwin.

RANGOON, February 11, 1823.

REV. AND DEAR SIR: My last to you was written just before we left Rangoon for Ava. While at Ava, yours of March last came to hand, and afforded me much consolation and encouragement. Since my return, I have received yours of July, the latest that has reached me from America. The magazines also have all been duly received. Many thanks for all your kindnesses, and thanks to God, who has excited so much interest for the Burman mission in the hearts of his dear children in far distant lands.

You will learn from my journal, forwarded herewith to the Corresponding Secretary, the particulars of our visit to Ava. Suffice it here to say that the Lord has been gracious to us beyond our expectation. My reception, as a minister of religion, has been very different from what it was before. A liberal and candid spirit seems to prevail among all the members of the royal family, and among many of the leading members of government. It is distinctly understood by the king, and by all who have any knowledge of me at all, that I am a thah-tha-nah-pyoo-tsayah, that is, a religion-propagating teacher; and yet I have been smiled on, and listened to, and, by the order of the king himself, have received from the chief public minister of state the grant of a small piece of ground, for the express purpose of building a kyoung, (a house appropriated to sacred characters.) It is my intention, therefore, to return thither as soon as Mrs. Judson arrives, who, I hear, has gone on to America. And in the mean time, I shall occupy myself in finishing the translation of the New Testament — a work which I left unfinished with great reluctance, and which I rejoice to have leisure to reassume.

During my absence, one of the best of our church members, the sister of Mah Men-la, was called from this world, to join, I trust, the church triumphant. She died in peace and joy, professing her belief in Jesus Christ, and saying that she should soon be with him in heaven.

During the whole of my residence at Ava, I was severely afflicted, at intervals, with the fever and ague. I did hope that a change of climate would effect my cure; but the disorder has followed me to Rangoon, and I am subject to it every other day. Brother Price was apprehensive that it would terminate fatally, having resisted every medical application, and become so deeply rooted; and he would have accompanied me hither, had I not dissuaded him. My only hope now is, that it will exhaust itself before my constitution is exhausted; but the Lord's will be done. I could wish to live to finish the New Testament, and I should also be happy to see a little church raised up in Ava, as there has been in Rangoon. But the ways of God are not as the ways of man. He does all things well. Glory be to his holy name forevermore.

Yours, very respectfully,

A. JUDSON, JR.

At the commencement of Brown University, 1823, the corporation of that institution conferred on Mr. Judson the honorary degree of Doctor in Divinity. Several years elapsed before he became acquainted with the fact. In May, 1828, he addressed the following letter to the editor of the Magazine:—

DEAR SIR: I beg to be allowed the privilege of requesting my correspondents and friends, through the medium of your magazine, no longer to apply to my name the title which was conferred on me in the year 1823 by the corporation of

Brown University, and which, with all deference and respect for that honorable body, I hereby resign.

Nearly three years elapsed before I was informed of the honor done me, and two years more have been suffered to pass, partly from the groundless idea that it was too late to decline the honor, and partly through fear of doing what might seem to reflect on those who have taken a different course, or be liable to the charge of affected singularity, or superstitious preciseness. But I am now convinced that the commands of Christ and the general spirit of the gospel are paramount to all prudential considerations, and I only regret that I have so long delayed to make this communication. Yours, &c.,

A. JUDSON.

This letter was, I believe, published at the time. Mr. Judson's wishes, however, in this respect, were unheeded, and it has been his fate, against his will, to be known as *Dr.* instead of *Mr.* Judson.

From a Letter to the Rev. D. Sharp, dated Rangoon, August 5, 1823.

It is with real satisfaction that I am able to inform you of the completion of the New Testament in Burman, about six weeks ago; since which I have added, by way of introduction, an epitome of the Old Testament, in twelve sections, consisting of a summary of Scripture history from the creation to the coming of Christ, and an abstract of the most important prophecies of the Messiah and his kingdom, from the Psalms, Isaiah, and other prophets. I trust this work will be found as valuable at present as the preceding; for though not, strictly speaking, the word of God, it is compiled almost entirely in the words of Scripture, is received by the converts with great eagerness, and found to be peculiarly interesting and instructive, and forms, moreover, a sort of text book, from which I am able to communicate much information on the history, types, and prophecies of the Old Testament in a systematic manner

CHAPTER X.

HOPEFUL PROSPECTS OF THE MISSION — PASSAGE UP THE IRRAWADI. — WAR BETWEEN THE ENGLISH AND BURMESE. — IMPRISONMENT OF DR. JUDSON AT AVA AND OUNG-PEN-LA. — HIS RELEASE. — PERSONAL REMINISCENCES.

1824—1826.

AT the close of the last chapter, the prospects of the mission seemed eminently favorable. Mrs. Judson was daily expected from America, in invigorated health, accompanied by Mr. and Mrs. Wade, two of the most devoted and successful laborers that have ever entered the missionary field. Mr. and Mrs. Hough had returned from Calcutta, and again united with their brethren at Rangoon. Dr. Judson had completed the translation of the New Testament into the Burmese language. A church of eighteen members had been gathered from the heathen, all of whom gave credible evidence of personal piety. Some of them had indicated both a desire and an aptitude for the ministry of the gospel; and every one of them, each in his appropriate sphere, was endeavoring to make known to others that religion of which he himself had felt the transforming effects. Christianity had thus not only been planted in Rangoon, but it had taken root, and was beginning to change the surrounding community into its own likeness. Yet all this had taken place without awakening, in any alarming degree, the spirit of persecution.

The prospect of success even in Ava was encouraging. A physician known to be associated with the teacher of the new religion had been ordered thither, and had been well received at court. Dr. Judson, who accompanied him, had resided there for several months, and been universally known as a "religion-propagating teacher." His character in this respect caused him no molestation. On the contrary, he was listened to with respectful attention by many persons holding high official rank, and some of them were inquiring about this new religion with more than common interest. When he proposed to leave Ava, the emperor himself condescended to express regret, and invited him to return at the earliest opportunity, accompanied by Mrs. Judson, and make Ava his permanent residence.

These indications of Providence seemed all to point directly to the establishment of a missionary station at Ava. The church at Rangoon would be sufficiently provided for by the presence and labors of Messrs. Wade and Hough and their wives. It had here within itself all the elements of increase. At Ava, the gospel had been heard respectfully by the most intelligent of its citizens. It seemed that a church might be planted there with less danger of persecution than even at Rangoon, while, if this could be done, the principle of religious toleration, from the example of the capital, would be established for the whole empire. The movement was perfectly in harmony with all Dr. Judson's rules of missionary action. Like the apostle Paul, his eye was ever fixed on "the regions beyond." He desired to go where Christ had not been named. When a church had been planted in Rangoon, he felt impelled to proceed with the message of salvation to Ava. Had he succeeded in establishing a church there, I doubt not that he would have moved still onward, to plant another church in some region yet more inaccessible. Such were the views of missionary enterprise which he ever inculcated upon his younger brethren, and which he ever exemplified in his own conduct.

Deeply impressed with these convictions, Dr. Judson had hastened with all speed to Rangoon to meet Mrs. Judson, who was daily expected there. When she arrived, the preparations for the passage up the river had been almost completed; and in a few days, they left Rangoon for Ava, little "knowing the things that should befall them there." There seemed in the whole horizon but one cloud, and that was no bigger than a man's hand. It by no means betokened an alarming tempest. There was, it is true, some reason to fear that a collision might ensue between the empire of Burmah and Great Britain. But the policy of Great Britain was known to be eminently pacific. They could not engage in war without enlarging their territory, and this result was not looked upon with favor by the government at home. A protracted war could not be anticipated; and, it being now well understood at Ava that the missionaries were not Englishmen, but Americans, it seemed highly probable that they would pass through the crisis, if it should arrive, without molestation.

Very soon, however, the indications became less encouraging. Before reaching Ava, they met Bandoola, the Burman general, on the river, hastening with a fleet of war boats and a large army, to invade the British province of Chittagong, where, it was alleged, Burman refugees were protected by British power. When they arrived at the capital, they were less favorably received than they had expected, and soon found themselves to be objects of suspicion. Suspicion, rendered sensitive by fear, soon ripened into hatred. All foreigners were at once arrested and thrown into prison. Imprisonment, among a semi-barbarous people, is something very different from confinement. It is confinement imbittered by every device of malicious and brutal cruelty. All this was endured for twenty-one months by a student of retired habits, unaccustomed to physical hardship, whose constitution had been already enfeebled by a protracted attack of the fever of the country. It seems almost miraculous that he did not sink under these intense and protracted sufferings.

And he would have sunk under them, had it not been that "an angel ministered unto him." Then were revealed those elements of character which designated Mrs. Judson as one of the most remarkable women of her age. She was the only European female in Ava, and the only foreigner who was not consigned to prison. Her whole time, with the exception of twenty days when she was confined by the birth of her child, was devoted to the alleviation of the sorrows of her husband and his fellow-prisoners. Perfectly familiar with the Burman language, of a presence which commanded respect even from savage barbarians, and encircled her with a moral atmosphere in which she walked unharmed in the midst of a hostile city with no earthly protector, she was universally spoken of as the guardian angel of that band of sufferers. Sometimes she appealed to the officers of government, but more frequently to their wives, and pleaded for compassion with an eloquence which even they could not resist. Fertile in resources, and wholly regardless of her own privations or exposure, she was incessantly occupied in alleviating the pain, or ministering to the wants, of those who had no other friend.

Rarely does it happen that the moral extremes of which our nature is susceptible are brought into so striking contrast as in the present instance. On the one hand might here have been seen the most degraded of mankind inflicting in sport the most horrid cruelties, month after month, upon their fellow-men, some of whom had sacrificed every earthly comfort for the good of their tormentors; and on the other hand there was seen, in the midst of this horde of ruffians, a lady, whose intelligence and refinement had quite lately won the admiration of the highest circles of the British metropolis, soothing the sorrows of the captive, ministering to the wants of the sick, providing and preparing food for the starving, consoling the dying with words of heavenly peace; heedless of meridian suns and midnight dews, though surrounded by infection, devoting herself with prodigal disinterestedness to the practice of heavenly charity, and sustaining the courage of men inured to danger and familiar with death by the example of her own dauntless resolution.

The knowledge of her deeds had reached the British army before the conclusion of hostilities. The men who had earned their laurels in the peninsular war were capable of appreciating such a character. She was received at the camp of Yandabo with honors such as would have befitted a lady of the most exalted rank. Sir Archibald Campbell, the commander-in-chief, treated her with parental kindness; and every thing that the army could command was made to minister to her comfort. Nor were the attentions of brave men ever more worthily bestowed; for even that army of war-worn veterans could not boast of a more heroic spirit than that which animated the slender and wasted form of Ann Hasseltine Judson.

I have inserted, without abridgment, the letters of Mrs. Judson, giving a narrative of the voyage to Ava, and the settlement of her husband and herself in that city, and also her letter to his brother, detailing at length the events of their captivity during the war. To these I am able to add many interesting particulars derived from conversations of Dr. Judson himself with Mrs. Emily C. Judson. I need not apologize for the length of these documents; for I do not remember any thing in the history of modern missions more deeply affecting.

Ava, February 10, 1824.

My dear Parents and Sisters: After two years and a half wandering, you will be pleased to hear that I have at last arrived at home, so far as this life is concerned, and am once more quietly and happily settled with Mr. Judson. When I retrace the scenes through which I have passed, the immense space I have traversed, and the various dangers, seen and unseen, from which I have been preserved, my heart is filled with gratitude and praise to that Being who has at all times been my Protector, and marked out all the way before me. Surely no one was ever more highly favored, no being was ever under greater obligations to make sacrifices for the promotion of God's glory, than I am at this moment. And I think I feel more than ever the importance of being spiritual and humble, and so to cherish the influences of the Holy Spirit, that in the communication of divine truth, powerful impressions may be made, and that I may no more wander from Him who is deserving of all my services and affections.

I wrote from Rangoon; but for fear my letters should not have arrived, I will mention a few things therein contained. We had a quick and pleasant passage from Calcutta to Rangoon. Mr. Judson's boat was all in readiness, my baggage was immediately taken from the ship to the boat, and in seven days from my arrival, we were on our way to the capital. Our boat was small and inconvenient; but the current at this season is so very strong, and the wind always against us, that our progress was slow indeed. The season, however, was cool and delightful; we were preserved from dangers by day and robbers by night, and arrived in safety in six weeks. The A-rah-wah-tee (Irrawadi) is a noble river; its banks every where covered with immortal beings, destined to the same eternity as ourselves. We often walked through the villages, and though we never received the least insult, always attracted universal attention. A foreign female was a sight never before beheld, and all were anxious that their friends and relatives should have a view. Crowds followed us through the villages, and some, who were less civilized than others, would run some way before us, in order to have a *long* look as we approached them. In one instance, the boat being some time in doubling a point we had walked over, we seated ourselves down, when the villagers, as usual, assembled, and Mr. Judson introduced the subject of religion. Several old men, who were present, entered into conversation, while the multitude was all attention. The apparent schoolmaster of the village coming up, Mr. Judson handed him a tract, and requested him to read. After proceeding some way, he remarked to the assembly that such a writing was worthy of being copied, and asked Mr. Judson to remain while he copied it. Mr. Judson informed him he might keep the tract, on condition he read it to all his neighbors. We could not but hope the Spirit of God would bless those few simple truths to the salvation of some of their souls.

Our boat was near being upset in passing through one of the rapids with which this river abounds. The rudder became entangled in the rocks, which brought the boat across the stream, and laid her on one side. The steersman, however, had presence of mind sufficient to cut the rudder from the boat, which caused her to right, without experiencing any other inconvenience than a thorough fright, and the loss of our breakfast, which was precipitated from the fireplace into the water, together with every thing on the outside of the boat.

On our arrival at Ava, we had more difficulties to encounter, and such as we had never before experienced. We had no home, no house to shelter us from the burning sun by day and the cold dews at night. Dr. Price had kindly met us on the way, and urged our taking up our residence with him; but his house was in such an unfinished state, and the walls so damp, (of brick, and just built,) that spending two or three hours threw me into a fever, and induced me to feel that it would be presumption to remain longer. We had but one alternative — to remain in the boat till we could build a small house on the spot of ground which the king gave Mr. Judson last year. And you will hardly believe it possible — for I almost doubt my senses — that, in just a fortnight from our arrival, we moved into a house built in that time, and which is sufficiently large to make us comfortable. It is in a most delightful situation, out of the dust of the town, and on the bank of the river. The spot of ground given by his majesty is small, being only one hundred and twenty feet long, and seventy-five wide; but it is our own, and is the most healthy situation I have seen. Our house is raised four feet from the ground, and consists of three small rooms and a veranda.

I hardly know how we shall bear the hot season, which is just commencing, as our house is built of boards, and before night is heated like an oven. Nothing but brick is a shelter from the heat of Ava, where the thermometer, even in the shade, frequently rises to a hundred and eight degrees. We have worship every evening in Burman, when a number of the natives assemble; and every Sabbath Mr. Judson preaches the other side of the river, in Dr. Price's house. We feel it an inestimable privilege, that amid all our discouragements we have the language, and are able constantly to communicate truths which can save the soul.

My female school has already commenced, with three little girls, who are learning to read, sew, &c. Two of them are sisters, and we have named them *Mary* and *Abby Hasseltine*.

One of them is to be supported with the money which the "Judson Association of Bradford Academy" have engaged to collect. They are fine children, and improve as rapidly as any children in the world. Their mother is deranged, and their father gave them to me to educate, so that I have been at no expense for them, excepting their food and clothes. I have already begun to make inquiries for children, and doubt not we shall be directed in regard to our school.

I have not yet been at the palace, the royal family all being absent. They returned to Amarapoora a day or two after our arrival, where they will remain till the new palace in this city is finished, when they will take possession in the usual form, and Ava in future will be their residence. My old friend, the lady of the viceroy of Rangoon, who died in my absence, came to the boat to see me immediately on being informed of my arrival. All her power and distinction ceased at the death of her husband, and she is now only a private woman. She is, however, a very sensible woman, and there is much more hope of her attending to the subject of religion now than when in public life. I intend to visit her frequently, and make it an object to fix her attention to the subject. In consequence of war with the Bengal government, foreigners are not so much esteemed at court as formerly. I know not what effect this war will have on our mission; but we must leave the event with Him who has hitherto directed us.

RANGOON, May 26, 1826.

MY BELOVED BROTHER: I commence this letter with the intention of giving you the particulars of our captivity and sufferings at Ava. How long my patience will allow my reviewing scenes of disgust and horror, the conclusion of this letter will determine. I had kept a journal of every thing that had transpired from our arrival at Ava, but destroyed it at the commencement of our difficulties.

The first certain intelligence we received of the declaration of war by the Burmese, was on our arrival at Tsen-pyoo-kywon, about a hundred miles this side of Ava, where part of the troops under the command of the celebrated Bandoola had encamped. As we proceeded on our journey, we met Bandoola himself with the remainder of h.s troops, gayly equipped, seated on his golden barge, and surrounded by a fleet of golden war boats, one of which was instantly despatched from the other side of the river to hail us, and make all necessary inquiries. We were allowed to proceed quietly on, when we had informed the messenger that we were Americans, *not English*, and were going to Ava in obedience to the command of his majesty.

On our arrival at the capital, we found that Dr. Price was out of favor at court, and that suspicion rested on most of the foreigners then at Ava. Your brother visited at the palace two or three times, but found the king's manner towards him very different from what it formerly had been ; and the queen, who had hitherto expressed wishes for my speedy arrival, now made no inquiries after me, nor intimated a wish to see me. Consequently, I made no effort to visit at the palace, though almost daily invited to visit some of the branches of the royal family, who were living in their own houses, out of the palace enclosure. Under these circumstances, we thought our most prudent course lay in prosecuting our original intention of building a house, and commencing missionary operations as occasions offered, thus endeavoring to convince the government that we had really nothing to do with the present war.

In two or three weeks after our arrival, the king, queen, all the members of the royal family, and most of the officers of government, returned to Amarapoora, in order to come and take possession of the new palace in the customary style. As there has been much misunderstanding relative to Ava and Amarapoora, both being called the capital of the Burmese empire, I will here remark, that the present Ava was formerly the seat of government; but soon after the old king had ascended the throne, it was forsaken, and a new palace built at Amarapoora, about six miles from Ava, in which he remained during his life. In the fourth year of the reign of the present king, Amarapoora was in its turn forsaken, and a new and beautiful palace built at Ava, which was *then* in ruins, but is *now the capital* of the Burmese empire. The king and royal family had been living in temporary buildings at Ava, during the completion of the new palace, which gave occasion for their returning to Amarapoora.

I dare not attempt a description of that splendid day, when majesty, with all its attendant glory, entered the gates of the golden city, and amid the acclamations of millions, I may say, took possession of the palace. The saupwars of the provinces bordering on China, all the viceroys and high officers of the kingdom, were assembled on the occasion, dressed in their robes of state, and ornamented with the insignia of their office. The white elephant, richly adorned with gold and jewels, was one of the most beautiful objects in the procession. The king and queen alone were unadorned, dressed in the simple garb of the country; they, hand in hand, entered the garden in which we had taken our seats, and where a banquet was prepared for their refreshment. All the riches and glory of the empire were on this day exhibited to view. The number and immense size of the elephants, the numerous horses, and great variety of vehicles of all descriptions, far surpassed any thing I have ever seen or imagined. Soon after his majesty had taken possession of the new palace, an order was issued that no foreigner should be allowed to enter, excepting Lanciego. We were a little alarmed at this, but concluded it was from political motives, and would not, perhaps, essentially affect us.

For several weeks nothing took place to alarm us, and we went on with our school. Mr. Judson preached every Sabbath; all the materials for building a brick house were procured, and the masons had made considerable progress in raising the building.

On the 23d of May, 1824, just as we had concluded worship at the doctor's house, the other side of the river, a messenger came to inform us that Rangoon was taken by the English. The intelligence produced a shock, in which was a mixture of fear and joy. Mr. Gouger, a young merchant residing at Ava, was then with us, and had much more reason to fear than the rest of us. We all, however, immediately returned to our house, and began to consider what was to be done. Mr. G.

went to Prince Thah-ya-wa-dee, the king's most influential brother, who informed him he need not give himself any uneasiness, as he had mentioned the subject to his majesty, who had replied, that "the few foreigners residing at Ava had nothing to do with the war, and should not be molested."

The government were now all in motion. An army of ten or twelve thousand men, under the command of the kyee-woon-gyee, were sent off in three or four days, and were to be joined by the sakyah-woon-gyee, who had previously been appointed viceroy of Rangoon, and who was on his way thither when the news of its attack reached him. No doubt was entertained of the defeat of the English; the only fear of the king was, that the foreigners, hearing of the advance of the Burmese troops, would be so alarmed as to flee on board their ships and depart, before there would be time to secure them as slaves. "Bring for me," said a wild young buck of the palace, "six kala-pyoos, [white strangers,] to row my boat." "And to me," said the lady of a woon-gyee, "send four white strangers to manage the affairs of my house, as I understand they are trusty servants." The war boats, in high glee, passed our house, the soldiers singing and dancing, and exhibiting gestures of the most joyous kind. "Poor fellows!" said we, "you will probably never dance again." And it so proved, for few, if any, ever again saw their native home.

As soon as the army were despatched, the government began to inquire the cause of the arrival of the strangers at Rangoon. There must be spies in the country, suggested some, who have invited them over. And who so likely to be spies as the Englishmen residing at Ava? A report was in circulation that Captain Laird, lately arrived, had brought Bengal papers which contained the intention of the English to take Rangoon, and it was kept a secret from his majesty. An inquiry was instituted. The three Englishmen, Gouger, Laird, and Rogers, were called and examined. It was found they had seen the papers, and were put in confinement, though not in prison. We now began to tremble for ourselves, and were in daily expectation of some dreadful event.

At length Mr. Judson and Dr. Price were summoned to a court of examination, where strict inquiry was made relative to all they knew. The great point seemed to be whether they had been in the habit of making communications to foreigners of the state of the country, &c. They answered, they had always written to their friends in America, but had no correspondence with English officers, or the Bengal government. After their examination they were not put in confinement, as the Englishmen had been, but were allowed to return to their houses. In examining the accounts of Mr. Gouger, it was found that Mr. Judson and Dr. Price had taken money of him to a considerable amount. Ignorant as were the Burmese of our mode of receiving money by orders on Bengal, this circumstance, to their suspicious minds, was a sufficient evidence that the missionaries were in the pay of the English, and very probably spies. It was thus represented to the king, who, in an angry tone, ordered the immediate arrest of the "two teachers."

On the 8th of June, just as we were preparing for dinner, in rushed an officer, holding a black book, with a dozen Burmans, accompanied by *one*, whom, from his spotted face, we knew to be an executioner, and a "son of the prison." "Where is the teacher?" was the first inquiry. Mr. Judson presented himself. "You are called by the king," said the officer — a form of speech always used when about to arrest a criminal. The spotted man instantly seized Mr. Judson, threw him on the floor, and produced the small cord, the instrument of torture. I caught hold of his arm. "Stay," said I; "I will give you money." "Take her too," said the officer; "she also is a foreigner." Mr. Judson, with an imploring look, begged they would let me remain till further orders. The scene was now shocking beyond description. The whole neighborhood had collected; the masons at work on the brick house threw down their tools, and ran; the little Burman children were screaming and crying; the Bengalee servants stood in amazement at the indignities offered their master; and the hardened executioner, with a kind of hellish joy, drew tight the cords, bound Mr. Judson fast, and dragged him off

I knew not whither. In vain I begged and entreated the spotted face to take the silver, and loosen the ropes; but he spurned my offers, and immediately departed. I gave the money, however, to Moung Ing to follow after, to make some further attempt to mitigate the torture of Mr. Judson; but instead of succeeding, when a few rods from the house, the unfeeling wretches again threw their prisoner on the ground, and drew the cords still tighter, so as almost to prevent respiration.

The officer and his gang proceeded on to the court house, where the governor of the city and officers were collected, one of whom read the order of the king to commit Mr. Judson to the death prison, into which he was soon hurled, the door closed, and Moung Ing saw no more. What a night was now before me! I retired into my room, and endeavored to obtain consolation from committing my case to God, and imploring fortitude and strength to suffer whatever awaited me. But the consolation of retirement was not long allowed me, for the magistrate of the place had come into the veranda, and continually called me to come out, and submit to his examination. But previously to going out, I destroyed all my letters, journals, and writings of every kind, lest they should disclose the fact that we had correspondents in England, and had minuted down every occurrence since our arrival in the country. When this work of destruction was finished, I went out, and submitted to the examination of the magistrate, who inquired very minutely of every thing I knew; then ordered the gates of the compound to be shut, no person to be allowed to go in or out, placed a guard of ten ruffians, to whom he gave a strict charge to keep me safe, and departed.

It was now dark. I retired to an inner room with my four little Burman girls, and barred the doors. The guard instantly ordered me to unbar the doors and come out, or they would break the house down. I obstinately refused to obey, and endeavored to intimidate them by threatening to complain of their conduct to higher authorities on the morrow. Finding me resolved in disregarding their orders, they took the two Bengalee servants, and confined them in the stocks in a very painful position. I could not endure this, but called the head man to the window, and promised to make them all a present in the morning, if they would release the servants. After much debate, and many severe threatenings, they consented, but seemed resolved to annoy me as much as possible. My unprotected, desolate state, my entire uncertainty of the fate of Mr. Judson, and the dreadful carousings and almost diabolical language of the guard, all conspired to make it by far the most distressing night I had ever passed. You may well imagine, my dear brother, that sleep was a stranger to my eyes, and peace and composure to my mind.

The next morning, I sent Moung Ing to ascertain the situation of your brother, and give him food, if still living. He soon returned, with the intelligence that Mr. Judson and all the white foreigners were confined in the *death prison*, with three pairs of iron fetters each, and fastened to a long pole, to prevent their moving! The point of my anguish now was, that I was a prisoner myself, and could make no efforts for the release of the missionaries. I begged and entreated the magistrate to allow me to go to some member of government to state my case; but he said he did not dare to consent, for fear I should make my escape. I next wrote a note to one of the king's sisters, with whom I had been intimate, requesting her to use her influence for the release of the teachers. The note was returned with this message; she "did not understand it;" which was a polite refusal to interfere; though I afterwards ascertained that she had an anxious desire to assist us, but dared not, on account of the queen. The day dragged heavily away, and another dreadful night was before me. I endeavored to soften the feelings of the guard, by giving them tea and cigars for the night; so that they allowed me to remain inside of my room without threatening, as they did the night before. But the idea of your brother being stretched on the bare floor, in irons and confinement, haunted my mind like a spectre, and prevented my obtaining any quiet sleep, though nature was almost exhausted.

On the third day, I sent a message to the governor of the

city, who has the entire direction of prison affairs, to allow me to visit him with a present. This had the desired effect, and he immediately sent orders to the guards, to permit my going into town. The governor received me pleasantly, and asked me what I wanted. I stated to him the situation of the foreigners, and particularly that of the teachers, who were Americans, and had nothing to do with the war. He told me it was not in his power to release them from prison or irons, but that he could make their situation more comfortable; there was his head officer, with whom I must consult, relative to the means. The officer, who proved to be one of the city writers, and whose countenance at the first glance presented the most perfect assemblage of all the evil passions attached to human nature, took me aside, and endeavored to convince me, that myself, as well as the prisoners, was entirely at his disposal; that our future comfort must depend on my liberality in regard to presents; and that these must be made in a private way, and unknown to any officer in the government! "What must I do," said I, "to obtain a mitigation of the present sufferings of the two teachers?" "Pay to me," said he, "two hundred ticals, [about a hundred dollars,] two pieces of fine cloth, and two pieces of handkerchiefs." I had taken money with me in the morning; our house being two miles from the prison, I could not easily return. This I offered to the writer, and begged he would not insist on the other articles, as they were not in my possession. He hesitated for some time; but fearing to lose the sight of so much money, he concluded to take it, promising to relieve the teachers from their most painful situation.

I then procured an order from the governor for my admittance into prison; but the sensations produced by meeting your brother in that *wretched, horrid* situation, and the affecting scene which ensued, I will not attempt to describe. Mr. Judson crawled to the door of the prison, — for I was never allowed to enter, — gave me some directions relative to his release; but before we could make any arrangement, I was ordered to depart by those iron-hearted jailers, who could not endure to see us enjoy the poor consolation of meeting in that miserable place. In vain I pleaded the order from the governor for my admittance; they again harshly repeated, "Depart, or we will pull you out." The same evening the missionaries, together with the other foreigners, who paid an equal sum, were taken out of the common prison, and confined in an open shed in the prison enclosure. Here I was allowed to send them food, and mats to sleep on, but was not permitted to enter again for several days.

My next object was to get a petition presented to the queen; but no person being admitted into the palace who was in disgrace with his majesty, I sought to present it through the medium of her brother's wife. I had visited her in better days, and received particular marks of her favor. But now times were altered; Mr. Judson was in prison, and I in distress, which was a sufficient reason for giving me a cold reception. I took a present of considerable value. She was lolling on her carpet as I entered, with her attendants around her. I waited not for the usual question to a suppliant, "What do you want?" but in a bold, earnest, yet respectful manner, stated our distresses and our wrongs, and begged her assistance. She partly raised her head, opened the present I had brought, and coolly replied, "Your case is not singular; all the foreigners are treated alike." "But it is singular," said I; "the teachers are Americans; they are ministers of religion, have nothing to do with war or politics, and came to Ava in obedience to the king's command. They have never done any thing to deserve such treatment, and is it right they should be treated thus?" "The king does as he pleases," said she; "I am not the king; what can I do?" "You can state their case to the queen, and obtain their release," replied I. "Place yourself in my situation; were you in America, your husband, innocent of crime, thrown into prison, in irons, and you a solitary, unprotected female, what would you do?" With a slight degree of feeling, she said, "I will present your petition; come again to-morrow." I returned to the house with considerable hope that the speedy release of the missionaries was at hand. But the next day, Mr. Gouger's property, to the amount of fifty thousand rupees, was taken and carried to the palace. The officers, on their return, politely informed me they should *visit our house* on the morrow. I felt obliged for this information, and accordingly made preparations to receive them, by secreting as many little articles as possible, together with considerable silver, as I knew, if the war should be protracted, we should be in a state of starvation without it. But my mind was in a dreadful state of agitation, lest it should be discovered, and cause my being thrown into prison. And had it been possible to procure money from any other quarter, I should not have ventured on such a step.

The following morning, the royal treasurer, the governor of the north gate of the palace, who was in future our steady friend, and another nobleman, attended by forty or fifty followers, came to take possession of all we had. I treated them civilly, gave them chairs to sit on, tea and sweetmeats for their refreshment; and justice obliges me to say that they conducted the business of confiscation with more regard to my feelings than I should have thought it possible for Burmese officers to exhibit. The three officers, with one of the royal secretaries, alone entered the house; their attendants were ordered to remain outside. They saw I was deeply affected, and apologized for what they were about to do by saying that it was painful for them to take possession of property not their own, but they were compelled thus to do by order of the king. "Where are your silver, gold, and jewels?" said the royal treasurer. "I have no gold or jewels; but here is the key of a trunk which contains the silver; do with it as you please." The trunk was produced, and the silver weighed. "This money," said I, "was collected in America, by the disciples of Christ, and sent here for the purpose of building a kyoung, [the name of a priest's dwelling,] and for our support while teaching the religion of Christ. Is it suitable that you should take it?" The Burmans are averse to taking what is offered in a religious point of view, which was the cause of my making the inquiry "We will state this circumstance to the king," said one of them, "and perhaps he will restore it. But is this all the silver you have?" I could not tell a falsehood. "The house is in your possession," I replied; "search for yourselves." "Have you not deposited silver with some person of your acquaintance?" "My acquaintances are all in prison; with whom should I deposit silver?" They next ordered my trunk and drawers to be examined. The secretary only was allowed to accompany me in this search. Every thing nice or curious which met his view was presented to the officers, for their decision whether it should be taken or retained. I begged they would not take our wearing apparel, as it would be disgraceful to take clothes partly worn into the possession of his majesty, and to us they were of unspeakable value. They assented, and took a list only, and did the same with the books, medicines, &c. My little work table and rocking chair, presents from my beloved brother, I rescued from their grasp, partly by artifice and partly through their ignorance. They left, also, many articles which were of inestimable value during our long imprisonment.

As soon as they had finished their search and departed, I hastened to the queen's brother, to hear what had been the fate of my petition, when, alas! all my hopes were dashed by his wife's coolly saying, "I stated your case to the queen, but her majesty replied, '*The teachers will not die; let them remain as they are.*'" My expectations had been so much excited, that this sentence was like a thunderclap to my feelings. For the truth at one glance assured me that if the queen refused assistance, who would dare to intercede for me? With a heavy heart I departed, and on my way home attempted to enter the prison gate, to communicate the sad tidings to your brother, but was harshly refused admittance; and for the ten days following, notwithstanding my daily efforts, I was not allowed to enter. We attempted to communicate by writing, and after being successful for a few days, it was discovered; the poor fellow who carried the communications was beaten and put in the stocks, and the circumstance cost me about ten dollars, besides two or three days of agony for fear of the consequences.

The officers who had taken possession of our property presented it to his majesty, saying, "Judson is a true teacher; we found nothing in his house but what belongs to priests. In addition to this money, there are an immense number of books, medicines, trunks of wearing apparel, &c., of which we have only taken a list. Shall we take them, or let them remain?" "Let them remain," said the king, "and put this property by itself, for it shall be restored to him again if he is found innocent." This was an allusion to the idea of his being a spy.

For two or three months following, I was subject to continual harassments, partly through my ignorance of police management, and partly through the insatiable desire of every petty officer to enrich himself through our misfortunes. When the officers came to our house, to confiscate our property, they insisted on knowing how much I had given the governor and prison officers to release the teachers from the inner prison. I honestly told them, and they demanded the sum from the governor, which threw him into a dreadful rage, and he threatened to put all the prisoners back into their original place. I went to him the next morning, and the first words with which he accosted me were, "You are very bad; why did you tell the royal treasurer that you had given me so much money?" "The treasurer inquired; what could I say?" I replied. "Say that you had given nothing," said he, "and I would have made the teachers comfortable in prison; but now I know not what will be their fate." "But I cannot tell a falsehood," I replied; "my religion differs from yours; it forbids prevarication; and had you stood by me with your knife raised, I could not have said what you suggest." His wife, who sat by his side, and who always, from this time, continued my firm friend, instantly said, "Very true; what else could she have done? I like such straightforward conduct; you must not," turning to the governor, "be angry with her." I then presented the governor with a beautiful opera glass I had just received from England, and begged his anger at me would not influence him to treat the prisoners with unkindness, and I would endeavor, from time to time, to make him such presents as would compensate for his loss. "You may intercede for your husband only; for your sake he shall remain where he is; but let the other prisoners take care of themselves." I pleaded hard for Dr. Price; but he would not listen, and, the same day, had him returned to the inner prison, where he remained ten days. He was then taken out, in consequence of the doctor's promising a piece of broadcloth, and my sending two pieces of handkerchiefs.

About this period, I was one day summoned to the Lutd'hau, in an official way. What new evil was before me I knew not, but was obliged to go. When arrived, I was allowed to *stand* at the bottom of the stairs, as no female is permitted to ascend the steps, or even to stand, but sit on the ground. Hundreds were collected around. The officer who presided, in an authoritative voice, began: "Speak the truth in answer to the questions I shall ask. If you speak true, no evil will follow; but if not, your life will not be spared. It is reported that you have committed to the care of a Burmese officer a string of pearls, a pair of diamond earrings, and a silver teapot. Is it true?" "It is not," I replied; "and if you or any other person can produce these articles, I refuse not to die." The officer again urged the necessity of "speaking true." I told him I had nothing more to say on the subject, but begged he would use his influence to obtain the release of Mr. Judson from prison.

I returned to the house with a heart much lighter than I went, though conscious of my perpetual exposure to such harassments. Notwithstanding the repulse I had met in my application to the queen, I could not remain without making continual effort for your brother's release, while there was the least probability of success. Time after time, my visits to the queen's sister-in-law were repeated, till she refused to answer a question, and told me by her looks I had better keep out of her presence. For the seven following months, hardly a day passed that I did not visit some one of the members of government, or branches of the royal family, in order to gain their influence in our behalf; but the only benefit resulting was, their encouraging promises preserved us from despair, and induced a hope of the speedy termination of our difficulties, which enabled us to bear our distresses better than we otherwise should have done. I ought, however, to mention that, by my repeated visits to the different members of government, I gained several friends, who were ready to assist me with articles of food, though in a private manner, and who used their influence in the palace to destroy the impression of our being in any way engaged in the present war. But no one dared to speak a word to the king or queen in favor of a foreigner, while there were such continual reports of the success of the English arms.

During these seven months, the continual extortions and oppressions to which your brother and the other white prisoners were subject are indescribable. Sometimes sums of money were demanded, sometimes pieces of cloth, and handkerchiefs; at other times an order would be issued that the white foreigners should not speak to each other, or have any communication with their friends without. Then, again, the servants were forbidden to carry in their food without an extra fee. Sometimes, for days and days together, I could not go into the prison till after dark, when I had two miles to walk in returning to the house. O, how many, many times have I returned from that dreary prison at nine o'clock at night, solitary, and worn out with fatigue and anxiety, and thrown myself down in that same rocking chair which you and Deacon L. provided for me in Boston, and endeavored to invent some new scheme for the release of the prisoners. Sometimes, for a moment or two, my thoughts would glance towards America, and my beloved friends there; but for nearly a year and a half, so entirely engrossed was every thought with present scenes and sufferings, that I seldom reflected on a single occurrence of my former life, or recollected that I had a friend in existence out of Ava.

You, my dear brother, who know my strong attachment to my friends, and how much pleasure I have hitherto experienced from retrospect, can judge from the above circumstances how intense were my sufferings. But the point, the acme of my distress, consisted in the awful uncertainty of our final fate. My prevailing opinion was, that my husband would suffer violent death, and that I should, of course, become a slave, and languish out a miserable though short existence in the tyrannic hands of some unfeeling monster. But the consolations of religion, in these trying circumstances, were neither "few nor small." It taught me to look beyond this world, to that rest, that peaceful, happy rest, where Jesus reigns, and oppression never enters. But how have I digressed from my relation! I will again return.

The war was now prosecuted with all the energy the Burmese government possessed. New troops were continually raised and sent down the river, and as frequent reports returned of their being all cut off. But that part of the Burmese army stationed in Arracan, under the command of Bandoola, had been more successful. Three hundred prisoners, at one time, were sent to the capital, as an evidence of the victory that had been gained. The king began to think that none but Bandoola understood the art of fighting with foreigners; consequently, his majesty recalled him, with the design of his taking command of the army that had been sent to Rangoon. On his arrival at Ava, he was received at court in the most flattering manner, and was the recipient of every favor in the power of the king and queen to bestow. He was, in fact, while at Ava, the acting king. I was resolved to apply to him for the release of the missionaries, though some members of government advised me not, lest he, being reminded of their existence, should issue an immediate order for their execution. But it was my last hope, and, as it proved, my last application.

Your brother wrote a petition privately, stating every circumstance that would have a tendency to interest him in our behalf. With fear and trembling I approached him, while surrounded by a crowd of flatterers; and one of his secretaries took the petition, and read it aloud. After hearing it, he spoke to me in an obliging manner, asked several questions relative to the teachers, said he would think of the subject, and bade me come again. I ran to the prison to communicate the favorable reception to Mr. Judson; and we both had sanguine hopes that his release was at hand. But the governor of the city expressed his amazement at my temerity, and said he doubted not it would be the means of destroying all the prisoners. In a day or two, however, I went again, and took a present of considerable value. Bandoola was not at home; but his lady, after ordering the present to be taken into another room, modestly informed me that she was ordered by her husband to make the following communication: that he was now very busily employed in making preparations for Rangoon, but that when he had retaken that place, and expelled the English, he would return and release all the prisoners.

Thus, again, were all our hopes dashed; and we felt that we could do nothing more, but sit down and submit to our lot. From this time we gave up all idea of being released from prison till the termination of the war; but I was still obliged to visit constantly some of the members of government, with little presents, particularly the governor of the city, for the purpose of making the situation of the prisoners tolerable. I generally spent the greater part of every other day at the governor's house, giving him minute information relative to American manners, customs, government, &c. He used to be so much gratified with my communications, as to feel greatly disappointed if any occurrence prevented my spending the usual hours at his house.

Some months after your brother's imprisonment, I was permitted to make a little bamboo room in the prison enclosure, where he could be much by himself, and where I was sometimes allowed to spend two or three hours. It so happened that the two months he occupied this place were the coldest of the year, when he would have suffered much in the open shed he had previously occupied. After the birth of your little niece, I was unable to visit the prison and the governor as before, and found I had lost considerable influence, previously gained; for he was not so forward to hear my petitions, when any difficulty occurred, as he formerly had been. When Maria was nearly two months old, her father one morning sent me word that he and all the white prisoners were put into the inner prison, in five pairs of fetters each, that his little room had been torn down, and his mat, pillow, &c., been taken by the jailers. This was to me a dreadful shock, as I thought at once it was only a prelude to greater evils.

I should have mentioned before this the defeat of Bandoola, his escape to Dan-a-byoo, the complete destruction of his army and loss of ammunition, and the consternation this intelligence produced at court. The English army had left Rangoon, and were advancing towards Prome, when these severe measures were taken with the prisoners.

I went immediately to the governor's house. He was not at home, but had ordered his wife to tell me, when I came, not to ask to have the additional fetters taken off, or the prisoners released, for *it could not be done.* I went to the prison gate, but was forbidden to enter. All was as still as death — not a white face to be seen, or a vestige of Mr. Judson's little room remaining. I was determined to see the governor, and know the cause of this additional oppression, and for this purpose returned into town the same evening, at an hour I knew he would be at home. He was in his audience room, and, as I entered, looked up without speaking, but exhibited a mixture of shame and affected anger in his countenance. I began by saying, " Your lordship has hitherto treated us with the kindness of a father. Our obligations to you are very great. We have looked to you for protection from oppression and cruelty. You have in many instances mitigated the sufferings of those unfortunate though innocent beings committed to your charge. You have promised me particularly that you would stand by me to the last, and though you should receive an order from the king, you would not put Mr. Judson to death. What crime has he committed to deserve such additional punishment?" The old man's hard heart was melted, for he wept like a child. "I pity you. Tsa-yah-ga-dau"—a name by which he always called me; "I knew you would make me feel; I therefore forbade your application. But you must believe me when I say I do not wish to increase the sufferings of the prisoners. When I am ordered to execute them, the least that I can do is, to put them out of sight. I will now tell you," continued he, "what I have never told you before—that three times I have received intimations from the queen's brother to assassinate all the white prisoners privately; but I would not do it. And I now repeat it, though I execute all the others, I will never execute your husband. But I cannot release him from his present confinement, and you must not ask it." I had never seen him manifest so much feeling, or so resolute in denying me a favor, which circumstance was an additional reason for thinking dreadful scenes were before us.

The situation of the prisoners was now distressing beyond description. It was at the commencement of the hot season. There were above a hundred prisoners shut up in one room, without a breath of air excepting from the cracks in the boards. I sometimes obtained permission to go to the door for five minutes, when my heart sickened at the wretchedness exhibited. The white prisoners, from incessant perspiration and loss of appetite, looked more like the dead than the living. I made daily applications to the governor, offering him money, which he refused; but all that I gained was permission for the foreigners to eat their food outside, and this continued but a short time.

It was at this period that the death of Bandoola was announced in the palace. The king heard it with silent amazement, and the queen, in eastern style, smote upon her breast, and cried, "Ama! ama!" (alas, alas.) Who could be found to fill his place? Who would venture, since the invincible Bandoola had been cut off? Such were the exclamations constantly heard in the streets of Ava. The common people were speaking *low* of a rebellion, in case more troops should be levied. For as yet the common people had borne the weight of the war; not a tical had been taken from the royal treasury. At length the pakan woon, who a few months before had been so far disgraced by the king as to be thrown into prison and irons, now offered himself to head a new army that should be raised on a different plan from those which had hitherto been raised, and assured the king, in the most confident manner, that he would conquer the English, and restore those places that had been taken in a very short time. He proposed that every soldier should receive a hundred ticals in advance, and he would obtain security for each man, as the money was to pass through his hands. It was afterwards found that he had taken, for his own use, ten ticals from every hundred. He was a man of enterprise and talents, though a violent enemy to all foreigners. His offers were accepted by the king and government, and all power immediately committed to him. One of the first exercises of his power was to arrest Lanciego and the Portuguese priest, who had hitherto remained unmolested, and cast them into prison, and to subject the native Portuguese and Bengalees to the most menial occupations. The whole town was in alarm, lest they should feel the effects of his power; and it was owing to the malignant representations of this man, that the white prisoners suffered such a change in their circumstances as I shall soon relate.

After continuing in the inner prison for more than a month, your brother was taken with a fever. I felt assured he would not live long, unless removed from that noisome place. To effect this, and in order to be near the prison, I removed from our house, and put up a small bamboo room in the governor's enclosure, which was nearly opposite the prison gate. Here I incessantly begged the governor to give me an order to take Mr. Judson out of the large prison, and place him in a more comfortable situation; and the old man, being worn out with my entreaties, at length gave me the order in an official form, and also gave orders to the head jailer to allow me to go in and out, all times of the day, to administer medicines, &c. I now felt happy indeed, and had Mr. Judson instantly removed into a little bamboo hovel, so low that neither of us could stand upright — but a palace in comparison with the place he had left.

Notwithstanding the order the governor had given for my admittance into prison, it was with the greatest difficulty that I could persuade the under jailer to open the gate. I used to carry Mr. Judson's food myself, for the sake of getting in, and would then remain an hour or two, unless driven out. We had been in this comfortable situation but two or three days when, one morning, having carried in Mr. Judson's breakfast, which, in consequence of fever, he was unable to take, I remained longer than usual, when the governor, in great haste, sent for me. I promised to return as soon as I had ascertained the governor's will, he being much alarmed at this unusual message. I was very agreeably disappointed when the governor informed me that he only wished to consult me about his watch, and seemed unusually pleasant and conversable. I found afterwards that his only object was to detain me until the dreadful scene about to take place in the prison was over. For when I left him to go to my room, one of the servants came running, and with a ghastly countenance, informed me that all the white prisoners were carried away. I would not believe the report, and instantly went back to the governor, who said he had just heard of it, but did not wish to tell me. I hastily ran into the street, hoping to get a glimpse of them before they were out of sight, but in this was disappointed. I ran first into one street, then another, inquiring of all I met; but no one would answer me. At length an old woman told me the white prisoners had gone towards the little river; for they were to be carried to Amarapoora. I then ran to the banks of the little river, about half a mile, but saw them not, and concluded the old woman had deceived me. Some of the friends of the foreigners went to the place of execution, but found them not. I then returned to the governor, to try to discover the cause of their removal, and the probability of their future fate. The old man assured me that he was ignorant of the intention of government to remove the foreigners till that morning;

that, since I went out, he had learned that the prisoners were to be sent to Amarapoora, but for what purpose he knew not. "I will send off a man immediately," said he, "to see what is to be done with them. You can do nothing more for your husband," continued he; "*take care of yourself.*" With a heavy heart I went to my room, and having no hope to excite me to exertion, I sank down almost in despair. For several days previous, I had been actively engaged in building my own little room, and making our hovel comfortable. My thoughts had been almost entirely occupied in contriving means to get into prison. But now I looked towards the gate with a kind of melancholy feeling, but no wish to enter. All was the stillness of death; no preparation of your brother's food, no expectation of meeting him at the usual dinner hour; all my employment, all my occupations, seemed to have ceased, and I had nothing left but the dreadful recollection that Mr. Judson was carried off, I knew not whither. It was one of the most insupportable days I ever passed. Towards night, however, I came to the determination to set off the next morning for Amarapoora, and for this purpose was obliged to go to our house out of town.

Never before had I suffered so much from fear in traversing the streets of Ava. The last words of the governor, "Take care of yourself," made me suspect there was some design with which I was unacquainted. I saw, also, he was afraid to have me go into the streets, and advised me to wait till dark, when he would send me in a cart, and a man to open the gates. I took two or three trunks of the most valuable articles, together with the medicine chest, to deposit in the house of the governor; and after committing the house and premises to our faithful Moung Ing and a Bengalee servant, who continued with us, though we were unable to pay his wages, I took leave, as I then thought probable, of our house in Ava forever.

On my return to the governor's, I found a servant of Mr. Gouger, who happened to be near the prison when the foreigners were led out, and followed on to see the end, who informed me that the prisoners had been carried before the lamine-woon, at Amarapoora, and were to be sent the next day to a village he knew not how far distant. My distress was a little relieved by the intelligence that our friend was yet alive; but still I knew not what was to become of him. The next morning I obtained a pass from government, and with my little Maria, who was then only three months old, Mary and Abby Hasseltine, two of the Burman children, and our Bengalee cook, who was the only one of the party that could afford me any assistance, I set off for Amarapoora. The day was dreadfully hot; but we obtained a covered boat, in which we were tolerably comfortable, till within two miles of the government house. I then procured a cart; but the violent motion, together with the dreadful heat and dust, made me almost distracted. But what was my disappointment, on my arriving at the court house, to find that the prisoners had been sent on two hours before, and that I must go in that uncomfortable mode four miles farther with little Maria in my arms, whom I held all the way from Ava. The cartman refused to go any further; and after waiting an hour in the burning sun, I procured another, and set off for that never-to-be-forgotten place, Oung-pen-la. I obtained a guide from the governor, and was conducted directly to the prison yard. But what a scene of wretchedness was presented to my view! The prison was an old, shattered building, without a roof; the fence was entirely destroyed; eight or ten Burmese were on the top of the building, trying to make something like a shelter with leaves; while under a little low projection outside of the prison sat the foreigners, chained together two and two, almost dead with suffering and fatigue. The first words of your brother were, "Why have you come? I hoped you would not follow, for you cannot live here." It was now dark. I had no refreshment for the suffering prisoners, or for myself, as I had expected to procure all that was necessary at the market of Amarapoora, and I had no shelter for the night. I asked one of the jailers if I might put up a little bamboo house near the prison; he said no, it was not customary. I then begged he would procure me a shelter for the night, when on the morrow I could find some place to live in. He took me to his house, in which there were only two small rooms — one in which he and his family lived; the other, which was then half full of grain, he offered to me; and in that little filthy place I spent the next six months of wretchedness. I procured some half-boiled water, instead of my tea, and, worn out with fatigue, laid myself down on a mat spread over the paddy, and endeavored to obtain a little refreshment from sleep. The next morning your brother gave me the following account of the brutal treatment he had received on being taken out of prison.

As soon as I had gone out at the call of the governor, one of the jailers rushed into Mr. Judson's little room, roughly seized him by the arm, pulled him out, stripped him of all his clothes excepting shirt and pantaloons, took his shoes, hat, and all his bedding, tore off his chains, tied a rope round his waist, and dragged him to the court house, where the other prisoners had previously been taken. They were then tied two and two, and delivered into the hands of the lamine-woon, who went on before them on horseback, while his slaves drove the prisoners, one of the slaves holding the rope which connected two of them together. It was in May, one of the hottest months in the year, and eleven o'clock in the day, so that the sun was intolerable indeed. They had proceeded only half a mile, when your brother's feet became blistered; and so great was his agony, even at this early period, that as they were crossing the little river, he ardently longed to throw himself into the water to be free from misery. But the sin attached to such an act alone prevented. They had then eight miles to walk. The sand and gravel were like burning coals to the feet of the prisoners, which soon became perfectly destitute of skin; and in this wretched state they were goaded on by their unfeeling drivers. Mr. Judson's debilitated state, in consequence of fever, and having taken no food that morning, rendered him less capable of bearing such hardships than the other prisoners. When about half way on their journey, as they stopped for water, your brother begged the lamine-woon to allow him to ride his horse a mile or two, as he could proceed no farther in that dreadful state. But a scornful, malignant look was all the reply that was made. He then requested Captain Laird, who was tied with him, and who was a strong, healthy man, to allow him to take hold of his shoulder, as he was fast sinking. This the kind-hearted man granted for a mile or two, but then found the additional burden insupportable. Just at that period, Mr. Gouger's Bengalee servant came up to them, and, seeing the distresses of your brother, took off his headdress, which was made of cloth, tore it in two, gave half to his master, and half to Mr. Judson, which he instantly wrapped round his wounded feet, as they were not allowed to rest even for a moment. The servant then offered his shoulder to Mr. Judson, who was almost carried by him the remainder of the way. Had it not been for the support and assistance of this man, your brother thinks he should have shared the fate of the poor Greek, who was one of their number, and, when taken out of prison that morning, was in perfect health. But he was a corpulent man, and the sun affected him so much that he fell down on the way. His inhuman drivers beat and dragged him until they themselves were wearied, when they procured a cart, in which he was carried the remaining two miles. But the poor creature expired in an hour or two after their arrival at the court house. The lamine-woon, seeing the distressing state of the prisoners, and that one of their number was dead, concluded they should go no farther that night; otherwise they would have been driven on until they reached Oung-pen-la the same day. An old shed was appointed for their abode during the night, but without even a mat or pillow, or any thing to cover them. The curiosity of the lamine-woon's wife induced her to make a visit to the prisoners, whose wretchedness considerably excited her compassion, and she ordered some fruit, sugar, and tamarinds for their refreshment; and the next morning, rice was prepared for them and, poor as it was, it was refreshing to the prisoners, who had been almost destitute of food the day before. Carts were also provided for their conveyance, as none of them were able to walk. All this time, the foreigners were entirely ignorant of what was to become of them; and when they arrived at Oung-pen-la, and saw the dilapidated state of the prison, they immediately, all as one, concluded that they were there to be burned, agreeably to the report which had previously been in circulation at Ava. They all endeavored to prepare themselves for the awful scene anticipated; and it was not until they saw preparations making for repairing the prison, that they had the least doubt that a cruel, lingering death awaited them. My arrival was in an hour or two after this.

The next morning, I arose, and endeavored to find something like food. But there was no market, and nothing to be procured. One of Dr. Price's friends, however, brought some cold rice and vegetable curry from Amarapoora, which, together with a cup of tea from Mr. Lanciego, answered for the breakfast of the prisoners; and for dinner we made a curry of dried salt fish, which a servant of Mr. Gouger had brought. All the money I could command in the world I had brought with me, secreted about my person; so you may judge what our prospects were, in case the war should continue long. But our heavenly Father was better to us than our fears; for, notwithstanding the constant extortions of the jailers during the whole six months we were at Oung-pen-la, and the frequent straits to which we were brought, we never really suffered for the want of money, though frequently for want of provisions, which were not procurable. Here at this place my personal bodily sufferings commenced. While your brother was confined in the city prison, I had been allowed to remain in our house, in which I had many conveniences left, and my health had continued good beyond all expectation. But now I had not a single article of convenience — not even a chair or seat of any kind, excepting a bamboo floor. The very morning after my arrival, Mary Hasseltine was taken with the small-pox, the natural way. She, though very young, was the only assistant I had in taking care of little Maria. But she now required all the time I could spare from Mr. Judson, whose fever still continued, in prison, and whose feet were so dreadfully mangled that for several days he was unable to move. I knew not what to do, for I could procure no assistance from the neighborhood, or medicine for the sufferers, but was all day long going backwards and forwards from the house to the prison with little Maria in my arms. Sometimes I was greatly relieved by leaving her for an hour, when asleep, by the side of her father, while I returned to the house to look after Mary, whose fever ran so high as to produce delirium. She was so completely covered with the small-pox, that there was no distinction in the pustules. As she was in the same little room with myself, I knew Maria would take it; I therefore inoculated her from another child, before Mary's had arrived at such a state as to be infectious. At the same time, I inoculated Abby and the jailer's children, who all had it so lightly as hardly to interrupt their play. But the inoculation in the arm of my poor little Maria did not take; she caught it of Mary, and had it the natural way. She was then only three months and a half old, and had been a most healthy child; but it was above three months before she perfectly recovered from the effects of this dreadful disorder.

You will recollect I never had the small-pox, but was vaccinated previously to leaving America. In consequence of being for so long a time constantly exposed, I had nearly a hundred pustules formed, though no previous symptoms of fever, &c. The jailer's children having had the small-pox so lightly, in consequence of inoculation, my fame was spread all over the village, and every child, young and old, who had not previously had it, was brought for inoculation. And although I knew nothing about the disorder, or the mode of treating it, I inoculated them all with a needle, and told them to take care of their diet — all the instructions I could give them. Mr. Judson's health was gradually restored, and he found himself much more comfortably situated than when in the city prison.

The prisoners were at first chained two and two; but as soon as the jailers could obtain chains sufficient, they were separated, and each prisoner had but one pair. The prison was repaired, a new fence made, and a large, airy shed erected in front of the prison, where the prisoners were allowed to remain during the day, though locked up in the little close prison at night. All the children recovered from the smallpox; but my watchings and fatigue, together with my miserable food, and more miserable lodgings, brought on one of the diseases of the country, which is almost always fatal to foreigners. My constitution seemed destroyed, and in a few days I became so weak as to be hardly able to walk to Mr. Judson's prison. In this debilitated state I set off in a cart for Ava, to procure medicines and some suitable food, leaving the cook to supply my place. I reached the house in safety, and for two or three days the disorder seemed at a stand; after which it attacked me so violently that I had no hopes of recovery left; and my only anxiety now was, to return to Oung-pen-la, to die near the prison. It was with the greatest difficulty that I obtained the medicine chest from the governor, and then had no one to administer medicine. I, however, got at the laudanum, and by taking two drops at a time for several hours, it so far checked the disorder as to enable me to get on board a boat, though so weak that I could not stand, and again set off for Oung-pen-la. The last four miles was in that painful conveyance, the cart, and in the midst of the rainy season, when the mud almost buries the oxen. You may form some idea of a Burmese cart, when I tell you their wheels are not constructed like ours, but are simply round thick planks with a hole in the middle, through which a pole, that supports the body, is thrust.

I just reached Oung pen-la when my strength seemed entirely exhausted. The good native cook came out to help me into the house; but so altered and emaciated was my appearance, that the poor fellow burst into tears at the first sight. I crawled on to the mat in the little room, to which I was confined for more than two months, and never perfectly recovered until I came to the English camp. At this period, when I was unable to take care of myself, or look after Mr. Judson, we must both have died, had it not been for the faithful and affectionate care of our Bengalee cook. A common Bengalee cook will do nothing but the simple business of cooking; but he seemed to forget his caste, and almost his own wants, in his efforts to serve us. He would provide, cook, and carry your brother's food, and then return and take care of me. I have frequently known him not to taste of food till near night, in consequence of having to go so far for wood and water, and in order to have Mr. Judson's dinner ready at the usual hour. He never complained, never asked for his wages, and never for a moment hesitated to go any where, or to perform any act we required. I take great pleasure in speaking of the faithful conduct of this servant, who is still with us, and I trust has been well rewarded for his services.

Our dear little Maria was the greatest sufferer at this time, my illness depriving her of her usual nourishment, and neither a nurse nor a drop of milk could be procured in the village. By making presents to the jailers, I obtained leave for Mr. Judson to come out of prison, and take the emaciated creature around the village, to beg a little nourishment from those mothers who had young children. Her cries in the night were heart-rending, when it was impossible to supply her wants. I now began to think the very afflictions of Job had come upon me. When in health, I could bear the various trials and vicissitudes through which I was called to pass. But to be confined with sickness, and unable to assist those who were so dear to me, when in distress, was almost too much for me to bear; and had it not been for the consolations of religion, and an assured conviction that every additional trial was ordered by infinite love and mercy, I must have sunk under my accumulated sufferings. Sometimes our jailers seemed a little softened at our distress, and, for several days together, allowed Mr. Judson to come to the house, which was to me an unspeakable consolation. Then, again, they would be as iron-hearted in their demands as though we were free from sufferings, and in affluent circumstances. The annoyance, the extortions, and oppressions, to which we were subject during our six months' residence in Oung-pen-la, are beyond enumeration or description.

It was some time after our arrival at Oung-pen-la that we heard of the execution of the pakan-woon, in consequence of which our lives were still preserved. For we afterwards ascertained that the white foreigners had been sent to Oung-pen-la for the express purpose of sacrificing them; and that he himself intended witnessing the horrid scene. We had frequently heard of his intended arrival at Oung-pen-la, but we had no idea of his diabolical purposes. He had raised an army of fifty thousand men, (a tenth part of whose advance pay was found in his house,) and expected to march against the English army in a short time, when he was suspected of high treason, and instantly executed, without the least examination. Perhaps no death in Ava ever produced such universal rejoicings as that of the pakan-woon. We never, to this day, hear his name mentioned but with an epithet of reproach or hatred. Another brother of the king was appointed to the command of the army now in readiness, but with no very sanguine expectations of success. Some weeks after the departure of these troops, two of the woon-gyees were sent down for the purpose of negotiating. But not being successful, the queen's brother, the *acting king* of the country, was prevailed on to go. Great expectations were raised in consequence; but his cowardice induced him to encamp his detachment of the army at a great distance from the English, and even at a distance from the main body of the Burmese army, whose head quarters were then at Maloun. Thus he effected nothing, though reports were continually reaching us that peace was nearly concluded.

The time at length arrived for our release from the dreary scenes of Oung-pen-la. A messenger from our friend, the governor of the north gate of the palace, informed us that an order had been given, the evening before, in the palace, for Mr. Judson's release. On the same evening an official order arrived; and, with a joyful heart, I set about preparing for our departure early the following morning. But an unexpected obstacle occurred, which made us fear that *I* should still be retained as a prisoner. The avaricious jailers, unwilling to lose their prey, insisted that, as my name was not included in the order, I should not go. In vain I urged that I was not sent there as a prisoner, and that they had no authority over me; they still determined I should not go, and forbade the villagers from letting me a cart. Mr. Judson was then taken out of prison, and brought to the jailers' house, where, by promises and threatenings, he finally gained their consent, on condition that we would leave the remaining part of our provisions we had recently received from Ava. It was noon before we were allowed to depart. When we reached Amarapoora, Mr. Judson was obliged to follow the guidance of the jailer, who conducted him to the governor of the city. Having made all necessary inquiries, the governor appointed another guard, which conveyed Mr. Judson to the court house in Ava, at which place he arrived some time in the night. I took my own course, procured a boat, and reached our house before dark.

My first object, the next morning, was to go in search of your brother; and I had the mortification to meet him again in prison, though not the death prison. I went immediately to my old friend, the governor of the city, who now was raised to the rank of a woon-gyee. He informed me that Mr. Judson was to be sent to the Burmese camp, to act as translator and interpreter; and that he was put in confinement for a short time only, till his affairs were settled. Early the following morning I went to this officer again, who told me that Mr. Judson had that moment received twenty ticals from government, with orders to go immediately on board a boat for Maloun, and that *he* had given him permission to stop a few moments at the house, it being on his way. I hastened back to the house, where Mr. Judson soon arrived, but was allowed to remain only a short time, while I could prepare food and clothing for future use. He was crowded into a little boat, where he had not room sufficient to lie down, and where his exposure to the cold, damp nights threw him into a violent fever, which had nearly ended all his sufferings. He arrived at Maloun on the third day, where, ill as he was, he was obliged to enter immediately on the work of translating. He remained at Maloun six weeks, suffering as much as he had at any time in prison, excepting he was not in irons, nor exposed to the insults of those cruel jailers.

For the first fortnight after his departure, my anxiety was less than it had been at any time previously since the commencement of our difficulties. I knew the Burmese officers at the camp would feel the value of Mr. Judson's services too much to allow their using any measures threatening his life. I thought his situation, also, would be much more comfortable than it really was; hence my anxiety was less. But my health, which had never been restored since that violent attack at Oung-pen-la, now daily declined, till I was seized with the spotted fever, with all its attendant horrors. I knew the nature of the fever from its commencement; and, from the shattered state of my constitution, together with the want of medical attendants, I concluded it must be fatal. The day I was taken with the fever, a Burmese nurse came and offered her services for Maria. This circumstance filled me with gratitude and confidence in God; for, though I had so long and so constantly made efforts to obtain a person of this description, I had never been able; when at the very time I most needed one, and without any exertion, a voluntary offer was made. My fever raged violently, and without any intermission. I began to think of settling my worldly affairs, and of committing my dear little Maria to the care of a Portuguese woman, when I lost my reason, and was insensible to all around me. At this dreadful period, Dr. Price was released from prison, and hearing of my illness, obtained permission to come and see me. He has since told me that my situation was the most distressing he had ever witnessed, and that he did not then think I should survive many hours. My hair was shaved, my head and feet covered with blisters, and Dr. Price ordered the

Bengalee servant who took care of me to endeavor to persuade me to take a little nourishment, which I had obstinately refused for several days. One of the first things I recollect was seeing this faithful servant standing by me, trying to induce me to take a little wine and water. I was, in fact, so far gone that the Burmese neighbors, who had come in to see me expire, said, " She is dead; and if the King of angels should come in, he could not recover her."

The fever, I afterwards understood, had run seventeen days when the blisters were applied. I now began to recover slowly, but it was more than a month after this before I had strength to stand. While in this weak, debilitated state, the servant who had followed your brother to the Burmese camp came in, and informed me that his master had arrived, and was conducted to the court house in town. I sent off a Burman to watch the movements of government, and to ascertain, if possible, in what way Mr. Judson was to be disposed of. He soon returned with the sad intelligence that he saw Mr. Judson go out of the palace yard, accompanied by two or three Burmans, who conducted him to one of the prisons, and that it was reported in town that he was to be sent back to the Oung-pen-la prison. I was too weak to bear ill tidings of any kind; but a shock so dreadful as this almost annihilated me. For some time I could hardly breathe, but at last gained sufficient composure to despatch Moung Ing to our friend, the governor of the north gate, and begged him to make *one more effort* for the release of Mr. Judson, and prevent his being sent back to the country prison, where I knew he must suffer much, as I could not follow. Moung Ing then went in search of Mr. Judson; and it was nearly dark when he found him, in the interior of an obscure prison. I had sent food early in the afternoon; but being unable to find him, the bearer had returned with it, which added another pang to my distresses, as I feared he was already sent to Oung-pen-la.

If I ever felt the value and efficacy of prayer, I did at this time. I could not rise from my couch; I could make no efforts to secure my husband; I could only plead with that great and powerful Being who has said, " Call upon me in the day of trouble, and *I will hear*, and thou shalt glorify me," and who made me at this time feel so powerfully this promise that I became quite composed, feeling assured that my prayers would be answered.

When Mr. Judson was sent from Maloun to Ava, it was within five minutes' notice, and without his knowledge of the cause. On his way up the river, he accidentally saw the communication made to government respecting him, which was simply this : " We have no further use for Yüdathan ; we therefore return him to the golden city." On arriving at the court house, there happened to be no one present who was acquainted with Mr. Judson. The presiding officer inquired from what place he had been sent to Maloun. He was answered, from Oung-pen-la. " Let him, then," said the officer, " be returned thither ; " when he was delivered to a guard and conducted to the place above mentioned, there to remain until he could be conveyed to Oung-pen-la. In the mean time, the governor of the north gate presented a petition to the high court of the empire, offered himself as Mr. Judson's security, obtained his release, and took him to his house, where he treated him with considerable kindness, and to which I was removed as soon as returning health would allow.

The advance of the English army towards the capital at this time threw the whole town into the greatest state of alarm, and convinced the government that some speedy measures must be taken to save the golden city. They had hitherto rejected all the overtures of Sir Archibald Campbell, imagining, until this late period, that they could in some way or other drive the English from the country. Mr. Judson and Dr. Price were daily called to the palace and consulted ; in fact, nothing was done without their approbation. Two English officers, also, who had lately been brought to Ava as prisoners, were continually consulted, and their good offices requested in endeavoring to persuade the British general to make peace on easier terms. It was finally concluded that Mr. Judson and one of the officers above mentioned should be sent immediately to the English camp, in order to negotiate. The danger attached to a situation so responsible, under a government so fickle as the Burmese, induced your brother to use every means possible to prevent his being sent. Dr. Price was not only willing, but desirous of going; this circumstance Mr. Judson represented to the members of government, and begged he might not be compelled to go, as Dr. Price could transact the business equally as well as himself. After some hesitation and deliberation, Dr. Price was appointed to accompany Dr. Sandford, one of the English officers, on condition that Mr. Judson would stand security for his return, while the other English officer, then in irons, should be security for Dr. Sandford. The king gave them a hundred ticals each to bear their expenses, (twenty-five of which Dr. Sandford generously sent to Mr. Gouger, still a prisoner at Oung-pen-la,) boats, men, and a Burmese officer to accompany them, though he ventured no farther than the Burman camp. With the most anxious solicitude the court waited the arrival of the messengers, but did not in the least relax in their exertions to fortify the city. Men and beasts were at work night and day, making new stockades and strengthening old ones, and whatever buildings were in their way were immediately torn down. Our house, with all that surrounded it, was levelled to the ground, and our beautiful little compound turned into a road and a place for the erection of cannon. All articles of value were conveyed out of town, and safely deposited in some other place.

At length the boat in which the ambassadors had been sent was seen approaching, a day earlier than was expected. As it advanced towards the city, the banks were lined by thousands, anxiously inquiring their success. But no answer was given; the government must first hear the news. The palace gates were crowded, the officers at the lut-d'hau were seated, when Dr. Price made the following communication: "The general and commissioners will make no alteration in their terms, except the hundred lacks [a lack is a hundred thousand] of rupees may be paid at four different times; the first twenty-five lacks to be paid within twelve days, or the army will continue their march." In addition to this, the prisoners were to be given up immediately. The general had commissioned Dr. Price to demand Mr. Judson, and myself, and little Maria. This was communicated to the king, who replied, " They are not English; they are my people, and shall not go." At this time I had no idea that we should ever be released from Ava. The government had learned the value of your brother's services, having employed him the last three months; and we both concluded they would never consent to our departure. The foreigners were again called to a consultation, to see what could be done. Dr. Price and Mr. Judson told them plainly that the English would never make peace on any other terms than those offered, and that it was in vain to go down again without the money. It was then proposed that a third part of the first sum demanded should be sent down immediately. Mr. Judson objected, and still said it would be useless. Some of the members of government then intimated that it was probable the teachers were on the side of the English, and did not try to make them take a smaller sum; and also threatened, if they did not make the English comply, they and their families should suffer.

In this interval, the fears of the government were considerably allayed by the offers of a general, by name Layar-thoo-yah, who desired to make one more attempt to conquer the English, and disperse them. He assured the king and government, that he could so fortify the ancient city of Pugan, as to make it impregnable, and that he would there defeat and destroy the English. His offers were heard; he marched to Pugan with a very considerable force, and made strong the fortifications. But the English took the city with perfect ease, and dispersed the Burmese army; while the general fled to Ava, and had the presumption to appear in the presence of the king, and demand new troops. The king, being enraged that he had ever listened to him for a moment, in consequence of which the negotiation had been delayed, the English general provoked, and the troops daily advancing, ordered the general to be immediately executed. The poor fellow was soon hurled from the palace, and beat all the way to the court house, when he was stripped of his rich apparel, bound with cords, and made to kneel and bow towards the palace. He was then delivered into the hands of the executioners, who, by their cruel treatment, put an end to his existence before they reached the place of execution.

The king caused it to be reported that this general was executed in consequence of disobeying his commands *" not to fight the English."*

Dr. Price was sent off the same night, with part of the prisoners, and with instructions to persuade the general to take six lacks instead of twenty-five. He returned in two or three days, with the appalling intelligence that the English general was very angry, refused to have any communication with him, and was now within a few days' march of the capital. The queen was greatly alarmed, and said the money should be raised immediately, if the English would only stop their march. The whole palace was in motion; gold and silver vessels were melted up; the king and queen superintended the weighing of a part of it, and were determined, if possible, to save their city. The silver was ready in the boats by the next evening; but they had so little confidence in the English, that, after all their alarm, they concluded to send down six lacks only, with the assurance that, if the English would stop where they then were, the remainder should be forthcoming immediately.

The government now did not even ask Mr. Judson the question whether he would go or not; but some of the officers took him by the arm, as he was walking in the street, and told him he must go immediately on board the boat, to accompany two Burmese officers, a woon-gyee and woon-douk, who were going down to make peace. Most of the English prisoners were sent at the same time. The general and commissioners would not receive the six lacks, neither would they stop their march; but promised, if the sum complete reached them before they should arrive at Ava, they would make peace.

The general also commissioned Mr. Judson to collect the remaining foreigners, of whatever country, and ask the question, before the Burmese government, whether they wished to go or stay. Those who expressed a wish to go should be delivered up immediately, or peace would not be made.

Mr. Judson reached Ava at midnight, had all the foreigners called the next morning, and the question asked. Some of the members of government said to him, " You will not leave us; you shall become a great man if you will remain." He then secured himself from the odium of saying that he wished to leave the service of his majesty, by recurring to the order of Sir Archibald, that whoever wished to leave Ava should be given up, and that I had expressed a wish to go, so that he of course must follow. The remaining part of the twenty-five lacks was soon collected; the prisoners at Oung-pen-la were all released, and either sent to their houses, or down the river to the English; and in two days from the time of Mr. Judson's return, we took an affectionate leave of the good-natured officer who had so long entertained us at his house, and who now accompanied us to the water side, and we then left forever the banks of Ava.

It was on a cool, moonlight evening, in the month of March, that with hearts filled with gratitude to God, and overflowing with joy at our prospects, we passed down the Irrawadi, surrounded by six or eight golden boats, and accompanied by all we had on earth. The thought that we had still to pass the Burman camp would sometimes occur to damp our joy, for we feared that some obstacle might there arise to retard our progress. Nor were we mistaken in our conjectures. We reached the camp about midnight, where we were detained two hours; the woon-gyee and high officers insisting that *we* should wait at the camp, while Dr. Price, who did not return to Ava with your brother, but remained at the camp, should go on with the money, and first ascertain whether peace would be made. The Burmese government still entertained the idea that, as soon as the English had received the money and prisoners, they would continue their march, and yet destroy the capital. We knew not but that some circumstance might occur to break off the negotiations. Mr. Judson therefore strenuously insisted that he would not remain, but go on immediately. The officers were finally prevailed on to consent, hoping much from Mr. Judson's assistance in making peace.

We now, for the first time for more than a year and a half, felt that we were free, and no longer subject to the oppressive yoke of the Burmese. And with what sensations of delight, on the next morning, did I behold the masts of the steamboat, the sure presage of being within the bounds of civilized life! As soon as our boat reached the shore, Brigadier A. and another officer came on board, congratulated us on our arrival, and invited us on board the steamboat, where I passed the remainder of the day; while your brother went on to meet the general, who, with a detachment of the army, had encamped at Yandabo, a few miles farther down the river. Mr. Judson returned in the evening, with an invitation from Sir Archibald to come immediately to his quarters, where I was the next morning introduced, and received with the greatest kindness by the general, who had a tent pitched for us near his own, took us to his own table, and treated us with the kindness of a father, rather than as strangers of another country.

We feel that our obligations to General Campbell can never be cancelled. Our final release from Ava, and our recovering all the property that had there been taken, was owing entirely to his efforts. His subsequent hospitality, and kind attention to the accommodations for our passage to Rangoon, have left an impression on our minds, which can never be effaced. We daily received the congratulation of the British officers, whose conduct towards us formed a striking contrast to that of the Burmese. I presume to say that no persons on earth were ever happier than we were during the fortnight we passed at the English camp. For several days, this single idea wholly occupied my mind — that we were out of the power of the Burmese government, and once more under the protection of the English. Our feelings continually dictated expressions like this: *What shall we render to the Lord for all his benefits towards us?*

The treaty of peace was soon concluded, signed by both parties, and a termination of hostilities publicly declared. We left Yandabo, after a fortnight's residence, and safely reached the mission house in Rangoon, after an absence of two years and three months.

A review of our trip to and adventures in Ava often excites the inquiry, Why were we permitted to go? What good has been effected? Why did I not listen to the advice of friends in Bengal, and remain there till the war was concluded? But all that we can say is, *It is not in man that walketh to direct his steps.* So far as my going round to Rangoon, at the time I did, was instrumental in bringing those heavy afflictions upon us, I can only state that, if I ever acted from a sense of duty in my life, it was at that time; for my conscience would not allow me any peace, when I thought of sending for your brother to come to Calcutta, in prospect of the approaching war. Our society at home have lost no property in consequence of our difficulties; but two years of precious time have been lost to the mission, unless some future advantage may be gained, in consequence of the severe discipline to which we ourselves have been subject. We are sometimes induced to think that the lesson we found so very hard to learn will have a beneficial effect through our lives, and that the mission may, in the end, be advanced rather than retarded.

We should have had no hesitation about remaining in Ava if no part of the Burmese empire had been ceded to the British. But as it was, we felt it would be an unnecessary exposure, besides the missionary field being much more limited, in consequence of intoleration. We now consider our future missionary prospects as bright indeed; and our only anxiety is, to be once more in that situation where our time will be exclusively devoted to the instruction of the heathen.

In a concluding paragraph, dated Amherst, July 27, Mrs. Judson adds, —

From the date, at the commencement of this long letter, you see, my dear brother, that my patience has continued for two months. I have frequently been induced to throw it aside altogether; but feeling assured that you and my other friends are expecting something of this kind, I am induced to send it, with all its imperfections. This letter, dreadful as are the scenes herein described, gives you but a faint idea of the awful reality. The anguish, the agony of mind, resulting from a thousand little circumstances impossible to be delineated on paper, can be known by those only who have been in similar situations. Pray for us, my dear brother and sister, that these heavy afflictions may not be in vain, but may be blessed to our spiritual good, and the advancement of Christ's cause among the heathen.

At the close of this long and melancholy narrative, we may appropriately introduce the following tribute to the benevolence and talents of Mrs. Judson, written by one of the English prisoners who were confined at Ava with Mr. Judson. It was published in a Calcutta paper, after the conclusion of the war.

Mrs. Judson was the author of those eloquent and forcible appeals to the government which prepared them by degrees for submission to terms of peace, never expected by any who knew the *hauteur* and inflexible pride of the Burman court.

And while on this subject, the overflowings of grateful feelings, on behalf of myself and fellow-prisoners, compel me to add a tribute of public thanks to that amiable and humane female, who, though living at a distance of two miles from our prison, without any means of conveyance, and very feeble in health, forgot her own comfort and infirmity, and almost every day visited us, sought out and administered to our wants, and contributed in every way to alleviate our misery.

While we were all left by the government destitute of food, she, with unwearied perseverance, by some means or other, obtained for us a constant supply.

When the tattered state of our clothes evinced the extremity of our distress, she was ever ready to replenish our scanty wardrobe.

When the unfeeling avarice of our keepers confined us inside, or made our feet fast in the stocks, she, like a ministering angel, never ceased her applications to the government, until she was authorized to communicate to us the grateful news of our enlargement, or of a respite from our galling oppressions.

Besides all this, it was unquestionably owing, in a chief degree, to the repeated eloquence, and forcible appeals of Mrs. Judson, that the untutored Burman was finally made willing to secure the welfare and happiness of his country, by a sincere peace.

Reminiscences of Conversations with Dr. Judson.

Mrs. Judson, in her letter to her brother, speaks of the cord as an "instrument of torture"—used not merely to confine the arms. It is small and hard, and may be so tied as to cut through the flesh, as in Mr. Judson's case it did to some extent. It is fastened around the two arms, at some distance above the elbow, and left to be played upon at the pleasure of the executioner. It may be drawn back with such force as to suspend respiration, which is its more special office. Very often a shoulder is dislocated; and not infrequently the blood gushes from the nostrils and mouth, and the poor victim drops dead in a few moments.

Dr. Price, in his journal, mentions a bamboo pole, on which, with more truth than elegance, he represents the prisoners as being "strung." It was a substitute for the stocks, all of which had been already appropriated, and, as it proved, a most torturing one. The foreigners were loaded with three pairs of fetters each, which confined their feet only a few inches apart. The bamboo was passed between their legs, and fastened at the ends; so that they were all obliged to lie in a row upon the floor, without a mattress, or even so much as the wooden block, which they begged might be granted them for a pillow. They were nine in number, and so closely crowded together, that the one who occupied the end of the pole esteemed himself peculiarly fortunate. One leg rested on the upper side of the long bamboo, and with all its weight of shackles pressed upon the limb below, producing, even after partial numbness had supervened, almost unendurable agony.

The death prison was constructed of boards, and was rather stronger than a common Burman dwelling house, though but little confidence was reposed in its strength. Hence the array of stocks and shackles, and the dreaded surveillance of insulting keepers. There were no windows, nor other means of admitting the air, except by such crevices as always exist in a simple board house, and only one small outer door. The common prison was crowded with occupants. The worst of criminals were huddled down beside the highest of state officers — perhaps the very judges who sat upon their crime the day before; for an autocrat, possessed of limitless and irresponsible power, thinks it a small thing to punish even a favorite by thrusting him temporarily into this place of degradation. It is well understood that all who are cast into the death prison are under the condemnation of death, though they may yet be saved by the clemency of the sovereign.

The missionaries were imprisoned in the month of June, and though the rains, which are later and much lighter at Ava than farther down the country, had commenced, their cooling influence was insufficient to counteract the sickening sense of suffocation to which the poisonous miasma rising from the damp earth contributed in a most dangerous degree. The prison was built on the ground, and so the consequences of a lack of ventilation were rendered doubly serious. Prisoners were continually dying of disease, as well as by violent treatment, and yet the place was always full. They came from the palace and from the robber's den; from the shop of the handicraftsman, whose power of execution had fallen short of his monarch's conception; and from the more aspiring roof of the merchant, sacrificed to his reputed wealth. Several sepoys, and occasionally English soldiers, swelled the lists of the miserable. These poor creatures, having no regular supply of food, were often brought to the very verge of starvation; and then, on some worship day, the women would come, as a religious duty, to the prison, with rice and fruit; and the miserable sufferers, maddened by starvation, would eat and die. "O, I dare not tell you," said Mr. Judson to me one day, "half the horrors I have seen and felt. They haunt me, when I am ill or sad, even now, and the simplest relation of them would do no good to either of our dreams."

The keepers of the prison were all branded criminals; some wearing the name of their crime burned into the flesh of their foreheads or breasts; others with a dark ring upon the cheek, or about the eye; and others still with mutilated noses, blind of an eye, or with their ears quite cut away. They are called "children of the prison," and form a distinct class, quite out of the way of reputable people, intermarrying only among themselves, and so perpetuating vice, while they are shut, both by their sentence and the horror with which they are regarded by all classes, without the pale of virtue. The cruelty, or other vicious inclination which led to the perpetration of the first crime, is now deepened and rendered indelible by constant familiarity with every species of human torture, until these creatures seem really to be actuated by some demoniac spirit. The head jailer, called by the prisoners the tiger cat, and branded in the breast *loo-that*, or *murderer*, was one of the most hideous and disgusting of his fraternity. He affected great jocularity, and was facetious even in the commission of his worst cruelties, bringing down his hammer with a jest when fastening manacles, putting his hated arms affectionately around the prisoners, and calling them his beloved children, to get a better opportunity to prick or pinch them, and withal studying torture as the most comical of arts.

One of the first things Mr. Judson inquired after, as soon as he and Mrs. Judson were allowed to meet and speak together in English, was the manuscript translation of the New Testament. Part of it had been printed, but there was a large portion, together with important emendations of the printed part, still in manuscript. Mrs. Judson had secreted it, with her silver and a few other articles of value, in the earth under the house. It was now the rainy season, and if the paper remained in this place any considerable length of time, it would be ruined by the mould. It was thought unsafe to allow a manuscript of this kind to remain in the house, from which every article was subject at any moment to be carried away, as, once examined, it would certainly be destroyed. The final conclusion was to sew the manuscript up in a pillow, so mean in its appearance, and so hard and uncomfortable withal, that even the avarice of a Burman would not covet it, while Mr. Judson himself should undertake the guardianship of the treasure. In reply to a remark afterwards made to him with regard to it, he said, "When people are loaded with chains, and sleep half the time on a bare board, their senses become so obtuse that they do not know the difference between a hard pillow and a soft one."

During the first seven months of Mr. Judson's imprisonment, there was but little change. The white men all wore three pairs of fetters; but they were suffered to walk about the prison yard, as well as they could with their ankles only a few inches apart, and always followed by keepers. They were from time to time subjected to almost innumerable annoyances, vexations, and extortions; and they were obliged to be the witnesses of wanton cruelties which they could not prevent, and of intense sufferings which they could not alleviate. For the most of the time, through Mrs. Judson's continual exertions, and by help of occasional presents, they were allowed to spend the day in the open shed in the yard, and Mrs. Judson was even permitted to build a little bamboo shelter for her husband, where he could be, some portion of the time, by himself. Mr. Judson was exceedingly nice in his personal habits, nice even to a fault; and this herding together, even if he had been permitted to choose his associates, would have been exceedingly unpleasant to him. They were not all, belonging as they did to five different nations, educated in his notions of cleanliness, and even he was often, from necessity, offensive to himself. Sometimes he was denied the use of water, and sometimes the admission of clothing was forbidden; and the act of dressing, with the ankles made fast by fetters, proved to be no simple art. With all his efforts, and the care taken by his wife of his wardrobe, he was sometimes in a very forlorn state. His food was such as Mrs. Judson could provide. Sometimes it came regularly, and sometimes they went very hungry. Sometimes, for weeks together, they had no food but rice, savored with gnapee — a certain preparation of fish, not always palatable to foreigners. But once, when a term of unusual quiet gave her time for the softer and more homely class of loving thoughts, Mrs. Judson made a great effort to surprise her husband with something that should remind him of home. She planned and labored, until, by the aid of buffalo beef and plantains, she actually concocted a mince pie. Unfortunately, as she thought, she could not go in person to the prison that day; and the dinner was brought by smiling Moung Ing, who seemed aware that some mystery must be wrapped up in that peculiar preparation of meat and fruit, though he had never seen the well-spread boards of Plymouth and Bradford. But the pretty little artifice only added another pang to a heart whose susceptibilities were as quick and deep, as, in the sight of the world, they were silent. When his wife had visited him in prison, and borne taunts and insults with and for him, they could be brave together; when she had stood up like an enchantress, winning the hearts of high and low, making savage jailers, and scarcely less savage nobles, weep; or moved, protected by her own dignity and sublimity of purpose, like a queen along the streets, his heart had throbbed with proud admiration; and he was almost able to thank God for the trials which had made a character so intrinsically noble shine forth with such peculiar brightness. But in this simple, homelike act, this little unpretending effusion of a loving heart, there was something so touching, so unlike the part she had just been acting, and yet so illustrative of what she really was, that he bowed his head upon his knees, and the tears flowed down to the chains about his ankles. What a happy man he might have been had this heavy woe been spared them! And what was coming next? Finally the scene changed, and there came over him a vision of the past. He saw again the home of his boyhood. His stern, strangely revered father, his gentle mother, his rosy, curly-haired sister, and pale young brother were gathered for the noonday meal, and he was once more among them. And so his fancy revelled there. Finally he lifted his head. O, the misery that surrounded him! He moved his feet, and the rattling of the heavy chains was as a death knell. He thrust the carefully prepared dinner into the hand of his associate, and as fast as his fetters would permit, hurried to his own little shed.

Mr. Judson was not naturally of an even temperament. Hopeful and earnest he was, beyond most men, and withal very persevering; but at this period of his life, and up to a much later time, he was subject to a desponding reaction, from which his faith in God, the ruling principle of his later years, was not now sufficiently ripe to set him entirely free. His peculiar mental conformation was eminently active; so that the passive suffering of his prison discipline was more galling than to a mind differently constituted. So long as he could contend with difficulties, he was appalled by nothing; but whatever he might have been in after life, he was at this time better fitted to *do* than to *endure*. For some time previous to the birth of poor little Maria, he had been filled with the gloomiest forebodings; and not without cause. His wife, from the peculiar customs of this land of semi-civilization, was more alone than she would have been among the wild Indian women of an American forest; and he could do nothing for her. When the dreaded crisis was past, and a pale, puny infant of twenty days was brought to his prison, no person, not thoroughly conversant with the secret springs of feeling which made his the richest heart that ever beat in human bosom, would be at all able to appreciate the scene. His first child slept beneath the waters of the Bay of Bengal, a victim to Anglo-Indian persecution, a baby martyr, without the martyr's conflict; the second, his "meek, blue-eyed Roger," had his bed in the jungle graveyard at Rangoon; and here came the third little wan stranger, to claim the first parental kiss from the midst of felon chains.

Mrs. Judson had long previous to this adopted the Burmese style of dress. Her rich Spanish complexion could never be mistaken for the tawny hue of the native; and her figure, of full medium height, appeared much taller and more commanding in a costume usually worn by women of inferior size. But her friend, the governor's wife, who presented her with the dress, had recommended the measure as a concession which would be sure to conciliate the people, and win them to a kindlier treatment of her. Behold her, then — her dark curls carefully straightened, drawn back from her forehead, and a fragrant cocoa blossom, drooping like a white plume from the knot upon the crown; her saffron vest thrown open to display the folds of crimson beneath; and a rich silken skirt, wrapped closely about her fine figure, parting at the ankle, and sloping back upon the floor. The clothing of the feet was not Burman, for the native sandal could not be worn except upon a bare foot. Behold her standing in the doorway, (for she was never permitted to enter the prison,) her little blue-eyed blossom wailing, as it almost always did, upon her bosom, and the chained father crawling forth to the meeting!

The following verses, of which the writer says, "They were composed in my mind at the time, and afterwards written down," commemorate this meeting: —

Lines addressed to an Infant Daughter, twenty days old, in the condemned Prison at Ava.

> Sleep, darling infant, sleep,
>   Hushed on thy mother's breast;
> Let no rude sound of clanking chains
>   Disturb thy balmy rest.

LINES TO HIS INFANT DAUGHTER.

Sleep, darling infant, sleep;
   Blest that thou canst not know
The pangs that rend thy parents' hearts,
   The keenness of their woe.

Sleep, darling infant, sleep;
   May Heaven its blessings shed,
In rich profusion, soft and sweet,
   On thine unconscious head!

Why ope thy little eyes?
   What would my darling see?
Thy sorrowing mother's bending form?
   Thy father's agony?

Wouldst view this drear abode,
   Where fettered felons lie,
And wonder that thy father here
   Should as a felon sigh?

Wouldst mark the dreadful sights,
   Which stoutest hearts appal —
The stocks, the cord, the fatal sword,
   The torturing iron mall?

No, darling infant, no!
   Thou seest them not at all;
Thou only mark'st the rays of light
   Which flicker on the wall.

Thine untaught infant eye
   Can nothing clearly see;
Sweet scenes of home and prison scenes
   Are all alike to thee.

Stretch, then, thy little arms,
   And roll thy vacant eye,
Reposing on thy mother's breast,
   In soft security.

Why ope thy paly lips?
   What would my darling say?

"My dear papa, why leave us thus?
    Why thus in prison stay?

"For poor mamma and I
    All lonely live at home,
And every day we watch and wait,
    And wish papa would come?"

No; all alike to thee
    Thy mother's grief or mirth;
Nor know'st thou one of all the ills
    Which mark thy mournful birth.

Thy lips one art alone,
    One loving, simple grace,
By nature's instinct have been taught:
    Seek, then, thy nestling-place!

Spread out thy little hand;
    Thy mother's bosom press,
And thus return, in grateful guise,
    Her more sincere caress.

Go, darling infant, go;
    Thine hour has passed away;
The jailer's harsh, discordant voice
    Forbids thy longer stay.

God grant that we may meet
    In happier times than this,
And with thine angel mother dear
    Enjoy domestic bliss.

But should the fearful clouds,
    Which Burmah's sky o'erspread,
Conduct the threatened vengeance down,
    On thy poor father's head, —

Where couldst thou shelter find?
    O, whither wouldst thou stray?
What hand would guide my darling's steps
    Along their dangerous way?

There is a God on high,
    The glorious King of kings;
'Tis he to whom thy mother prays,
    Whose love she sits and sings.

That glorious God, so kind,
    Has sent his Son to save
Our ruined race from sin and death,
    And raise them from the grave.

And to that gracious God,
    My darling I commend;
Be thou the helpless orphan's stay,
    Her Father and her Friend.

Inspire her infant heart
    The Saviour's love to know,
And guide her through this dreary world,
    This wilderness of woe.

Thou sleep'st again, my lamb,
    Nor heed'st nor song nor prayer:
Go, sleeping in thy mother's arms,
    Safe in a mother's care.

And when, in future years,
    Thou know'st thy father's tongue,
These lines will show thee how he felt,
    How o'er his babe he sung.

To Maria Eliza Butterworth Judson, born at Ava, January 26, 1825.

The following versification of the Lord's Prayer was composed a few weeks later. It illustrates the nature of the subjects which occupied the thoughts of the missionary during this long-protracted agony. It is said by the author to be comprised in fewer words than the original Greek, and in two more only than the common translation:—

Our Father God, who art in heaven,
    All hallowed be thy name.

> Thy kingdom come; thy will be done,
>   In earth and heaven the same.
>
> Give us, this day, our daily bread;
>   And, as we those forgive
> Who sin against us, so may we
>   Forgiving grace receive.
>
> Into temptation lead us not;
>   From evil set us free;
> The kingdom, power, and glory, Lord,
>   Ever belong to thee.
>
> <small>Prison, Ava, March, 1825.</small>

The foreigners had spent about seven months in prison, when suddenly a change came. One day a band of men rushed into the prison yard, and while some seized the white prisoners, and added two more pairs of fetters to the three they already wore, others began tearing down Mrs. Judson's little bamboo room, snatching up pillows and mattresses, and whatever other articles came within their reach. At last the prisoners, after having half the clothing torn from their persons, were thrust into the common prison, and, with a bamboo between their legs, again stretched upon the bare floor. Here were more than a hundred miserable wretches, shut from every breath of air except such as could find its way between the crevices in the boards, groaning with various tortures, and rattling their chains, as they groped in the gray light, and writhed and twisted themselves, as much as was in their power, from side to side, in the vain endeavor to obtain some ease by change of position. It was the commencement of the hot season, and the heat was not lessened by the fevered breaths of that crowd of sufferers, nor the close air purified by the exhalations which arose from their bodies. Night came, but brought with it no rest. A whisper had passed around the prison, whether through malice or accident, that the foreigners would be led out to execution at three in the night; and the effect on the little band was not so much in accordance with natural temperament as the transforming principle of faith. Bold men were cowards, and weak men grew strong. At first, Mr. Judson felt a pang of regret that he was to go at last without saying farewell to his unsuspecting wife and child. But gradually the feeling changed, and he would not have had it different if he could. She had left him in comparative comfort that day; she would come the next, and find him beyond her care. It would be a terrible shock at first; but she would be spared much anxious suffering, and he could almost fancy that she would soon learn to rejoice that he was safe in glory. As for herself, the Burmans had always treated her with some respect; she seemed to have gained immunity from personal insult, while her intrepidity had won their admiration; and he did not believe that even the rudest of them would dare to do her harm. No; fruitful in resources as she had proved herself, she would get an appointment to carry some message of peace to the English, and so place herself under their protection. It would be a blessing to her and to his child, if he was removed from them; and he thanked God that his time was so near at hand. He felt thankful, too, that the execution was to take place in the night. He should pass his own door on the way. There he might breathe his silent farewell, while she was spared the parting agony. He thought of Burmah, too, even then. The English would most likely be conquerors; and then there would be nothing to hinder the propagation of Christianity. He even recollected — so calm and dispassionate were his thoughts — some passages in his translation capable of a better rendering; and then he speculated on the pillow he had lost that day, weighing the probabilities of its ever falling into his wife's hands, so that the manuscript would be recovered. And then he imagined that she did not find it, and went off into a visionary scene of its being brought to light years afterwards, which he smiled at when he gave a sketch of these emotions, and did not fully describe. At length the fatal hour drew nigh. They had no means of ascertaining it precisely, but they knew that it could not be very far distant. They waited with increased solemnity. Then they prayed together Mr. Judson's voice for all of them, and then he, and probably each of the others, prayed separately. And still they waited, in awful expectancy. The hour passed by, — they felt it *must* be passed, — and there was no unusual movement in the prison. Still they expected and waited, till finally there woke a glimmering of hope, a possibility that they had been deceived. And so, hoping, and doubting, and fearing, they lingered on, till the opening of the door assured them of what they had long suspected. It was morning. Then the jailer came; and, in answer to their questions, chucked them mockingly under the chin, and told them, O no; he could not spare his beloved children yet, just after — kicking the bamboo as he spoke, till all the chains rattled, and the five rows of fetters dashed together, pinching sharply the flesh that they caught between them — just after he had taken so much trouble to procure them fitting ornaments.

After Mr. Judson had been about a month in the loathsome inner prison, he was attacked by a slow fever, which threatened to destroy his life. His guardian angel was, as ever, on the alert; but it was in vain that she entreated permission to rebuild his room in the prison yard. About this time the poor sufferers were astonished by a most singular accession to their numbers. Something like a year previous to the commencement of the war, the king had received from some foreigner a present of a lion. The noble beast had been a particular favorite with him, and an object of great interest at court. But it was now whispered about, and with mysterious meaning in the whispers, that the English bore a lion upon their standard. The disgraceful defeat of Bandoola, his alarming final fall, and the utter inefficiency of the hardiest Burman troops before these charmed warriors, were matters of grave conference, and strange glances were cast towards the king's noble pet; but for a time no one dared to speak. The matter was first broached by the queen's brother, an ignorant, brutal fellow, who owed his elevation, from the lot of a common fishmonger, entirely to his clever, intriguing sister's power over the king. He was positive that the English had a demoniac ally in the palace, in the shape of this regal-looking beast, which had entirely won the heart of the king. The pakan-woon, a man of more sense, but, like all Burmans, superstitious, seconded his opinions; and other counsellors, now that they durst speak, came in with floods of argument and testimony. The king repelled the idea of any connection between his favorite and the enemy as absurd in the extreme, but at last consented to the animal's being sent to the death prison, though he expressly stipulated that it should not be slain without his order. The queen's brother, however, gave secret directions to the keepers not to furnish the animal with food; and so merciless was he well known to be in the execution of his vengeance, that they dared not disobey him, even to please the king. The cage, all newly ironed and barricaded, as though some unusual resistance was expected, was placed in the prison yard, close against the principal building. And now commenced a new and fearful scene of misery. The unhappy prisoners had seen *men* starved, and beaten, and smothered, and strangled to death, then dragged by the feet from the door, and thrust, like dogs, into some shallow pit, or left for wild dogs to devour; and they thought they had gained a fearful familiarity with every species of wretchedness. But there was something almost supernatural in this new horror — a gradually starving lion. Day after day, the noble beast writhed in the pangs of hunger, parched with thirst, and bruised and bleeding with his fearful struggles, while his roarings seemed to shake the prison to its foundations, and sent a thrill of indescribable terror to the hearts of the occupants. The jailer said it was the British lion ineffectually struggling against the conquering Burmans; though even his facetious features were somewhat elongated by superstitious fears. Sometimes a compassionate woman would steal to the cage after dark, and thrust a morsel of food between the bars; but it was necessarily a trifle to the powerful beast, and served only to increase his ravings. At other times one of the keepers would throw pails of water over him, which would be greeted with almost human shrieks of pleasure, though it only served to lengthen for a little the terrible term of suffering. At last the scene was over. The skeleton of the poor beast was dragged from its cage, and buried with more care than many a poor human skeleton had been before.

The next time Mrs. Judson came to the prison door, and her husband crawled to meet her — crawled with the upper part of his body, having his feet still attached to the moveless bamboo — he had a new plan to broach. He told her of the empty lion's cage — what a comfortable retreat it might be made for him, while the fever lasted, and begged her intercession with the governor; for he had entreated the comic jailer in vain. The " cat " refused to listen for a moment to such an insult to royalty. Mrs. Judson's application was successful; and with feelings of deep gratitude to God for such a mercy, the sick man was removed from his loathsome quarters to the better accommodations of the lion's cage.

I ought to have stated before that the keeper, to whose share Mr. Judson's old pillow fell on the day they were so unceremoniously thrust into the inner prison, had afterwards exchanged it for a better one, wondering, no doubt, at the odd taste of the white man. When he was again robbed of his clothes and bedding, on the day he was driven away to Oung-pen-la, one of the ruffians deliberately untied the mat which was used as a cover to the precious pillow, and threw the apparently worthless roll of hard cotton away. Some hours after, Moung Ing, stumbling upon this one relic of the vanished prisoners, carried it to the house as a token; and, several months from that time, the manuscript which now makes a part of the Burmese Bible was found within, uninjured.

It will be recollected that Mr. Judson, at the time of his removal to Oung-pen-la, was very much reduced by fever, and that this was the hottest season of the year. Having his wife as a link between himself and the humanity which could not well find existence in such a den, he had avoided some of the careless habits from which his fellow-prisoners had nothing without to preserve them, and consequently he was exposed to greater suffering in that bloody, burning march. He had always kept his person covered, so that, in a very short time, his shoulders were blistered by the heat of the sun. His companions had long ago thrown aside shoes and stockings as a useless encumbrance; but he had never parted from his till that morning, when they were torn away. The terrible result I have no heart to tell. He carried the marks, as well as those of the shackles on the ankles, to the last. He used sometimes to speak to me of the time when he was occasionally permitted to come from the prison to minister to his sick wife, and when he carried poor little wailing Maria from door to door, still with but a few inches of chain between his shackled feet, a beggar at the breasts of pitying mothers.

They remained at Oung-pen-la six months, when Mr. Judson was, for the first time, released from his irons, to be employed as translator and interpreter to the Burmans. From the first, he had been particularly careful not to take any part in political affairs; for, however the war might end, he did not wish the Burmans to receive an impression that he was in the interests of the English. He felt that it would be wrong to endanger his influence as a religious teacher by taking any step which would be likely to render him obnoxious even to a conquered people. But now he had no choice. His own wishes in the matter were not consulted, any more than they had been when he was first thrown into prison. He was probably selected for the office because there was no one who could be better trusted, although it was evident that not the slightest confidence was reposed in him. He was carried to Ava under guard, kept in prison two days, and then, without being permitted to visit his own house but a few moments, was guarded like a prisoner to the boat. Mrs. Judson had hastily prepared a few such articles as she thought necessary to his comfort; but either through the malice, or cupidity, or carelessness of his keepers, nothing but his mattress, pillow, and one blanket could be found. The boat was very small, without a cover, and so crowded that he had not room to lie down. He remained here three days, exposed to the scorching sun by day, and the heavy November dews by night, with no sustenance but a bag of refuse rice, broken and mildewed, for which he was expected to evince the highest gratitude. When he arrived at Maloun, he was so ill as to be almost helpless. The banks of the Irrawadi, at Maloun, as at Ava, are bordered for rods with beds of white, glittering sand, which assumes, in the sunlight, an intense metallic glare, and reflects such heat as might come from a burning furnace. On this sand, half way between the river and the camp, a small bamboo hovel had been erected for the reception of the still carefully watched and guarded translator. There was no aperture for the admittance of air, and he could not roll up the matting which composed the sides of his little shelter without admitting that intolerable white glitter; while the heat reflected from the burning sand penetrated the fragile bamboo braids, and aided in a more alarming development of the fever contracted in his passage down the river. It was in vain that he represented his condition to the officers who came to summon him to the presence of the Burman general. They chose to consider him stubborn, and told him that means would be used to make him obedient to their master's call, and make him work, too, in spite of his pretences. But when they found that he really could not move, they brought papers to his floorless hovel, and insisted on an explanation; while he writhed beneath the torture, and wished himself back to Ava in his chains, or that the fever which was searing his brain would only make him quite mad. The last wish was mercifully granted; for he finally became unconscious of every thing, except a coming and going of sandalled feet, the solemn entrance of a shaven crown and yellow robe, and a very indistinct impression that he was being conveyed from the prison at Oung-pen-la, to be burned alive. When his consciousness returned, he was lying alone in a little room made by suspending a mat from the projecting eaves of a cook house, whither he had been removed less, probably, from compassion than selfish interest. With the cessation of intense physical suffering, even before strength had begun to return, there came a feeling of intellectual vigor and activity characteristic of his nature; and long before even his persecutors thought him fit for labor, he had been busy in arranging his plans for the future. His thorough appreciation of the Burmese character made it very easy to see the mortal terror that the military leaders at Maloun were in; and he resolved by degrees to accustom their thoughts to such concessions as he knew they would soon be called on to make. The native mind, treacherous and suspicious in the main, has yet a fine vein of truth and honesty running through it; and he believed that they would be able in time to distinguish him, true friend as he really was, from the designing agent of the enemy, which they supposed him to be.

In the mean time, papers were occasionally brought to his bed, for advice or explanation; and so he had time to win a large share of confidence before he was able to enter fully upon the duties of a translator. These duties, with those of interpreter and adviser, he soon found to be sufficiently arduous; for the suspicious Burmans obstinately withheld all confidence in the integrity of their conquerors, and, moreover, invested every newspaper paragraph from Calcutta with the dignity of a state document. It was a difficult task to set forth to unaccustomed ears and hearts those high principles of honor which actuate civilized nations; and the attempt usually won more admiration for the speaker than confidence in the truth of his subject. He was often interrupted by such remarks as, "That is noble," "That is as it should be;" but the exclamation would be immediately followed by an incredulous shake of the head, and, "But the teacher dreams; he has a celestial spirit, and so he thinks himself in the land of the Celestials." One definite object he had in view was, in his estimation, more difficult than any other. He had no doubt that the English would retain, if not the whole lower country, at least the port of Rangoon, as, indeed, for the good of both nations, they ought to have done; and he labored to prepare the way for this mortifying loss of territory.

In the mean time, he was far from being overwhelmed by physical comforts. His allowance was only twenty ticals, and this, with the utmost economy, was exhausted in a month. He had long since become accustomed to the Burmese style of cookery; but his recent illness rendered the crude vegetable diet, with its pungent acids and spices, more than usually unsuited to him. The nights, too, were very cold; and the heavy fog, which rested on the river till nine in the morning, seemed, under cover of the darkness, to assume the chilliness of ice. At last he was driven to the necessity of begging a blanket. He was presented, as a special mark of esteem,— because, as he was assured, it had been ascertained that he was a true friend to Burmah,— with a thick cotton rug, about large enough to cover a child of six years. Taking some bamboo twigs for thread, and a penknife for a needle, he stitched his new acquisition to the centre of his blanket, and so, by dint of frequent shiftings from side to side, alternate drawings up of the feet, and crouchings of the shoulders, and other little ingenious contrivances for lessening his bulk, he managed to keep half of his person at a time in a state of tolerable warmth. Here he remained about six weeks, when, in consequence of the advance of the English from Prome, he was hurriedly sent back to Ava. It was late in the night when he arrived, and he was taken through the streets directly past his own door. A feeble light glimmered within, assuring him that it was not altogether deserted; but yet what might not have occurred in those six weeks! He entreated permission to enter but for five minutes; he threatened, he bribed, he appealed to their humanity, for he knew that even they, hard as they seemed, must have humanity somewhere; but all without success. His conductors, with some show of feeling, assured him that they had orders to take him directly to the court house, and that they dared not disobey. He crouched down in an outbuilding until morning, when, after a slight examination, he was placed under guard in an out-of-the-way shed, which served as a temporary prison. At night of the same day, Moung Ing found him in this obscure place, where he had been all day without food. While conversing with the faithful Burman, Mr. Judson once or twice fancied there was something in his words or manner, or perhaps both, a little puzzling; but the impression was only momentary, and the very sight of this messenger from his wife relieved him of a burden of apprehension. He immediately despatched Moung Ing to the friendly governor, for aid in his new difficulties, instructing him carefully as to his words and behavior, and, in the joy of his heart, bade him tell the tsayah-ga-dau to keep up courage one day more; it was almost certain he should be with her on the next. As soon as the messenger was gone, Mr. Judson's thoughts immediately recurred to the singularity of his behavior, scarcely observable at the time, but now assuming much importance. His wife was doubtless well, though Moung Ing had certainly not been very explicit when inquired of; she *must* be well, for had she not sent several messages, and herself suggested the application to the governor? The child, too, was well; he had said that unhesitatingly. Why had he hesitated in the other case? Could it be, could it really be, that any thing serious had befallen her, and they had concealed it from him? But no; those messages! He remembered, however, (it all came to him too clearly now,) how ostentatiously the good-natured Burman had paraded one of those messages whenever he asked a question; and yet, think as he would, they all resolved themselves into two — she longed to see him, and she recommended an application to the governor. The messenger had certainly behaved strangely, and he had been strangely blinded. These two simple phrases had been repeated so often, and in such variety of style, that they had been made to appear a dozen, and to contain a world of meaning; and for the time he was fully satisfied. "She must be living," he repeated to himself; "there is ample proof of that." "She must *have been* living," answered a withering doubt within, "when she gave the directions to Moung Ing." After that one thought, he had no disposition to sleep. The tedious night at length dragged itself away; and, though the governor sent for him as early as could reasonably be expected in the morning, a strange, vague apprehension seemed to concentrate whole ages in those few early hours. The kind old man had become his security with the government, and set him free. With a step more fleet than for the last two years he had practised, and in spite of the maimed ankles, which sometimes almost refused their office, he hurried along the street to his beloved home. The door stood invitingly open, and, without having been seen by any one, he entered. The first object which met his eye was a fat, half-naked Burman woman, squatting in the ashes beside a pan of coals, and holding on her knees a wan baby, so begrimed with dirt that it did not occur to the father it could be his own. He gave but one hasty look, and hurried to the next room. Across the foot of the bed, as though she had fallen there, lay a human object, that, at the first glance, was scarcely more recognizable than his child. The face was of a ghastly paleness, the features sharp, and the whole form shrunken almost to the last degree of emaciation. The glossy black curls had all been shorn from the finely-shaped head, which was now covered by a close-fitting cotton cap, of the coarsest and — unlike any thing usually coming in contact with that head — not the cleanest kind. The whole room presented an appearance of the very extreme of wretchedness, more harrowing to the feelings than can be told. There lay the devoted wife, who had followed him so unweariedly from prison to prison, ever alleviating his distresses, without even common hireling attendance. He knew, by the very arrangement of the room, and by the expression of sheer animality on the face of the woman who held his child, that the Bengalee cook had been her only nurse. The wearied sleeper was awakened by a breath that came too near her cheek. Perhaps a falling tear might have been added; for, steady as were those eyes in difficulties, dauntless in dangers, and stern when conscience frowned, they were well used to tender tears.

Of Mr. Judson's employment by the government I know but little more than Mrs. Judson has told. He was not inclined to speak boastingly; his fault was rather in the opposite extreme; and yet, when he said any thing, it was always evident that he was an important agent. He kept clear from every thing of the sort as long as possible, for the reason before mentioned — he did not wish to implicate himself with the suspicious Burmese as a friend of their enemies, lest it might detract from his influence as a religious teacher. He emphatically wished "to know nothing among them save Jesus Christ and him crucified." As soon as he did use his influence, however, it was of weight. His very reluctance increased his importance, and his deep insight into character generally, and especially that of the Burmese, led him usually to touch the right key. One of the British officers of whom Mrs. Judson speaks, when writing of these things afterwards, mentions Mr. Judson as "possessed of a quick, chivalrous sense of honor, which made him a noble representative of the English character, and which could not fail of impressing even the rude barbarians among whom he was thrown."

One evening several persons at our house were repeating anecdotes of what different men in different ages had regarded as the highest type of sensuous enjoyment; that is, enjoyment derived from outward circumstances. "Pooh!" said Mr. Judson; "these men were not qualified to judge. I know of a much higher pleasure than that. What do you think of floating down the Irrawadi, on a cool, moonlight evening, with your wife by your side, and your baby in your arms, free — all free? But *you* cannot understand it, either; it needs a twenty-one months' qualification; and I can never regret my twenty-one months of misery, when I recall that one delicious thrill. I think I have had a better appreciation of what heaven may be ever since." And so, I have no doubt, he had.

The reception of a lady was an incident in the English camp; and Mrs. Judson's fame had gone before her. No one better than a true-born Englishman can discern precisely the measure of attention grateful to a woman in her situation; and there were innumerable minute touches in General Campbell's conduct which fixed her gratitude, and more still that of her husband on her account. It was not that his son was sent with the staff officers who came to escort her from the steamer; nor that unexpected honors, in military guise, waited her on the shore, where she was received by Sir Archibald in person; nor that her tent was larger and more commodious than his own, with the very agreeable addition of a veranda; but it was a certain fatherly kindness and genuine heart interest, which made her feel as though she was receiving all these favors from a friend.

An incident that occurred a few days after the landing of the prisoners is perhaps worthy of notice. General Campbell was to give a dinner to the Burmese commissioners, and he chose to make it an affair of some pomp and magnificence. At a given order, almost as by magic, the camp was turned into a scene of festivity, with such a profusion of gold and crimson, and floating banners, as is thought most pleasing to an oriental eye. When the dinner hour arrived, the company marched in couples, to the music of the band, toward the table, led by the general, who walked alone. As they came opposite the tent with the veranda before it, suddenly the music ceased, the whole procession stood still, and while the wondering Burmans turned their eager eyes in every direction, doubtful as to what would be the next act in the little drama, so curious to them as strangers, the general entered the tent. In a moment he reappeared with a lady on his arm, — no stranger to the conscious commissioners, — whom he led to the table, and seated at his own right hand. The abashed commissioners slid into their seats shrinkingly, where they sat as though transfixed by a mixture of astonishment and fear. " I fancy these gentlemen must be old acquaintances of yours, Mrs. Judson," General Campbell remarked, amused by what he began to suspect, though he did not fully understand it; " and, judging from their appearance, you must have treated them very ill." Mrs. Judson smiled. The Burmans could not understand the remark, but they evidently considered themselves the subject of it, and their faces were blank with consternation.

"What is the matter with yonder owner of the pointed beard?" pursued Sir Archibald; "he seems to be seized with an ague fit."

"I do not know," answered Mrs. Judson, fixing her eyes on the trembler, with perhaps a mischievous enjoyment of his anxiety, "unless his memory may be too busy. He is an old acquaintance of mine, and may probably infer danger to himself from seeing me under your protection."

She then proceeded to relate, how, when her husband was suffering from fever, in the stifled air of the inner prison, with five pairs of fetters about his ankles, she had walked several miles to this man's house to ask a favor. She had left home early in the morning; but was kept waiting so long that it was noonday before she proffered her request, and received a rough refusal. She was turning sorrowfully away, when his attention was attracted by the silk umbrella she carried in her hand, and he instantly seized upon it. It was in vain that she represented the danger of her walking home without it; told him she had brought no money, and could not buy any thing to shelter her from the sun; and begged that, if he took that, he would at least furnish her with a paper one, to protect her from the scorching heat. He laughed, and turning the very suffering that had wasted her into a jest, told her it was only stout people who were in danger of a sunstroke — the sun could not find such as she; and so turned her from the door.

Expressions of indignation burst from the lips of the listening officers; and try to restrain them as they would, indignant glances did somewhat detract from that high tone of courtesy which it is an Englishman's, and especially an English officer's, pride to preserve in all matters of hospitality. The poor Burman, conscience-taught, seemed to understand every thing that was passing, and his features were distorted with fear; while his face, from which the perspiration oozed painfully, appeared, through his tawny skin, of a deathly paleness. It was not in a woman's heart to do other than pity him; and Mrs. Judson remarked softly, in Burmese, that he had nothing to fear, and then repeated the remark to Sir Archibald. The conversation immediately became general, and every means was taken to reassure the timorous guests, but with little success. There sat the lady, whom all but one of them had personally treated with indignity, at the right hand of power, and her husband, just released from his chains, close beyond; and they doubtless felt conscious that if they and their lady wives were in such a position, they would ask the heads of their enemies, and the request would be granted.

"I never thought I was over and above vindictive," remarked Mr. Judson, when he told the story; "but really it was one of the richest scenes I ever beheld."

A British officer, Major Calder Campbell, describing "an adventure in Ava" in the year 1826, gives a beautiful and affecting description of Mrs. Judson. Major Campbell, then a lieutenant, when descending the Irrawadi River in a canoe manned by Burmans, was attacked in the night, while asleep, by his faithless boatmen, and severely wounded and robbed. When waiting on the beach with much anxiety and distress for the passage of some friendly bark, a row boat was seen approaching.

Signals of distress were made, and a skiff sent to his assistance. The following is the language of the writer: —

"We were taken on board. My eyes first rested on the thin, attenuated form of a lady — a white lady! the first white woman I had seen for more than a year! She was standing on the little deck of the row boat, leaning on the arm of a sickly-looking gentleman with an intellectual cast of countenance, in whom I at once recognized the husband or the brother.

"His dress and bearing pointed him out as a missionary. I have said that I had not beheld a white female for many months; and now the soothing accents of female words fell upon my ears like a household hymn of my youth.

"My wound was tenderly dressed, my head bound up, and I was laid upon a sofa bed. With what a thankful heart did I breathe forth a blessing on these kind Samaritans! With what delight did I drink in the mild, gentle sounds of that sweet woman's voice, as she pressed me to recruit my strength with some of that beverage 'which cheers, but not inebriates!' She was seated in a large sort of swinging chair, of American construction, in which her slight, emaciated, but graceful form appeared almost ethereal. Yet, with much of heaven, there were still the breathings of earthly feeling about her; for at her feet rested a babe, a little, wan baby, on which her eyes often turned with all a mother's love; and gazing frequently upon her delicate features, with a fond yet fearful glance, was that meek missionary, her husband. Her face was pale, very pale, with that expression of deep and serious thought which speaks of the strong and vigorous mind within the frail and perishing body; her brown hair was braided over a placid and holy brow; but her hands — those small, lily hands — were quite beautiful; beautiful they were, and very wan; for ah, they told of disease — of death — death in all its transparent grace — when the sickly blood shines through the clear skin, even as the bright poison lights up the Venetian glass which it is about to shatter. That lady was Mrs. Judson, whose long captivity and severe hardships amongst the Burmese have since been detailed in her published journals.

"I remained two days with them; two delightful days they were to me. Mrs. Judson's powers of conversation were of the first order, and the many affecting anecdotes that she gave us of their long and cruel bondage, their struggles in the cause of religion, and their adventures during a long residence at the court of Ava, gained a heightened interest from the beautiful, energetic simplicity of her language, as well as from the certainty I felt that so fragile a flower as she in very truth was, had but a brief season to linger on earth.

"Why is it that we grieve to think of the approaching death of the young, the virtuous, the ready? Alas! it is the selfishness of human nature that would keep to itself the purest and sweetest gifts of Heaven, to encounter the blasts and the blights of a world where we *see* them, rather than that they should be transplanted to a happier region, *where we see them not.*

"When I left the kind Judsons, I did so with regret.

When I looked my last on her mild, worn countenance, as she issued some instructions to my new set of boatmen, I felt my eyes fill with prophetic tears. They were not perceived. We parted, and we never met again; nor is it likely that the wounded subaltern was ever again thought of by those who had succored him. Mrs. Judson and her child died soon after the cessation of hostilities."

CHAPTER XI.

MISSION TRANSFERRED TO THE TENASSERIM PROVINCES. — REMOVES TO AMHERST. — EMBASSY TO AVA. — SYSTEM OF MISSIONARY REGULATIONS. — DEATH OF MRS. JUDSON. — DEATH OF HIS ONLY CHILD. — REMOVES TO MAULMAIN. — DEATH OF HIS FATHER.

1826-1827.

Upon Dr. Judson's return to Rangoon, after leaving the camp at Yandabo, he found the city invested by the Peguans, who had seized this opportunity for attempting to regain their independence. Every thing was in utter confusion. The mission house was a ruin; the disciples had fled; and it was evident that some other place must now be selected as the scene of missionary labor. It is true that the king had requested Dr. Judson to remain at Ava, and had promised him honors and rewards; but he had refused to grant religious toleration to his subjects. For a long time the lower provinces, which had been in possession of the British, must suffer severely from the vindictive jealousy of the monarch. The portions of Burmah which had been ceded to the British were inhabited by the same races as the other parts of the empire. In these the gospel might be preached; here missions might be established, not merely by sufferance, but under the fostering care of a Christian government. Every thing conspired to point out the Tenasserim provinces as the future seat of the mission; at least until some change should take place in the political condition of the Burman empire.

Dr. Judson, who had rendered so important services at the treaty of Yandabo, and who was better ac quainted with the Burman language and character than any other European, was invited to proceed from Rangoon with the civil commissioner, Mr. Crawfurd, to select the site of the new capital for the ceded provinces. This invitation he accepted. Proceeding in a steamer to the mouth of the Salwen, in company with the commissioner, he examined various localities from Point Kyaikamee to Maulmain. It was at the former place that the most desirable situation was found, and there it was determined that a town should be established. It was accordingly selected for that purpose in the name of the British government, and the Honorable East India Company, and, as a compliment to the then governor general, was named Amherst.

Here it was intended to establish the capital of the Tenasserim provinces, and here it would have been established but for an unfortunate misunderstanding between the civil commissioner and the commander-in-chief. Sir Archibald Campbell considered Maulmain, a small town twenty-seven miles farther up the river, the most favorable military position. Here he, therefore, established his head quarters, and erected barracks for the troops. This determined the direction in which population should flow. Maulmain became the capital. Amherst declined, and, in spite of its commercial advantages, has remained to the present time an insignificant town. When the course of events became thus determined, Mr. Crawfurd resigned the civil government of the provinces, and the aid of a most intelligent and competent officer was lost to the mission.

As soon, however, as the site of Amherst was selected, Dr. Judson determined to remove thither with his family. On the 2d of July, 1826, he arrived there with Mrs. Judson, who was very kindly received by Captain Fenwick, the military officer of the station. The following letters relate to these events: —

To the Corresponding Secretary.

STEAM VESSEL, OFF KYAIKAMEE, April 1, 1826.

MY DEAR SIR: I left Rangoon about one o'clock yesterday, in company with Mr. Crawfurd, commissioner of the governor general, on an exploring expedition to the upper parts of the provinces lately ceded by the Burmese government to the British. This morning, made the Kyaikamee temple, perched on the highest part of a ledge of rocks, which projects into the sea from a high bluff crowned with large trees, at the very entrance of the Salwen or Martaban River. After several hours spent in examining the shoals and rocks, and ascertaining a safe entrance, we found good anchorage, inside the rocky promontory, about one hundred and fifty yards from the shore. Just at night, set our feet on some of the rocks, which at present impede the free entrance of a boat, and with some difficulty reached the beach, ascended the high ground, and looked round on a place, which, though now covered with woods, and exhibiting no marks of having ever been inhabited, except the remains of a few old pagodas and wells, appears to be, from vicinity to the sea, good anchorage ground, and connection with an extensive interior, well calculated to be the site of a new town, the future seat of government.

April 2. Out early in the morning, with the animation of new discoverers — Mr. Crawfurd and other gentlemen of the party aspiring to the honor of founding a town which shall rival the most celebrated ports of the East, and extend the interest and honor of their king and country; myself, while far from being indifferent to the same objects, yet animated by higher hopes and more extended prospects. Discovered a small river, two miles above the point, called the Kalyen or Wâgaree, from a small village of that name, a few miles from its mouth. Proceeded up the river in the steam vessel, viewed several places on the banks, and at night returned to our old station.

April 3. Went up the eastern branch of the Salwen River to Martaban, on the Burmese side, but still occupied by British troops, nearly thirty miles from its mouth. Found not sufficient water for large ships, and concluded, therefore, at once, that no place up the river would answer for the new settlement. Just below Martaban, the Ataran, Gyne, and Salwen unite, and form a beautiful expanse of water; on one side the town of Martaban, on the other the district of Maulmain, where it had been originally proposed to form the new settlement, the country appearing fertile, and the distant prospects, on every side, bounded by ranges of high mountains, covered with wood, and replete, as we were told, with mineral treasure. All of us regretted the want of deep water in the channel leading to this delightful spot, yet perfectly reconciled to a port at Kyaikamee, from the assurance that all the productions of the interior may be conveyed thither by these same streams, with as much facility as to any part of Maulmain.

April 4. Went up the Salwen, about twenty miles above Martaban. The features of the country, as we advanced, became more marked and diversified, evidently capable also of a high degree of cultivation. Villagers removing from the western to the eastern bank, to enjoy the protection of the British government. Went ashore, and explored a very curious temple, partially subterranean, and filled with a most astonishing number and variety of images. At night returned to Martaban.

April 5. Accompanied by Captain Fenwick, civil superintendent of these parts, we retraced our course between the fertile island of Balu and the eastern coast, and resumed our old station off Kyaikamee, which, notwithstanding its present rough and wild appearance, evidently possesses greater advantages and capabilities than any other place we have seen in these parts.

April 6. Repaired to the beach under a bold cliff, on the

north-western side of the promontory, in company with the civil and military authorities present, when, by command of the commissioner, the British flag was hoisted, and, under fire of a royal salute and discharge of musketry, the place was taken possession of in the name of the King and the Honorable Company, and the ceremonies concluded by reading the sixtieth chapter of Isaiah, and presenting an appropriate prayer. Designation of the new place — *Amherst.*

April 7. Traversed the woods, and marked out some of the outlines. Observed the tracks of tigers, buffaloes, deer, and wild hogs. Another trip up the Salwen. Towards night, employed in translating into Burmese a proclamation of the commissioner to the inhabitants of the adjoining districts.

April 8, afternoon. Took leave of Amherst, on return to Rangoon.

April 9. Having strong west wind all the way, made slow progress, and anchored just below Rangoon late at night.

April 14. Mrs. Judson and myself conclude to be the first settlers in Amherst. I have taken down the zayat, (may the blessing of God rest on it, as in days of old,) and intend to send the boards by an early conveyance, to form a temporary shelter during the approaching rainy season. We are promised a passage in the steam vessel, which will leave this in the course of ten days.

Affectionately yours,
A. JUDSON, JR.

When the treaty of Yandabo was negotiated, it was stipulated that an additional commercial treaty should be contracted between the British and Burman governments. Mr. Crawfurd was appointed envoy on behalf of the governor general in council, to conduct this negotiation. He had become intimately acquainted with Dr. Judson, and was exceedingly desirous of securing his assistance in this embassy to Ava. For a long time Dr. Judson resisted every solicitation. At last, Mr. Crawfurd promised to use every effort to procure the insertion of an article in the treaty which should guaranty to all the subjects of the king the right of religious liberty. The hope that so desirable an end might be attained decided Dr. Judson, at last, to accept the appointment. He would not, however, have come to this conclusion but for the opinion of his wife, who decidedly favored it.

The emolument accruing from this service would, however, be what missionaries would consider large. Here, then, was a principle involved for which no precedent existed in the management of American missions. Ought a missionary to be allowed to enter, for a time, into any other service? and if this were, under any circumstances, allowed, to whom should the remuneration belong? — to himself, or to the missionary board? A difference of opinion on this subject led to a most unpleasant discussion between the missionaries at Serampore and their brethren at home, which terminated in a total separation of the parties from each other. Dr. Judson saw that this was the time for the settlement of the question. He conceived that the whole time of the missionary was to be consecrated to the work of propagating the gospel; that the board at home became responsible for his whole support, and therefore that he could not, with propriety, enter into any other engagements without their consent, or, in special emergencies, the consent of his associates; and that whatever remuneration should accrue from his services was to be considered not his own property, but the property of the board. He saw also that a decision on this subject would become more universally binding, if it were proposed by him on the eve of entering upon an engagement which would be both honorable and lucrative. With these views he wrote immediately to the board, and suggested the rules on this subject by which this and all future cases should be decided. They were adopted in this country without alteration, and remain unchanged to the present moment.

In consequence of this decision, Dr. Judson made over to the board five thousand two hundred rupees, the sum allowed him by the governor general in council, in consideration of his services at the treaty of Yandabo, and as a member of the embassy to Ava, and also two thousand rupees, the avails of presents made to him at Ava. This was frequently spoken of as a donation to the mission. He, however, never so considered it. In conveying it to the board, he only acted in conformity with the principles which he had adopted, and by which he believed every missionary should be governed. If he had retained it, no one could have found just cause of complaint; for during these months but little could have been done for the mission. He appreciated, however, the value of the principle, and refused to receive any higher remuneration than was received by his brethren, considering all the surplus the rightful property of the mission.

To the Corresponding Secretary.

RANGOON, June 10, 1826.

REV. SIR: It has, for some time, appeared to me necessary, in order to prevent the improper appropriation and lavish waste of the mission funds, and to prevent missionaries from pursuing measures with a view to their own emolument, while ostensibly engaged in missionary work, that a system of regulations should be adopted by the board or the managing committee, and made binding on all the missionaries in their employ. Experience has shown that regulations adopted by missionaries themselves, though subsequently sanctioned by higher authority, are not sufficiently binding; nor is that mode of proceeding so proper as to have the regulations emanate from the managing powers.

With these views, I take the liberty of submitting to your consideration the accompanying paper, No. I. The regulations therein contained may be thought by some too lax, and by others too strict. I can only say that they are the result of many years' experience, and a very extensive acquaintance with missionaries of various denominations, the relations which have subsisted between them and their employers, and the rules by which they have been governed. In framing the system of regulations now presented, I have had a particular view to the numerous difficulties and differences which have arisen between missionaries and managers of missions, few only of which are generally known, and have endeavored to preserve the balance of power between the parties, so as to infringe neither the natural rights of the one, nor the directing and controlling power of the other.

The accompanying paper, No. II., contains a resolution which I propose for adoption, conformably to the third article of the regulations. The rates of allowance therein stated are rather higher than those originally fixed by the missionaries in Rangoon, where, on account of the exportation of money being strictly prohibited by the Burmese government, the exchange was generally twenty or thirty per cent. in favor of Bengal. In the ceded provinces, as there will be no restriction on the exportation of specie, the exchange will probably be at par.

I have only to add that, if the regulations now submitted meet your approbation, the sooner copies are forwarded to the several missionaries for their signature, the sooner, I trust, existing evils will be remedied.

Yours faithfully,
A. JUDSON, JR.

No. I.

Regulations of the Managing Committee of the Board of Missions of the American Baptist Convention. To be subscribed by all persons entering the service of the board, and to be forwarded for signature to all persons previously in service.

1. No missionary receiving pecuniary support from the board shall engage in any secular business for the purpose of personal emolument; and not at all, unless, in the opinion of the board, the great object of the mission can be best promoted thereby.

2. No such missionary shall appropriate to himself the avails of his labor, or the compensation he may receive for service of any kind; but all avails of labor, and all presents or payments made in consideration of services performed, shall be placed to the credit of the board: Provided, that nothing in this article shall be construed to affect private property, inheritances, or personal favors, not made in compensation of service.

3. All missionaries supported by the board shall, with their wives and children, be considered as having claims on the mission fund for equal support in similar circumstances, the rates of allowance being fixed *by the board*, and the claims of widows and orphans being not invalidated by the death of the head of their family.

4. In regard to missionaries who support themselves from the income of their estates, or in any way not inconsistent with their missionary profession, they shall be considered members of the mission equally with those who receive pecuniary support, and, therefore, equally subject to the instructions and general regulations of the board.

5. Every missionary, however supported, shall transmit to the board, in a journal or series of letters, a regular account of the manner in which he spends his time and performs the duties of his profession.

6. Missionaries stationed in the same place or vicinity, who

shall form a voluntary compact for that purpose, shall be a committee of the board, for the appropriation and disposal of money and property intrusted to them by the board, the Christian public, or private individuals, and for the general management of missionary affairs.

7. If a missionary persist in violating any of the above regulations, it shall be the indispensable duty of his associates in the mission to give full information to the board.

No. II.

Resolution of the Board or the Managing Committee.

Resolved, That, in regard to missionaries stationed in the provinces lately ceded to the British, south and east of the Salwen River, the monthly allowance for their personal expenses, exclusive of appropriations for building or house rent, conveyance on mission business, and other expenses of a public nature, be, for a single man one hundred and ten, for a married man one hundred and fifty, for a child twelve, and for a widow or single woman seventy-five rupees per month, payable in Bengal.

To a Friend.

Rangoon, July 12, 1826.

My dear Sir: Your very handsome present of three hundred rupees arrived most opportunely to enable Mrs. Judson to build a temporary mission house, and set up a small school at Amherst; for which purposes no appropriation had been made by our managing committee at home. I left her there, a few days ago, in the house of Captain Fenwick, civil superintendent, who immediately on our arrival vacated it for her present accommodation, and who exerted himself in every possible way to render her situation comfortable during my absence.

We found several of the native converts who had preceded us to that place, and built the first native houses that encroached on the jungle, and disturbed the deer and wild fowl which had been the undisputed occupants of the peninsula.

Two of the men, whose names you may recollect, Moung Shwa-ba and Moung Ing, I have long intended for assistants in the mission, and I have now advised that one of them be immediately employed in the school, and the other as an itinerant missionary among the new settlers.

Mrs. Judson is delighted with her situation and prospects, though all around her is yet wild, and she can expect but very little society at present. There are about fifty houses, chiefly native, exclusive of the military cantonment, and officers' houses, about a mile distant, on the west side of the peninsula; but after the rainy season, the influx of native population will probably be very great. The harbor proves to be safe and commodious, and the place evidently possesses capabilities and resources which must render it, in time, a point of considerable importance.

It was with great reluctance that I left Amherst and returned to this place, to accompany the embassy to Ava, according to my engagement with Mr. Crawfurd — an engagement which he obtained by long solicitation, and finally by holding out a temptation that I could not, or rather thought it not my duty to resist; he pledged himself to use his utmost interest to secure in the commercial treaty which he is commissioned to negotiate with the court at Ava, an article in favor of religious toleration, on principles of reciprocity; the Burman government engaging not to persecute their subjects who may embrace the Christian religion, and the British government securing a similar privilege to their subjects in behalf of the religion of Gaudama. I sincerely hope that the business of the embassy will be accomplished in three or four months, and that I shall reach Amherst and recommence missionary operations in November next.

Your donation to the mission, and that of Mr. ———, I regard as peculiarly valuable, because uninfluenced by *solicitation*, personal attachment, or desire of human praise, and therefore affording assurance of having originated in those motives which alone are acceptable in the sight of our blessed Lord; assurance also of being accompanied and followed by that spirit of prayer for the mission which invests the donation with its greatest value.

Mrs. Judson and myself feel much gratified that our missionary efforts have attracted your notice, and obtained your approbation; and, begging for a continued interest in your good wishes and prayers,

I remain, my dear sir,
Yours with much affection and respect,
A. JUDSON, JR.

To the Corresponding Secretary.

RANGOON, July 31, 1826.

REV. AND DEAR SIR: At the date of my last, the 10th of June, I was waiting for an opportunity of removing to Amherst. Since then, the commissioner, Mr. Crawfurd, who is appointed to negotiate a secondary treaty with the court of Ava, renewed his proposal for me to accompany the embassy, and pledged himself, in case of my complying, to use his interest to procure the insertion of an article in the treaty favorable to religious toleration — an object which I have had at heart so many years, and which, though now, on account of the opening in the south provinces, not so necessary as formerly, is yet greatly favorable to the gradual introduction of religion into all parts of the country, from the station which we propose occupying. With these views, I thought it my duty to accept the offer. Desirous, however, of making a commencement in the new place as early as possible, and unwilling to disappoint the native converts, who had left this in the full expectation of our immediately following them, I accompanied Mrs. Judson and family thither, in the end of last month; and after seeing them comfortably settled, in a temporary house belonging to Captain Fenwick, civil superintendent of the place, which he kindly vacated for Mrs. Judson's accommodation, I returned to Rangoon the 9th instant.

The new town has made some progress during the rains. About fifty native houses, Burmese, Chinese, and India-Mussulman, and three or four European, exclusive of barracks for the troops and officers' houses, compose the infant settlement.

As soon as the favorable season commences, it will increase rapidly, in consequence of large emigrations from Rangoon. Numerous villages are even now springing up on the eastern side of the Salwen, and there can be no doubt that the whole region will eventually be filled with native population. The harbor of Amherst proves to be safe and commodious; large forests of teak have been discovered in the interior, thereby insuring it a place of trade; the situation of the settlement, expo ed at all seasons to the sea breeze, must be healthy, and the mission, I may venture to say, will receive the decided patronage of government. The management of all the ceded provinces will probably be intrusted to Mr. Crawfurd, one of the most enlightened, intelligent, liberal men I have ever met; one most eminently qualified to discharge the highest and most responsible duties of government.

The embassy will leave this for Ava on the receipt of final orders from Bengal, which are daily expected. I hope that the object of the embassy will be obtained in the course of three or four months, and that I shall be able to reach Amherst and recommence missionary operations in November next.

Yours faithfully,

A. JUDSON, JR.

Mr. Judson, on the 5th of July, left Mrs. Judson and his family at Amherst, to embark for Rangoon on his way to Ava, in the suite of Mr. Crawfurd, the British envoy. It was not until the 30th of September that he arrived at the capital, where the negotiations were to be conducted. He soon found, to his mortification, that no provision in favor of religious toleration could be secured. His labor, therefore, so far as this result was concerned, was fruitless; and he was constrained to spend his time in a service in which he felt very small interest, and which could contribute but very little to the happiness or prosperity of either nation. The Burmans were ignorant of their own interest, incapable of appreciating honorable motives, afraid of the wisdom, as they had been of the prowess, of their conquerors, and seemed governed by one maxim only, which was, to agree to as little as possible. To labor in conducting a negotiation under such circumstances must have been, to a man of Dr. Judson's aspirations, sufficiently irksome.

But the worst was yet to come. On the 24th of November, he heard of the death of Mrs. Judson. She died at Amherst, on the 24th of October, 1826, in the thirty-seventh year of her age. The being whom he loved better than all else on earth, who had been so intimately associated with him in all his plans of benevolence, and who had borne so important a part in their accomplishment; to whose devoted love, consummate tact, and heroic resolution, for twenty-one months, he had been indebted not only for his life, but for all that rendered life endurable; a woman who was the acknowledged ornament of every circle in which she had moved, — had, in an unexpected moment, been removed from him forever. She had sickened and died among strangers. A few native Christian women were her only female attendants. The voice which might have soothed her agony could not administer to her the consolations of the gospel. Other hands than his had smoothed her pillow, received her messages of love, closed her dying eyes, and consigned her to the house appointed for all the living. Her last words were spoken of him, and her last request to Dr. Richardson, her medical attendant, was, that he would convey to her husband her earnest entreaty that he would never consent to enter the service of the British government, but confine himself exclusively to the duties of his religious mission. It is very rare that so many elements of exquisite sadness are concentrated in one bereavement. The narrative of these mournful events is best conveyed by his own pen.

To his Sister.

AVA, December 7, 1826.

Weep with me, my dear sister and parents, for my beloved wife is no more. She died at Amherst, the 24th of October last, of remittent fever, and is buried near the spot where she first landed; and "they have put up a small, rude fence around the grave, to protect it from incautious intrusion." There lies, enclosed in a coffin, the form of her I so much loved — the wife of my youth, the source and centre of my domestic happiness.

She had just built a small house, and moved into it three weeks before she was taken ill; and she writes, "May God preserve and bless you, and restore you in safety to *your old and new home*, is the prayer of your affectionate Ann.' Alas! the new home only remains for me; my old home is broken up forever. Even little Maria is too young to recognize her papa, and, before I see her, will have forgotten her mamma, who loved her so much, and took such care of her. Ah, little, ungrateful babe, who will ever love you like your own mamma, whom you have so soon forgotten? Let us go, my child, to her grave, and plant some flowers there, and water them with our tears, and wait for her resurrection at the last day; for her spirit has been conveyed by angels to Abraham's bosom, and is now existing in paradise with the spirits of the just made perfect. And she will come again, and resume the form which now moulders in the grave. Then she will be bright as the sun, beautiful as an angel, immortal as the Saviour. And all of us who are entitled to immortality by a union to the same immortal Head will live together with her in the enjoyment of everlasting life.

We will not, then, mourn as those who have no hope; "for if we believe that Jesus died and rose again, even so them also that sleep in Jesus will God bring with him."

Yet, notwithstanding the consolations of the gospel, grief claims its right, and tears their course; and I must subscribe myself

Your brother, in the deepest sorrow,

A. JUDSON, JR.

To the Corresponding Secretary, Rev. Dr. Bolles.

AVA, December 7, 1826.

REV. AND DEAR SIR: My last was dated at Rangoon, while waiting to accompany the embassy to Ava. We were detained until the 1st of September, and arrived here the 28th, though we were not admitted to an audience with the king till the 20th of the ensuing month.

In the very commencement of negotiations, I ascertained that it would be impossible to effect any thing in favor of religious toleration, in consequence of the extraordinary ground assumed by the Burmese commissioners. Reluctant as the government has ever been to enter into any stipulations with a foreign power, they resolved to do nothing more than they were obliged to by the treaty of Yandabo; and as that required them to make a "commercial treaty," they resolved to confine the discussions to points strictly commercial; so that, instead of a treaty of twenty-two articles, calculated to place the relations of the two countries on the most liberal and friendly footing, the treaty just concluded is confined to four, and those utterly insignificant.

So far, therefore, as I had a view to the attainment of religious toleration in accompanying the embassy, I have entirely failed. I feel the disappointment more deeply on account of the many tedious delays which have already occurred, and which we anticipate during our return; so that, instead of four or five months, I shall be absent from home seven or eight.

But, above all, the news of the death of my beloved wife has not only thrown a gloom over all my future prospects, but has forever imbittered my recollections of the present journey, in consequence of which I have been absent from her dying bed, and prevented from affording the spiritual comfort which her lonely circumstances peculiarly required, and of contributing to avert the fatal catastrophe which has deprived me of one of the first of women, the best of wives.

I commend myself and motherless child to your sympathy and prayers, and remain

Yours, in the deepest sorrow,

A. JUDSON, JR.

To Mrs. Hasseltine, of Bradford, Mass.

AVA, December 7, 1826.

DEAR MOTHER HASSELTINE: This letter, though intended for the whole family, I address particularly to you; for it is a mother's heart that will be most deeply interested in its melancholy details. I propose to give you, at different times, some account of my great, irreparable loss, of which you will have heard before receiving this letter.

I left your daughter, my beloved wife, at Amherst, the 5th of July last, in good health, comfortably situated, happy in being out of the reach of our savage oppressors, and animated in prospect of a field of missionary labor opening under the auspices of British protection. It affords me some comfort that she not only consented to my leaving her, for the purpose of joining the present embassy to Ava, but uniformly gave her advice in favor of the measure, whenever I hesitated concerning my duty. Accordingly I left her. On the 5th of July I saw her for the last time. Our parting was much less painful than many others had been. We had been preserved through so many trials and vicissitudes, that a separation of three or four months, attended with no hazards to either party, seemed a light thing. We parted, therefore, with cheerful hearts, confident of a speedy reunion, and indulging fond anticipations of future years of domestic happiness. After my return to Rangoon, and subsequent arrival at Ava, I received several letters from her, written in her usual style, and exhibiting no subject of regret or apprehension, except the declining health of our little daughter,

Maria. Her last was dated the 14th of September. She says, "I have this day moved into the new house, and, for the first time since we were broken up at Ava, feel myself at home. The house is large and convenient, and if you were here I should feel quite happy. The native population is increasing very fast, and things wear rather a favorable aspect. Moung Ing's school has commenced with ten scholars, and more are expected. Poor little Maria is still feeble. I sometimes hope she is getting better; then again she declines to her former weakness. When I ask her where papa is, she always starts up, and points towards the sea. The servants behave very well, and I have no trouble about any thing, excepting you and Maria. Pray take care of yourself, particularly as it regards the intermittent fever at Ava. May God preserve and bless you, and restore you in safety to your new and old home, is the prayer of your affectionate Ann."

On the 3d of October, Captain F., civil superintendent of Amherst, writes, "Mrs. Judson is extremely well." Why she did not write herself by the same opportunity, I know not. On the 18th, the same gentleman writes, "I can hardly think it right to tell you that Mrs. Judson has had an attack of fever, as before this reaches you she will, I sincerely trust, be quite well, as it has not been so severe as to reduce her. This was occasioned by too close attendance on the child. However, her cares have been rewarded in a most extraordinary manner, as the poor babe at one time was so reduced that no rational hope could be entertained of its recovery; but at present a most favorable change has taken place, and she has improved wonderfully. Mrs. Judson had no fever last night, so that the intermission is now complete." The tenor of this letter was such as to make my mind quite easy, both as it regarded the mother and the child. My next communication was a letter with a black seal, handed me by a person, saying he was sorry to have to inform me of the death of the child. I know not whether this was a mistake on his part, or kindly intended to prepare my mind for the real intelligence. I went into my room, and opened the letter with feelings of gratitude and joy, that at any rate the mother was spared. It was from Mr. B., assistant superintendent of Amherst, dated the 26th of October, and began thus:—

MY DEAR SIR: To one who has suffered so much, and with such exemplary fortitude, there needs but little preface to tell a tale of distress. It were cruel indeed to torture you with doubt and suspense. To sum up the unhappy tidings in a few words, *Mrs. Judson is no more.*

At intervals I got through with the dreadful letter, and proceed to give you the substance as indelibly engraven on my heart:—

Early in the month she was attacked with a most violent fever. From the first she felt a strong presentiment that she should not recover, and on the 24th, about eight in the evening, she expired. Dr. R. was quite assiduous in his attentions, both as friend and physician. Captain F. procured her the services of a European woman from the 45th regiment; and be assured all was done that could be done to comfort her in her sufferings, and to smooth the passage to the grave. We all deeply feel the loss of this excellent lady, whose shortness of residence among us was yet sufficiently long to impress us with a deep sense of her worth and virtues. It was not until about the 20th that Dr. R. began seriously to suspect danger. Before that period the fever had abated at intervals; but its last approach baffled all medical skill. On the morning of the 23d, Mrs. Judson spoke for the last time. The disease had then completed its conquest, and from that time up to the moment of dissolution, she lay nearly motionless, and apparently quite insensible. Yesterday morning I assisted in the last melancholy office of putting her mortal remains in the coffin, and in the evening her funeral was attended by all the European officers now resident here. We have buried her near the spot where she first landed, and I have put up a small, rude fence around the grave, to protect it from incautious intrusions. Your little girl, Maria, is much better. Mrs. W. has taken charge of her, and I hope she will continue to thrive under her care.

Two days later, Captain Fenwick writes thus to a friend in Rangoon:—

I trust that you will be able to find means to inform our friend of the dreadful loss he has suffered. Mrs. Judson had slight attacks of fever from the 8th or 9th instant, but we had no reason to apprehend the fatal result. I saw her on the 18th, and at that time she was free from fever, scarcely, if at all, reduced. I was obliged to go up the country on a sudden business, and did not hear of her danger until my return on the 24th, on which day she breathed her last, at 8 P. M. I shall not attempt to give you an account of the gloom which the death of this most amiable woman has thrown over our small society. You, who were so well acquainted with her, must feel her loss more deeply; but we had just known her long enough to value her acquaintance as a blessing in this remote corner. I dread the effect it will have on poor Judson. I am sure you will take every care that this mournful intelligence may be opened to him as carefully as possible.

The only other communication on this subject, that has reached me, is the following line from Sir Archibald Campbell to the envoy: "Poor Judson will be dreadfully distressed at the loss of his good and amiable wife. She died the other day at Amherst, of remittent fever, eighteen days ill."

You perceive that I have no account whatever of the state of her mind, in view of death and eternity, or of her wishes concerning her darling babe, whom she loved most intensely. I hope to glean some information on these points from the physician who attended her, and the native converts who must have been occasionally present.

I will not trouble you, my dear mother, with an account of my own private feelings — the bitter, heart-rending anguish, which for some days would admit of no mitigation, and the comfort which the gospel subsequently afforded — the gospel of Jesus Christ, which brings life and immortality to light. Blessed assurance, — and let us apply it afresh to our hearts, — that, while I am writing and you perusing these lines, her spirit is resting and rejoicing in the heavenly paradise, —

> "Where glories shine, and pleasures roll
> That charm, delight, transport the soul;
> And every panting wish shall be
> Possessed of boundless bliss in thee."

And there, my dear mother, we also shall soon be, uniting and participating in the felicities of heaven with her for whom we now mourn. "Amen. Even so, come, Lord Jesus."

AMHERST, February 4, 1827.

Amid the desolation that death has made, I take up my pen once more to address the mother of my beloved Ann. I am sitting in the house she built, in the room where she breathed her last, and at a window from which I see the tree that stands at the head of her grave, and the top of the "small rude fence" which they have put up "to protect it from incautious intrusion."

Mr. and Mrs. Wade are living in the house, having arrived here about a month after Ann's death; and Mrs. Wade has taken charge of my poor motherless Maria. I was unable to get any accounts of the child at Rangoon; and it was only on my arriving here, the 24th ultimo, that I learned she was still alive. Mr. Wade met me at the landing-place, and as I passed on to the house, one and another of the native Christians came out, and when they saw me they began to weep. At length we reached the house; and I almost expected to see my love coming out to meet me, as usual. But no; I saw only in the arms of Mrs. Wade a poor little puny child, who could not recognize her weeping father, and from whose infant mind had long been erased all recollection of the mother who loved her so much.

She turned away from me in alarm, and I, obliged to seek comfort elsewhere, found my way to the grave. But who ever obtained comfort there? Thence I went to the house, in which I left her, and looked at the spot where we last knelt in prayer, and where we exchanged the parting kiss.

The doctor who attended her has removed to another station, and the only information I can obtain is such as the native Christians are able to communicate.

It seems that her head was much affected during her last days, and she said but little. She sometimes complained thus: "The teacher is long in coming; and the new missionaries are long in coming; I must die alone, and leave my little one; but as it is the will of God, I acquiesce in his will. I am not afraid of death, but I am afraid I shall not be able to bear these pains. Tell the teacher that the disease was most violent, and I could not write; tell him how I suffered and died; tell him all that you see; and take care of the house and things until he returns." When she was unable to notice any thing else, she would still call the child to her, and charge the nurse to be kind to it, and indulge it in every thing, until its father shall return. The last day or two, she lay almost senseless and motionless, on one side, her head reclining on her arm, her eyes closed; and at eight in the evening, with one exclamation of distress in the Burman language, she ceased to breathe.

February 7. I have been on a visit to the physician who attended her in her illness. He has the character of a kind, attentive, and skilful practitioner; and his communications to me have been rather consoling. I am now convinced that every thing possible was done, and that, had I been present myself, I could not have essentially contributed to avert the fatal termination of the disease. The doctor was with her twice a day, and frequently spent the greater part of the night by her side. He says that, from the first attack of the fever she was persuaded she should not recover; but that her mind was uniformly tranquil and happy in the prospect of death. She only expressed occasional regret at leaving her child, and the native Christian schools, before her husband, or another missionary family, could arrive. The last two days she was free from pain. On her attention being roused by reiterated questions, she replied, "I feel quite well, only very weak." These were her last words.

The doctor is decidedly of opinion that the fatal termination of the fever is not to be ascribed to the localities of the new settlement, but chiefly to the weakness of her constitution, occasioned by the severe privations and long-protracted sufferings she endured at Ava. O, with what meekness, and patience, and magnanimity, and Christian fortitude, she bore those sufferings! And can I wish they had been less? Can I sacri legiously wish to rob her crown of a single gem? Much she saw and suffered of the evil of this evil world, and eminently was she qualified to relish and enjoy the pure and holy rest into which she has entered. True, she has been taken from a sphere in which she was singularly qualified, by her natural disposition, her winning manners, her devoted zeal, and her perfect acquaintance with the language, to be extensively serviceable to the cause of Christ; true, she has been torn from her husband's bleeding heart, and from her darling babe; but infinite wisdom and love have presided, as ever, in this most afflicting dispensation. Faith decides that it is all right, and the decision of faith eternity will soon confirm.

I have only time to add — for I am writing in great haste, with very short notice of the present opportunity of sending to Bengal — that poor little Maria, though very feeble, is, I hope, recovering from her long illness. She began indeed to recover, while under the care of the lady who kindly took charge of her, at her mother's death; but when, after Mr. Wade's arrival, she was brought back to this house, she seemed to think that she had returned to her former home, and had found in Mrs. Wade her own mother. And certainly the most tender, affectionate care is not wanting to confirm her in this idea.

I remain, my dear mother,
Yours, in the deepest sorrow,
A. JUDSON, JR.

Dr. Judson returned to Amherst January 24, 1827, and joined the family of Mr. and Mrs. Wade, who had arrived there November 23, 1826, about a month after Mrs. Judson's death. Mrs. Wade had assumed the charge of the feeble infant, and she watched over it with a mother's fondness until its brief course was completed. On the 7th of April, Mr. and Mrs. Boardman joined the mission. The health of Mrs. Boardman, however, soon rendered it necessary for them to proceed to Maulmain for medical advice. It was found desirable to establish a branch of the mission in that place, and they remained for that purpose. The fortunes of Amherst continuing to decline, Dr. Judson, in August, removed thither. In November, Mr. and Mrs. Wade, with the native Christians at Amherst, followed them; and henceforward Maulmain became the chief seat of the Burman mission.

The work which had been so prosperously commenced at Rangoon had now to be done over again. A few of the converts, whom war and the cholera had spared, were gathered around them; but to the population at large the missionaries were entire strangers. They were wild Burmans, such as they had at first met at Rangoon. There were, however, now several European missionaries. The New Testament had been translated, and portions of it, together with several tracts, had been printed. A spirit of Christian zeal had manifested itself among some of the converts, which gave good promise of success. The work of preaching the gospel was recommenced, and, as before, converts were added to them of such as should be saved. These events are narrated at large in the following journals and letters: —

Journal.

January 24, 1827. Arrived at Amherst, and detached myself from the suite of the envoy. Was happy to find that Mr. and Mrs. Wade had previously arrived, and were occupying the house built by Mrs. Judson. Mrs. Wade had also taken charge of my daughter Maria, now two years old. As I passed from the landing-place to the house, the native Christians came out to meet me, and they welcomed me with the voice of lamentation; for my presence reminded them of the great loss they had sustained in the death of Mrs. Judson. There are four only in the place, Moung Shwa-ba and Moung

Ing, Mah Men-la and Mah Doke. The rest of the baptized are scattered in different parts of the country. The teacher Moung Shwa-gnong died of the cholera, on his way down from Ava, at the close of the war. Three of the disciples remained in Rangoon, until the place was evacuated by the British, and then failed in their attempts to obtain a passage hither.

On our way we stopped a few days at Rangoon. The place was invested by the Peguans, who have raised the standard of rebellion, and taken possession of several towns in the lower part of the country. From one of the highest roofs within the stockade I obtained a view of the mission house, which afforded us shelter so many years. It is now quite in ruins, nothing remaining but the posts and part of the roof. All the houses in the suburbs, and by the river side, are completely swept away. It is not probable, however, that the Peguans will succeed in establishing their independence, or even in getting possession of Rangoon.

We find Amherst in a state of decay, owing to Sir Archibald Campbell having fixed his head quarters at Maulmain, twenty-five miles up the river. Most of the Burmese emigrants have settled in that vicinity. But as the river is not navigable for vessels of any size, Amherst must be the port, and as soon as it receives the fostering care of government, will probably become a flourishing town.

January 28, Lord's day. This day I recommenced worship in Burmese, after an intermission of two years and a half. About twenty persons were present, and among the rest Mah Loon-byay, wife of a French trader from Rangoon, settled in this place. She has been for some months in the habit of meeting with the native Christians, for the purpose of worship.

February 3. Attended the funeral of Abby, daughter of Moung Shwa-ba. She and her elder sister, Mary, were the first girls with whom Mrs. Judson commenced the female school, previous to the late war. They have been with us ever since. Mrs. Wade intends to go on with the school, and has now several girls under her care.

February 4, Lord's day. Worship as last Lord's day Commenced commenting on the epitome of the Old Testament. In the evening administered the Lord's supper. Seven communicants present.

February 10. A few days ago, went up to Maulmain, to pay my respects to Sir Archibald Campbell, and also to obtain an interview with Dr. R., who attended Mrs. Judson in her last illness. Sir Archibald encourages our removing to his favorite station; but as we are already settled here, we feel disposed to wait a little, until we see what the supreme government intends to do for the place.

February 11, Lord's day. After worship, had some particular conversation with Mah Loon-byay, who intimated her wish to become a full disciple by being baptized. Endeavored to explain to her the necessity of the new birth, without which baptism would avail her nothing.

February 13. At the evening meeting, which is attended by the native Christians Tuesdays and Fridays, Moung Ing expressed his desire to undertake a missionary excursion to Tavoy and Mergui. We were all particularly pleased with the proposal, as originating with himself, and indicating a state of mind particularly favorable to the spread of the gospel.

February 25, Lord's day. After the usual worship, we set apart Moung Ing for the work to which we trust he is called by the Spirit of God, appointing him a preacher of the gospel and teacher of the Christian religion, without the charge of any church or power to administer the ordinances — an appointment similar to that which, in our churches, commonly precedes ordination as a pastor or evangelist, in the higher sense of the word. And being thus commended to the grace of God, he embarked on a native boat bound to Tavoy. May the divine Spirit accompany, and guide, and prosper the first Burman preacher we have ever sent forth.

March 13. Received a letter from Moung Ing, dated the 2d instant, informing us of his arrival at Tavoy, five days from this place, and of his attempt to communicate the gospel to the boat people, who listened in silence, without contradicting or reviling.

April 14. We have been much occupied of late in completing the mat houses which Mrs. Judson had begun, and in clearing away the trees and underwood in the vicinity of the mission premises. We have now room for myself and brother Wade's family, and have nearly finished a house for the female school, which will also afford temporary accommodation for brother Boardman's family on their first arrival.

The case of Mah Loon-byay has become very encouraging. In her latest conversation with Mrs. Wade, she gave considerable evidence of having received the grace of God. One of her daughters, also, about twelve years old, professes to be anxious for the salvation of her soul, and desirous of becoming a disciple of Jesus Christ.

A letter from Moung Ing informs us that, after remaining a few days at Tavoy, he proceeded by sea to Mergui, his former residence. He met with a favorable reception from several at Tavoy, and one householder said it would be a good plan to build a zayat by the wayside for the preaching of the gospel.

April 20. Returned from Maulmain, whither I went in quest of medical aid for my daughter, accompanied by Mrs. Wade. Happy to meet with Mr. Boardman and family, who had arrived during our absence.

April 22, Lord's day. Three hopeful inquirers, beside Mah Loon-byay, deserve notice — Moung Dwah, husband of Mah Doke, Moung Thah-pyoo,* a poor man belonging to Moung Shwa-ba, and Moung Myat-poo, son-in-law of a Peguan chief, who emigrated from Rangoon with his followers, and died in this place. They have regularly attended worship on Lord's day, and thereby manifested some regard to religion. At the close of the discourse to-day, which treated of the wisdom, righteousness, sanctification, and redemption which Christ is to all believers, Moung Myat-poo broke out into some audible expressions of satisfaction. This led to some conversation after worship, in which he professed a desire to know more of this religion; "for," said he, "the more I understand it, the better I like it."

* Ko-Thah-byoo, the first Karen convert.

April 24. My little daughter Maria breathed her last, aged two years and three months, and her emancipated spirit fled, I trust, to the arms of her fond mother.

April 29, Lord's day. In consequence of the funeral, several of our Burmese acquaintances in the village came a few evenings in succession, according to their custom, and I endeavored to improve the opportunity in preaching to them Jesus Christ, the resurrection and the life. Three respectable men, friends of Moung Myat-poo, were of the number. They all came again to-day, and attended both morning and evening worship. They profess to be quite convinced of the truth of the Christian religion, but I fear they are deficient in true repentance.

April 30. A letter from Moung Ing informed us of his arrival at Mergui. He conducts public worship every Lord's day, and has commonly four or five auditors, some of whom also attend the daily family worship. His present residence being very obscure, he is about building a small house by the wayside, which will cost, he says, fourteen or fifteen rupees; and, among other means of attracting company, he proposes to prepare and suspend a religious writing in front of his house. But, he adds, while man devises, God's pleasure alone will be accomplished; and under this impression he desires to persevere in his work.

May 6, Lord's day. Had a long conversation with Mah Loon-byay, in which we became satisfied that she is a subject of renewing grace. She received her first religious impressions in Rangoon, several years ago, during a season of great domestic affliction, when, not finding any comfort at the Roman Catholic church, to which, in consequence of some of her ancestors being of foreign extraction, she considered herself attached, she began to visit at the mission house. After her removal to Amherst, her former impressions were deepened; and, though her religious experience has never been so clear and decided as that of some others, we trust that she is a growing Christian, and ought to be admitted to those sources of nourishment which the Great Shepherd has provided for the sustenance of his flock.

DEATH OF HIS ONLY CHILD. 429

Moung Myat-poo, mentioned April 22 and 29, was, as usual, present at worship. From being a noisy, talkative man, of assumed airs and consequence, he has become quiet, and modest, and docile. Mah Men-la, who lives near him, speaks in his favor. She says that, ever since he began to attend worship, he has forsaken the habits of intemperance he had contracted, and spends much of his time in reading our books and conversing on religious subjects.

May 8. Returned from a visit to brother Boardman at Maulmain, who went up, a few days ago, on account of Mrs. Boardman's health, and now thinks of remaining there for the present. Sir Archibald having offered us ground for a mission station, we fixed upon a site about three quarters of a mile south of the military cantonments, commanding a view of the river, and contiguous to a large native town.

May 15. In the evening, at the stated prayer meeting, the case of Mah Loon-byay was laid before the church, and we agreed to receive her into fellowship, on being baptized.

May 20, Lord's day. Mah Loon-byay was accordingly baptized.

May 26. Brother Boardman and family have been with us a few days, during which we have discussed many points relative to our missionary operations, and made some arrangement concerning the outward affairs of the mission.

To Mrs. Hasseltine.

AMHERST, April 26, 1827.

DEAR MOTHER HASSELTINE: My little Maria lies by the side of her fond mother. The complaint to which she was subject several months proved incurable. She had the best medical advice; and the kind care of Mrs. Wade could not have been, in any respect, exceeded by that of her own mother. But all our efforts, and prayers, and tears could not propitiate the cruel disease; the work of death went forward, and after the usual process, excruciating to a parent's heart, she ceased to breathe on the 24th instant, at 3 o'clock, P. M., aged two years and three months. We then closed her faded eyes, and bound up her discolored lips, where the dark touch of death first appeared, and folded her little hands on her cold breast. The next morning we made her last bed in the small enclosure that surrounds her mother's lonely grave. Together they rest in hope, under the hope tree, (*hopiá,*) which stands at the head of the graves; and together, I trust, their spirits are rejoicing after a short separation of precisely six months.

And I am left alone in the wide world. My own dear family I have buried; one in Rangoon, and two in Amherst. What remains for me but to hold myself in readiness to follow the dear departed to that blessed world,

"Where my best friends, my kindred, dwell,
Where God, my Saviour, reigns"?

I remain, my dear mother, yours,
A. JUDSON.

To the Rev. D. Sharp.

AMHERST, May 5, 1827.

MY DEAR SIR: You are doubtless acquainted with the measures we have taken in regard to the formation of a new mission station at this place.

The final disposal of the ceded provinces on this coast is still rather uncertain, the question having been referred to the decision of the Court of Directors. But it is generally understood that the Burmese government has behaved so ill, since the war, in not complying with the terms of the treaty, and in giving the envoy, Mr. Crawfurd, a most ungracious reception at court, that these provinces cannot be restored to their former masters, and that the difficulty attending their erection into an independent principality, or transferring them to any neighboring power, will render their final retention necessary, though the British government uniformly profess their reluctance to extend their Indian territories.

The fate of this port is still more dubious, in consequence of Sir Archibald Campbell's having fixed his head quarters at

Maulmain, twenty-five miles up the river, and of the uncertainty whether Mr. Crawfurd, or any person interested in the prosperity of Amherst, will be placed in civil charge here.

When I first determined on settling here, it was understood that all the heads of government were unanimous in the purpose of making this the capital of the ceded provinces; but an unhappy misunderstanding took place; and though this is admitted to be the most pleasant place, the most salubrious, the most centrical, the best, and indeed the only port, (for ships cannot go up the river,) Sir Archibald pronounced Maulmain the best military station, and the whole tide of Burmese emigration has flowed thither.

On brother Wade's arrival, and my return from Ava, as we had a house here which Mrs. Judson had begun, we continued to occupy it, and wait for the openings of Providence. On brother Boardman's arrival, he had occasion to go up to Maulmain to obtain medical assistance for Mrs. Boardman, and according to an arrangement we have made, he will probably remain there for the present. Sir Archibald has repeatedly offered us ground for a mission station; and we are pleased with having a footing at both places, that we may, with greater facility, occupy that which will become the permanent seat of government, or perhaps both, if the native population of both, and other circumstances, shall appear to warrant such a division of our strength.

The expense of building such mat houses as our present necessities require is not large. We have expended about three hundred dollars in Amherst, and have sufficient accommodation for myself and brother Wade's family, besides a commodious zayat for the female school. And even this appropriation has not been made from the funds furnished from America, but from donations made us for the express purpose of building. Since the close of the war, I have been able, from money paid me by the British government, presents lately made me at Ava, and donations to the mission, to pay into the funds of the board above four thousand dollars, which, after deducting such expenses as our regulations allow, together with the last donation from Madras, I have remitted to Mr. Pearce, of Calcutta.

The long interruption of our missionary work, occasioned by our troubles at Ava, the domestic calamities which have since overwhelmed me in quick succession, and the hitherto unfavorable circumstances of Amherst, have operated to prevent my returning with much ardor to my usual occupations. I am, however, endeavoring to do a little. We have a small assembly of twenty-five or thirty on Lord's days, and our daily family worship is not unfrequently attended by a few inquirers. One woman desires to profess our religion, and has lately given some satisfactory evidence that she is sincere. A few respectable men declare themselves convinced of the truth of the Christian religion; but we discern yet no traces of the renewing influences of the Spirit on their hearts.

Three only of the Rangoon converts are now with us. The rest are dead or scattered in different parts of the country. So far as I have been able to ascertain the circumstances of those who died in my absence, and those who still remain, I believe that, with the exception of two, who were excluded from the church in Rangoon for neglecting to attend worship, none of the baptized have disgraced their holy profession. I do not, of course, speak of two or three cases which required temporary church discipline.

Moung Ing lately went on a mission to Mergui, (Bike,) the place of his former residence, where he has set up Christian worship, and has, he writes me, several inquirers.

I commend my sorrows to your sympathetic remembrance, and, begging an interest in your prayers, remain,

My dear sir,

Yours faithfully,

A. JUDSON.

To the Corresponding Secretary.

AMHERST, June 21, 1827.

REV. AND DEAR SIR: When brother Boardman was last here, we were on the point of writing a joint letter, recommending a reënforcement of missionaries to be sent out to these provinces. But it then remained doubtful whether Mr. Crawfurd, the late envoy to Ava, and the founder of Amherst, would be appointed to the government of this place — a measure which we considered indicative of the intention of the supreme government of Bengal, so far as the question rests with them, to retain this part of the ceded provinces. We have now ascertained that he is appointed, and may be expected here in a few weeks. This circumstance, together with the present state of negotiation between the British and Burmese governments, too tedious to be detailed, and a variety of other considerations, render it quite certain in our minds that these provinces, at least the seaports, will be permanently annexed to the territories of the East India Company.

In this view we recommend them, as a very promising field of missionary labor.

The principal towns are Maulmain, Amherst, Yay, Tavoy, and Mergui. Maulmain itself contains a native population of fifteen or twenty thousand. Amherst is still small. Yay contains perhaps three thousand, but no census has yet been taken. Tavoy contains, according to the census, eight thousand; the whole district twenty-five thousand. Mergui contains three thousand, and the adjoining villages about the same number. It is not, however, the immediate population that we would insist on, but the consideration that, while these provinces contain a population sufficient for all missionary operations, they are really as much a part of Burmah as Rangoon or Ava; and therefore it is to be hoped that the influence of the gospel preached here will ultimately be felt through the whole country.

The climate of all this coast is decidedly salubrious; more so, perhaps, than any other part of India; and communication will always be maintained with Bengal, by way of Amherst.

In regard to the number required, we should say *not less than three.* Five could be disposed of to the greatest advan tage, namely, two at Tavoy, two at Mergui or Yay, and one more at Maulmain.

We remain,
Rev. and dear sir,
Yours faithfully,
A. JUDSON.
J. WADE.

P. S. We cannot wait to communicate with brother Boardman without losing the present opportunity of sending to Bengal, which, we are told, is the last that will occur for some time. We know that his sentiments on the subject of this letter perfectly accord with ours.

Second postscript. Siam is also a noble field for missions. The capital, Bangkok, is only twenty miles from the sea, and is itself a port. Constant communication is maintained with Singapore, just at the extremity of the Siamese and Malayan peninsula; and between Singapore and Bengal ships are constantly passing. See "Singapore," in Chapin's Missionary Gazetteer.

Bangkok is now unoccupied, but the London Independents are looking that way.

I know not what to say about the coast of Arracan, it has proved so extremely unhealthy. Sandoway, however, is said to be salubrious; and other places, when cleared and settled, will doubtless be so. It was rumored that the insalubrity of the climate would occasion the country being delivered up to the Burmese, or erected into a separate principality; but the new title of the governor general, *Earl of Arracan*, shows that, at home, they value the acquisition.

Dr. Morrison wrote, many years ago, that an American mission, in his opinion, would be less suspected in China than an English one. The Chinese perfectly understood the difference between the two nations; and the trade with America is direct, furnishing means of constant communication.

I had the honor of submitting these considerations, many years ago, to the former board, as well as the state of Siam and the Sandwich Islands, then unoccupied; but they excited no attention.

A. JUDSON.

Journal.

AMHERST, July 3, 1827.

For a month past I have been chiefly employed in revising the New Testament, in several points which were not satisfactorily settled when the translation was made. Have also completed two catechisms for the use of Burman schools, the one astronomical, in thirty-eight questions and answers, the other geographical, in eighty-nine, accompanied by a map of the world, with Burman names.

5. Commenced a translation of the book of Psalms.

9. Received letters from Moung Ing, dated Mergui, June 12, in which he says that he is preaching the gospel to all he meets — in the streets, in houses, in zayats. Some contradict, some revile, some say, "These words are good, but the religion is too hard for us."

Among several little incidents mentioned by Moung Ing, I select the following: "One day I met a woman who praised the meritorious efficacy of religious offerings. I preached to her the vanity of such offerings, and the truth of Jesus Christ. The woman repeated my words to her husband. Soon after, as I was passing by, the husband called me in, and invited me to preach there. Next Sunday I went to the house, and found they had invited about fifteen of the neighbors to hear me preach. In the midst of preaching, some rose up and went away; some staid and listened till I had finished, among whom there are three or four persons who continue to appear well. The householder's name is Moung Pyoo, and his wife's name Mah Thwai." One Moung Nwai, also, a man of Portuguese extraction, appears to be a sincere inquirer.

One of us having been requested by a friend in Bengal to procure a collection of sea shells, we mentioned it in writing to Moung Ing, to which he replies, in a postscript, "In regard to what you say about sea shells, if I can conveniently collect some, I will do so; but as this is a worldly concern, I shall not bestow any effort upon it, and probably shall not effect much" — a resolution not, perhaps, unworthy the attention of missionaries of a higher order.

11. Received letters from America, the first that have been written since my release from imprisonment. Was much gratified to find that, in recommencing the work of translating, I was anticipating the particular wishes of the board.

Maulmain, August 12, Lord's day. Yesterday came up to this place, on a visit to brother Boardman. To-day, attempted public worship, as usual, but had no native worshipper, except Moung Myat-poo, from Amherst. He staid the greater part of the day, and gave considerable evidence of being truly attached to religion. In the afternoon, Moung Tau-lay, a native chief in this village, and Moung Mau, brother Boardman's teacher, of whom he has a little hope, came in, and listened with some attention.

15. Spent several hours with Moung Bo, an old Rangoon acquaintance, in discussing the external evidences of the Christian religion. Some of the arguments appeared to convince his understanding, but his heart remains unaffected.

19, Lord's day. Had a novel assembly of thirteen, all, except Moung Mau, ignorant of the first principles of Christianity. They paid uncommon attention, and proposed several questions, which occasioned a desultory and animated conversation of some hours. One old Pharisee expressed his fear that all his good works were nugatory, and declared his sincere desire to know the real truth.

September 9, Lord's day. Still at Maulmain, as we have nearly given up all hope of Amherst's becoming a town, since Mr. Crawfurd has declined the government of these provinces.

16, Lord's day. Had an assembly of about a dozen. One man, by name Moung Pan-pyoo, a sedate, steady person, and a strict observer of the Boodhist religion, listened and conversed in such a manner as raised some hope that he is well disposed towards the truth.

This morning, heard of the death of our excellent sister

Mah Men-la, at Amherst — an event which we have been expecting for several days. She was taken ill before I left Amherst, with a species of dropsy. When her case became dangerous, she was removed to the mission house: "after which," says a letter dated September 3, "she indulged but little hope of recovery. She therefore made her will, and gave up every worldly care. In her will she bequeathed fifty rupees to her brother, the husband of Mah Doke, one hundred and fifty to the missionaries, and the remainder (two hundred, perhaps,) to her two adopted boys, with the exception of a few articles to a niece in Rangoon, and a few other articles to be given away in charity. She has left the boys in our charge, most earnestly desiring and praying that they may be brought up in the Christian religion. No one influenced her to give us any part of her little property, nor had we the least idea that she intended to do so, until she desired Moung Shwa-ba to write an article to that effect.

"When her will was written, she said, 'Now I have done with all worldly things.' Since that, she has enjoyed great peace of mind. She does not express a doubt that her name is written in heaven, and that she is hastening to a blissful immortality. She suffers considerable pain with much patience, and, in order to fortify her mind, often compares her sufferings to those of her divine Master. She is not inclined to converse much; but how delighted *you* would be to hear her, now and then, talk of entering heaven, and *of meeting Mrs. Judson*, and other pious friends! The other day, after having dwelt for some time on the delightful subject, and mentioned the names of all the friends she should rejoice to meet, not omitting *dear little Maria*, she stopped short, and exclaimed, 'But first of all, I shall hasten to where my Saviour sits, and fall down, and worship and adore him, for his great love in sending the teachers to show me the way to heaven.' She says that she feels a choice in her mind to die now, rather than to be restored to health, but desires that the will of God may be done. She was much gratified with your letter to-day, and now seems more reconciled to the idea of not seeing you again on earth. I feel it a pleasure to do any thing for her, she is so grateful and affectionate." Letters received this morning add, "While the funeral procession is moving towards the house appointed for all living, I sit down to inform you that last evening, about nine o'clock, Mah Men-la's happy spirit took its flight to her native skies. Her departure was quiet and serene, without a groan or sigh, or even a gasp, to distort her smiling countenance. She had often said that, to her, death had no terrors: and, though insensible at last, she seemed to bid him welcome. A large concourse of people attended the funeral services; and we have been much gratified by this general respect shown to our departed sister."

October 2. We have been lately clearing up part of our ground contiguous to the road, and removing some of the native houses, with a view to building a house for brother Wade and myself, as we have now concluded to abandon Amherst altogether, with the little enclosure, the hope tree, and the graves which contain the mouldering remains of all that were dearest to me on earth.

MAULMAIN, October 7, 1827.

Lord's day. A succession of company from morning till afternoon. In the last party were some individuals who listened with much seriousness, particularly Moung Gway, a man of some distinction. This is his second visit, and his whole appearance indicated real earnestness.

19. Had the pleasure of seeing Moung Ing, who has just returned from Mergui. Spent the evening in hearing him relate his adventures. The latter part of his residence there, he daily occupied a zayat, in a central part of the town, and made pretty extensive communications of the gospel. Beside some cases mentioned in his letters, he now mentions the case of Moung Nay, from Rangoon, who appeared the most promising of all. But he found none who was willing to accompany him back to this place, though some expressed a desire to do

so, in order to see the foreign teachers, and become more acquainted with their religion.

21, Lord's day. Moung Shoon and Moung Pan-pyoo, two of our principal workmen, were with me a great part of the day, and I cannot but hope that they are seriously inquiring after the truth. I pressed them to attend a prayer meeting in the evening, with myself and Moung Ing, but they were unwilling to commit themselves so far.

November 14. Have been extremely busy the last month, in getting the new house ready to occupy. On the 10th, went down to Amherst; and to-day removed hither, with Mr. and Mrs. Wade. Moung Shwa-ba, Moung Ing, and eleven of the female scholars accompany us, as well as the two boys, left in our charge by Mah Men-la. Mah Doke and her husband will follow us in a few days, together with Moung Myat-poo, and several families connected with him. As to Mah Loon-byay, she is obliged to remain behind, on account of her husband.

25, Lord's day. We have arranged a large room in the front of the house, in the manner of a zayat, and to-day set up worship, in the old Rangoon fashion; and a busy day it has been. About seventy persons, great and small, attended worship in the forenoon; after which twenty or thirty women followed Mrs. Wade into another room, and listened to her instructions. In the evening we had about thirty; and after worship some animated conversation ensued, in which Mah Doke's husband, Moung Dwah, came out very decidedly on the side of Christianity. Moung Ing has a good degree of missionary spirit, and affords much assistance in the work.

26. This evening we had rather an encouraging season. Several of the neighbors came in, so that there was an assembly of a dozen, beside the school. After worship, had some particular conversation with Moung Dwah, in which he gave considerable evidence of being a converted man. He declares that he loves the religion of Christ, because he is sure it is the true religion, and confers inestimable benefits. He says it is about six weeks, or two months, since his mind became quite

decided. His wife says, that so long ago he began to read the Scriptures more attentively, and requested her to pray for and with him, which she did for some days, when he began to pray in the family himself. These things she related, at the time, to Mrs. Wade, with tears of joy. Moung Thah-oung also, an old Rangoon neighbor, and violent opposer, has just come up from Amherst, with a view to removing here, having, as he says, become convinced that his former opposition was wrong, and that the religion of Christ is worthy consideration and acceptance.

9, Lord's day. I cannot help recording the name of Ka-ning-tsoo. He is one of the most respectable of our neighbors — a venerable, white-headed old man, called a Thoo-dau-goung, (saint,) on account of his conscientious life and meritorious deeds; formerly rich, but now poor; once a pharisee, but lately disposed to change his character. He occasionally attends our evening worship, and seems to be opening his mind to the influence of divine truth. We feel much interested in him, and daily pray for his precious soul.

11. Moung Noo, another of our neighbors, the youngest of four brethren, came in last Sunday, just at night; and after hearing some plain truths, he staid during evening worship, and paid uncommon attention. This morning he came again, and this evening again. After worship, he inquired with feeling, "What shall I do to be saved?" "Believe on the Lord Jesus Christ." "I do believe. I do believe. This religion is right. I have been all wrong. What shall I now do?" "If you have begun to believe, let your faith increase. Attend worship. Keep the Lord's day. Become the Saviour's servant. Do all his will. Give yourself, soul and body, into his hands. Will you do so?" "I will, I will. But I do not know all his will." "Read the Scriptures." "I can read Talaing only, not Burman." "Come then, and we will read to you. Come every day to worship, and at all times of day, and we will instruct you."

The case of this poor man is the case of a large majority of the population of these parts. They understand the Scriptures in Burman when read, but cannot read themselves. And I felt the necessity of having the Scriptures constantly read in some public place — in a word, of setting up a reading zayat, to be occupied by one of the native Christians.

12. Conversed with Moung Shwa-ba, on the project of a reading zayat, and he entered into it with some interest. We concluded therefore to put up a shed on the wayside, in the vicinity of the house, and employ him on account of the mission half of the time, the other half of his time being devoted to the female school. Moung Ing is to be continued in the service of the mission exclusively, as an itinerant throughout the place, and an assistant to brother Wade, n the preaching zayat, which he is about setting up.

16, Lord's day. Moung Shwa-ba commenced his operations in the reading zayat, and had several listeners. In the course of the day, had several opportunities of preaching the gospel to a great many. In an excursion through the north part of the place, met Moung Ing, engaged in the same way. He is growing a most valuable assistant. He takes up the business without instigation, and appears to be deeply interested in the spread of the gospel. Moung Dwah, also, is growing in zeal and attachment to the cause. I trust it will not be long before he is baptized.

31. Though considerable missionary work has been done for several days past, I have noted nothing in the journal; but the close of the year reminds me of this as well as many other delinquencies.

The means which are at present using for the spread of truth, may be said to be four: 1st. Public worship on Lord's days. This commences at half past ten o'clock in the forenoon, and is attended by the members of the mission, the scholars, the native converts, and inquirers, and occasionally some of the neighbors and travellers; the assembly varying from twenty to seventy or more. The worship consists of a set form of adoration and praise, followed by an extempore disccurse, or rather harangue, for it is commonly very desultory, suited to the nature of the assembly; and the exercises are closed with prayer. After the assembly breaks up, several remain, and we frequently have religious conversation and discussion for several hours. 2d. The daily evening worship. This is intended for our own family, the scholars, the Christians that live around us, and such of the neighbors as wish to attend. The attendance, including the children, averages about twenty. We begin with reading a portion of Scripture — explain — exhort — and conclude with prayer. After worship I spend the evening with those who are willing to remain, particularly the converts, and endeavor to make the conversation instructive and profitable to them. In the mean time, the women repair to another room, and receive the instruction of Mrs. Wade; and this, together with the female school, conducted by Mrs. Wade and Mrs. Boardman, (brother Boardman has also just commenced a school for boys,) may be called the third means. The fourth is brother Wade's zayat, about half a mile south of the mission house, on the principal road leading from Maulmain to Tavoy-zoo. He goes regularly after breakfast, and spends the day. But his adventures he will relate in his own journal. I hope in a few days to be able to add the fifth head, namely, a small zayat at Koung-zay-kyoon, about two miles and a half north of our present residence, a very populous part of the town, where I intend to spend the day, making an occasional exchange with brother Wade.

As to success — our most hopeful inquirer, Moung Myat-poo, with his extensive connections, has found it inconvenient to remove from Amherst; and for him we can only hope and pray. Moung Dwah, brother of Mah Men-la, and husband of Mah Doke, gives very satisfactory evidence of being a true disciple. He is constant in attending worship every day, besides his own family worship, and has lately requested to be admitted into the church. He will probably be the first baptized in the waters of Maulmain. The second is Moung Thah-byoo, (mentioned April 22,) a Karen by nation, imperfectly acquainted with the Burman language, and possessed of very ordinary abilities. He has been about us several months, and we hope that his mind, though exceedingly dark and ignorant, has begun to discern the excellence of the religion of Christ. The third is Mah Lah, concerning whom my principal acquaintance is derived from Mrs. Wade. She is most constant in improving every opportunity of attending worship, and gives considerable evidence of loving the gospel. Both the last have requested baptism. Next in order comes the priest, whom brother Wade has doubtless mentioned in his journal. He visits the zayat every day; has been to the house once, and spent a few hours with me. He appears to be almost convinced of the truth, but cannot yet think of giving up the merits of thirty-seven years of clerical austerity. Kaning-tsoo, mentioned the 9th instant, remains about the same. There are two or three more, who attend worship occasionally, and give us some reason to hope that their attention has been so far excited as to consider the Christian religion, with some conviction of its truth and excellence. I ought not to forget the children in the school, two or three of whom, and particularly one, by name Mee A, have manifested much tenderness of feeling, and desire to obtain an interest in Christ.

To his Mother and Sister.

MAULMAIN, December 13, 1827.

MY DEAR MOTHER AND SISTER: Yours of the 5th February last reached me a few days ago, and gave me the particulars of that solemn event which has laid the venerable head of our family in the silent dust. "Death, like an overflowing stream, sweeps us away" into the ocean of eternity. You have heard, from my letters of December 7, '26, and May 3, '27, of the ravages which death has made in my own dear family. I am left alone in this wide wilderness, to wait all the days of my appointed time, till my own change come. I pray earnestly that you may both enjoy much of the divine presence, in your solitary, bereaved circumstances, and that both you and I may be preparing, under the repeated strokes of our heavenly Father's hand, to follow the dear departed ones, and enter upon the high enjoyment of everlasting life.

Your affectionate son and brother,

A. JUDSON.

CHAPTER XII.

LABORS AT MAULMAIN.—ORDINATION OF BURMESE PASTORS—MUNIFICENT GIFT.—LETTER TO SIR ARCHIBALD CAMPBELL.—VIEWS OF HIGHER ATTAINMENTS IN RELIGION.—PREPARATION OF WORKS FOR THE PRESS.—SECLUSION.

1828–1830.

THE period comprised in the present chapter is marked by some of the most characteristic events in the life of Dr. Judson. They are, for the most part, narrated with sufficient minuteness in his journal and letters. A few introductory remarks may, however, serve to connect them together in a more continuous whole.

We have seen that Dr. Judson had succeeded in establishing a flourishing church in Rangoon, and had removed to Ava for the purpose of carrying the gospel to "regions beyond," as well as to make an attempt to secure to the empire some degree of religious toleration. These cherished prospects were all ruined by the war. The church in Rangoon was dispersed; the missionaries whom he had left there barely escaped with their lives; the government had become imbittered against all foreigners; and he and his wife had passed through a trial such as has, I believe, happened to no other modern missionaries. The whole work was to be recommenced; but with, the advantage of a perfect knowledge of the language, and under the fostering care of the British government.

This change of circumstances, however, made no alteration in his plans of labor. Experience had taught him to adhere with greater strictness to the example of missionary effort contained in the Acts of the Apostles. Mr. Wade and he at once erected zayats at different parts of the town, and each made the *viva voce* preaching of the gospel his chief occupation. Dr. Judson was, of course, engaged constantly in the work of translation; but he devoted to it only the intervals which occurred between his preaching services and his conversations with passers by. The result was the same as at Rangoon. Very soon one and another became deeply interested in the subject of personal religion. Some of the old converts from Rangoon removed to Maulmain, and aided in extending the knowledge of the gospel. A Christian church was soon formed, which continues until the present day.

From the close of the war to his removal to Maulmain, Dr. Judson had been intimately associated with many of the civil and military officers of the British government. When the seat of the chief commissioner was established at that place, this intimacy for some time continued; and he was frequently the honored and cherished guest of the gentlemen to whom the care of the ceded provinces was committed. He, however, soon perceived that engagements of this kind, from being mere relaxation, began to engross too much of that time the whole of which he had devoted exclusively to the Burmans. In a matter of duty, he was incapable of doing a thing by halves. He immediately resolved to cut off every thing like fashionable intercourse with his English friends — a resolution to which he steadfastly adhered to the close of his life. The first person to whom he communicated his intention of never again dining out of the mission was Sir Archibald Campbell himself. The announcement created of course a variety of impressions in the small society of Maulmain. Some regretted that so agreeable a man should become a mere devotee; others believed that sorrow for the loss of his wife had made him mad; while others, who understood him better, honored what they considered his self-immolation in a good cause; and, on the whole, he was regarded with a sort of reverential sympathy. In subsequent years, his separation from general society came to be regarded, both by the English and even by his brethren, as a personal peculiarity, resulting, in part, from religious asceticism, and partly from want of interest in those around him. This opinion was wide of the truth. No one enjoyed intelligent and cultivated society more keenly than he; and he surrendered it only in obedience to those principles by which he designed to govern his life. He was, however, always punctilious in the performance of those simpler civilities which required no sacrifice of precious time; and he was on intimate terms with nearly all the civil commissioners stationed on that coast, standing to most of them in the relation of a confidential adviser.

As additional missionaries were sent out by the board, they naturally came first to Maulmain. While there may have been some propriety in sending them to that point to learn the rudiments of their missionary work, and to become acquainted with the customs of the East, Dr. Judson was, from the first to the last, most earnestly opposed to the concentration of missionary effort, either in this or in any other place. He was in favor of attacking the enemy at every accessible point. His eye was fixed on the whole heathen world; and he labored incessantly to induce his brethren to occupy every promising field that presented itself in that part of India. It was at his suggestion, I believe, that Dr. Jones established the mission in Siam, Mr. Brown that in Asam, and Mr. Boardman that at Tavoy. These were all brethren to whom Dr. Judson was strongly attached, and to be deprived of their coöperation and society was to him a sore bereavement; but he rightly judged them all to be eminently qualified to lay the foundations of new missions, and, as was his wont, he sacrificed all personal considerations to the cause in which he had embarked.

He applied to himself the same rule by which he supposed every missionary should be governed. As soon as there were men at Maulmain able to perform the labor at that station, he left it to plant the gospel in other districts. In this spirit, he removed to Rangoon to aid Mr. and Mrs. Wade, who were there laboring alone. Here, however, he was not satisfied, but pushed on to Prome, the ancient seat of Burman power, determining there to unfold the standard of the cross. Here he labored with considerable prospect of success, until he was ordered away by the government at Ava. He went forth on this mission attended only by a few native converts, in the spirit of an apostle; and his farewell to Prome, as he looked upon it for the last time, reminds us of our Lord's pathetic lamentation over Jerusalem.

When his mission here was abruptly terminated by order of the government, he returned to Rangoon; and a great and an effectual door was, for a while, opened for him in that city. The demand for tracts and portions of the Scriptures was great beyond all precedent. Persons from all parts of the empire were earnestly desiring writings which would explain to them the new religion. To this work he devoted himself with characteristic energy, at the same time translating the Scriptures, and preaching the gospel. A knowledge of the new religion was thus carried to the interior; and from the seed then sown have arisen those incipient churches found so frequently in the lower part of the empire.

Journal.

Maulmain, January 2, 1828. Spent the day in brother Wade's zayat, he being otherwise engaged. Considerable company all day. The priest present most of the time. Tells every body that he comes daily to investigate the new religion, speaks in our favor on all occasions, but will not own that he has any thought of changing his profession.

January 6, Lord's day. Not a very interesting day; the assembly rather thin, but in the evening had some gratifying conversation with Mah Lah, and obtained satisfactory evidence that she, as well as Moung Dwah, has experienced divine grace.

January 11. Commenced operations in the Koung-zay-kyoon zayat, and had literally a crowd of company, without any intermission, through the day. Among the rest, one Moung San-lone, who has received some instructions from Moung Ing, appeared to drink in the truth. Two others, whose names I know not, staid from morning till night, and manifested that inquisitive spirit which, I feel persuaded, will bring them again.

January 12. The two last, Moung Tau and Moung Yay, were with me nearly all day; but San-lone, I am sorry to find, has suddenly gone off to Rangoon on business, and will be absent several days. In the evening, Moung Dwah and Mah Lah were examined for admission into the church, and fully approved.

January 13, Lord's day. A pretty full assembly at morning worship. Much gratified to see Moung Tau and Moung Yay, who, with Moung En, a very sensible young man from Koung-zay-kyoon, and Moung Myat-kyau, brother of the chief of that district, and two or three others, remained several hours, and maintained a most interesting and profitable discussion of many points of Christian doctrine. All these that have been named, together with Moung San-lone, may be considered hopeful inquirers.

January 14. Company at the zayat through the day. Towards night, Moung San-lone came in, having been disappointed in his attempt to go to Rangoon. He manifests a spirit of sincere, anxious inquiry. He says that he desires, above all things, to find the light; but it seems to him that the farther he advances the more dark and sinful he becomes. After I left the zayat, he told Moung Ing that he wanted to come and live near us, that he might devote himself more entirely to the investigation of religious truth.

January 15. A crowded zayat all day. Obliged to talk incessantly. One Oo San-lone, a blind man of some note among his neighbors, took the lead in conversation. The other, Moung San-lone, is evidently improving in disposition to the gospel.

January 17. Had worship in the house, as on Lord's days. Not a very large assembly, but some of the most promising inquirers were present. After the exercises, Moung Dwah and Mah Lah received baptism. Moung Thah-vyoo, who had been absent on business several days, happened to come in at the time, and requested leave to join them; but we advised him to wait a little.

At night Moung San-lone declared that he fully approved of the Christian religion in all its parts, but felt his mind so weak and dark that he knew not how to encounter the reproach and ridicule which would ensue on embracing it.

January 25. For several days past the attendance at the Koung-zay-kyoon zayat has varied from ten to twenty through the day. Moung Myat-kyau, brother of the chief of the district, has been gradually advancing in religious knowledge and decision of character, until I begin to indulge a hope that he is a subject of divine grace. Mah Men, an old acquaintance of Mah Mee of Rangoon, came to the zayat a few days ago, and listened with such eagerness and approbation as inclined me to think that she had obtained some love to the truth before she removed to this place. Her husband is a decided opposer. The opposition throughout the district and the whole place is becoming more open. At the same time, the number of listeners and inquirers is multiplying, and the excitement in favor of religion is evidently increasing. Moung San-lone, the most hopeful inquirer, has gone to Rangoon, and will be absent several days.

March 20. Since the last date, all the inquirers mentioned then, and on the 17th preceding, have been advancing slowly. Some or other of them attend the zayat every day. Moung Shway-pan and Ko Man-poke must also be added to the list. The latter, an elderly man of some respectability, appears to be really attached to the truth, but is yet very timid in his professions. Mah Men is treated harshly by her husband, and seldom dares to come near us. Moung San-lone, on his return from Rangoon, was accompanied by his father-in-law, Oo Pai by name, a very active, intelligent old man, who drank in the truth with singular avidity. On his return to Rangoon he took an affectionate leave of me, promising to remove his family hither, if at all practicable. We hear that our old friend Moung Thah-a is now in Rangoon, and that there are several of the old inquirers who listen to his instructions.

But my particular object in taking up my pen this morning was to mention the case of Moung Shway-pwen, a bright young man of twenty, who professes to have received the truth about fourteen years ago. On first hearing the gospel at the zayat, it sank into his heart; but as he lived at some distance, we saw him occasionally only. A few days ago, he removed hither, and took up his abode with Moung Ing, that he might devote himself entirely to the attainment of the one thing needful. His experience has been uncommonly clear and rapid; and having outstripped all the older inquirers, he this morning followed his Lord into the watery grave.

March 23, Lord's day. After the forenoon worship, Moung Myat-kyau, Moung San-lone, and Moung En, requested baptism; and after the Lord's supper in the evening, they were examined before the church, and approved.

March 29. Brother and sister Boardman left us for Tavoy, with the cordial approbation of all the members of the mission, accompanied by Moung Shwa-pwen, and Ko Thah-byoo, the Karen, who also has lately been approved by the church, but not baptized.

March 30, Lord's day. The three persons mentioned last Lord's day were baptized. Three others, Moung Yay, Moung Shway-pan, and Ko Man-poke, attended all the exercises of the day; and they give considerable evidence of being really converted. Mah Moo also, a poor woman, who has occasionally attended the instructions of Mrs. Wade, must be mentioned as a very hopeful character. Mah Men is, I hope, a decided Christian, but is seldom able to attend, on account of her husband. Moung Tau, who has been sometimes mentioned among the inquirers, has become rather deistical of late; but we do not despair of him. May the Lord pour out his Holy Spirit upon our hearts, and upon the inhabitants of Maulmain.

April 20. Received a letter from Moung Thah-a, of Rangoon, stating the names of thirteen men and three women who are disciples of Jesus, "but secretly, for fear of the Jews." In the number I recognize my old friend "the teacher Oo Oung-det, of the village of Kambet," and two or three others whom I formerly knew; but most of them are new cases.

May 31. The last two months I have spent at the zayat, with scarcely the exception of a single day; and I seldom have been without the company of some of the Christians, or the hopeful inquirers. In the latter class we count eight or ten, adding to those mentioned above Moung San-lone the second, a young man of ordinary abilities, but warmly attached to the cause, and Moung Bo, noticed once in the annals of the Rangoon mission, a man of the first distinction in point of talents, erudition, general information, and extensive influence.

His progress has been so slow that I have not mentioned him before; but he has attended me ever since the zayat was opened, his house being on the opposite side of the street. He was an intimate friend of Moung Shwa-gnong, and has apparently been going through a process similar to what my dear brother, now, I trust, in heaven, experienced. He has relinquished Boodhism, and got through with Deism and Unitarianism, and now appears to be near the truth. Many a time, when contemplating his hard, unbending features, and listening to his tones of dogmatism and pride, I have said in my heart, "Canst thou ever kneel, a humble suppliant, at the foot of the cross?" But he has lately manifested some disposition to yield, and assures me that he does pray in secret.

To conclude this paper, I hope that the light is gradually spreading around us, more extensively, perhaps, from brother Wade's zayat than from mine, that being in a situation to catch visitors from all parts of the country, while mine is chiefly confined to the immediate vicinity. And I hope also that the Spirit of God is operating, in some cases, on the minds of our hearers. All those who have been baptized in this place, as well as those who came with us, give us great and increasing satisfaction. It is, I think, rather characteristic of Burman converts, that they are slow in making up their minds to embrace a new religion; but the point once settled is settled forever.

To the Corresponding Secretary.

MAULMAIN, May 31, 1828.

REV. AND DEAR SIR: When I left America, I brought with me a considerable sum of money, the avails of my own earnings, and the gifts of my relatives and personal friends. This money has been accumulating, at interest, for many years, under the management of a kind friend to the mission, and occasionally receiving accessions from other quarters, particularly at the close of the late war, until it amounts to twelve thousand rupees. I now beg leave to present it to the board, or rather to Him "who loved us, and washed us from our sins in his own blood." I am taking measures to have the money paid to the agent of the board, and the payment will, I trust, be effected by the end of this year.

I would suggest, lest a temporary suspension of the necessity of remitting money should occasion some relaxation of the usual efforts made to meet the current expenses of the mission, whether it may not be advisable to invest a sum equivalent to that which I now pay the agent, viz., six thousand dollars, as part of a permanent fund. But this I leave entirely to the discretion of the board.

Yours, faithfully,
A Missionary.

P. S. It is not from an affected desire of concealment that the writer has subscribed himself "A Missionary." He is sensible that the tenor of the letter will, to those who are acquainted with the state of the mission, sufficiently betray him. But this is not the case with the public in general; and so far as it may be thought desirable not to throw away the influence of example, it is quite sufficient to tell the public that the money is given by a missionary, without specifying the individual.

Journal.

July 28, 1828. Yesterday, five persons were baptized, whose names and characters are as follows: —

1. McDonald, a native Hindoo, twenty-eight years of age. He renounced heathenism a few years ago, and was christened by an English clergyman on the Madras coast. His first profession of Christianity was probably sincere; but, within a few months, he became acquainted with some persons whose communications unsettled his mind, and reduced him to a state of darkness and perplexity for several years. When he came to this coast, about a year ago, he assumed the English dress, and, in correspondence with his former friends in Madras and Bengal, he made many attempts to

disseminate erroneous sentiments in all classes of society, but happily without the slightest success. One morning, about a fortnight ago, he came to the zayat, and heard the doctrines of implicit faith in the word of God, and of regeneration by the power of the Holy Spirit — doctrines which were quite new, and at the same time quite satisfactory to his soul. He yielded at once to the force of truth, and became, to all appearance, a humble, teachable disciple of the divine Son. He understands Burman enough to join in our worship, and, on his requesting baptism, we had no hesitation about receiving him into our little number. He brought with him, yesterday, a large bundle, which, he informed us, contained the tracts and publications which had given him so much trouble; and when he was baptized, he buried them, with his former character, in the watery grave.

2. Moung Shway-pan, whose name has been sometimes mentioned in the journal as a hopeful inquirer. He has been a constant attendant at the zayat ever since it was built, and is a pretty fair specimen of a cautious Burman, who turns a thing over ten thousand times before he takes it, but, when once he takes it, holds it forever. He accordingly appears now very firm and decided.

3. Mai Nyo, an aged female, above eighty. She says she was a little girl when the great Alompra subverted the kingdom of Pegu, and established the present Burman dynasty, so that she has lived under eight successive monarchs. She became acquainted with Mrs. Wade three or four months ago; and though she is bitterly opposed by her relatives, on whom she is quite dependent, and though she has been, especially of late years, a devotee in religious duties, she has renounced all for Christ, and with tottering steps, bending under the infirmities of age, has done homage to the King of kings in the baptismal stream.

4. Mah-ree, (Mary Hasseltine,) about twelve years old, daughter of Moung Shwa-ba, and the only girl that survives of the female school which Mrs. Judson commenced at Ava.

5. Meh Aa, of the same age and standing as Mah-ree.

These two girls are the first fruits of an incipient revival in the school, similar to those glorious revivals which distinguish our beloved native land. May the Holy Spirit be poured out more copiously on our own hearts, on the children of the school, and on all the inhabitants of Maulmain.

While I have my English pen in hand, — an event which rarely occurs, — I would say a word concerning Ko Myat-kyau, who was baptized last March, especially as we have considered him an assistant in the mission since that time.

He is, as I have mentioned, a brother of the first native chief in the place, nearly fifty years of age, of most respectable rank in society, more so than any other that has been baptized, possessed of a clear mind, considerable native eloquence, and an uncommon degree of mental and bodily activity. His literary attainments are scanty; but he has command of handsome language, particularly that which is current in the higher classes of society. He has been an inquirer after truth many years, and has diligently investigated the systems of Boodh, of Brahma, and of Mahomet. At length, he embraced the religion of Jesus Christ with all his heart and soul, manifesting more zeal and ardor than commonly characterize his cool, considerate countrymen. He has suffered as much persecution as can be openly inflicted under British government. All his relations and friends joined in a most appalling cry against him; his wife commenced a suit for divorce; and his brother publicly declared that, if he had the power of life and death, he would instantly wipe out with his blood the disgrace brought upon the family. Our friend bore it all with the meekness of a lamb, and conducted himself with such forbearance and Christian love that the tide has begun to turn in his favor. His wife has relinquished her suit, and begins to listen to the word; his brother has become silent; and some few of the relatives begin to speak in our favor.

It ought to be added that Ko Myat-kyau has given up all worldly business, and devoted himself to assisting us in our missionary work. For this he is particularly fitted by his undissembled humility. It gives us great pleasure to see him sometimes sitting on a level with some poor beggar woman, endeavoring, in language intelligible to her dark mind, to communicate some idea of the mysteries of redeeming love.

But in commending Ko Myat-kyau, I would not forget our old tried friends, Moung Ing and Moung Shwa-ba. The former says it is his meat and drink to preach the gospel, and when, for some time, he has no good opportunity, he feels like a person deprived of his necessary food. The latter has been lately growing in habitual self-denial and holiness of heart; his prayers savor of heavenly communion; and it was through a word from him, spoken in season to his daughter Mah-ree, that the revival commenced in the female school.

August 3, Lord's day. We baptized Mee Tan-goung, Mee Nen-mah, and Mee Nen-yay, three girls from the school, whose cases are rendered interesting by the considerable knowledge they have acquired, in the course of a few months, by the distinctness of their religious experience, and by the violent persecution they have suffered from their respective parents and relatives. Mee Tan-goung's case is particularly interesting, when contrasted with that of her elder sister, Mee Lau, who, after experiencing very clear and pungent convictions of divine truth, has at length been induced, by alternate promises and threatenings, deliberately to reject the Saviour of sinners, and join her mother's party.

Another girl, Mee Pike, who gives us satisfactory evidence of being converted, was brought before the church this day; but her mother being a member of the church, it was thought, by some, that she was perhaps influenced by her mother's example, rather than by the convictions of her own mind, and we could not get a clear vote for her admission.

An elderly man, Ko Shan, was also presented; but his replies were so indistinct, that he was rejected by an overwhelming majority.

Moung San-lone the second, mentioned May 31, was accepted for baptism next Lord's day.

4. Mee Tan-goung's mother came early in the morning,

before any of us were up, and having made her elder daughter, Mee Lau, open the door of the school zayat, she fell upon her younger daughter, abusing and beating her, until, fearing that she should alarm the house, she went off. Soon after, however, she came again, and finding her daughter outside, she beat her on the head with an umbrella, and threatened to sell her for a slave. She then went into town, and after raising a tumult in the market-place, and declaring that her daughter had entered into a religion which prevented her lying and cheating, so that she was quite lost to all purposes of trade, she carried the alarming tale to the mothers of the other two girls who were baptized yesterday. One of them, the mother of Mee Nen-mah, who has been most violent heretofore, came in a rage to Mrs. Wade, (brother Wade and myself being absent at our zayats,) and after using as bad language as she dared, she ran down to the school room, seized her daughter by the hair, and dragged her out doors towards a pile of wood, where she would soon have armed herself with a weapon, had not Mrs. Wade interfered, and rescued the victim; upon which the mother went off, muttering vengeance. The girls bore all this abuse in silent submission, and really manifested something of the spirit of martyrs. All three are taken into the house for the present, lest their infuriated relatives should make an assault upon them by night.

Poor Mee Aa, baptized Sunday before last, lives in great fear. She is daily expecting her mother from Amherst, who will, no doubt, take her away instantly, and use all the means in her power to make her renounce the Christian religion.

August 10, Lord's day. Ko Shan, having satisfied us all, during the past week, that his unfavorable appearance last Lord's day was owing more to his want of language to express his ideas, (being a Taling, and but little acquainted with the Burman,) than to his want of grace was this day reëxamined and accepted. Mee Pike also was accepted; and these, together with Moung San-lone the second, received baptism.

Two other girls, younger than those that have been baptized, appear to have obtained light and hope in Christ.

PLAN FOR SUPPLYING THE TREASURY. 459

"Out of the mouth of babes and sucklings thou hast perfected praise." One of them, Mee Youk, about eight years old, gives as clear, satisfactory evidence of real conversion as any of the older girls. The other, Mee Kway, like our departed Meh Shway-ee, was rescued at Amherst from miserable slavery. She has hitherto given us very little pleasure, but is now led to see that she has been an uncommonly wicked child, and to feel a humble, penitent disposition.

24, Lord's day. Mee Youk received baptism, though her brother, a young man, threatens to beat her to death.

September 21, Lord's day. We baptized Oo Peen-yah, Pandarram, and Mee Kway; the first a respectable person, about fifty years of age, a native of Tavoy, by profession a doctor; the second a Hindoo from the Madras coast, a doctor also, and astrologer, quite ignorant of English and Burman, and brought to the knowledge of the truth through the instrumentality of McDonald, and the New Testament in Tamil, which he has had in his hand, day and night, for the last six weeks; the third the little girl mentioned August 10.

In the afternoon we partook of the Lord's supper, with twenty native communicants, four being absent from illness or other causes, besides those at Rangoon and Tavoy.

To the Corresponding Secretary.

MAULMAIN, September 1, 1828.

REV. AND DEAR SIR: Since it is to be ascribed to the want of money, rather than to that of men, that the Baptists in the United States of America make such feeble efforts to send the gospel through the world, inasmuch as the want of money prevents the managers of missions from presenting those invitations and encouragements which would be gladly embraced by many young men who are waiting the call of Providence, we feel the importance of recurring practically to the golden rule, *that every individual do his duty* in furnishing those means which are absolutely necessary to carry on the great war with the prince of darkness and his legions in this fallen world. Feeling, also, that missionaries and ministers are under peculiar obligations, beyond any other classes of Christians, *to take the lead in contributing of their substance*, and encouraged by our Saviour's commendation of the poor widow in the gospel, we have entered on a course of living which will, we hope, enable us to offer our two mites; and we propose, therefore, to relinquish annually one twentieth of the allowance which we receive from the board of missions.

We respectfully suggest that a similar proposal be made to the Baptist ministers in the United States; and we engage that, as soon as it shall appear that one hundred ministers, including ourselves, have resolved to transmit annually to the treasurer of the American Baptist Board of Foreign Missions one twentieth of all their regular income, whether derived from their salaries or estates, we will relinquish a second twentieth of our allowance, that is, one tenth of the whole.

And lest it be said that we now receive high allowances, and can therefore afford to make some retrenchment, we state, not by way of ostentation, but merely to meet the remark, that, considering our allowances cover all our personal expenses except building or house rent, conveyance on mission business, and charges for medical attendance, we receive less than any English missionaries of any denomination, in any part of the East, and as little as any American missionaries in those parts, notwithstanding the expense of living on this coast is probably greater than at a majority of other stations.

We remain,
Yours faithfully,
A. JUDSON,
J. WADE.

Journal continued.

October 6, 1828. We baptized Oo Pay, Mah Kai, Mah Toon, and Mah Lan. The first is a respectable man, about sixty years of age. He was obliged to leave his house day before yesterday, and take refuge with us, his wife and family made such an uproar about his heretical intentions. But last night a pressing message came for him to return, upon which he made them a visit, and they promised to behave better. They only begged that after he was baptized, he would not go about the neighborhood proclaiming that Gaudama is not the true God, as others who enter the new religion are apt to do.

The second is the mother of Mee Aa, of whom the daughter was so much afraid, as mentioned under August 4. Soon after that date, Mee Aa came trembling, one morning, to Mrs. Wade, with the alarming news that her mother had just arrived at the landing-place, with the intention, doubtless, of taking her away by force; and what should she do? She was told to go and meet her mother, and to pray as she went. But the poor girl need not have been alarmed. She had been incessantly praying for her mother ever since she had learned to pray for herself; and God had heard her prayers, and softened her mother's heart. So when she heard that her daughter was actually baptized, she only made up a queer face, like a person choking, and said, "It was *so*, was it not? I hear that some quite die under the operation." This speech we all considered encouraging. And, accordingly, she soon settled down among us, drank in the truth from her daughter's lips, and then followed her example.

The third is the eldest daughter of Mah Lah; and the fourth, wife of our assistant, Moung Ing.

November 2. Ko Thah-a arrived from Rangoon. His story is rather interesting, but too long to be given in detail. At the close of the war, in the year 1826, he spent a few months at a large village in the neighborhood of Shwa-doung; and there, devoting himself to the preaching of the word, he produced a very considerable excitement. Several professed to believe in the Christian religion; and three of the most promising received baptism at his hands. Some others requested the same favor; but he became alarmed at his own temerity, and declined their repeated applications. The villagers, in time, returned to the vicinity of Rangoon, whence they had fled at the commencement of the war. He also returned to Rangoon, his former residence, and continued to disseminate the truth, but in a more cautious and covert manner. He has now come hither to inquire what he shall do with those who wish to be baptized, and to get some instructions concerning his own duty. He says that he cannot stay long, for when he came away the converts and inquirers begged him to return soon, and his heart is evidently with his little flock, which he has left in yonder wilderness. Let us pray for Ko Thah-a, and the remnant in Rangoon. For, though the tree seemed for a time cut down, "the stump of the roots was left in the earth, with a band of iron and brass, in the tender grass of the field."

November 30. We baptized Moung Dwa, Moung Shoon, and Matthew. Moung Dwa is a native of Arracan, formerly a gross reviler and blasphemer, but now zealous for the truth. Moung Shoon is a merchant of some property, and very respectable connections. Matthew (alias Ram Sammy, that is, god Ram) is a Hindoo, of the same class with Pandarram, mentioned September 21. We have not been in the habit of changing Burman names, as they are generally destitute of any bad signification; but the names of the Hindoos are sometimes (as in the present case) utterly abominable, and require to be cast off, with all their other abominations.

December 7. We baptized Mah Tee, wife of Ko Man-poke, who has been a very hopeful inquirer for nearly a year, but cannot yet fully make up his mind. Mah Tee would have joined the party last Lord's day, had not her husband, poor man, been unwilling to have her go before him. She has been very anxious about it several days; and, though she is of a most amiable disposition, and they have been a very happy couple for twenty-five years, she told him that this was a business which concerned her eternal interests; that she believed in Christ with all her heart, and could not wait for him; and upon this he gave a reluctant consent. She appears to have attained an uncommon share of divine grace.

December 14. We baptized Thomas, (making the thirtieth received this year,) a Hindoo of the same class and character with Matthew, mentioned above.

The four Hindoo converts having all taken Burman wives, without any ceremony of marriage at all, we thought proper to require them to be married in a Christian manner; but none of their wives give any evidence of being piously inclined.

January 4, 1829, Lord's day. We commence this year with an auspicious event — the ordination of Ko Thah-a as pastor of the church in Rangoon, to which place he expects to depart by an early conveyance. He has been so evidently called of God to the ministry that we have not felt at liberty to hesitate or deliberate about the matter. But, if it had been left to us to select one of all the converts to be the first Christian pastor among his countrymen, Ko Thah-a is the man we should have chosen. His age, (fifty-seven,) his steadiness and weight of character, his attainments in Burman literature, which, though not, perhaps, necessary, seem desirable in one who is taking up arms against the religion of his country, and his humble devotedness to the sacred work, all conspire to make us acquiesce with readiness and gratitude in the divine appointment.

Letter to Sir Archibald Campbell.

MAULMAIN, January 8, 1829.

MY DEAR SIR : A few days ago I heard of your intention to leave this place on your return home.

When I reflect on your many kindnesses to me and my beloved wife, now, I trust, in heaven, from the time I first saw you at Yebbay to the present moment, and on the many pleasant interviews with which I have been honored, it is natural that I should feel a desire to express my gratitude for your goodness, and my regret at your departure. But, besides that desire, I have, for a few days, had an impression on my mind which I cannot avoid, and dare not counteract. I would fain say a few words to you on a subject which you have probably never had a friend faithful enough to present plainly to your mind. I feel that I write under the influence of a higher power ; and I beg that if my words offend you, you will still have the charity to believe that I am influenced by none other than the most disinterested, affectionate, and respectful sentiments. And though you should at first be displeased, I cannot but hope that you will sometimes suffer the question to intrude on your most retired moments, whether the words I speak are not the words of eternal truth.

But why should I proceed with hesitation and fear? Why give way to an unbelieving heart? He who inclines me to write will incline your heart to receive my words. If even a heathen monarch appointed one of his courtiers to accost him every morning with the warning salutation, "Philip, thou must die," surely Sir Archibald Campbell, of a Christian country and Christian habits, will be willing, for a moment, to turn away his ear from the voice of flattery, and listen to the monitory voice of sober truth.

And yet true religion is a very different thing from all that you have probably been acquainted with. True religion is seldom to be found among mitred prelates and high dignitaries. It consists not in attachment to any particular church, nor in the observance of any particular forms of worship. Nor does it consist in a mere abstinence from flagrant crimes, a mere conformity to the rules of honesty and honor. True religion consists in a reunion of the soul to that great, omnipresent, infinite Being, from whom we have all become alienated, in consequence of the fall. In our natural state, we spend our days in seeking the wealth and honors of this life, which we yet know to be but short and transitory, and we become too forgetful of that awful eternity to which we are rapidly hastening. So great is the blinding influence of sin, so successful are the fatal machinations of the god of this world, that when we cannot stay the near approach of death and eternity, we still endeavor to quiet our conscience and pacify our fears by vague and indefinite ideas of the mercy of God, and by the hope that it will be well with us hereafter, though the still voice within whispers that all is wrong; and thus we are apt to suffer year after year to pass away, while we drink the intoxicating draught of pleasure, or climb the height of human ambition.

O Sir Archibald, the glittering colors of this world will soon fade away; the bubbles of life will soon burst and disappear; the cold grave will soon close upon our worldly enjoyments, and honors, and aspirings; and where then will our souls be?

God's own eternal Son, the Lord Jesus Christ, came down from heaven to rescue us from the delusion of this world, the power of sin, and the doom of the impenitent. But "unless we have the spirit of Christ, we are none of his." His own divine lips have declared, "Except a man be born again, he cannot see the kingdom of God." And the ambassador of Christianity must not hesitate to declare this solemn truth, plainly and fearlessly, to the king and the beggar, the rich and the poor, if he would clear his own conscience, and manifest true love to their souls.

Allow me, then, to say to thee, Sir Archibald, Turn away thine eye from the fleeting shadows, and thine ear from the empty sounds of earth. Open the eye of thy mind to the uncreated beauties of that divine Being who is ever with thee, and ever waiting to be gracious. Listen to the call of his Holy Spirit. Give thine heart to the Friend and Lover of man, who hung and died on the cross to redeem us from eternal woe, and thou shalt find such peace and sweetness as thou hast never yet conceived of. Thou wilt be astonished that thou couldst have lived so many years ignorant of such transcendent beauty, insensible to those excellences which fill heaven with rapture, and in some instances make a heaven of earth. But if thou wilt not give thy heart to God, thou wilt never find true happiness here, thou wilt never see his face in peace.

I do not suppose that, amid your present hurry, you will find leisure to pay any attention to the topic I now present. But perhaps when oceans have intervened between us, when resting in the bosom of your own native land, the truths of this letter may, through the divine blessing, find their way to your heart.

Farewell, Sir Archibald, and while all around you flatter and praise, while the plaudits of your king and country sound in your ears believe that there is one person, humble and unknown, who prays in his retirement for your immortal soul; whose chief desire is to see you on the great day invested, not with the insignia of earthly monarchs, but with the glorious crown of eternal life, and who desires ever to subscribe himself,

    With heartfelt affection and respect,
        Your sincere friend and faithful servant,
            A. JUDSON.

To the Corresponding Secretary.

            MAULMAIN, January 27, 1829.

REV. AND DEAR SIR: Your letters of May and June, 1828, came to hand last evening. In my previous communications, I have, I believe, anticipated every point that you mention, except that of an application to the Bible Society; and even on that point it is rather singular, that, only three days previous to receiving your last, I was conning over a letter of the very purport that you suggest — with this difference, however, that I thought of making application for the premium only, which is usually granted for the first translation of the New Testament, viz., five hundred pounds. As to the Old Testament, I am sorry that I have inadvertently led you to suppose that the translation was rapidly advancing. When I mentioned commencing the Psalms, it was not with an immediate view of doing any more than that book, though I hope, in time, if life be spared, to go on with the rest. But even that book is not yet done. The truth is, that when I settled here, I found, that what with death, and what with dispersion, I had no church about me to read even the New Testament. I gave up study, therefore, and spent nearly a year in a little shed, projecting into one of the dirtiest, noisiest public streets of the place. Brother Wade did the same in another quarter. The consequence has been, that as God owns the truth, though preached by the most unworthy creatures, a considerable impression has been made on the place; a small church has been collected; the number of inquirers is increasing; and the opposition is most outrageous. I never saw any thing like it in Rangoon, for there we did nothing in public. The mass of the population, particularly in parts where converts have been made, show all the rage of chained wild beasts. But to return. My ideas of translating are very different from those of some missionaries, better men than myself, but mistaken, I think, in this particular. I consider it the work of a man's whole life to procure a *really good* translation of even the New Testament in an untried language. I could write much on this subject, but I have neither time nor disposition. I would only say that, in many instances, missionary labor has been dreadfully misdirected, and hundreds of thousands most foolishly thrown away. As to us, we wish to proceed, *slow* and *sure*, and to see to it that whatever we do, in regard to the inspired word, is *well done*. About four months ago, being convinced that the New Testament, notwithstanding all my labor upon it, was still in a very imperfect state, brother Wade and myself undertook a thorough revision. We have now done one quarter of it; and I have some hope that by the time the printer and press arrive, we shall be able to warrant the whole. After that, we propose to work and rework at the precious book of Psalms, until we can venture to warrant that also. And so, God willing, and giving us life and strength, we hope to go on. But we beg still to be allowed to feel, that our great work is to preach the gospel *viva voce*, and build up the glorious kingdom of Christ among this people. To this end, we consider a good translation of the New Testament, the Psalms, and some other portions of the Old Testament, essentially necessary — the whole very desirable.

I am extremely sorry to hear that there are no young men ready to come out. There are only three of us, and death is hovering around. May I be allowed to say a word in favor of brother ———, though I have not heard of him for two years? From some letters that I have seen, and the accounts given by brothers Wade and Boardman, I cannot help regretting that circumstances prevented his being sent out. And may I be allowed to add, though it is, perhaps, going beyond my province, that possibly the board may have become too particular in their choice of missionaries? Good, humble, pious, self-denying, judicious men will perhaps do more good than brilliant geniuses and men of great literary attainment.

Yours, faithfully,
A. JUDSON.

Journal continued.

January 11, 1829. Pastor Thah-a took leave of us for his charge in Rangoon. We love him as a brother missionary — a humble, conscientious, faithful servant of the Lord Jesus. During his visit he has endeared himself to us all; and we should gladly detain him here, were he not evidently called to labor in another part of the vineyard. May he be made faithful unto death, and then receive the crown of life.

25. Last Lord's day, another god Ram (see November 30) was divested of his attributes, and rose out of the water plain John. He is a Talinga man, but understands Tamil enough to join with the other Hindoos who speak that language. To-day we expected another Hindoo, but he was detained for some reasons unknown to us, and we made up a small female party, consisting of Mah See, Mah Gatee, and Mah Kyan, all decided and hearty in the cause, amid a torrent of threatening and abuse. The first is the wife of Moung San-lone, second; but her elder brother, and her priest, and other acquaintance are all alive on the occasion. The husbands of the other two are both opposers, and have threatened their wives with every thing bad if they enter the new religion. They expect to suffer as soon as their husbands hear of the deeds of this day. We feel most for Mah Kyan, who has a child at her breast, an only child; and her husband has declared that he will not only turn her off, but take the child away from her, and provide it another nurse. After they were baptized, they said that their minds were very happy; come life, come death, they were disciples of the Lord Jesus Christ for life and forever.

February 8. We baptized Moung Zu-thee, who has been

an inquirer several months, but has only lately given us much encouragement. He appears now to have embraced the religion most cordially.

22. We baptized Thomas the second, (referred to January 25.) He has been kept back a month, through the opposition of certain Roman Catholics, with whom he was in some way connected.

We have also ordained Moung Ing, pastor of the church at Amherst. That church consisted of three — Mah Loonbyay, who was baptized while we lived there, and has never left the place; Mah Kai, and her daughter, Mee A, who have lately moved thither. To these are now added Pastor Moung Ing, and his wife, Mah Lan. May the five become five hundred. May the seed formerly sown in weakness and tears yet spring up and bear fruit. May the last efforts of the one we have lost, whose setting rays sunk in death beneath the hope tree, prove not to have been in vain; and may the prayers which ascended from her dying bed be yet heard and answered in blessings upon Amherst.

26. A letter from Moung Thah-a, of Rangoon. He states that he has baptized Ko Thah-doke, who has long given satisfactory evidence of piety; and that two others, relatives of Moung Kywet-nee, one of the three baptized up the country, have requested baptism, and their case is before the church. He divides his time between Rangoon and the villages of Kam-bet and Anan-ben, where the later converts live.

March 5. Several other letters from the members of the church in Rangoon; and among the rest, one from Mah Ing, mentioned in the last pages of the history of the Burman mission, in the year 1822, but not heard of for several succeeding years. She expresses her joy on meeting with the teacher Thah-a, and receiving instruction from him concerning the religion of Christ, to which she professes to have maintained a permanent attachment.

8. We baptized Mah Zu-ga-len, a blind woman, related to Mah Tee, a person of good sense and decided piety.

22. Three English soldiers followed their Lord and Master

into the watery grave. They have been in the habit of attending certain evening meetings, in which we have lately indulged ourselves a little, though averse to every interruption to native work. These soldiers we have not received into the Maulmain church, but have recognized them to be the Baptist church in his majesty's 45th regiment.

May 29. I perceive that I have neglected my journal for a long time, having been chiefly engaged in going forward with the revision of the New Testament. Brother and sister Wade have done all the itinerating; and many interesting tales they have to tell at night, but I believe they put very little on paper. Truth is spreading slowly on every side; prejudices are weakening; opposition is growing more violent in some parts, and in other parts it seems subsiding. The husband of Mah Kyan, who tore his infant from the mother's breast, and pursued his poor wife through the street with a great knife, has become a lamb. He has made a comfortable place in his house for Mrs. Wade to sit and receive company, to the great annoyance of other opposers in that quarter. Mah Gatee has persuaded her husband to come and live near us, that they may attend the daily evening worship, though his mother is still outrageous. They are a young, interesting couple, very fond of one another. It was a great trial for poor Mah Gatee to be baptized against his will.

We have received five since the last date — Moung Tau-ma-gnay and Mah San, the first couple that we have had the pleasure of baptizing together; Moung Toot, brother of Mah San, and Moung Gatee, a young man of some promise; Mah Poot, wife of Moung Zu-thee, wild as the woods, and formerly as mischievous as possible; and Ko Man-poke, husband of Mah Tee, (see December 7,) a steady, excellent old man, a considerable scholar in the Taling language. He has translated all our Burmese tracts into the Taling, and will perhaps be encouraged to go on with some parts of the New Testament. We consider him as one of the most valuable accessions to the cause that we have ever received; and his wife stands almost unrivalled among the female converts. She always accompanies Mrs. Wade, and is of inestimable use in explaining things in the Taling to those who cannot well understand the Burmese; and that is the case with a great part of the population of British Pegu.

No case of church discipline has yet occurred; but Mah Kai, at Amherst, occasions us much sorrow. We hear that her husband forces her to follow him to the house of Rimmon, and that she there bows down, when I fear she has not Naaman's excuse for so doing. Two of the Hindoo members also give us trouble, and we fear that their case must come before the church. Instances of irregularity and sin do sometimes occur; but our efforts in the way of private exhortation and persuasion have been hitherto blessed to the promotion of that repentance and reformation which make amends for all.

June 7, Lord's day. Several applications for baptism have lately been refused, the applicants being relatives of professors of religion, and influenced, we fear, by the example and persuasion of others, rather than by the impulse of grace. To-day, however, a clear case occurred — an old lady, eighty years of age, mother-in-law of a petty chief, who is one of our bitterest opposers. She commenced her inquiries several months ago with a great deal of timidity. And though she has acquired a little courage, and is a person of considerable presence, she almost trembles under a sense of the great responsibility of changing her religion. Such being her character, the promptness with which she answered our questions, before the church, affected us even to tears. "How old are you, mother?" "Eighty years." "Can you, at such an age, renounce the religion that you have followed all your life long?" "I see that it is false, and I renounce it all." "Why do you wish to be baptized into the religion of Jesus Christ?" "I have very, very many sins; and I love the Lord, who saves from sin." "Perhaps your son-in-law, on hearing that you have been baptized, will abuse you, and turn you out of doors." "I have another son-in-law, to whom I will flee." "But he also is an opposer: suppose that you should meet with the same treatment there." "You will, I think, let me come and live near you." We made no reply, willing that she should prove her sincerity by bearing the brunt alone. Her name is Mai Hlah. Behold this venerable woman, severing, at her time of life, all the ties which bind her to a large circle of connections and friends, hazarding the loss of a comfortable, respectable situation, the loss of character, the loss of a shelter for her grey head, throwing herself on the charity of certain foreigners, and all for the sake of " the Lord who saves from sin." O, blessed efficacy of the love of Christ!

12. A letter from Ko Thah-a of Rangoon. Last Lord's day he baptized Moung Au and Moung Shwa-bo, inhabitants of Pah-zoon-doung, the former residence of Moung Shwa-gnong.

August 12. Since the last date, we have baptized two persons — Ko Zen, a relative of Ko Man-poke, and Mah Ta-kau, wife of Ko Shan. Mai Hlah, mentioned above, soon after her baptism, left her son-in-law's house, where she had been living, and took refuge with her elder daughter, Mah Men, mentioned formerly as a hopeful inquirer, but subsequently delinquent. She begins now to give some evidence of grace; and even her husband has become rather favorably disposed.

Letters from Rangoon mention the baptism of two more persons, distant relatives of Thah-a. All the converts behave well, and the number of inquirers is increasing. But the chief of Kam-bet has commenced a course of petty oppression, in consequence of which the disciples are obliged to be silent in that quarter.

The doctor Oo Yan, whose name sometimes occurred in the annals of the Rangoon mission, is no more. He appeared once to be very near the kingdom of heaven; but, alas for his poor soul! the fear of man finally prevailed.

August 29. A letter from Rangoon mentions the baptism of two others, one of them a nephew of Mah Men-la. It appears, also, that a nephew of Thah-a was baptized several months ago, of whom we had not before heard; so that the church at present consists of eleven members baptized by the present pastor, besides three or four who remain of the old stock.

To his Mother and Sister.

Maulmain, March 19, 1829.

My dear Mother and Sister: Your letters of May last I have just received. I think it probable that, soon after you wrote, you received mine of December, 1827, in answer to yours of February, same year, and which contained, as well as I knew how, a quitclaim, as you requested. In regard to the twenty dollars, I have no occasion for the money, and present it to you, my sister, in remembrance of that handful of money which you gave me when we parted in Boston for the last time. But I give it on the express condition that you appropriate part of it to purchase for yourself the Life of Lady Guion, a work which was published in New York, in the year 1820, in one volume 8vo. Lincoln and Edmands will, doubtless, be able to get it for you. And I hope you will read it diligently, and endeavor to imitate that most excellent saint, so far as she was right. Two other books that I would particularly recommend to you are Law's Serious Call, and his Treatise on Christian Perfection.

As to you, my dear mother, do not think that I can ever forget you. When I used to carry about my poor little Maria, I thought how much my mother loved her little Adoniram, and carried him about, and took care of him. And though he has now grown almost out of her knowledge, and been parted many years, and will probably see her no more on earth, he never can forget how much he owes to his own dear mother. It is my comfort that, if truly united to Christ, we shall, at last, meet on the bright plains of heaven, where all our infirmities, and griefs, and sins will have fled away forever.

I shall never need any pecuniary aid from either of you. I thank you for your kind offers, but you can help me in no other way than by your prayers.

My dear sister, I shall never forget the years of childhood; and now I regard you as a sister in Christ, and therefore doubly dear. Perhaps, if mother should be taken away before you, you might scrape together your little property, and find your way out to me. You would soon pick up enough of the language to make yourself very useful in various ways, particularly in the girls' school, which Mrs. Wade has been obliged to give up, she has so much to do among the women. Pray daily to God that he would show you the way in which you can be most useful to his cause, the little while you have to live in this probationary state. Don't think of living for yourself, but for Him who has died for your soul.

May God bless you both here below, and prepare you for all his will, and for his heavenly glory, is the prayer of

Your ever affectionate,
A. JUDSON.

May 14, 1829.

1. Observe the seven seasons of secret prayer every day.

2. "Set a watch before my mouth, and keep the door of my lips."

3. See the hand of God in all events, and thereby become reconciled to his dispensations.

4. Embrace every opportunity of exercising kind feelings, and doing good to others, especially to the household of faith.

5. Consult the internal monitor on every occasion, and instantly comply with his dictates.

6. Believe in the doctrine of perfect sanctification attainable in this life.

To his Sister.

MAULMAIN, May 28, 1829.

MY DEAR SISTER: Yours of October 16th last arrived yesterday. In regard to the quitclaim, it is impossible for me to ascertain, at this distance, what particular forms are required by the laws of the United States. But if you, or brother, or any person will send me such an instrument as the case requires, I will complete and return it. I am rather glad, however, that the first did not answer, because I have now a request to make which I doubt whether you would comply with, if I did not make your compliance a condition of my returning you the said instrument. My request is, that you will entirely destroy all my old letters which are in your and mother's hands, unless it be three or four of the later ones, which you may wish to keep as mementoes. There are several reasons for this measure, which it would take too much time to detail. Suffice it to say, that I am so very desirous of effecting a complete destruction of all my old writings, that you must allow me to say positively, (as the only means of bringing you to terms,) that I cannot send you the instrument you desire until I have an assurance, under your hand, that there is nothing remaining, except as mentioned above.

I should exceedingly rejoice to be once more in the old mansion house at Plymouth, and sit and converse with my own dear mother and sister; but that time can never come. Let us look forward to a happy meeting in the mansions of our Father's house on high. I am afraid that poor Elnathan will not be of our happy number. Let us all pray more fervently for him, and perhaps our prayers will at last be heard. I have not had a letter from him for a long time.

With never-ceasing love to mother, I remain,
Your affectionate brother,
A. JUDSON.

To the Corresponding Secretary.

MAULMAIN, June 19, 1829.

MY DEAR SIR: I propose, from this date, to lessen my usual allowance by one quarter, finding, from experience, that my present mode of living will admit the retrenchment; this arrangement not to interfere with the proposals made under date of September last, concerning the one twentieth and one tenth.

Yours faithfully,
A. JUDSON.

To Mrs. Hasseltine.

The Solitary's Lament.

"Together let us sweetly live,
    Together let us die,
And hand in hand those crowns receive
    That wait us in the sky."

Thus Anne and I, for many a year,
    Together raised our prayer;
One half reached Heaven's propitious ear,
    One half was lost in air.

She found a distant, lonely grave,
    Her foreign friends among;
No kindred spirit came to save,
    None o'er her death bed hung.

Her dying thoughts we fain would know;
    But who the tale can tell,
Save only that she met the foe,
    And where they met she fell.

And when I came, and saw her not
    In all the place around,
They pointed out a grassy spot,
    Where she lay under ground.

And soon another loved one fled,
    And sought her mother's side;
In vain I stayed her drooping head;
    She panted, gasped, and died.

Thus one in beauty's bright array,
    And one all poor and pale,
Have left alike the realms of day,
    And wandered down the vale, —

The vale of death, so dark and drear,
    Where all things are forgot;
Where lie they whom I loved so dear;
    I call — they answer not.

O, bitter cup which God has given!
  Where can relief be found?
Anon I lift my eyes to heaven,
  Anon in tears they're drowned.

Yet He who conquered death and hell
  Our Friend at last will stand;
And all whom he befriends shall dwell
  In Canaan's happy and, —

Shall joyful meet, no more to part,
  No more be forced to sigh,
That death will chill the warmest heart,
  And rend the closest tie.

Such promise throws a rainbow bright
  Death's darkest storm above,
And bids us catch the heaven-born light,
  And praise the God of love.

MY DEAR MOTHER HASSELTINE: I wrote the above lines some time ago, and intended to add a longer postscript; but find myself pressed for time at the present moment.

It is a long time since I had a line from any of your family. I hope you will not quite forget me, but believe me ever,

Yours most affectionately,

A. JUDSON.

August 17, 1829.

Journal.

November 29, 1829. Since my last, we have finished revising the New Testament and the Epitome of the Old — a work in which we have been closely engaged for above a year. We have also prepared for the press several smaller works, viz.: —

1. The Catechism of Religion. This has already passed through two editions in Burmese. It has also been translated and printed into Siamese, and translated into Taling or Peguan.

2. The View of the Christian Religion, thoroughly revised

for a fourth edition in Burmese. It has also been translated into Taling and Siamese.

3. The Liturgy of the Burman Church.
4. The Baptismal Service.
5. The Marriage Service.
6. The Funeral Service; the three last consisting chiefly of extracts from Scripture.
7. The Teacher's Guide; or, a Digest of those parts of the New Testament which relate to the Duty of Teachers of Religion, designed particularly for Native Pastors.
8. A Catechism of Astronomy.
9. A Catechism of Geography.
10. A Table of Chronological History, or a Register of principal Events from the Creation to the present Time.
11. The Memoir of Mee Shway-ee.
12. The Golden Balance; or, the Christian and Boodhist Systems contrasted. This has been translated into Taling.

The Gospel of St. Matthew was also translated into Siamese by Mrs. Judson, and is now being translated into Taling by Ko Man-poke, our assistant in that department.

Mah Men, mentioned August 13, daughter of Mai Hlah, has been baptized, and Mah Men-san, half sister of Mah Tee, resident at Pah-ouk, a village between this and Amherst. Four European soldiers also have joined the little church in the English forty-fifth regiment. Between ten and twenty attend our English worship Lord's day morning and evening, and Friday evening, some of whom are very hopeful inquirers.

As to the Hindoo branch of the church, composed of six members, we found them so ignorant of both English and Burmese as to be neither capable nor desirous of attending worship with us; and we therefore set them off as a distinct church. But the principal member, he who acted as interpreter, and in whom we had most confidence, having proved a very fickle, unsteady character, and ceased to be in the employ of the mission, and some of the others having moved away, we have no hope, at present, of doing any thing further in that department.

At Rangoon, five more have been baptized — three men and two women. Poor Mah Ing, mentioned March 5, had finally requested baptism, and been accepted by the church; but previous to the administration, she was taken ill with a fever, and died. We have heard, also, of the baptism of three more Karens at Tavoy, since brother Boardman's return.

In regard to Amherst, the prospect is quite dark. Moung Ing has had no success at all, though he has not been wanting in diligence and faithfulness. At length we advised him to remove to Tavoy. He, however, preferred Rangoon, and is now coöperating with Ko Thah-a. His wife remained behind. Her conduct has been very exceptionable since her baptism, and soon after her husband's departure, she became openly vicious. She is now suspended from communion — the first case of church discipline that has occurred amongst the native members.

December 31. Since my last, Moung Poo, husband of Mah Men-san, mentioned November 29, has been baptized at Pah-ouk, and last Lord's day three more soldiers were baptized in this place, making twenty-eight individuals this year; not quite so many as were baptized last year, besides which, ten of the number are Englishmen. However, Rangoon furnishes a reënforcement of seventeen Burmans, (four lately,) and Tavoy another reënforcement of eight, mostly Karens, making a total of fifty-three.

Our Taling translator has added the Gospel of St. Matthew to his little stock of tracts, and we have just appointed a committee to unite with him in examining and revising his work.

January 15, 1830. Brother and sister Bennett arrived last night, with their two children — all quite well.

To his Sister.

MAULMAIN, December 21, 1829.

MY DEAR SISTER: I have just received yours of May 25 last, giving an account of Elnathan's death, and also Dr. Sewall's detail of his dying exercises. Perhaps you have not seen Dr. Sewall's letter. It closes thus: "A few hours before his death, and when he was so low as to be unable to converse or to move, he suddenly raised himself up, and clasping his hands, with an expression of joy in his countenance, cried, '*Peace, peace!*' and then he sunk down, without the power of utterance. About ten minutes before he expired, it was said to him, 'If you feel the peace of God in your soul, open your eyes.' He opened his eyes, and soon after expired, and, as we believe, in the triumphs of faith." When I read this account, I went into my little room, and could only shed tears of joy, my heart full of gratitude, and my tongue of praise. I have felt most anxious about him for a long time; to hear at last that there is some good reason to conclude that he has gone to heaven is enough. So we are dying, one after another. We shall all be there, I trust, before long. I send you and mother a little tract, which I beg you will study prayerfully. Let me urge you frequently to reëxamine the foundation of your hope. O, it is a solemn thing to die — an awful thing to go into eternity, and discover that we have been deceiving ourselves! Let us depend upon it that nothing but real faith in Christ, *proved to be genuine by a holy life*, can support us at last. That faith which consists merely in a correct belief of the doctrines of grace, and prompts to no self-denial, — that faith which allows us to spend all our days in serving self, content with merely refraining from outward sins, and attending to the ordinary duties of religion, — is no faith at all. O, let me beg of you to look well into this matter! And let me beg my dear mother, in her old age, and in view of the near approach of death and eternity, to examine again and again whether her faith is of the right kind. Is it that faith which gives her more enjoyment in Jesus, from day to day, than she finds in any thing else?

May God bless you both is the fervent prayer of
Your affectionate brother,
A. JUDSON.

To the Rev. Professor Knowles.

MAULMAIN, December 21, 1829.

DEAR BROTHER KNOWLES: Yours of October 9 and May 25 I have received, together with a dozen of the Memoir, and the books pertaining to biblical criticism, &c., that you mention. The box containing the books and sundry articles for the school has been forwarded from Bengal, where brother Bennett remains, of whose arrival we have just heard.

For some of the books that have now arrived I have longed, the past year or two, beyond the power of language to express. We have just finished our final revision of the New Testament, and I am contemplating a return to Rangoon. I have felt a more than ordinary incitement to do so; but whether it is from God, and whether it is certainly my duty, I cannot fully decide. My brethren approve of the measure; but they did not propose it, and I sometimes fear that their approbation is mere acquiescence. May the Lord direct.

In regard to the Memoir, it becomes me not to expatiate. I would only say that I am extremely gratified, perhaps too much so, with the execution of the work in all its parts. Some inaccuracies will, of course, be noticed by those who are personally acquainted with the scenes and events described; but they are not important. It may, however, be well for me to mention, with a view to some future edition, that Amherst is situated at the mouth of the river, and that the population of all British Pegu, as we sometimes term the ceded provinces on this coast, does not probably exceed one hundred thousand.

Yours most affectionately,
A. JUDSON.

To Mrs. J. W., a Friend of Mrs. Ann H. Judson, London.

MAULMAIN, December 22, 1829.

MY DEAR MRS. W.: The return of the birthday of my beloved, sainted Ann, reminds me of her friends, and particularly of you, one of her dearest and best. Your letter, also, of the 10th of April last, is lying before me. The inquiries in that letter you will find all answered in the Memoir published by Mr. Knowles, a copy of which has doubtless reached you. You will notice some inaccuracies in the accounts of these provinces. For instance, Amherst is situated at the mouth of the river, and the population of all British Pegu does not probably exceed one hundred thousand. The coloring, also, of our present missionary prospects is much too high. Concerning some other inaccuracies it becomes not me to speak.

Mrs. Judson's accounts of you I have listened to, and your letters to her I have read with much pleasure. But O that you were as eminent in piety as you are distinguished by beauty, talents, and elegant accomplishments. Let me beg of you not to rest contented with the commonplace religion that is now prevalent. Let me respectfully call your attention to the example of such women as Madame Chantal, Madame Bourignon, and Lady Guion. I have really learned to lament the early death of my beloved wife, chiefly because it has deprived me of an opportunity of leading her into paths that I have but lately discovered myself; discovered, I say, not entered. God give me grace for the latter. How much, my dear madam, beloved friend of my beloved Ann, have I to say to you on the subject I have now introduced! But I must forbear. I have relinquished almost all foreign correspondence for above a year; and, really, my principal object in taking up my pen just now is to enclose a little tract,* which, being printed in Bengal only, you have probably not seen. The author, it seems, from not affixing his name, desires to remain unknown.

Your affectionate brother in Christ,

A. JUDSON.

MAULMAIN, October 24, 1828.

MY DEAR SISTERS M. AND A.: You see from the date that it is the second anniversary of the triumph of death over

---

* The Threefold Cord. See Appendix.

all my hopes of earthly bliss. I have this day moved into a small cottage, which I have built in the woods, away from the haunts of men. It proves a stormy evening, and the desolation around me accords with the desolate state of my own mind, where grief for the dear departed combines with sorrow for present sin, and my tears flow at the same time over the forsaken grave of my love and over the loathsome sepulchre of my own heart.

October 24, 1829.

And now the third anniversary returns, and finds me in the same cottage, except it has been removed nearer the mission house, to make way for a government building. I live alone. When I wish to be quite so, Mrs. W. sends me my food; at other times I am within the sound of a bell that calls me to meals.

"Blest who, far from all mankind,
This world's shadows left behind,
Hears from heaven a gentle strain,
Whispering love, and loves again."

But O, that strain I have hitherto listened in vain to hear, or rather have not listened aright, and therefore cannot hear.

Have either of you learned the art of real communion with God, and can you teach me the first principles? God is to me the Great Unknown. I believe in him, but I find him not.

March, 1830.

Since writing the above, dear brother and sister Wade have left me for Rangoon, and I have found new friends in brother and sister Bennett. Thus one scene succeeds another, and draws on to the final catastrophe. It is long since I have had a line from B., and I fancy you have about forgotten me by this time. So fare ye well, and may blessings ever rest on you both, and on your parents, and on all the branches of the family.

Your affectionate brother,

A. JUDSON.

Continuation of his Journal.

March 4, 1830. Since my last we have baptized two native women and two Europeans, Mrs. B. and a soldier from the forty-fifth regiment. Dear brother and sister Wade left us for Rangoon the 21st of last month. A day or two after their arrival, brother Wade writes, "The Christians soon heard of us, and Ko Thah-a and a number of his flock came to see us, and appeared very well. Some who live at a distance we have not yet seen." Sister Wade writes, "I have been surrounded with visitors almost all the time since we arrived, and feel it such a luxury to have all the women understand and speak good Burmese! I had intended to have given you a particular account of all the disciples, and others whom we have seen, but I feel scarcely able to hold my pen, from weakness and fatigue; and, as we hope to see you soon, I will only say that we are in general much pleased with the state of things here, and think that God is with our native brother and the little church."

CHAPTER XIII.

REVISITS RANGOON. — PASSAGE TO PROME. — SOJOURN AT PROME. — RESIDENCE AT RANGOON. — PROGRESS IN TRANSLATING THE SCRIPTURES. — RETURN TO MAULMAIN. — REVIEW OF HIS AUSTERITIES. — THE KARENS.

1830-1831.

Journal.

Maulmain, March 22, 1830. I am now contemplating a visit to Rangoon. Mrs. Boardman is here, and we expect that brother Boardman will remove hither shortly.

Our reëntering Burmah is an experiment which we are making with fear and trembling. Accounts from brother and sister Wade are rather encouraging. They both give it as their decided opinion that I ought to join them immediately; not merely with a view to Rangoon, but to the neighboring towns, and to all that are afar off, even as many as the Lord our God shall render accessible.

The number of native inquirers in this place has lately rather increased. There are about five or six that I hope are near the kingdom of heaven, and as many more among the Europeans.

April 18. Some encouraging appearances of late have made me unwilling to leave the place until brother Boardman should have actually arrived. One more European, a soldier, has received baptism, and two natives, Moung Dan, a young man, related to several of the Taling disciples, and Mah Poo, wife of McDonald. To-day, two lads, whose parents are members of the church, and who both give some evidence of grace, received a final examination, but were rejected by a few dissenting votes.

In the afternoon, we were surprised by a visit from brother Wade, who has had another severe attack of the liver complaint, and has come round for a change. Three persons have been lately baptized in Rangoon, and there are many inquirers.

April 21. A letter from brother Boardman, informing us that he will soon be here. I conclude, therefore, to accompany brother Wade on his return to Rangoon.

Rangoon, May 2. Arrived in this place, and took up my abode for a few days, in brother Wade's hired house, in the midst of the town, where we have a great deal of company, some of whom will, we hope, hear and live.

May 18. Thinking it better to reside in different places, for the more extensive diffusion of truth, we had a small building put up, for about fifty rupees, just without the enclosure of the town, in a place of considerable resort; but the neighboring priests made so much opposition that we were obliged to desist, and we conclude to remove the building to the old mission premises, though the neighborhood is deserted.

The governor of the town, formerly the "a-twen-woon Moung K.," has received me very kindly, and invited me to stay under his protection.

Brother and sister Wade have several hopeful inquirers. My principal one is a Thah-tay, a person of some little rank, whom we formerly knew at Tsa-gaing. He is an intimate friend of my old protector, the north commandant of the palace, and is here, for a few days, on some government business. He visits us almost every day, and appears, for the first time, to be pleased with the truth, though he has heard something of it for years. All the disciples that I have seen in this place appear to have grace. A spirit of inquiry is more prevalent, and more boldly indulged, than formerly, and I feel that we have reason to thank God for all the past, and take courage for the time to come.

May 23. The Thah-tay is about leaving us for Ava. At his suggestion, I send by him letters to my former acquaintance, the north commandant of the palace, and the Prince Myen-zaing.

May 25. I have not yet moved out to the new house, nor even seen it; for every day deepens the conviction in my mind that I am not in the place where God would have me be. It was to the interior, and not to Rangoon, that my mind was turned long before I left Maulmain; and while I feel that brother and sister Wade are in the right place, I feel that I am called elsewhere. Under these impressions, I am about proceeding up the river, accompanied by Moung Ing, Moung En, Moung Dway, Moung Dan, baptized April 4, and little Moung Like, mentioned April 18, not yet baptized. The boat on which we embark will take us to Prome, the great half-way place between this and Ava, and there I hope and pray that the Lord will show us what to do.

To Mr. C. Bennett.

RANGOON, May 25, 1830.

DEAR BROTHER BENNETT: I have received both yours of May 9 and 14, with the specimens of types, &c. I think that the new character is very handsome, and that it is extremely desirable the whole fount should be finished in the same style. But in regard to questions pertaining to the printing department, I do not feel competent to give any advice. I hope you will act according to your best judgment, assisted by the advice of brother Boardman and other brethren that may be with you. . . . I expect in a day or two to leave this for the interior. The place that I have immediately in view is Prome. Moung En goes with me; and I wish to say to you and Mrs. Bennett, in behalf of his wife, that, in case she should cease to be in the employ of Mrs. Bennett, and should be in need of some money for habitation or support, you will please to let her have what is proper, and put it to my account. Moung En is desirous of returning to take care of his wife; but he is also desirous of going with me; and as he is the only person of my party who has any acquaintance with that part of the country, I am desirous of taking him. And, on my promising to write to you as above, he has concluded to accompany me, with the expectation of being absent from Maulmain about three months from the present time. Moung Dway also accompanies me, and Moung Dan and Moung Like. None of these get any wages. The latter is not yet baptized, but he appears pretty well. Pastor Ing wants to go up the country; but he is just now taken ill, and I think it will prove an intimation of the will of God that he is not to go at present. I asked Pastor Thah-a to go; but he thinks it quite impossible, on account of having so many irons in the fire, — that is, hopeful inquirers, — that he must stay to bring forward and baptize. And he is as solicitous and busy as a hen pressing about her chickens. It is quite refreshing to hear him talk on the subject, and see what a nice, careful old shepherd he makes. The Lord bless his soul, and the souls of his flock!

I am glad to hear that you are getting on in the language. I beg you will always make every thing yield to that, until you find yourself at home among the natives. I trust that I need not exhort dear sister Bennett on this subject. I should truly rejoice to see you all a little while. I daily remember little Elsina, but I suppose she has forgotten her old uncle. The Lord bless you evermore!

A. JUDSON.

Letter to the Missionaries at Rangoon and Maulmain, and the Corresponding Secretary in Boston, U. S.

PROME, June 15, 1830.

DEAR BRETHREN AND SISTERS: Foreseeing that, during my residence in the interior of the country, I shall be desirous of writing many letters to my beloved brethren and sisters in Rangoon and Maulmain, in addition to my usual correspondence with the board, and desirous of spending as little time as possible in such employment, I propose to blend all my communications in one; and, as I have usually sent my journal in duplicate, I shall now send one copy to Rangoon, to be transmitted thence to Maulmain, and thence to America, and the other copy I shall send to America by the most direct conveyance.

I proceed, accordingly, to give you some account of my

adventures since leaving Rangoon on the 29th of last month. The afternoon of that day, we reached Tix-theet, twelve or fifteen miles distant, and, the tide being against us, we remained there several hours. I went on shore, entered into conversation with several, and gave away a dozen of the old tracts; and it was amusing and gratifying to see the groups of boatmen, about sunset, employed in reading and listening to the truth; and some would be constantly coming to our boat for a tract. I could have given away a hundred to advantage; for, though the village contains but very few houses, it is a place of rendezvous for a multitude of small trading boats. At midnight we reached the cluster of villages about Pau-ling, containing, I should suppose, a population as large as that of Rangoon. In the morning I went on shore at Kat-tee-yah, and spent a couple of hours in preaching to little assemblies, and distributed about thirty of the old catechism. I could have given away two hundred with perfect ease, and to the greatest advantage; for they would have spread from this central place into every part of the country. It is my way to produce a few tracts or catechisms, and after reading and talking a little, and getting the company to feel kindly, I offer one to the most attentive auditor present; and on showing some reluctance to give to every person, and on making them promise to read attentively, and consider, and pray, they get furious to obtain a tract, many hands are eagerly stretched out, and "Give me one, give me one," resounds from all sides. On the 31st we reached Gnettong, near the great river. Just became engaged with a few people, when the master of our boat concluded to proceed farther. Gave away two tracts. One of them fell into the hands of a respectable elderly man, who, having read part of it, followed us, in a small boat, to ask for something more; and I gave him a copy of Matthew. Just at dark, reached Yan-gen-tsan-yah, at the entrance of the great river, the Irrawadi, fifty or sixty miles from Rangoon.

For several days after entering the Irrawadi, I did nothing, scarcely, on account of the rainy weather and other unfavorable circumstances. At Hen-tha-dah, ninety miles from Rangoon, I walked through the place, though it was very wet, and gave away a few tracts. Moung En found some relations on shore, at whose house he and another of the disciples slept; and they did something in the evening.

The night of the 6th of June we spent at Yay-gen, a pretty large village, just below Ka-noung, on the opposite side of the river. Here the native country of the tamarind tree commences, the banks of the river become high and pleasant, nature assumes a more interesting and commanding aspect, and, at this distance, even the character of the people always seems to me to be a little more elevated. Immediately on landing I went through the place, but without any success, and was just coming off, when I descried Moung Ing, with half a dozen about him. I drew near, and very soon had a large and respectable assembly, to whom I held forth, and distributed about thirty tracts and catechisms. Several pursued us to the boat, and begged very hard; and we continued to give away to small parties who came in succession, and occupied an empty boat which lay between us and the shore, till late in the evening, when our captain pushed off into the river to get rid of the annoyance. However, it would not answer; for they came to the shore, and called out, "Teacher, are you asleep? We want a writing to get by heart." And, on being promised one if they would come and get it, they contrived to push off a long canoe which lay between us and the said empty boat, and got so near that they could reach a paper stuck in the end of a long pole. This continued till nine o'clock at night. Once, during the evening, our captain went on shore; and he said that in almost every house there was some one at a lamp, reading aloud one of our papers. I felt some desire to pray that it might not be all in vain. It cost us not less than sixty tracts and catechisms. Write to Maulmain for several hundred, and ask brother Bennett to get ready to print another edition. I have already given away one quarter of my whole stock; and I shall have to send to you for a supply before long.

We passed the large towns of Ka-noung, Myan-oung, and Kyan-gen, without being able to do any thing. But at Kyce-thai, a pretty large place, I went on shore, and got the start of the boat by about an hour, which time I improved under a shed, in the midst of an attentive crowd. I gave away several tracts. Some of the people followed me to the boat, begging the captain to stay all night. And after we had pushed off, a little boat pursued us, with a small offering of rice and beans, begging another tract. It was quite dark when we arrived at Shway-doung, one of the most populous places in the country. Above Shway-doung, we came to the flourishing villages of Pyouk-tsik and Mendai, divided by a small creek. The latter is our captain's home, and he wished to stay a day or two, before going to Prome, which is only a few miles distant. The people at Mendai seemed disposed to cavil, and some of them treated me rather uncivilly. I gave away not many tracts. Moung Ing went out to Men-yoo-ah, near which is the residence of the celebrated Toung-dwen teacher, the head of a sect of heretics in this part of the country; and in that neighborhood he found our old friend Mah Zoo, baptized formerly in Rangoon. The next morning she came to the boat, accompanied by Mah Wenyo, widow of Moung Long, the one-eyed metaphysician formerly mentioned in the annals of the Rangoon mission, who now declares herself a Christian, and one Mah Ping, a very hopeful inquirer. These women all begged me to stop one day, while they could return and consult their male relations, whether it would not be better to invite me to come to their village at once, without proceeding to Prome. So I consented, and they went off. In the afternoon of that day, I had a crowded zayat on shore. One man appeared to be impressed. But there were many cavillers, and some discouraging signs. At night the women came back, and with many tears said, that the chief men of the village were afraid to entertain a foreigner, lest, in case of war with the English, they should be involved. The next morning the wife of the governor in these parts, having heard of me, sent to the boat for a tract; several other people also came on the same errand, until we left the place, which we did about noon; and at night, the wind being contrary, we reached this place, about one hundred and seventy miles from Rangoon. I landed, and found Mr. M., the only European residing here; and he invited me to stay with him a few days, until I could get settled. The next morning I left the boat, and repaired to his house. He immediately took me to the governess of the town, whose husband has lately been summoned to Ava. In her presence I found the deputy governor and a number of people. I read and preached to them. They applauded my style of reading, &c., but seemed to be more taken with the sound than the sense. The governess, however, was evidently impressed. She begged for the tract, that she might get it copied. I presented it to her, and she received it thankfully. Thence I proceeded to various places in search of a house to be let, but was unsuccessful. The people are afraid to have any connection with a foreigner. Ever since Major Burney passed up to Ava, the country has been full of all manner of rumors and fears. The very face of a white man spreads general alarm. Mr. M. has been accused of being a spy, though nothing can be more false; and it was even proposed to put him in confinement. I find that the same suspicion is generally felt towards me. I foresee that people will be afraid to come near me, and that my usefulness here will, on that account, be greatly impeded. Add to this that the town has been so dreadfully oppressed to pay their contingent of the government debt, that poverty, distress, and terror, are the order of the day. However, the walls of Jerusalem have sometimes been built in troublous times.

Failing in my attempt to hire a house, I went in search of a vacant spot to build on. Fell in with two of the first officers of the place, and had a little friendly conversation. Found, in the heart of the town, an old, dismantled zayat, in front of a pagoda, with a little vacant ground around it. Went to the deputy governor, presented him with a tract, and warned him not to be intoxicated with worldly splendor, for life was short, &c. He read part of the tract, and said that my words were very proper. One of my people respectfully requested leave to repair the old zayat for the residence of the kalah pong-gyee, until he should proceed to Ava. The governor was disposed to be kind; but fearing, I suppose, for the reasons above mentioned, to do any thing on his own responsibility, said that he would bring forward my business in the court house, the next day, before the assembled authorities of the place.

Notwithstanding this promise, however, nothing was done the next day; and it being Lord's day, I staid at home, had usual worship with my people, and tried to study patience and Thomas à Kempis in the shattered house that Mr. M. occupies, with the rain beating in on every side.

On Monday, that is, yesterday, I went myself to the court house, and found the magistrates assembled, each sitting at his post, in Burman style, and the deputy governor in the centre. He pretended not to see or know me. I waited some time, and in an interval of business addressed some of the inferior magistrates. An inquiry rose who I was, and what I wanted. The deputy governor began slyly to assist me; and after considerable conversation, it was unanimously agreed that I should be permitted to take possession of the old zayat, and repair it for my present residence. From the court house I went to survey my new estate. I find it to be forty-five feet long, and twenty wide. The posts and the main parts of the roof and floor, being of teak, are still extant; but it is all overgrown with wild creepers, and makes, on the whole, a pretty venerable ruin. It stands on holy ground, occupying one corner of the enclosure of a pagoda; which corner I am to surround with a fence, and thus have an enclosure about four times larger than the ruin itself. This morning I am sending out people to beg materials and engage workmen to make the place habitable as soon as possible.

I am very glad to hear that brother Bennett is leading the worship of the European assembly, when brother Boardman's ill health prevents him. Go on in this good work. You have an evident call from God and man. As to the ideas you entertain of your own unfitness, they are quite correct; but if you thought you were fit, it would clearly prove that you were more unfit than you are.

How much I love you all, dear brethren and sisters, and disciples, I cannot tell. And did I not expect soon to meet you in heaven, and be happy with you forever, I should be quite unwilling to live an exile, far from you, in this dark land.

A. JUDSON.

PROME, June 26, 1830.

DEAR BRETHREN AND SISTERS: To-day I have taken possession of the old zayat allowed me by government, as stated in my last. Part of it we have enclosed in rooms, and the other part we have left open for the reception of company. Several people accosted us, as they passed. "So you have moved, have you? We shall come and see you before long." There are at present no hopeful inquirers; but some visitors from Men-dai and Men-yoo-ah approximate towards that character.

June 27, Lord's day. After usual worship with the disciples, I went to spend the day, it being Burman day of worship, at the great Shway San-dau pagoda, which is the same to Prome that Shway Da-gong is to Rangoon, and Kyaik Than-lan to Maulmain. The zayat which we occupied had many visitors, and some heard with attention.

July 2. A great change has taken place in the minds of government people towards me. Satan has industriously circulated a report that I am a spy in pay of the British. Last night the deputy governor sent to inquire my name and title. This morning I waited on him, and on the lady governess, but met with a very cold reception at both places. The deputy governor is probably reporting me to Ava, and what the consequences will be, I know not. Several visitors, who began to listen with some favorable disposition, have suddenly fallen off. To-day I have had no company at all.

July 3. Pastor Ing returned from a visit to Men-yoo-ah.

He says that the same suspicion is spreading all over the country. Even the women mentioned in my last were afraid to have any communication with him. By forcing his way, he managed to sleep two nights at the house of the Toung-dwen teacher, and had some conversation with him and his people on the subject of religion. But the teacher, though not a regular Boodhist, feels his consequence, as the head of a sect, and is perhaps as far from candid consideration as the most bigoted priest. Pastor Ing says that the country is full of villages, and there is some disposition to listen to religion, but that in the present state of the public mind, if I should make the tour of those parts, as I had some intention of doing, there is not a house where the owner would dare to ask me to sit down at the entrance of the door.

Feel extremely dejected this evening. Never so heartily willing to enter into my rest, yet willing to offer, and I do, with some peculiar feelings, offer, my poor life to the Lord Jesus Christ, to do and to suffer whatever he shall appoint, during my few remaining days. My followers feel some courage yet; for they have, I hope, a little faith, and they know, also, that whatever storm comes, it will beat upon their teacher first.

July 4, Lord's day. Another Burman day of worship, and a great day, being the first day of Lent, a season which continues three months. After usual worship, took a stroll through the place. All smiles and looks of welcome are passed away; people view me with an evil eye, and suffer their dogs to bark at me unchecked. Near Shway San-dau, the zayats were crowded with devout-faced worshippers. I found a vacant place under a shed built over a large brick idol, and, sitting down on the ground, I held converse with small parties, who came around in succession. Some company, also, morning and evening, at home. I cannot but hope that two persons have this day obtained some discovery of the way of salvation through a crucified Saviour. But it is really affecting to see a poor native when he first feels the pinch of truth. On one side he sees hell; on the other side, ridicule, reproach, confiscation of goods, imprisonment, and death.

July 7. Moung A, one of the persons last mentioned, comes every day. He seems to be quite taken with the Christian religion, but says he cannot think of embracing it until the learned and the great lead the way.

July 8. Many visitors through the day, in consequence of a festival held in the vicinity. Moung A begins to speak decidedly for Christ.

July 9. Having agreed that two or three of our number shall go out every day, in different directions, and preach the gospel, whether the people will hear or forbear, my lot fell in a public zayat, about a mile from home, near Shway San-dau, where I had an uninterrupted succession of hearers from morning till night. Pastor Ing and Moung Dway were successfully engaged in another quarter, and Moung En had some company at home. I presume that a hundred and fifty people have this day heard the gospel intelligibly, who never heard it before.

July 10. The same as yesterday, except that, being ill, I left the zayat about noon. Moung A was with me in the afternoon. His case is becoming extremely interesting. He is a bright young man, with a small family, formerly belonged to Cæsar's household, and bore a considerable title, which was forfeited through false accusation. He began last night to pray to the eternal God.

July 11, Lord's day. Several came in during worship, and behaved decently, though they would not put themselves into a devotional posture, or join in the responses. One man, in particular, professed to be excessively delighted with the new and wonderful things which he heard. Moung A present at evening worship, but he remains in a very critical state. No wine to be procured in this place, on which account we are unable to unite with the other churches, this day, in partaking of the Lord's supper.

July 12. A Burman day of worship. In the morning, received private information that the deputy governor, as I conjectured, did actually report me to Ava. If any order be given immediately, whether favorable or unfavorable, it may be expected in the course of a fortnight. Felt rather dejected, but endeavored to put my trust in God, and resolve to work while the day lasts. The zayats being all full of worshippers, I took my seat on a brick under the shed over the great idol, and, from morning till night, crowd succeeded crowd. Some became outrageously angry, and some listened with delight. "Some said, He is a good man; but others said, Nay, he deceiveth the people." About noon, heard Moung Dway's voice on the other side of the idol. Pastor Ing was busy in another quarter. At home, Moung En received a visit from Myat-pyoo, one of the two persons mentioned on the 4th. He is sixty-nine years old, a little deaf, very timid and retiring. My expectations of him are not disappointed. He says that he thinks this is the true religion, and the only one that provides a way of escape from hell, of which he is exceedingly afraid, in consequence of his many, many sins.

July 13. Took up my position at my favorite zayat. It stands at the crossing of two great roads, the one leading from the river side to Shway San-dau, and the other from the town to the place of burying, or rather burning, the dead. Several funeral processions pass every day, and many of the followers, in going or returning, stop at my zayat to rest. To-day there was a funeral of distinction, and all the officers of government, with their respective suites, attended. In consequence of this, the crowd around me was greater than ever before. But they were not hearers of the right stamp. Most of them, being adherents of government, were rude, insolent, and wicked in the extreme. A few considerate persons remained till night, particularly one man, on whose account I also remained, though dreadfully exhausted. He has been with me two days, and I have a little hope that he begins to feel the force of truth.

July 14. Another day of hard conflict. The enemy begins to be alarmed, and his forces come on fresh and fierce, while we, few in number, have to sustain the combat without any human reënforcement. The spirit is willing, but the flesh is weak. At night, felt an entire prostration of strength, so much so that I was unable to go through with the evening service as usual.

July 15. Staid at home, and had some company, who listened well. Oo Myat-pyoo appears to have taken the religion of Christ into his heart. He and Moung A bid fair to be the first fruits of the mission here.

Moung Dway is about returning to Rangoon and Maulmain. He will take Moung Like with him, so that I shall have no other assistants besides Pastor Ing and Moung En, Moung Dan being useful in the kitchen department only. I hope, however, that Moung Dway's business will be facilitated by all parties, so that he will be able to rejoin me before long.

July 16. Moung San-lone has just arrived from Rangoon, and proposes staying with me a while. I close this to forward by Moung Dway.

A. JUDSON.

PROME, August 23, 1830.

DEAR BRETHREN AND SISTERS: Tired of minuting down the events of each day, I have written nothing since my last date, July 16. My time has been spent in the same way as stated in the first part of that month. At one period the whole town seemed to be roused to listen to the news of an eternal God, the mission of his Son, the Lord Jesus Christ, and the way of salvation through his atonement. A considerable proportion of the hearers became favorably disposed. At length the enemy assumed a threatening aspect; the poor people became frightened; many sent back the tracts they had received; and there was a general falling off at the zayats. I was summoned to undergo a long examination at the court house, not, however, on the subject of religion, but concerning all my past life since I have been in Burmah. The result was forwarded to Ava. The magistrates still preserve a perfect neutrality, in consequence of the absence of the governor. At Ava I have been regarded as a suspicious character ever since I deserted them at the close of the war, and went over to the British. I know not what impressions the governor of this place will there receive, or how he will feel towards me when he is informed of the noise I have made in Prome during his absence.

On hearing of the declining health of brother Boardman, and brother Wade's intention of leaving Rangoon for Maulmain, I had some thoughts of returning immediately to Rangoon. But on further consideration and prayer, I feel that I must work while the day lasts at Prome. I have some company at the zayats every day, and crowds on days of worship. Most of the hearers are opposers; but I observe in distant corners those who listen with eagerness. There are five persons who have, I trust, obtained a little grace; but in the present dark time, they give no satisfactory evidence.

August 30. Since my last letters from Rangoon, I think continually of brother Boardman, and the great loss we are threatened with. May the Lord direct and support him and our dear sister.

September 8. The rise of the river has, for several days, prevented my going to the zayats; they being situated in a distant part of the town. I have employed myself in revising brother Wade's Investigator, and send herewith a clean copy. In return, I hope to be favored with a few hundred printed copies. It is a piece of great merit, and ought to be brought to bear on the enemy without delay. An edition of three thousand will not be too large. I have already sent down some corrections for brother Boardman's Ship of Grace. That piece is well written, but not so well adapted for present service. It is, however, acceptable among the converts; and I should be glad to see it in print, especially if the author should be taken away, that, being dead, he may yet speak. His Scripture extracts, I have no doubt, will be as judicious as can be made; and the work ought to be put into immediate circulation.

We have had one new inquirer of a most promising appearance, a secretary of the deputy governor. He had repeatedly visited me at the zayats; at length he came to the house, and finally began to attend our evening worship. But alas! as has been the case with all our good inquirers, he met, I suppose, with some violent threatening, and a few days ago, suddenly and entirely disappeared. Old Oo Myat-pyoo, mentioned July 15, sends me word, that he reads our writings every day, and thinks of us constantly, but begs we will never mention to any person that he formerly visited us. As for Moung A. he has privately left the place altogether, for what reason we cannot ascertain. You can have no idea of the fear of government which pervades all classes. I never saw so much of it before.

My present expectation is, that the way will be clear for me to leave this for Rangoon the latter part of this month.

A. JUDSON.

From Major H. Burney's Journal.

AVA, September 1, 1830.

The ministers requested my advice as to the measures which they ought to pursue with respect to Dr. Judson, who, they said, is come up to Prome, and is there distributing tracts among the inhabitants, and abusing the Burmese religion, much to the annoyance of the king. I told them that Dr. Judson is now exclusively devoted to missionary pursuits; that I possess no power or authority over him, but that I know him to be a very pious and good man, and one not likely to injure the Burmese king or government in any manner. The ministers replied that the king is much vexed with Dr. Judson for the zeal with which he is distributing among the people writings in which the Burmese faith is held forth to contempt, and that his majesty is anxious to remove him from Prome. I said that the Burmese king and government have always enjoyed a high reputation among civilized nations for the toleration which they have shown to all religious faiths; that there are thousands, in Europe and America, who would be much hurt and disappointed to hear of any change in the liberal policy hitherto observed by the King of Ava, and that I hoped the ministers would not think of molesting or injuring

Dr. Judson, as such a proceeding would offend and displease good men of all nations. They replied that it was for this reason, to avoid hurting Dr. Judson, that they had consulted me; and they proposed that I should write and advise Dr. Judson of the king's sentiments towards him. I reiterated my assurances that Dr. Judson is in no way connected with me or my government, and that I can issue no orders to him; and I begged the ministers to leave him alone, which, however, they said they could not, as his majesty had expressed himself much displeased with his conduct. I consented at last to write to Dr. Judson, but I told the ministers to recollect that I had no right to interfere with him, who would, notwithstanding any letter he might receive from me, act in whatever manner his own judgment and conscience might dictate. The ministers begged of me only to recommend Dr. Judson to return to Rangoon, and confine his missionary labors within that city.

Letter to the Missionaries at Rangoon and Maulmain, and the Corresponding Secretary in Boston, U. S.

BELOW PROME, September 18, 1830.

Afloat on my own little boat, manned by none other than my three disciples, I take leave of Prome and her towering god Shway San-dau, at whose base I have been laboring, with not the kindest intentions, for the last three months and a half. Too firmly founded art thou, old pile, to be overthrown just at present; but the children of those who now plaster thee with gold will yet pull thee down, nor leave one brick upon another.

The government writer Moung Kywet-nee, who recommenced visiting us a few days ago, has been hanging about us for two hours, lamenting our departure; and he is now sitting alone at the water's edge, looking after our boat as it floats down the stream. "Mark me as your disciple; I pray to God every day; do you also pray for me; as soon as I can get free from my present engagements, I intend to come down to Rangoon," are some of his last expressions.

The sun is just setting. We could not get our boat ready earlier in the day; and, as it is Saturday evening, we intend to proceed as far as Men-dai, in order to spend the Lord's day there. There is no period of my missionary life that I review with more satisfaction, or, rather, with less dissatisfaction, than my sojourn in Prome. This city was founded several hundred years before the Christian era. Through how many ages have the successive generations of its dark inhabitants lived and died, without the slightest knowledge of the Great Eternal, and the only way of salvation which he has provided! At length, in the year 1830, it was ordered that a missionary of the cross should sit down in the heart of the city, and from day to day, for above three months, should pour forth divine truth in language which, if not eloquent and acceptable, was at least intelligible to all ranks. What a wonderful phenomenon must this have been to celestial beings, who gaze upon the works and dispensations of God in this lower world! It was necessary to the accomplishment of the divine purpose, that, after so many centuries of darkness, there should be such an exhibition of light as has been made, and no more. Thousands have heard of God who never, nor their ancestors, heard before. Frequently, in passing through the streets, and in taking my seat in the zayats, I have felt such a solemnity and awe on my spirit as almost prevented me from opening my lips to communicate the momentous message with which I was charged. How the preacher has preached, and how the hearers have heard, the day of judgment will show. O, how many will find their everlasting chains more tight and intolerable on account of the very warnings and entreaties they have received from my lips! But what more can be done than has been done? Though warned and entreated, they have wilfully, obstinately, and blasphemously refused to listen. But, blessed be God, there are some whose faces I expect to see at the right hand of the great Judge. The young man just mentioned, the carpenter Moung Shway-hlah, a poor man, by name Moung Oo, in addition to some others mentioned in former letters, give us reason to hope that they have received the truth in good and honest hearts. Many also there are who have become so far enlightened that I am sure they never can bow the knee to Shway San-dau, without a distressing conviction that they are in the wrong way. Farewell to thee, Prome! Willingly would I have spent my last breath in thee and for thee. But thy sons ask me not to stay; and I must preach the gospel to other cities also, for therefore am I sent. Read the five hundred tracts that I have left with thee. Pray to the God and Saviour that I have told thee of. And if hereafter thou call me, though in the lowest whisper, and it reach me in the very extremities of the empire, I will joyfully listen, and come back to thee.

MEN-DAI, September 19.

Spent the day in the zayat which I formerly occupied. The crowds were very noisy, but some listened with attention. Distributed nearly a hundred tracts. Mai Goo came from her village with two other women, one of whom appears to have grace. But Mah Wen-yo and Mah Ping were not seasonably apprised of our arrival. Just at night, dropped down to a small village below Men-dai, that we might have a little evening worship by ourselves.

NEAR RANGOON, September 24.

We have distributed four hundred tracts between this and Men-dai, having touched at many of the principal places, and spent an hour or two, or a night, as we could make it convenient. We should have stopped oftener and staid longer had not our stock of tracts become exhausted. My people, also, began to be impatient at the restless nights we were obliged to spend, on account of the insufferable annoyance of mosquitoes on the banks of the river in the lower country at this season of the year.

September 25. Came in sight of my old acquaintance, Shway Da-gong; landed once more in Rangoon; found letters from Maulmain, saying that brother Boardman is considerably better, for which I desire to thank God; repaired to the house lately occupied by brother Wade. Since his departure, I find that some efforts have been made to check the progress of religious inquiry. At one time men were stationed at a little distance, on each side of the house, to threaten those who visited the place, and take away the tracts they had received. Reports were circulated that government was about to make a public example of heretics; the crowds that used to come for tracts all disappeared, and Pastor Thah-a, who continued to occupy the house, became intimidated, and retreated to his own obscure dwelling. Things are, therefore, at a very low ebb; but we trust in God that the tide will flow again in its own appointed time.

September 26, Lord's day. Very few present at worship. All the women actually afraid to come, lest they should be apprehended by government.

October 3, Lord's day. Have seen most of the disciples and several inquirers during the past week. The case of Ko San deserves particular notice. He is a respectable elderly man, residing in a village north of Ava. Twelve years ago a copy of the first edition of the first tract found its way thither, and he treasured it up as the truth. At subsequent times he occasionally met with disciples, particularly during the war, when some of them fled beyond Ava, with the rest of the population. The more he heard of the Christian religion, the better he liked it. He has now concluded to remove to Rangoon. His wife is of the same mind with himself; and when they arrive, will both, he says, request baptism.

Moung Kywet-nee, one of Pastor Thah-a's disciples, baptized up the country, and now living at Kam-bai, (not Kam-bet, as written formerly,) in this vicinity, a disciple that I have never seen before, pleases me much. He appears to be a steady, conscientious Christian. Moung Bike, an inquirer from Anan-ben, a village beyond Kam-bai, where there are two disciples, has made me a visit for the first time, and spent a night. He has twice requested baptism; but Pastor Thah-a says that he is deficient in humility and meekness, so that the poor man is obliged to wait. In my view he appears pretty well. Moung Thah-doke, another disciple from a village beyond Anan-ben, appears well. But there are two of Thah-a's flock that are very delinquent, and he has but little hope of reclaiming them.

To-day my faithful Moung En leaves me for Maulmain, where his wife is. Ko Ing and Moung Dan still remain with me, and I have taken Moung Shway-too, a bright young man, baptized by Thah-a, into the family, instead of Moung En.

October 8. Have just received intelligence that about the 1st of September the king issued an order that I should be removed from Prome, "being exceedingly annoyed that I was there, in the interior of the country, distributing papers, and abusing the Burmese religion." The woon-gyees, being unwilling to proceed to extremities, made application to Major Burney, the British resident at Ava, who assured them that he had no control over me; that I was in no way connected with the British government, but employed exclusively in the duties of my profession; and he begged them not to proceed to adopt a measure which would be condemned as intolerant by good men of all countries. They said, however, that his majesty's order was peremptory, and that it was necessary for me to confine my labors within the limits of Rangoon. Major Burney then consented to write me on the subject.

A. JUDSON.

A Visit to Mr. Judson in 1830.*

Being unexpectedly in Rangoon, in the autumn of 1830, and hearing that the justly celebrated American missionary, good Mr. Judson, was still there, with indefatigable zeal prosecuting his "labor of love" in the conversion of the Burmese, I was extremely anxious to see him; and, having informed ourselves that a visit from English travellers would not be deemed a disagreeable intrusion, the captain, his wife, and myself, immediately proceeded to Mr. Judson's house.

It was a Burman habitation, to which we had to ascend by a ladder; and we entered a large, low room through a space like a trap door. The beams of the roof were uncovered, and the window frames were open, after the fashion of Burman

---

* By Miss Emma Roberts, author of Scenes and Characteristics of Hindoostan.

houses. The furniture consisted of a table in the centre of the room, a few stools, and a desk, with writings and books neatly arranged on one side. We were soon seated, and were most anxious to hear all that the good man had to say, who, in a resigned tone, spoke of his departed wife in a manner which plainly showed he had set his affections "where alone true joy can be found." He dwelt with much pleasure on the translation of the Bible into the Burmese language. He had completed the New Testament, and was then as far as the Psalms in the Old Testament, which having finished, he said he trusted it would be the will of his heavenly Father to call him to his everlasting home.

Of the conversions going on amongst the Burmans he spoke with certainty, not doubting that when the flame of Christianity did burst forth, it would surprise even him by its extent and brilliancy. As we were thus conversing, the bats, which frequent the houses at Rangoon, began to take their evening round, and whirled closer and closer, till they came in almost disagreeable contact with our heads; and the flap of the heavy wings so near us interrupting the conversation, we at length reluctantly took our leave and departed. And this, thought I, as I descended the dark ladder, is the solitary abode of Judson, whom after ages shall designate, most justly, the great and the good. It is the abode of one of whom the world is not worthy; of one who has been imprisoned, chained, and starved, and yet who dares still to prosecute his work in the midst of the people who have thus treated him. America may indeed be proud of having given birth to so excellent and admirable a man, who, amidst the trials, sufferings, and bereavements with which it has pleased Heaven to afflict him, still stands with his lamp brightly burning, waiting his Lord's coming.

If there be any man of whom we may without presumption feel assured that we will hear the joyful words, "Well done, thou good and faithful servant," it is certainly the picus Judson, the great and persevering founder of Christianity in a land of dark idolatry and superstition.

To Mr. Bennett.

RANGOON, September 20, 1830.

DEAR BROTHER BENNETT: I write a line to beg most earnestly that you will not, after receiving this, suffer a single vessel to leave the port of Maulmain without having on board five hundred of the View, and two hundred and fifty of the Balance, also a few hundred of the Catechism of Religion. A few copies of the Three Sciences will be acceptable, but there is no demand at all for the Prayers. Don't hesitate about paying for the freight. Better make some arrangement with some mercantile person for the regular transportation of such packages and boxes of tracts, &c., as we may from time to time require. I began this letter in great haste, expecting every moment a person to call for it. But I will continue to write until he comes. Yours of August 28 is before me. I rejoice in all your work. May you be strengthened to go on. I am particularly glad to hear of the average of hours per day. Adhere to such a rule, and you will ultimately pass the highest Alps. I wrote to Maulmain last night, but did not mention the want of tracts, thinking on my first arrival here there was some stock on hand. But on rummaging the boxes to-day, I find only about fifty of the new tracts, and a couple of bundles of the old, and about twenty of the Balance; so that we shall be completely exhausted, however fast you run after receiving this. But I must stop. Love to dear sister Bennett and Elsina. Yours ever,

A. JUDSON.

Letter to Mrs. Bennett, with an Extract from Thomas a Kempis, Book. IV. Chapter VIII., translated from the Latin Edition.

RANGOON, October 11, 1830.

MY DEAR SISTER: I send you this extract, not because I think you have not given yourself to God, (that is a matter between him and your own soul,) but to stir up your pure mind by way of remembrance. May the reading of it be more blessed to your soul than the translating and transcribing of it have been to mine. Remember, I pray you, that word of

Brainerd, "Do not think it enough to live at the rate of common Christians." True, they will call you uncharitable and censorious; but what is the opinion of poor worms of the dust, that it should deter us from our duty? Remember that other word of the same holy man, "Time is but a moment, life a vapor, and all its enjoyments but empty bubbles and fleeting blasts of wind." The first duty of every lover of Christ is to enter constantly within the veil, offering himself a sacrifice to God, to obtain some sensible communion with the great Invisible; and his second, to come forth with a shining face, as Moses, and be ready to speak and do whatever God, by his word, providence, and indwelling Spirit, shall appoint. If we reverse this order, and wear out our lives in the most indefatigable services, without an habitual sense of holy unction and divine communion, God may, indeed, in mercy to souls, bless our labors in some degree, but our own souls, though just saved, will suffer great, irreparable loss, through all eternity.

I sometimes try to pray for little Elsina, that the first dawn of her intellect may be accompanied with the dawn of heavenly light. Perhaps, if you pray a few words with her alone every day, and endeavor to direct the first thoughts of her young and tender mind to the crucified Saviour, she will grow up a better saint than her own mother.

With love to brother Bennett, I remain

Your affectionate brother,

A. JUDSON.

To the Missionaries at Maulmain, particularly Mr. Bennett.

RANGOON, November 13, 1830.

DEAR BRETHREN: I wrote you lately by Ko Ing, since which I have received yours by Moung En. We continue to distribute about forty tracts a day, and should gladly double the number if we could depend on a supply from Maulmain. By tracts I mean not the single sheets or handbills,* containing merely a scrap of Scripture, which, being wholly inade-

---

* Two pages tracts of Scripture Extracts.

quate to give any full idea of the Christian religion, it is impossible to mock any poor soul with, when he holds out his hand for such spiritual food as his case requires. They do well enough among the converts, and if you find they are useful in your parts, I shall be happy to send you back those I have on hand, for there is no demand for that article here in the present state of the mission. . . . But by tracts I mean the View, the Catechism, the Balance, and the Investigator. I earnestly beg the brethren to wake up to the importance of sending a regular supply of all these articles. How long we shall be allowed a footing in Rangoon is very uncertain. While a missionary is here, a constant stream ought to be poured into the place. Rangoon is the key of the country. From this place tracts go into every quarter. I could write sheets on the subject, but I trust that it is unnecessary. Six weeks have elapsed since I wrote for the Balance, and for a few only, as I did not wish to distress any one, and though it was then out of print, it is not yet put to press. And why? Because the Epitome has been in the way. I am glad the Epitome is printed; but after all, we shall not give away one a week of that article. The state of things does not immediately require it. But of the Balance I shall give away one hundred a week. There are daily calls for it. During the last six weeks I should have given away one thousand of the Balance, and they would now be circulating all over the country. I found twenty in the house on my arrival, and have been dealing them out like drops of heart's blood. There are few left. I did expect some by Moung En; but alas! out popped two bundles of *scrippets*.* The *book* of Scripture Extracts, however, I am thankful for. I do not write this with any disposition to find fault. I am sure you have done all for the best; and I feel for brother Bennett in his labors at the press. I only blame myself that I have not been more explicit, and written more urgently on the subject.

Yours ever,   A. JUDSON.

---

* The two page tracts mentioned above.

To the Missionaries at Maulmain.

Rangoon, November 16, 1830.

Dear Brethren: We were obliged to give away ninety-five tracts and Scriptures yesterday, besides refusing several. This morning I took twenty in my hand, as usual, and though I avoided streets, and kept to the jungle, and walked as fast as possible, yet, notwithstanding every precaution, they fleeced me of fifteen by sunrise. We shall not be able to stand it longer than fifteen or twenty days at this rate. They come from all parts of the country, and the thing is spreading and increasing every day. I hope you will not fail me in the hour of need. We want thousands of the Catechism, the View, the Balance, and the Investigator. Next to these we shall want a thousand or two of the Gospel of Luke, that is, after the Scripture Extracts are done, which will be shortly, if you will only send them along. I am more and more convinced that Burmah is to be evangelized by tracts and portions of Scripture. They are a reading people beyond any other in India. The press is the grand engine for Burmah. Every pull of brother Bennett at the press sends another ray of light through the darkness of the empire. I write in a hurry, for I am in the middle of the sixty-fifth Psalm; and though I keep snug in the garret, I have had within an hour one man from Mad-dee-yah, who has come for tracts, having heard the gospel from one of the disciples at Prome, a writer from Kyouk-mau, brought hither by your inquirer Moung Louk, a disciple from An-au-len, and Moung Hming, from Pan-ta-nau, who requests baptism, and brings also a message and request for tracts from Nah-kau-dau, who says he heard about Jesus Christ from a foreigner* at Prome. And, as I am alive, here comes at this moment a priest and his followers. So farewell.

Yours,

A. Judson.

---

* "Judson himself," says Mr. Bennett, in a note.

To the Corresponding Secretary.

RANGOON, November 21, 1830.

DEAR SIR: Since my return to this place, I have chiefly confined myself to the garret of the house we occupy, in order to get a little time to go on with the translation of the Psalms, which was begun three years ago, but has been hitherto postponed for more important missionary work, which was ever pressing upon us. Some of the disciples occupy the front part of the house below, and receive company and distribute tracts and portions of Scripture. The more hopeful visitors are shown the way up stairs. But notwithstanding this arrangement, I am interrupted above half my time. People find their way to me from all parts of the country, and some, I trust, return with that light in their heads, and that love in their hearts, and that truth in their hands, which will operate as a little leaven, until the whole mass is leavened.

Two have been lately added to the church in Rangoon — one of them the husband of a female disciple, whom he formerly persecuted for her religion, but whose example he has now followed; the other an old woman of seventy-four, who has met with violent opposition from a host of children and grandchildren, who for a time confined her, lest she should be baptized; and at last she was baptized by stealth. On her return from the water, in wet clothes, she suddenly met three of her sons, grown men, who, it seems, were suspecting some mischief. At first she thought of avoiding them; but feeling very happy that she was now a full disciple, life and death, praise and abuse, became, at the moment, indifferent to her; she met them courageously, and to their rude questions, "What have you been about, mother?" she mildly and promptly replied, "I have been baptized into the religion of the Lord Jesus Christ, to the entire renunciation of the religion of our ancestors." The young men appeared to be astonished, and, contrary to her fears, refrained from all abusive treatment, and suffered her to proceed home quietly, as if nothing had happened. There are a few others, who seem to be near the kingdom of heaven; but weakness of faith and the fear of men keep them back.

Ko Ing left me, a few days ago, on an excursion to Tavoy and Mergui. I hope that he will accompany brother Boardman in his proposed return to the former place, and assist him in baptizing several Karens, who are waiting there to profess the Christian religion. Moung En has returned from Maulmain, and taken Ko Ing's place; and of all the disciples I have yet employed, he seems to be the best qualified to receive promiscuous company. He was, when I first knew him, extremely irritable. He was frequently betrayed into a passion, at the Goung-zay-gyoon zayat. But now he bears with imperturbable composure, and a smiling countenance, the floods of contradiction and abuse which sometimes pour upon him. Nor is he ever so much in his element, as when surrounded by a large company, some contradicting and some approving. Moung Mo also, one of Ko Thah-a's converts, has been on a visit to the villages on the other side of the river. He was absent ten days, and distributed three hundred tracts. From his account, the fields in that quarter also are quite ready for the harvest.

To Mrs. Bennett.

RANGOON, December 10, 1830.

DEAR SISTER BENNETT: It is with heartfelt pleasure that I find myself able, at last, to beg your acceptance of a copy of the Life of Lady Guion. And it is my most fervent prayer that this and all other means of grace may be abundantly blessed to you and dear brother Bennett. I love you both most sincerely, and hope shortly to be happy with you in the world of light, where we shall understand many mysteries, which now seem dark to our dark minds. However, we have a glimpse of that light which shineth more and more to the perfect day. . . . I thank you for your kind letter, and wish I had time and grace to make a more worthy return. I hope you will pray for me, for you have not such inveterate habits to struggle with as I have contracted through a long course of religious sinning. O, my past years in Rangoon are spectres to haunt my soul; and they seem to laugh at me as they shake the chains they have riveted on me. I can now do little more than beg my younger brethren and sisters not to live as I have done, until the Ethiopian becomes so black that his skin cannot be changed. And yet I have sometimes sweet peace in Jesus, which the world can neither give nor take away. O, the freeness, the richness of divine grace, through the blood of the cross!

Your affectionate, unworthy brother,

A. JUDSON.

To the Corresponding Secretary.

RANGOON, December 20, 1830.

REV. AND DEAR SIR: I am happy to inform the board that my health, which was rather impaired some time ago, is now quite good; so that I should not feel justified in accepting their invitation to return home.

At the same time, the kind feeling which dictated the invitation, and the affection, though undeserved, which breathes in every line, have made an indelible impression on my heart. I must confess that, in meditating on the subject, I have felt an almost unconquerable desire to become personally acquainted with my beloved patrons and correspondents, the members of the board, as well as to rove once more over the hills and valleys of my own native land, to recognize the still surviving companions of my youth, and to witness the wide-spread and daily-increasing glories of Emanuel's kingdom, in that land of liberty, blessed of heaven with temporal and spiritual blessings above all others.

However, I anticipate a happier meeting, brighter plains, friends the same, but more lovely and beloved; and I expect soon to witness, yea, enjoy, that glory in comparison of which all on earth is but a shadow. With that anticipation I content myself, assured that we shall not then regret any instance of self-denial or suffering endured for the Lord of life and glory.

Your affectionate friend and faithful servant,

A. JUDSON.

To Mr. Bennett.

Rangoon, December 24, 1830.

Dear Brother Bennett: Your remittances of the *needful*, under dates the 14th and 19th instant, have relieved in some measure my distresses, which, however, would not have risen to such a degree, had not the people here told me that the Hebe and La Belle were the only small vessels running between the ports; and I then concluded that you were all gone to sleep. I beg ten thousand pardons for thinking so; and if you could only know how grateful I feel for the present kind supplies, and for the kinder promise of better things in future, namely, the Balance, the Investigator, and the View, you would be convinced that I am a very good creature. I am happy to hear that you get on so well in reading; I see that you begin to spout Burman too. . . . I am glad to hear that you are enlarging the office, and writing for a colleague. Keep moving; never doubt we shall bring up in the right place.

I send you enclosed all the lampblack I can procure in Rangoon. You see it purports to be of the "very best" kind. You say you wrote for ink last September! When you want any thing from Bengal, you must learn to write six months before you need the article, and send one letter per month regularly until you receive it. I suppose you did not even send a duplicate. However, you will learn in time how we do things in the East. The Memoir of Payson that you speak of I have. It is a most precious work.

With love to Mrs. Bennett,

Yours affectionately,

A. Judson.

Rangoon, January 6, 1831.

Dear Brother Bennett: I have just received yours of the 25th December, and the two parcels of tracts by the Hebe. The contents of these parcels I value. . . . I do not object to a *box* of books occasionally, but I should prefer parcels, as a general thing, for the reason mentioned formerly;

and for the same reason I should much prefer having them sent by native boats; but I know not how you can manage that, unless when native Christians give information. If once, however, some of the native boat owners, who continually pass between the two places, should know that for every parcel they conveyed from your house to my house they would receive half a rupee, I presume you would frequently have voluntary application; and that arrangement would save us both some trouble, besides avoiding the inspection and hue and cry at the custom house. You can't send too many of the Scripture Extracts, (together or in two parts,) the Septenary, the Investigator, the Balance, the View, and the Catechism. Send by every opportunity. Don't be afraid that I shall give away the large books without care, and as fast as you send them. I want a stock on hand of the larger articles; and, indeed, I want to be laying in a stock of all the articles against the great March festival, when, if things go on prosperously, I shall want ten thousand on hand at the very least.

I have had a good letter from sister Boardman, giving an account of the wonders of divine grace at Tavoy; but I suppose you have heard all.

With love to your dear wife,
Yours affectionately,
A. JUDSON.

To the Missionaries at Maulmain.

RANGOON, January 25, 1831.

DEAR BRETHREN: I have attentively read your letter by A, and formed some acquaintance with the man, and endeavored to lay the subject before God in prayer; and I do not find myself at liberty to attempt to remove the cross which the Lord Jesus has kindly laid upon your backs. I beg you will be more grateful for the favor than you appear to be. Particularly I would exhort brother Bennett to remember, among other things, the example of the Abbé de Paris, who, after having tried various modes of self-denial, in order to subdue his spirit, and gain the victory over the world, at length selected a crazy man to be the inmate of his miserable hovel. Now, though I am doubtful about self-inflicted austerities, I am quite sure that evangelical self-denial eminently consists in bearing patiently and gratefully all the inconveniences and pain which God in his providence brings upon us, without making the least attempt to remove them, unless destructive of life or health, or, in one word, capacity for usefulness.

RANGOON, February 1, 1831.

DEAR BRETHREN: The great festival falls this year on the 25th. Alas! alas! what shall I do? I beg and entreat that you will not give any tracts in the vicinity of Maulmain until after the 1st of March; but let every thing that can possibly be got ready be sent with all possible expedition to this place. I do beg you will all make one effort, and, if possible, send me fifteen or twenty thousand tracts between this and the 25th or 28th. The festival will last several days. I have lost all hope of hoarding up my present stock. We have been obliged to give away above one thousand within the last three days. It is not here as at Maulmain, where a great many are destroyed. Here, I am persuaded, after a great deal of inquiry, not one in a hundred is destroyed. The people are eager to get tracts. We don't give to every one we meet, as you do, but to those only who ask earnestly. Don't think the tracts you print, and stitch, and trim, with a great deal of labor, and send here, are lost. I trust that the most of them will come to light at the day of judgment.

I send this by Sanlone, who goes around in Moung Gway's boat. He, and perhaps the same boat, will return soon; I hope in time for the festival. Send every thing you possibly can, and by every other boat or vessel after receiving this.

In great haste, yours,
A. JUDSON.

To Mr. Bennett.

RANGOON, February 7, 1831.

DEAR BROTHER BENNETT: I wrote lately by Moung Sanlone, saying that the great festival falls on the 25th instant, and begging that, until that time, no tracts might be circulated in your quarter, but that every thing, that could be got ready should be sent hither. If you listen to that petition, well; if not, to repeat it, with all the urgency of a dying man, would be of no use. We were giving away at the rate of three or four hundred per day, until I became alarmed, and reduced the allowance to two hundred. We are just, therefore, keeping our heads above water. But we have no hopes of being ready for the festival unless you pour in fifteen or twenty thousand more, between this time and that. We have had none since the arrival of Moung En. He and A brought good supplies; but alas! no Views, and but few Balances and Investigators. O, when will the time come that I shall have as much as I want, and *of the right kind!* I have labored to very great disadvantage ever since I came down from Prome, for want of the *right kind* of supply. If, instead of printing such a variety, the brethren had aimed only at furnishing a sufficient supply of the necessaries of life, how much better it would have been! I should not then have been left for months without the Balance, or any equivalent, nor be left, as I now am, month after month, without the View — the staple commodity. How distressing it is, when the poor people come crying for the elements of the Christian religion, to be obliged to give them one of the small numbers of the Scripture Extracts, which singly can give them no idea! By the way, I beg you will send no more of No. 8: it is just good for nothing, in the present state of things. I do not write thus by way of finding fault with my brethren; I am quite sure that you have meant all for the best. I have made too many mistakes, and criminal ones too, all my life long, to allow me to find fault with others. I only hope that things will now be kept in such a train as to prevent my being reduced again to the straits I have been in for several months. When you have made arrangements to insure a supply of the *four standard articles,* so that we can always have as many of such kind, and of all the kinds, as the state of the market requires, I would recommend to the brethren to issue a small edition of three thousand of the First Epistle of John. I once thought of Luke; but if you take hold of that, we shall be left to starve again, for want of the necessaries of life. You say that there are fourteen hundred of the Scripture Extracts remaining; and these, stitched together or in two parts, will answer to give in cases where something more than the four standards is required. As to the Septenary, I would suggest that it is to be kept for special cases, and not distributed promiscuously, for you will not want to print another edition immediately. It was not intended for general circulation, but to be kept on hand for the converts and hopeful inquirers. As to your plan of printing the Catechism and View *together* it is most excellent. You cannot furnish too many of that article. As to the Balance, it is now all the rage, particularly with *the cut.* I suppose you cannot clap the cut on the covers of those that have it not. It doubles the value. I presume that from fifty to one hundred per day inquire particularly for the Balance, and we are obliged to turn them off with something very inadequate to their exigency. Is not this most awful? Only contrast the countenance of one who has No. 8 forced upon him instead of the Balance, and goes away feeling very "gritty," with the countenance of another, who seizes upon the desired article, gloats upon the interesting *Bennett cut,* and goes away almost screaming and jumping for joy.

I see, on reperusing your letter, that you speak of a second edition of the Septenary. I have no objection, provided it does not deprive us again of the necessaries of life. I hope, however, you will not abandon the study of the language. The proverb of the "cat and her skin" I do not like. I have a much better one from the first authority. "My son," said the head jailer of the death prison at Ava to an under jailer, who was complaining that they could get no more out of a poor fellow whom they had been tormenting for several days, his wife and house being completely stripped — "my son," said the venerable old man, "be sure you have never wrung a rag so dry but that another twist will bring another drop." . . . Love to Mrs. Bennett and family.

        Yours, A. JUDSON.

To the Missionaries in Maulmain.

        RANGOON, March 3, 1831.

DEAR BRETHREN AND SISTERS: I am grieved that sister Wade, after running down to Amherst, and deriving a little benefit during a few days' stay, thinks she must return, and probably has by this time returned, because sister Bennett is quite worn out, "having every thing to do." Now, it appears to me that the better way to have remedied that evil would have been for sister Bennett to run away from all her cares, and take the air at Amherst too.

Mrs. Jones, I hear, is also ill, and Mrs. Kincaid has not, I believe, much health to spare. Now, as you have two months of very trying weather to sustain, I earnestly beg that you will all take into serious consideration the propriety of repairing Landale's house forthwith, or some other, and placing one or two of the ladies, by turns, to keep the post, until the rainy season sets in. Mrs. Wade, I humbly conceive, ought to be immediately apprehended and sent back as a deserter. And certainly no one ought to hesitate a moment at leaving mission or domestic cares for the preservation of health. When our best beloved are once laid in the cold grave, no cries, or tears, or remorse, will bring them back. Many faithful servants and handmaids of the Lord might have been spared many years, had they only relaxed before they made their last effort.

If you have a house at Amherst during the hot season, some of the brethren, too, may be benefited by an excursion thither. Brother Bennett will certainly need a week's relaxation, there or somewhere else. . . . However, I only submit these hasty thoughts for your consideration. You are on the spot, and know better than I what is necessary and proper. May God preserve your precious lives many years; for, though the prospect of death may not be grievous, but joyous, "the harvest is plenteous, and the laborers are few."

Yours most affectionately,
A. JUDSON.

To Mr. Bennett.

RANGOON, March 3, 1831.

DEAR BROTHER BENNETT: I am in great distress. The View has been out several days. It failed us in the midst of the festival. Why some were not ready to be sent by the Hebe, when the arrival would have been so opportune, I cannot conceive. We had been on a short allowance of one hundred per day for several days, and were nearly exhausted, when, on the morning of the 22d, the splendid consignment of Moung San-lone arrived. On that day, Tuesday, we gave away three hundred; on Wednesday, eight hundred; on Thursday, nine hundred; on Friday, the full moon, seven hundred; on Saturday, eleven hundred; on Sunday, eight hundred; on Monday, five hundred. On Tuesday, the immense crowd of boats began to move off. Moung San-lone, second, had been petitioning for two thousand, with which to proceed a few miles up the river, and supply the departing boats. I could not listen to him, when, at the critical moment, the Hebe hove in sight, with your second consignment, and I sent off a couple of disciples with twelve hundred, but no View. On the same day we gave away, at the house, six hundred; on Wednesday, seven hundred; on Thursday, to-day, five hundred. I have been trying for two days to reduce the allowance, but in vain. And even if I could reduce it to two hundred, which is the utmost I hope for, how many days should I hold out? I have no Views, only six hundred of the Balance, ditto Catechism, about one hundred and fifty of the Investigator, a few Septenaries and Scripture Extracts. That is all; for we do not consider the Epitome a suitable thing to give away promiscuously to people who have never heard a word of the gospel. Now you see, do you not, that I am in distress? In a very few days, unless we have a fresh supply, we shall have to shut up the house, and send away the hungry souls without giving the crumb of a Catechism. It is true that we have had a glorious festival; but when a famishing man sees pale hunger advancing with rapid strides, it affords him no relief to reflect that he feasted sumptuously a week ago. We have had a glorious festival, for which I feel under infinite obligation to you; and as you have begun to run well, I hope nothing will hinder you from prosecuting the race. I have the greatest hope that in a very few days a supply will arrive. As to the Investigator, I begin to hesitate about giving it promiscuously. It is an excellent work, but appears to be rather too straightforward for the present state of Burmah. It gives more offence than the Balance. The latter work, being cast in a hypothetical shape, is less offensive. I think of proposing a large edition of the Balance, say twenty thousand. . . .

Yours affectionately,
A. Judson.

Rangoon, March 16, 1831.

Dear Brother Bennett: Your last box of "pills" has quite relieved my distress, and I perceive as yet no symptom of a return, the thermometer being down to one hundred, in consequence of a persevering application of refrigerants. Pretty work for a missionary! Next box of pills you send, please enclose one compounded of five hundred Catechisms.

. . . . . .

March 30.

Your splendid consignment came to hand this morning. I feel as rich as Crœsus. But I am sorry to say (perhaps you will be glad) that, for some reason or other, the tide seems to be turning. There are now comparatively few applications for tracts, and I shall not need any other supplies just *at present*. Never, however, hesitate to send a few, at least, when a good opportunity offers, especially by native boats, if it is only to encourage the trade. Little Sanlone went off with five hundred a few days ago, to be present at the annual festival of Shway Man-dan, in old Pegu, which took place the 21st instant. If the present consignment had then arrived, he would have taken two thousand or more. I expect him back every day. Pastor Thah-a and Shway-too start to-morrow morning with a few hundred for the villages of Kam-bai, &c.

Poor little Elsina seems to be ill all the time. I expect she will be quite a shadow when I come to see her again, if that ever takes place. However, if your children live at all, it is a favor that not every one enjoys in this climate.

Yours affectionately,
A. JUDSON.

RANGOON, April 17, 1831.

DEAR BROTHER BENNETT: . . . The demand for tracts at the house is much less than formerly; but during my morning walks I give away, every day, between forty and fifty, on earnest solicitation. The priests are good customers.

Since the call for tracts is not so great as formerly, I do hope that you will turn your attention to the language. Do let me urge you to do a little task every day. The greatest mountain will in time disappear, if a cart load is taken away every morning. When you get the language, you will be interested and happy in your work, but not without.

As to the other matter, the land of Beulah lies beyond the valley of the shadow of death. Many Christians spend all their days in a continual bustle, doing good. They are too busy to find either the valley or Beulah. "Virtues they have, but are full of the life and attractions of nature, and unacquainted with the paths of mortification and death." Let us die as soon as possible, and by whatever process God shall appoint. And when we are dead to the world, and nature, and self, we shall begin to live to God.

Yours affectionately,
A. JUDSON.

To the Corresponding Secretary.

RANGOON, February 5, 1831.

REV. AND DEAR SIR: Since my return from Prome, I have been chiefly employed in finishing the Psalms, the Song of Solomon, and the book of Daniel, all of which were begun some time ago. These, with an Epitome of History and Prophecy, are all the parts of the Old Testament that are yet translated. I propose next to enter upon Isaiah.

During the past year there have been baptized twelve at Maulmain, seven at Rangoon, and twenty-eight at Tavoy; in all forty-seven, five of whom are Europeans, and the rest natives. Three have been finally excluded, and a few are under censure.

Since the beginning of the year, one young man, by name Moung Shway-gnong, has been baptized here, three or four Europeans at Maulmain, and four Karens at Tavoy.

The most prominent feature in the mission at present is the surprising spirit of inquiry that is spreading every where, through the whole length and breadth of the land. I sometimes feel alarmed, like a person who sees a mighty engine beginning to move, over which he knows he has no control. Our house is frequently crowded with company; but I am obliged to leave them to Moung En, one of the best of assistants, in order to get time for the translation. Is this right? Happy is the missionary who goes to a country where the Bible is translated to his hand.

When we can obtain a sufficient supply of tracts from Maulmain, which is not half the time, we give away between two and three hundred per day, *giving to none but those who ask.* The government still preserve neutrality. We have been once accused before the viceroy, by a deputation from two subordinate departments of government; but his excellency rejected the accusation with indignation. He is not, however, favorably disposed to the Christian religion, but merely wishes to preserve peace, being a quiet, good-natured man. And it is scarcely known to government that there are any native converts, all our acts of worship being conducted in private.

To the Corresponding Secretary.

RANGOON, February 28, 1831.

REV. AND DEAR SIR: One of the brightest luminaries of Burmah is extinguished; dear brother Boardman has gone to his eternal rest. I have heard no particulars, except that he died on returning from his last expedition to the Karen villages, within one day's march of Tavoy. He fell gloriously at the head of his troops, in the arms of victory; thirty-eight wild Karens having been brought into the camp of King Jesus since the beginning of the year, besides the thirty-two that were brought in during the two preceding years. Disabled by mortal wounds, he was obliged, through the whole of his last expedition, to be carried on a litter; but his presence was a host, and the Holy Spirit accompanied his dying whispers with almighty influence. Such a death, next to that of martyrdom, must be glorious in the eyes of Heaven. Well may we rest assured that a triumphal crown awaits him on the great day, and "Well done, good and faithful Boardman, enter thou into the joy of thy Lord." I have great confidence in sister Boardman, that she will not desert her husband's post, but carry on the work which he has gloriously begun.

In connection with this subject, I would suggest a doubt on the advisableness of sending out missionaries of a consumptive habit. Three of my companions, now dead, were subject to some pulmonary affection before they left America. Colman, it is true, died prematurely of another disorder; but I have always thought that, if he had escaped the Arracan fever, he would not have survived many years. Price also died of consumption, though he had no symptoms of that disorder on first arriving. I have understood, however, that it is hereditary in his family. This mission, therefore, has been peculiarly unfortunate. The four male missionaries who have died were probably *all of them* consumptive before they left home. Such persons, instead of laboring in their own language, where they might be directly useful, spend their little span in toiling to acquire a foreign language, and then sink into the grave. Another consequence is, that Burmah, which is the healthiest country of the East, next to Ceylon, is liable to be considered peculiarly unhealthy, and some are perhaps deterred by this consideration from offering themselves to the service. I would further remark, however, that a slender, feeble habit of body is perhaps no objection. A person of such a habit is, indeed, more likely to survive in an eastern climate than one who is very stout and fat. Freedom from hereditary taint, particularly as it regards pulmonary affection, is the principal desideratum. The idea that a warm climate is favorable to persons of consumptive habit, is correct in some cases, but not where a rainy season is to be encountered every year. Let those young men who have a predisposition to consumption, and this is the case with many of our theological students, consider themselves debarred from the privilege of preaching Christ to the heathen of the East. But at the same time, *let all the rest feel themselves under greater obligation* to listen to the heart-melting, soul-stirring cry, which the varied population of this great country, the Shans, the Karens, the Talings, the Burmese, and the Arracanese are now sending forth from their towns, and villages, and hamlets, their mountains, their valleys, and their woods, " COME AND SAVE US, FOR WE ARE SINKING INTO HELL."

March 4. The great annual festival of Shway Dagong is just past, during which I have distributed nearly ten thousand tracts, *giving to none but those who ask*. Priests and people, from the remotest regions, are alike eager to get our writings. I should have given away double the number, if I could have obtained sufficient supplies. But poor brother Bennett cannot, single handed, with bad type, and not yet familiar with Burmese printing, answer all the demands which we make upon him, from different quarters. May God forgive all those who desert us in our extremity. May he save them all. But surely, if any sin will lie with crushing weight on the trembling, shrinking soul, when grim death draws near, if any sin will clothe the face of the final Judge with an angry frown, withering up the last hope of the condemned, in irremediable, everlasting despair, it is the sin of turning a deaf ear to the plaintive cry of ten millions of immortal beings, who, by their darkness and misery, cry, day and night, "*Come to our rescue, ye bright sons and daughters of America,* COME AND SAVE US, FOR WE ARE SINKING INTO HELL."

I am, however, most grateful and happy that three new missionaries, with their wives, have lately arrived, and are now applying themselves to the language, and preparing to come up to the help of the Lord against the mighty. May he preserve their lives many years, and make them more successful and blessed than their predecessors.

To Mrs. Boardman.

RANGOON, March 4, 1831.

MY DEAR SISTER: You are now drinking the bitter cup whose dregs I am somewhat acquainted with. And though, for some time, you have been aware of its approach, I venture to say that it is far bitterer than you expected. It is common for persons in your situation to refuse all consolation, to cling to the dead, and to fear that they shall too soon forget the dear object of their affections. But don't be concerned. I can assure you that months and months of heart-rending anguish are before you, whether you will or not. I can only advise you to take the cup with both hands, and sit down quietly to the bitter repast which God has appointed for your sanctification. As to your beloved, you *know* that all his tears are wiped away, and that the diadem which encircles his brow outshines the sun. Little Sarah and the other have again found their father, not the frail, sinful mortal that they left on earth, but an immortal saint, a magnificent, majestic king. What more can you desire for them? While, therefore, your tears flow, let a due proportion be tears of joy. Yet take the bitter cup with both hands, and sit down to your repast. You will soon learn a secret, that there is sweetness at the bottom. You will find it the sweetest cup that you ever tasted in all your life. You will find heaven coming near to you, and familiarity with your husband's voice will be a connecting link, drawing you almost within the sphere of celestial music.

I think, from what I know of your mind, that you will not desert the post, but remain to carry on the work which he gloriously began. The Karens of Tavoy regard you as their spiritual mother; and the dying prayers of your beloved are waiting to be answered in blessings on your instructions.

As to little Georgie, who has now no earthly father to care for him, you cannot, of course, part with him at present. But if you should wish to send him home, I pledge myself to use what little influence I have in procuring for him all those advantages of education which your fondest wishes can desire. Or if you should be prematurely taken away, and should condescend, on your dying bed, to commit him to me, by the briefest line or verbal message, I hereby pledge my fidelity to receive and treat him as my own son, to send him home in the best time and way, to provide for his education, and to watch over him as long as I live. More than this I cannot do, and less would be unworthy of the merits of his parents.

As to yourself, I know of nothing that I can do for you. It occurs, however, to say, that I hope you will feel no uneasiness, or think it necessary to make any inquiries, about your support. By our regulations, a widow is entitled to seventy rupees a month, and a child ten rupees. But as Mr. Beeby may not understand this matter, I enclose a note to him, which you can forward or suppress, as you think proper.

You will, moreover, receive ere long a reply from the board to the application which Mr. Boardman made on this subject.

I remain, dear sister,
Your sympathizing brother,
A. JUDSON.

P. S. I should be glad to know that my letter of six weeks or two months ago reached brother Boardman before he died.

To the Rev. Mr. Grow, of Thompson, Conn.

RANGOON, March 4, 1831.

REV. AND DEAR BROTHER: Your letter of the 19th July last is before me, and your fifty dollars are in the hands of Mr.

Jones, at Maulmain, who writes me that he is ready to pay it to my order. The sentiments expressed in your letter are cheering and encouraging to my heart. I wish that all Baptist ministers felt so, and would all make such presents, though I should prefer their being made directly to the board. My gratitude, however, in both cases is sincere.

The great annual festival is just past, during which multitudes come from the remotest parts of the country to worship at the great Shway Dagong pagoda, in this place, where it is believed that several real hairs of Gaudama are enshrined. During the festival, I have given away nearly ten thousand tracts, giving to none but those who ask. I presume there have been six thousand applications at the house. Some come two or three months' journey, from the borders of Siam and China — " Sir, we hear that there is an eternal hell. We are afraid of it. Do give us a writing that will tell us how to escape it." Others come from the frontiers of Kathay, a hundred miles north of Ava — " Sir, we have seen a writing that tells about an eternal God. Are you the man that gives away such writings? If so, pray give us one, for we want to know the truth before we die." Others come from the interior of the country, where the name of Jesus Christ is a little known — " Are you Jesus Christ's man? Give us a writing that tells about Jesus Christ." Brother Bennett works day and night at the press; but he is unable to supply us; for the call is great at Maulmain and Tavoy, as well as here, and his types are very poor, and he has no efficient help. The fact is, that we are very weak, and have to complain that hitherto we have not been well supported from home. It is most distressing to find, when we are almost worn out, and are sinking, one after another, into the grave, that many of our brethren in Christ at home are just as hard and immovable as rocks; just as cold and repulsive as the mountains of ice in the polar seas. But whatever they do, we cannot sit still, and see the dear Burmans, flesh and blood like ourselves, and like ourselves possessed of immortal souls, that will shine forever in heaven, or burn forever in hell — we cannot see them go down to perdition without doing our very utmost to save them. And thanks be to God, our labors are not in vain. We have three lovely churches, and about two hundred baptized converts, and some are in glory. A spirit of religious inquiry is extensively spreading throughout the country, and the signs of the times indicate that the great renovation of Burmah is drawing near. O, if we had about twenty more versed in the language, and means to spread schools, and tracts, and Bibles, to any extent, how happy I should be! But those rocks and those icy mountains have crushed us down for many years. However, I must not leave my work to write letters. It is seldom that I write a letter home, except my journal, and that I am obliged to do. I took up my pen merely to acknowledge your kindness, and behold I have scratched out a long letter, which I hope you will excuse, and believe me,

In haste, your affectionate brother in Christ,

A. JUDSON.

To the Corresponding Secretary.

RANGOON, May 22, 1831.

REV. AND DEAR SIR: I am surprised to see that my last date is three months ago. The truth is, I have been so absorbed in translating, that I have been hardly sensible of the lapse of time. I am just finishing the books of Isaiah and Genesis, having kept them along together, the one by way of refreshment after the toil of the other. I have done but little missionary work, except distributing tracts and superintending the native assistants. But as Genesis, Psalms, Solomon's Song, Isaiah, and Daniel, some of the most important books of the Old Testament, are now just done, I propose to change my course of labor. Moung En is settled with me, having brought his wife, Mah Nen-yay, from Maulmain. His department is to receive company at the house. His wife assists her husband, and also teaches a small school of four children at present, two of them belonging to Moung Sanlone, formerly of Maulmain, but now settled in Rangoon. Moung Sanlone the second, (or Tsan-lone, as I will write his name in future to distinguish it from the other) is becoming a valuable assistant. It is his business to go about the place, distribute tracts, and converse wherever he can get an opportunity; and he sometimes makes short excursions to the neighboring villages. He frequently meets with very rough treatment, which, as far as I can learn, he bears well.

It has been my habit for several months past to perambulate the streets every morning about sunrise, distributing tracts to those who ask. At first I gave away fifteen or twenty a day. The average has now risen to seventy. We think, from inquiry and observation, that very few are destroyed. They are in almost every house, and are read in private. The truth is unquestionably spreading. Were it not for the fear of government, I think the spread in this place would be rapid. There are a good many hopeful inquirers, but when they arrive at a certain point, their visits become few and far between. They see the Rubicon before them, and dare not pass. The number of such persons is continually increasing. This cannot last always. God will, I trust, make a bridge to facilitate their passage.

I hear that brother Wade has raised up a church of fourteen Karens, in the neighborhood of Maulmain, and that brother Kincaid and brother Jones have large and attentive assemblies from the army. Pour out, O Lord, thy Holy Spirit upon all our feeble efforts, that we may be more successful, and upon thy baptized people at home, that they may begin at last to wake up to the subject of missions, even though they have been sleeping these eighteen years — not to say centuries.*

June 6. I hear that three more natives and three Europeans have joined the church in Maulmain. But at the same time, I am distressed to hear that Mrs. Wade is rapidly sink-

* The man of sin sleeps not, nor his father. Witness one bishop and two priests lately arrived from Prome, by way of the Red Sea, in addition to four others in the country. Two of them are just proceeding to Ava. I hear also that they are building a church at Maulmain.

ing, and that nothing can save her life but a long voyage. To this measure her attending physician, Dr. Brown, has long urged her. But her extreme reluctance "to leave all she loves below the skies, and go off," seemed to be an insuperable objection. At length the brethren met, and formally advised her to go home immediately, and brother Wade to accompany her, partly on account of his own health, which is daily getting worse. A copy of their resolution they sent to me, and I have sent back my entire approbation. I should not wonder if they were now on their way to Bengal. I hope they are.

I have also written to the brethren to know what I shall do with myself in the mean time. I know not whether they can keep the press moving without me. And though they can, what will become of the native flock in Maulmain? What of the Karens? What of all the people in the ceded provinces, from Tenasserim to the frontiers of China? What of all the people from Rangoon to Ava? I am startled and terrified to find that, by several unexpected moves, I am left, as it were, alone; there being not another foreigner in all the country that can preach the gospel to the perishing millions, north and south, or feed the infant churches, except, indeed, Mrs. Bennett, who has begun to take the management of the female meetings. My prayers to God and my entreaties to my brethren at home seem to have equal efficacy. Since the last missionaries left home, I perceive no further signs of life. All seem to have gone to slumbering and sleeping. However, it is a comfort that those last arrived are on the ground; and I cannot but sanguinely hope that dear brother and sister Wade will, in due time, return with renovated health and a fresh reënforcement.

A. JUDSON.

Journal.

Rangoon, June 18, 1831. I have been employed several days in studying Professor Stuart's Commentary on the Hebrews, and revising my translation of that Epistle.

I have received letters from Maulmain, in answer to my

inquiries. Brother Wade being obliged to leave for the present, the brethren recommended my removing to Maulmain. I return the favor by recommending the removal of one of the brethren to this place.

July 20. I have just finished the first part of Exodus, that is, twenty chapters, as an appendix to Genesis. I now shut up my translating books, having received the gratifying intelligence from brother Jones, that he will be ready to relieve this post on the 25th, soon after which I shall embark for Maulmain. Though we have had a very great number of inquirers, and some of them very hopeful, we have had but few baptisms. Many of them come from a distance, and return, I trust, to spread the light around them; but we see them no more for the present.

I have sent Moung Shway-doke with three thousand tracts up the Laing River, which breaks off from the Rangoon outlet a little above Rangoon, and joins the great River Tingdau, below Prome. It passes through a populous part of the country, where the word of life has never yet been published. Moung Sanlone has left me this morning, with twenty-five hundred tracts, to visit the neighborhood of old Pegu, on the east; and Moung Shway-too will shortly leave with three thousand, for the large towns of Pan-ta-nau and Bassein, on the west. These disbursements have reduced me to my last thousand, with which we shall endeavor to hold out, in expectation of the reënforcement which is near at hand.

July 23. I had the pleasure of welcoming brother and sister Jones.

Left Rangoon, July 26, and on the 11th of August, after a very tedious passage, reached the mission premises at Maulmain, where I had no sooner set foot than I found myself surrounded by a crowd of native Christians, children of the school and members of the mission; and our joy was reciprocal. Find there are continual accessions to the European church under the care of brother Kincaid, some encouraging news from the Karens in the north, but prospects among the native population of Maulmain rather dark.

Pencilled Fragments, without Date.

Topics to encourage Prayer.

Wrestling Jacob.
Friend at midnight.
The unjust judge.
Satan fights neither with small nor great, save only with the spirit of prayer.

An effort made in aridity, in wandering of thought, under a strong tendency to some other occupation, is more pleasing to God, and helps the soul forward in grace more than a long prayer without temptation.

Whatever others do, let my life be a life of prayer.

Get the King's daughter, and you get all; the grace of devotion is the daughter of God.

1. Self-denial.
2. Do nothing from your own will, but all from the will of God.
3. The Holy Spirit is the soul of the ransomed soul. — *Fenelon.*
4. Keep turning the soul to God until it habitually rest in God. — *Guion.*
5. Strive after the spirit of prayer, rather than to pray. — *Kempis.*
6. Keep the cross of Christ in view.
7. Listen to the voice within.

Points of Self-denial.

1. The passion for neatness, uniformity, and order, in arrangement of things — in dress, in writing, in grounds.
2. A disposition to suffer annoyance from little improprieties in the behavior and conversation of others.
3. A desire to appear to advantage, to get honor and avoid shame. "*Come shame*, come sorrow," &c.
4. A desire for personal ease and comfort, and a reluctance to suffer inconvenience.
5. Unwillingness to bear contradiction.

In several of the foregoing letters, it may have been observed that allusion is made to the works of Lady Guion and some other distinguished quietists of the Catholic church. The attachment of Dr. Judson to writings of this class, some of the sentiments which he embraced, and the rules of living which he adopted, were, at the time, a source of uneasiness to many of his friends. Even now they are somewhat unwillingly called to remembrance, or are alluded to as facts which prove that his tendencies were imaginative and mystical, and that the soundness of his judgment is by no means to be relied upon. I consider it my duty — and I perform it with pleasure — to state the facts of the case just as they occurred, offering at the close such suggestions as the narrative has awakened in my own mind.

It will be borne in recollection that Dr. Judson had, a short time before, suffered an imprisonment of twenty-one months in Ava, under circumstances which rendered the preservation of his life almost miraculous. While his health was still suffering from the effects of this captivity, his wife, whom he loved almost to idolatry, was taken from him, and he returned to a desolate home, to lay by her side, under the hope tree, the only child that she had left him. He proceeded steadily and earnestly with his work, as though none of this had happened; but it is, I suppose, to be remembered that Christians and missionaries have the same physical nature, the same brain and nerves, and the same domestic affections, as other men. While Dr. Judson, in all this, bowed to the will of his Father in heaven with unquestioning submission, the pain which his sensitive nature endured must have been as great as could be borne without producing derangement. The world had lost for him all its charms; and he looked upon it only as a field for the discharge of duty. His thoughts all tended to the heaven where were gathered all, both created and uncreated, that he most dearly loved. The realities of eternity were ever present to his mind; and there naturally arose within him a desire, amounting to a passion, to become assimilated as nearly as it was possible to those whom he loved, who were now without sin. He meditated on the delineations and the examples of Christian character contained in the New Testament, and compared them with the standard of piety by which the moral efforts of the disciples of Christ are now limited; and he became convinced that religious men might arrive at vastly higher attainments in holiness if they earnestly and honestly desired it. Having come to this conclusion, he at once determined to reduce his theory to practice, and seek for the nearest and most constant communion with God of which his nature was capable.

He devoted himself to this work with characteristic energy. It is to be observed, however, that the discipline to which he subjected himself was merely the means to an end. He desired to subdue every impulse, and to conquer every habit, which interfered with supreme love to God and disinterested love to man. While he was thus mortifying the sensual, he was also cultivating the spiritual by earnest devotion and the exercise of self-denying charity. The means to which he resorted were such as proved him to be most thoroughly in earnest, and singularly capable of conforming his practice to the principles of duty by which he was governed.

He resolved to overcome every form of selfishness

and cultivate in his soul the largest measure of love to man. He observed that missions were languishing for want of funds, and, as no human being was dependent on him for support, he gave to the board his whole patrimonial estate. His love of order and neatness was excessive, and liable to interfere with his labors among the filthy Karens. He overcame this tendency by ministering to the sick under the most revolting diseases. In youth, he had cherished an intense desire for reputation; and even his father had cultivated, rather than repressed, this infirmity. The severe dispensations which had been meted out to him had, in a great measure, corrected this propensity; but there yet lingered within him a desire for posthumous reputation. To mortify this weakness, he caused all his correspondence, so far as it was in his power, to be destroyed, and committed to the flames a letter of thanks for his services from the governor general of India, together with several other documents of a similar character. He went still farther. He desired to subdue every appetite that might interfere with perfect consecration of the soul to God. He therefore built in the edge of the jungle a bamboo house, which he called the "hermitage," where he lived upon rice for weeks together, mingling in no society, and seeing only those persons who came to him for religious instruction, that thus he might render his intense love for his friends perfectly subordinate to his love to God. This time was devoted to prayer and the work of translating the Scriptures. To these austerities was added the habit of frequent fasting, which, in fact, he continued to the close of his life. He had suffered much from a peculiar form of dread of death — not the separation of the soul from the body, or any doubt of ultimate acceptance with God, but a nervous shrinking from decay and corruption — the mildewing and mouldering in dark, damp, silent ghastliness. He believed this to be the result of pride and self-love; and, in order to mortify and subdue it, he had a grave dug, and would sit by the verge of it, and look into it, imagining how each feature and limb would appear days, months, and years after he had lain there. Once, when worn out with translations, and really needing rest, he went over the hills into the thick jungle, far beyond all human habitation, though still overlooked by a moss-grown pagoda, so distant that even the strictest devotee of Gaudama never thought of visiting it. To this place he brought his Bible, and sat down under the wild jungle trees to read, and meditate, and pray, and at night returned to the "hermitage." The next morning, when he went to his retreat, he found a rude bamboo seat in the place, and the branches of the trees woven for a canopy over his head. He never knew to whom he was indebted for this watchfulness; but Ko En informed Mrs. Judson that it was Ko Dwah,* the deacon, whose fear of tigers was so far overcome by his

---

* This man was devotedly attached to Dr. Judson. Both were taken sick at nearly the same time, so that during their illness they met but once, and the old deacon could not, with the other disciples, accompany the dying pastor to the wharf. As soon as Dr. Judson removed, the house which he occupied, and which had long been condemned by Dr. Morton for its unhealthiness, was removed. Ko Dwah was not aware of the circumstance, though living in the vicinity, until the spot was left bare. He then insisted on leaving his bed to look upon the ruin. He hobbled on his staff across the road, ascended the chapel steps with great difficulty, and then sitting down, rested his chin on his palms, and burst into a loud, wild sort of lamentation, like the wailing at a funeral. Neither mind nor body ever recovered from the shock, though he lingered on for some time longer.

affection, that he braved the dangers of the dusk to accomplish his pious purpose. This place of resort was considered by the natives so dangerous, that Dr. Judson's preservation during the forty days which he spent there, partaking of no food except a little rice, was regarded by them as a repetition of the miracle of Daniel.

In this manner were several months of this part of the life of Dr. Judson spent. The whole energy of his nature was directed to the attainment of perfect self-government and intimate communion with God. His labors in the translation were, however, not intermitted. He strove to impose these austerities on no one else; but to his intimate friends he frequently spoke of the necessity of aiming at a higher degree of sanctification than was commonly attained. He censured no one — a virtue not always in practice, either by ascetics or by self-indulgent Christians. The more he examined his own heart, and tested his own motives, the farther did he seem removed from that perfect holiness to which he aspired. He did not, I believe, ever conceive himself to have arrived at the perfection which he sought; but, had he been suffered to entertain any doubts of his acceptance with God, he must have become instantly insane. He was spared this trial. He had never any doubt of his title to a heavenly inheritance; and all his desire was, the better to prepare himself to enjoy it. In subsequent life, though he looked back upon this portion of his moral history with trembling, yet he firmly believed that he had derived from it benefits which could not, perhaps, otherwise have been attained. Those who knew him best trace to this period that unusual self-possession, that victory over the allurements of the world, that habitual tendency of the soul towards the realities of eternity, and that loving trust in God under the most discouraging circumstances, which so distinctly marked the remainder of his career.

If, now, we reflect upon this passage in the life of Dr. Judson, I think we shall be convinced that it is by no means deserving of the sort of remark to which it has given rise. He was striving for the same attainments which President Edwards, Payson, Baxter, Bishop Wilson, and a multitude of others, whose lives are considered worthy models for Christian imitation, most earnestly sought after. His labors were more intense, and his austerities more painful, than many of these holy men underwent; but this arose from the self-sacrificing energy of his nature, modified, at the time, by the condition of his nervous system — shattered almost to insanity by sickness, captivity, torture, and the severest of all bereavements.

But we are not obliged to rest our defence of this part of Dr. Judson's conduct even here. We may go farther, and ask, What was the object which he so earnestly desired? It was the highest attainment in virtue, in supreme love to God, and universal charity to man. Can any object be more worthy of an intelligent and accountable being? By what means did he attempt to cultivate his moral nature? By prayer, the mortification of the appetites, and the practice of charity. These are certainly suitable means, and such as the Scriptures, and men who love the Scriptures best, have ever recommended. Our Saviour declares that, unless we deny ourselves, we cannot enter his kingdom. But it is said that Dr. Judson carried his obedience to these precepts to excess. We ask, Did he carry them to such an excess as to injure his neighbor? If not, his neighbor has surely no reason to complain. Did he, in consequence of these austerities, neglect any duty devolving upon him, either as a Christian or as a missionary? His visit to Prome and Rangoon occurred during this very period; can any thing be more cheerful, more kind, or more natural than his letters from these places? But it may be asked, Do you advise us all to live in this manner? I answer, Did Dr. Judson ever advise it? He held himself up as a model to no one. He never even proposed to himself permanently such a mode of life. He only adopted it *for a time*, as a means of moral improvement by which the whole of his future life might be rendered more in harmony with the perfect example of the Saviour whom he worshipped. If there is any thing in which a man should be left to act specially for himself, it must be in that part of his conduct which pertains to his relations to God. If there be any course of action which he should be allowed to pursue without censure, it must be that in which he is striving to cultivate most assiduously love to God and charity to man. If we believe the means which a brother adopts to be unwise, let us, by our example, teach him something better. But, whatever opinion we may form of the means, certainly no rightly-constituted mind can contemplate without reverence an immortal spirit making the most strenuous efforts in its power to attain to near resemblance to the Author and Exemplar of all moral perfection.

If, then, it be asked whether we advise disciples of Christ to follow Dr. Judson's example in these respects, we answer, By no means. We do, however advise them to seek as earnestly as he did the subjugation of the appetites and passions, and the most intimate communion possible between the soul and God. As to the means to be employed, let each one judge for himself. Among the most successful of them will, I think, be found some modification of those to which he resorted — self-denial, renunciation of the maxims, amusements, and practices of the men who are manifestly living for this present world, almsgiving, and personal labor in the various departments of charity, all being pervaded by a spirit of fervent devotion. In debating about the means, let us not lose sight of the object to be attained; and because we disapprove of digging a grave and sitting by the side of it, let us not yield ourselves without resistance to the lust of the flesh, the lust of the eyes, and the pride of life.

In the preceding pages, mention is made of the Karens, a people in whom Dr. Judson became deeply interested, and whom he frequently visited on missionary tours in their native jungles. The following notice of their character and habits, taken from Mrs. Emily C. Judson's Life of Mrs. Sarah B. Judson, was made under the eye of Dr. Judson himself.

The Karens have for many years been known to American Christians, and have shared deeply in their sympathies. Different opinions respecting their origin have from time to time been advanced; but who they are, or whence they came, if not indigenous to the Burmese wilderness, is still a mystery, even to themselves. Distant resemblances have been traced between the Karens and several mountain tribes to the north of Burmah; but nothing satisfactory with regard to their identity has yet been ascertained, and the whole subject is one of loose conjecture. Their numbers have also been variously estimated. By a census of the Tenasserim provinces, taken in 1839, the Karens and Toung-thoos (the latter a small hill tribe, not easily distinguished by a casual observer) were ascertained to number thirteen thousand five hundred and three. This estimate includes those of both races, from the province of Maulmain on the north to Tavoy, and thence to Mergui on the south; but since that time the number of Karens has been considerably increased by immigration, especially in the vicinity of Maulmain. They are probably four or five times as numerous in the southern part of Burmah, where they occupy a strip of territory lying between Rangoon and Bassein, and extending along the borders of Arracan; while a third division, still more numerous, people a range of hills stretching off to the north-east, as far as Toung-oo, an inland city half way between Rangoon and Ava. They are a rude, wandering race, drawing their principal support from the streams that flow through their valleys, and from the natural products of their native mountains. They migrate in small parties, and, when they have found a favorable spot, fire the underbrush, and erect a cluster of three or four huts on the ashes. In the intervals of procuring food, the men have frequent occasion to hew out a canoe or weave a basket; and the women manufacture a kind of cotton cloth, which furnishes material for the clothing of the family. Here they remain until they have exhausted the resources of the surrounding forest, when they seek out another spot, and repeat the same process.

The Karens are a meek, peaceful race, simple and credulous, with many of the softer virtues, and few flagrant vices. Though greatly addicted to drunkenness, extremely filthy and indolent in their habits, their morals, in other respects, are superior to many more civilized races. Their traditions, like those of several tribes of American Indians, are a curious medley of truth and absurdity; but they have some tolerably definite ideas of a Great Being, who governs the universe; and many of their traditionary precepts bear a striking resemblance to those of the gospel. They have various petty superstitions; but, with the exception of a small division, known to the Burmans as the Taling Karens, and to the missionaries as

Pwos or Shos, they have never adopted Boodhism; the oppressive treatment which they have received at the hands of their Burmese rulers probably contributing to increase their aversion to idolatry.

Soon after the arrival of the first Burmese missionary in Rangoon, his attention was attracted by small parties of strange, wild-looking men, clad in unshapely garments, who from time to time straggled past his residence. He was told that they were called Karens; that they were more numerous than any similar tribe in the vicinity, and as untamable as the wild cow of the mountains. He was further told that they shrunk from association with other men, seldom entering a town, except on compulsion; and that, therefore, any attempt to bring them within the sphere of his influence would prove unsuccessful. His earnest inquiries, however, awakened an interest in the minds of the Burmese converts; and one of them, finding, during the war, a poor Karen bond servant in Rangoon, paid his debt, and thus became, according to the custom of the country, his temporary master. When peace was restored, he was brought to the missionaries on the Tenasserim coast, and instructed in the principles of the Christian religion. He eventually became the subject of regenerating grace, and proved a faithful and efficient evangelist. Through this man, who will be recognized as Ko Thah-byu, access was gained to others of his countrymen, and they listened with ready interest. They were naturally docile; they had no long-cherished prejudices and time-honored customs to fetter them; and their traditions taught them to look for the arrival of white-faced foreigners from the West, who would make them acquainted with the true God. The missionaries, in their first communications with the Karens, were obliged to employ a Burmese interpreter; and, notwithstanding the disadvantages under which they labored, the truth spread with great rapidity. Soon, however, Messrs. Wade and Mason devoted themselves to the acquisition of the language, and the former conferred an inestimable blessing on the race by reducing it to writing. This gave a fresh impetus to the spread of Christianity. The wild men and women, in their mountain homes, found a new employment; and they entered upon it with enthusiastic avidity. They had never before supposed their language capable of being represented by signs, like other languages; and they felt themselves, from being a tribe of crushed, down-trodden slaves, suddenly elevated into a nation, with every facility for possessing a national literature. This had a tendency to check their roving propensities; and, under the protection of the British government, they began to cultivate a few simple arts, though the most civilized among them still refuse to congregate in towns, and it is unusual to find a village that numbers more than five or six houses. Their first reading books consisted of detached portions of the gospel; and the Holy Spirit gave to the truth thus communicated regenerating power. Churches sprang up, dotting the wilderness like so many lighted tapers; and far back among the rocky fastnesses of the mountains, where foreign foot has never trod, the light is already kindled, and will continue to increase in brilliancy, till one of the darkest corners of the earth shall be completely illuminated.

END OF VOL. I.

www.ingramcontent.com/pod-product-compliance
Lightning Source LLC
Chambersburg PA
CBHW030329240426
43661CB00052B/1569